W. Shott

The Letter to the
COLOSSIANS

EDUARD SCHWEIZER

The Letter to the
COLOSSIANS

A COMMENTARY

translated by Andrew Chester

Augsburg Publishing House

Minneapolis, Minnesota

The Letter to the Colossians

First published 1976 by Benziger Verlag, Zürich
and Neukirchener Verlag, Neukirchen-Vluyn,
in the Evangelisch-Katholischer Kommentar (EKK) series.

First published in English 1982
by Augsburg Publishing House in the USA,
and in Great Britain by
SPCK
Holy Trinity Church
Marylebone Road
London NW1 4DU

ISBN 0 281 03856 2 (SPCK)

ISBN 0 8066 1893 0 (Augsburg)

Library of Congress Catalog Card No. 81-65657

PRINTED IN THE USA

To my good friends
of both Protestant and Catholic confessions
in the United Theological Faculty in Melbourne (Australia)
and the entire Sacrae Theologiae Collegium
as a small token of gratitude
for the great honour they bestowed by conferring
upon me the title and privileges of Doctor of Theology
on 3 October 1975

Contents

Abbreviations 9

Preface 10

Introduction 13
1. The Community in Colossae   13
2. The Author   15
3. The Date and Place of Composition   24

Commentary 27
  I. The Opening Address (1:1-8) 27
    1. Assurance of Grace (1:1-2)   27
    2. Thanksgiving (1:3-8)   31

  II. Laying the Foundation (1:9–2:23) 39
    1. Intercession (1:9-11)   39
    2. The Hymn and its Setting (1:12-23)   45
    3. World Mission as Revelation of the
       Mystery (1:24-29)   98
    4. The Apostle's Involvement for the Community
       (2:1-5)   115
    5. The Confrontation with the Colossian Philosophy
       (2:6-23)   121
    Excursus: The Colossian Philosophy   125

  III. The Life that Comes from Faith 3:1–4:6) 171
    1. The New Life as an Undertaking (3:1-4)   171
    2. The Old and the New Man (3:5-11)   181
    3. Life in Christ's World (3:12-17)   203
    4. Christ in the Sphere of Marriage, Family,
       and Work (3:18–4:1)   212
    Excursus: The Household Rules   213
    5. The Call to Intercession and
       Missionary Responsibility (4:2-6)   230

IV. The Conclusion of the Letter: Greetings (4:7-18) 236

The Impact of Colossians 245
   I. Introduction 245

  II. Christology: The Father and the Son 246
     1. Christ as the Wisdom of God   246
     2. First-Born of All Creation, Image of the
       Invisible God (1:15)   250
     3. The Two Natures   252
     4. Christ in the Old Testament   255
     5. The Function of the Statements about Christ   257

 III. Soteriology: The Son and the World 259
     1. Incarnation of the Logos as Salvation
       for the world   259
     2. Universal Redemption?   260

  IV. Ethics 277
     1. General   277
     2. The Polemical Sections   278
     3. The Call to Worship Addressed to All the Members
       of the Community   281
     4. The Household Rules   282
     5. Ethical Implications   286

Outlook 290
    The Epistle to the Colossians in History   290
    The Epistles to the Colossians in Its Setting   293
    The Epistle to the Colossians Today   298

Bibliography 303

Index of Subjects 313

Index of References 316

Abbreviations

Abbreviations for sources and literature from antiquity follow those given by G. Kittel, ed. *Theological Dictionary of the New Testament* (Grand Rapids and London, Eerdmans, 1964) xvi-xl. The abbreviations used for periodicals, compilations, etc. follow those suggested by the Society of Biblical Literature and those given in *Internationalen Abkürzungsverzeichnis für Theologie und Grenzgebiete*, (S. Schwertner, ed., Berlin, 1974).

Commentaries included in the Bibliography are cited simply by the author's name and the page number. When the section cited refers to a verse in Colossians other than that immediately under discussion, then that is given as well. All other literature is cited by author's name, one or two key words of the title, and page number. In the case of sources and literature from antiquity and various periods of church history, the citation is given according to the book, chapter, and section or original pagination.

Preface

"With a heartfelt sigh, and able to breathe freely again now that the crushing weight had been removed, I laid their works aside;" thus de Wette, 5 expressed his profound sense of relief at having discharged his duty in reading the commentaries on Colossians. I can only hope that not too many readers of the present commentary will give vent to similar feelings.

This commentary is intended to be *ecumenical*. However, it is ecumenical not in the sense that the discussion is primarily concerned with points at issue between the denominations. In the joint work undertaken by the EKK team in recent years, for which we are profoundly indebted above all to the Swiss and German publishing houses (Benziger Verlag and Neukirchener Verlag), it has become clear that the boundaries between denominations are being crossed and only in rare instances do specifically denominational differences become evident in their interpretation of the text. This commentary is ecumenical in the sense that I am indebted for a great deal of what is contained in it to what has been achieved at the joint EKK sessions. In particular in considering the hymn (1:15-20) I have learned to see something new from discussion with Catholic colleagues. Above all, Rudolf Schnackenburg has been a companion and friend throughout the whole endeavor, and he read and commented on the first draft.

The interpretation is intended to be *theological*. Again, however, this is not so in the sense that dogmatic questions are discussed extensively. I know only too well the limits imposed upon exegetes.

It is theological rather in the sense that no section has been written without having first been preached. I have also deliberately included in the Summaries a number of bold images, which can be expressed better in a sermon, because I think that pointed formulations show, most of all in those sections directed towards the practice of proclamation, where the author has allowed himself to be moved by the text. Thus for myself, for instance, Schleiermacher's sermons, with all their formulations that are questionable for the present day, provided an invigorating change when set alongside the "correct" modern commentaries.

Further, the interpretation is deliberately intended to be *historical*. Once more, this is not meant in the sense that a survey of times long since past has been provided. It is intended rather in the sense that I have expended a great deal of time and energy on research into the relevant historical background. This can often restrain interpreters from reading into the text their own preconceived notions. In my ten years of working for the EKK (which came into being in 1966 as a result of a suggestion that I made to the Neukirchener Verlag), it has become apparent how difficult critical historical work has proved to be at the present time. This is certainly the case when, as here, the intention is that the work be carried out in a consciously theological way and that it should at the same time reach into the sphere of both Protestant and Catholic communities.

It is perhaps valid to apply to this work the words which Father Jacobus, in Hermann Hesse's *Glass Bead Game* says to the young Josef Knecht, also in a sort of ecumenical dialogue: "To pursue history means to give oneself up to chaos, and yet to keep one's faith in order and reason. It is a very serious task, young man, and perhaps a tragic one." I would like, in the following pages, to offer an invitation to a faith of this sort, a faith which is not lightly to be lived and yet which offers real life. This cannot come about in any other way except by both author and reader alike undertaking the "very serious and perhaps tragic task."

Without the efforts of my assistant, Hans Weder, who checked many references and read the proofs, the book could not possibly have been made ready for publication so soon. The clerical help faithfully provided by Frau Anneliese Blum was also greatly appreciated. My profound thanks are due to them both, as also to all my friends in the EKK team. My wife and children and also my grandchildren have time and again called me back to different dimensions of life, and this as well has enriched the work. Indeed, I can no longer conceive of the commentary, especially as far as it is directed toward the proclamation to the world at the present time, without also thinking of many discussions with my wife during our strolls through the woods. Hence it is that my heartfelt thanks to God, for all the people who have accompanied me during the course of this work, should be set over everything that follows.

Zürich, Easter Sunday, 18 April 1976   *Eduard Schweizer*

Introduction

1. The Community in Colossae

Colossae is situated some two hundred kilometers from the sea, on the great eastern trade-route from Ephesus to Miletus. It is located in the valley of the Lycus, a tributary of the Meander, and lies at the end of a gorge some sixteen kilometers upstream from Laodicea and twenty from Hierapolis. At first Colossae was an important center (Xenophon I 2.6) of the wool-industry, which also included dyeing and weaving (Strabo XII 8.16; Pliny, *Hist.Nat.* XXI 51); the subsequent fate of the city is uncertain. It is not clear whether Strabo XII 8.13 describes it as a "small town," since there is a lacuna in the text at this point. Whereas Laodicea and Hierapolis are also both attested to in Christian sources, the former by Rev. 1:11; 3:14, the latter by Papias (Eusebius, *Hist. Eccl.* III 36.2), Colossae vanishes from our literary sources after A.D. 61. It was in this year that Laodicea was destroyed by an earthquake (Tacitus, *Annals* 14.27).

Eusebius, writing in the fourth century, informs us that Colossae—along with Laodicea and Hierapolis—was completely destroyed by an earthquake—and he also seems to have had the Nero period in mind.[1] However, we do not know whether this account is correct. All that can be said for certain is that Laodicea was rebuilt and

---

1. *Chronicon*, ed. R. Helm, Berlin, 1956, 183; 1:21f. The passage, translated c. 380 by Jerome, seems (according to the lemmata) to go back to a Greek text and even at that stage to have related to the description of Nero. Orosius, *Historia adversus paganos* VII, 7.12 (PL 31:7.11) repeats the information, and it is also cited by Calvin (122, argumentum). Eusebius and Orosius are mentioned by Gomarus (547a).

prospered, whereas we hear no more of Colossae. Its existence is
proved, however, by coins of the second and third centuries.[2]
Hierapolis, situated on the north side of the river, was famed for
its mineral springs and renowned as a center of Phrygian mystery
cults (Strabo XIII 4, 14), although at the time of the Epistle to the
Colossians an Apollo-Archegetes cult may have replaced that of the
mother goddess.[3] After Antiochus III had established Jewish communities in these three towns, they each harbored a sizeable Jewish
population; according to Cicero, it may have been more than 10,000.[4]

Epaphras (1:7; 4:12) was a Gentile-Christian who also devoted
his energies to the communities in Laodicea and Hierapolis (4:13).
It was through him that Colossians, themselves Gentiles (1:21, 27;
2:13; 3:5, 7)[5] before their baptism (2:11f.), heard the gospel proclaimed by Paul (1:23, 28); and it was this gospel which took them
out of the dominion of darkness and into light. What they have
heard bears fruit among them (1:5); the word is alive among them
in their singing of spiritual songs. But the word lives also in their
conscious share of responsibility for the non-Christian world around
them (3:16; 4:5). And yet the Colossians are threatened by a
philosophy, which is competing for their favor (2:4, 8; cf. the excursus to 2:8). Neither they nor the Laodiceans know Paul personally (2:1). At the present time he is suffering (1:24) as a prisoner
(4:3, 18), and has been largely forsaken by Jewish-Christian fellow

2. D. Magie, *Roman Rule in Asia
Minor*, Princeton 1950, 986, cf. 126f.,
985. According to the *British Museum
Catlogue of the Greek Coins (and
Medals)*, vol. *Phrygia*, London 1906,
154-7, Colossae is expressly mentioned
on coins of the reign of Antoninus Pius
(A.D. 138-61), and up until c. A.D. 217.
There are however few such, and only
the offices of the γραμματεύς (under
Antoninus Pius) and ἄρχων (under
M. Aurelius) appear. Unfortunately
one inscription which mentions many
of the offices cannot be dated (W. M.
Ramsay, *The Cities and Bishoprics of
Phrygia*, Oxford 1895, 212). Pliny,
Hist. Nat. 5.105, no longer refers to
Colossae alongside Laodicea and Hierapolis; he does mention it at 5.145,
but the usage of the old name Celae-
nae for Apameia shows that his report

concerns something in the past; 31.29
speaks only of the fossils found at
Colossae. Cf. Houlden, 119; Reicke,
Rev. Exp. 70. 430-2. Melanchthon
(*Enarratio* 365) cites Eutropius: "Laodicea and Colossae were destroyed
by an earthquake a year after the
death of Paul."
3. Magie (note 2 above) 987f.
4. *Pro Flacco* 28 =*Or.* VI/2, 224f.;
Lightfoot, 20; Lohse, 9.
5. It is true that "idolatry" is used in
its metaphorical sense; yet vices that
are typically heathen are mentioned,
and 1:21 is hardly an expression that
would be used of former Jews. "Uncircumcision" in 2:13 could be understood in a spiritual sense (but see the
commentary on this verse); however,
the expression "Gentiles" in 1:27 is
taken up by "you."

workers (4:11). The link with the Colossians is for that reason all the more important for him; he is present with them in spirit and he hopes for their intercessions (4:3). Just as Epaphras has already joined Paul from Colossae (1:8), so will Tychicus, together with Onesimus, go to Colossae from Paul as the bearer of the letter (4:7f.). Mark, of whom they have already been informed, will visit them later (4:10). Further, it is recommended that there should be an exchange of letters with the Laodiceans, for whom greetings are included (4:15f.).

2. The Author

A problem that particularly concerns us is the immediately apparent and intimate relationship between the Epistle to the Colossians and that to the Ephesians. Although the opposite opinion is on occasion maintained, the Epistle to the Ephesians is, nonetheless, dependent upon Colossians; this question must, accordingly, be discussed in the Introduction thereto.[6] First of all, Colossians has every appearance of being a genuine Pauline epistle. As in 2 Cor. 1:1 and Phil. 1:1 (cf. 1 Thess. 1:1) Paul and Timothy are named as those who are sending the letter. 1:23, in the same way as 2 Cor. 10:1, points to Paul as the actual author. 4:18 contains his own personal signature, in the same way as 1 Cor. 16:21; Gal. 6:11; Philemon 19. The letter also begins, as is customary with Paul, with the experiences of the community, and seeks to proceed from there, without basing its argument on established formulas of Christian teaching. The imperative of ethical admonition is, as in Paul, founded on the indicative of the promise of salvation (2:6; 3:1-4).

The structure of the Epistle to the Colossians roughly corresponds to that of Romans: there is a dogmatic section, which lays the foundation of the letter and ends with the discussion of a special problem of contemporary concern (in the case of Romans, that of the special role of Israel, in the case of our present Epistle, that of the Colossian philosophy), there then follows the ethical section (3:1–4:6), which is introduced both in Col. 3:1-4 and Rom. 12:1f., by reference to the first part; both sections are framed by the Introduction (Preamble, Thanksgiving, and Intercession, with reference

6. E.G. Synge, 56; cf. R. Schnackenburg in EKK. For the most recent survey of the various hypotheses see J. B. Polhill, "The Relationship between Ephesians and Colossians," *Rev. Exp.* 70 (1975) 439-50. On this whole section cf. at greater length: Schweizer, "Letter."

to the life of the community, 1:1-8) and the concluding passage,
with personal notes and greetings (4:7-18).[7] The letter also contains
typically Pauline expressions and turns of phrase; there are some
such that are not found, but that is equally true of genuine Pauline
Epistles. Many of the words in this letter which are found nowhere
else in the New Testament stem from the Hymn that is cited, or are
connected with the philosophy that is being opposed; they cannot,
therefore, be adduced to prove anything.[8] This could also account
for theological differences.

That the congregation has already been raised from the dead,
that their hope is already laid up in heaven awaiting them, that
their Lord has already disarmed all powers and authorities, whereas
the not-yet theme is expressed only once (in 3:2f.), all this could
be offered as an answer to the fear of the congregation that after
death they would not attain to the exalted Christ (cf. p. 133). The
danger of a libertine-enthusiastic misunderstanding was less of a
threat amongst the Colossian rigorists than it was with the Corinthians.[9] Again, the origin of the concept of Christ as the head of
the church could be explained just as easily by reference to Paul as
it could by reference to a later writing (cf. p. 82f.). The fact that
there is still no kind of hierarchical church order apparent, that no
role is ascribed to a leader of the community[10] in the struggle against
the intruding philosophy, and that an abundant life in the "word of
Christ" and in spiritual songs of praise is presumed to obtain for
the entire congregation (3:16), do indeed all prove nothing by
themselves. However, all this is more easily intelligible at a time
that is not so very far removed from that of Paul himself.

More difficult to explain in a Pauline Epistle are the sufferings of

---

7. So, more or less, Lohse, 3f.; he does
however mark off 1:11 as ending one
section and 1:12 as beginning another.
It is of course possible to designate
3:1-4 as a transitional section (Ludwig, Verfasser, 57), and it may also be
asked whether the polemic in 2:6-23
should not be separated off as a distinct middle section on its own
(Lähnemann, Kolosserbrief, 61f.; similarly Zeilinger, Der Erstgeborene,
61f.). However, on the one hand po-
lemics have already played a part
earlier in the letter, while on the
other hand 2:10-15 provides the dog-

matic basis for the ethical exhortation
in 3:1-4, 9-15.
8. The evidence is assembled in Lohse,
85-7.
9. It is true, however, that Moule's
warning, that 3:5, 8 also have opposing dangers in view (RevExp. 70, 483-
6) should not go unheeded.
10. Lohse, 179; S. Schulz, Die Mitte
der Schrift, Stuttgart 1976, 89; Lähnemann, Kolosserbrief, 58. In the polemic of 2:8-23 there is also no reference back to the apostleship (ibid. 53,
n102).

the apostle which are endured for the benefit of the church, and which fulfil what is still lacking in the sufferings of Christ (1:24). This does indeed go far beyond what is found in Rom. 15:15-21. In the latter, passages from the prophets are interpreted afresh, and above all the whole weight is laid on the activity of Christ (Rom. 15:18; cf. 1 Cor. 15:9f.). Here the apostle's service in the gospel has already been given great prominence in 1:23, by means of "I, Paul," and again in 1:26f. through the schema of revelation (v. p. 107).[11] The fact that the apostle now reveals to the heathen what had for aeons remained concealed exceeds in essence what has been said at 1 Cor. 2:6-16. None of this is impossible with Paul, but it is at all events striking.

2:17 is really difficult. The explanation of the law as a shadow of the future fulfilment can be found in Heb. 8:5; 10:1, but not in Paul. Certainly Paul can also speak positively of the law (Rom. 7:12; Gal. 3:24); but he immediately corrects expressions such as these by maintaining that the good law in fact leads to captivity and enslavement (Rom. 7:22-24; 8:2; Gal. 4:1-3). It must be said that in the whole of the Epistle to the Colossians there is no discussion of law, commandment, righteousness, or justification. This would not in itself be impossible for Paul,[12] but it is almost unthinkable in a letter that is fighting against rigorists. Again, it is highly improbable that the apostle reacts in a different way against what are perhaps purely Gentile precepts than he does against Jewish commandments, in view of Gal. 4:8-11, where, as in Col. 2:16f., it is the holding of festivals that is discussed; it is all the more improbable since Col. 2:16 even mentions the Sabbath.

Even more remarkable in a Pauline Epistle would be the almost complete lack of references to the Spirit (cf. pp. 38f.). This would still be conceivable in face of an effervescent enthusiasm, since it is

11. "I, Paul" is found in Philemon 19, in a reference to the apostle's financial obligation, where it is as necessary as an IOU; otherwise it occurs in 2 Cor. 10:1 and Gal. 5:2, in keeping with the style, to introduce an ethical admonition (U. B. Müller, *Prophetie und Predigt im Neuen Testament,* 1975 (SNT 10) 132f.) and in 1 Thess. 2:18 as a reference, required by the sense, to Paul as the subject of the clause. For the rest, the name Paul appears only where he takes it up, as a slogan bandied about by the Corinthians (1 Cor. 1:12f.; 3:4f., 22), except in addresses and greetings. The emphatic "I" of Rom. 15:14 lays stress precisely on the fellowship of the apostle with those whom he addresses, and not his own special position. The schema of revelation is found otherwise only in deutero-Pauline writings (Rom. 16:25-7; Eph. 3:4-12; cf. 1 Tim. 3:16).

12. Νόμος is not found in 2 Cor.

easier to formulate and control Christological statements, if the appeal to the Spirit becomes problematic. However, an enthusiasm of this kind certainly did not exist in the Colossian community; on the contrary, the apostle has to assure them that they have already risen from the dead, that they do already live "above."

Differences of style may be explained individually. Again, however, the differences vis-à-vis Paul abound in Colossians, even in words which are completely unemphasized, but particularly in the way in which synonymous expressions are combined, genitives are strung together, explanations are pedantically added (which is . . . !), and in the formation of long and difficult sentences instead of the style of arguing with or talking to the reader.[13] A comprehensive stylistic analysis decides the issue, since it shows that every observation leads to one uniform result.[14] The sentence structure reveals how lacking in structure the Epistle is, and how hypotaxis and indeed all logical connection are largely absent. The train of thought is associative, scarcely ordered, and in any case not in such a way that the reader is needed as a partner in dialogue on a conceptual journey. The rhetorical devices that the author uses are a style that expresses full assurance ("everything" is especially favored), appended interpretations, circumstantial details with "in" and a substantive, and genitives headed up on top of each other. So the conclusion is clear; a mass of observations that can be proved statistically and evaluated carefully produce a uniform picture, and point to an author who, although following Paul completely in

---

13. Lohse, 87-90. On ὅ ἐστιν cf. note 17 to 2:8-9.
14. Bujard, *Untersuchungen*. In addition to the evidence cited in Lohse, the following points are also noteworthy: infinitive constructions are found in Paul two to four times as frequently; further, final infinitives, as also those constructed with the characteristic Pauline formula εἰς τό, are lacking only in Philemon and Col. (ibid. 53-6); participles carrying on to a new statement of the text are found, on a conservative reckoning, to occur 31 times altogether in the Pauline Epistles and 25 times in Col. (ibid. 61); relative clauses loosely strung together, often with καί after the pronoun, are much more frequent in Col. than in Paul (ibid. 68-70); modal circumstantial phrases with *en* and the substantive are a usage very much favored in Col.; indeed Col. may, in proportion to its length, be the richest work in antiquity in its use of *en* (ibid. 127f.). Ludwig (*Verfasser*) corroborates this conclusion: a circumstantial phrase with *en* serves 11 times in Col. to bring an idea to its conclusion, whereas in the whole of the Pauline Epistles this happens only 6 times (ibid. 39). Sanders, *JBL* 85, 28-45 notes, vis-à-vis the genuine Paulines, the far greater number of combinations of two or more phrases, which otherwise in Paul are to be found separated.

vocabulary and theological concepts, differs from him altogether in his mode of argument. The letter can neither have been written nor dictated by Paul.

Can it be *post-Pauline*, as it is now usually taken to be? Deliberate forgeries were made, from good and not so good motives from the sixth century B.C. onwards, even within Judaism, which smuggled favorable views concerning Old Testament monotheism and other matters into classical writings; later on, Christians treated Jewish works in a corresponding way.[15] Imitation of style was widespread, and was practiced in the rhetorical schools. Devices commonly used in forgery included mentioning the name in the middle of the letter and alluding to personal authorship.[16] Here, however, the imitation of style could derive from the author being on intimate terms with Paul; while the mention of Paul's name could merely be intended to distinguish the apostle from Timothy, who is mentioned along with him in the opening verses; and the allusion to personal authorship could be an unconscious repetition of the same sentence in 1 Cor. 16:21 (cf. also Philemon 19).

Against post-Pauline authorship it must first be noted that Colossae, after A.D. 61, seems to have been destroyed and only to have been repopulated to an insignificant extent (v. p. 13)—if appearances do not deceive! However, the personal notes and greetings in 4:7-18 present considerable problems. The fact that Epaphras is recommended to the community (1:7; 4:12f.) would be intelligible as the legitimation of a successor. The brief allusions to Paul's imprisonment (4:3, 18), and to the few Jewish-Christian fellow-workers remaining faithful with him (4:11) could belong to the image of the suffering apostle. Again, the strong emphasis on his suffering for the good of the church in 1:24 may be intended directly as a remem-

---

15. W. Speyer, *Die literarische Fälschung im Altertum,* 1971 *(HKAW 1/2)* 105f., 131-49, 155-60, 232-8. Forged letters were especially favored (ibid. 57f., 83, 140 etc.).

16. Ibid. 82, 84f., 46, 56f. In a similar way to what is found in 2 Thess. 3:17 (cf. 2:2; 2 Peter 1:16-18; 3:1), the thirteenth (pseudo-)Platonic Epistle (360A) explains: "The opening of this letter should be proof to you that this Epistle derives from me" (ibid.

58, cf. 50). On the whole question, cf. N. Brox, "Zu den persönlichen Notizen der Pastoralbriefe," *BZ* 13 (1969) 76-94; id., "Zum Problemstand in der Erforschung der altchristlichen Pseudepigraphie," *Kairos* 15 (1973) 10-23; id., "Zur pseudepigraphischen Rahmung des ersten Petrusbriefes," *BZ* 19 (1975) 78-96; id., *Falsche Verfasserangaben. Zur Erklärung der frühchristlichen Pseudepigraphie,* 1975 (SBS 79).

brance for his martyr's death.[17] But three or four Jewish-Christians and a great number of Gentile Christians are mentioned by name; the apostle, therefore, has certainly not been forsaken by his co-workers.

It is, however, the customary notes and greetings that make incredible the thesis of a post-Pauline origin for the letter. They must have been gathered together in an extraordinarily artificial fashion from the material in the Epistle to Philemon in order to give Colossians the appearance of authenticity. The three Jewish-Christians also appear as the first three in Philemon 23f., after the Gentile-Christian Epaphras who is made especially prominent; provided, that is, that instead of "Epaphras, my fellow prisoner in Christ Jesus, . . . Mark, Aristarchus" one reads "Epaphras, my fellow prisoner in Christ, . . . Jesus, Mark, Aristarchus." There, however, they are found in a different sequence, without further details and without the surname Justus ("the just"). Likewise, Luke and Demas are found together in Philemon 24, again in reverse order and without the information provided in Col. 4:14. Archippus (Col. 4:17), contrast, is mentioned at the beginning of Philemon (v. 2), and Onesimus (Col. 4:9) plays the most important role in Philemon 10ff. This means, then, that apart from the addressees, Philemon and Apphia (Philemon 1f.), everyone who is mentioned there appears again here, usually in a different order; and all of those who send greetings here in Colossians are mentioned in Philemon as well.

Tychicus (Col. 4:7), who in Philemon 23f. is not reckoned among those who send greetings, and Nympha, who appears only in Col. 4:15 along with the house church gathered together there (probably in Laodicea), would have to have been invented or copied from another tradition (Acts 20:4). In the case of an authentic Pauline epistle, Tychicus would either be the bearer of both Colossians and Philemon, or otherwise be absent at the time of the writing of Philemon. Furthermore, there would then be mention of a "letter from Laodicea," which would scarcely still be known after the death of Paul. Nor can there be any special purpose behind these names and notes. Should, perhaps, some faithful disciples of Paul be recommended to the post-Pauline church? But it is highly unlikely that all those mentioned in Philemon belonged to this category.

Thus, neither the person of the apostle nor the place and manner

17. H. M. Schenke, "Das Weiterwirk-   Erbes durch die Paulusschule," *NTS*
en des Paulus und die Pflege seines   21 (1975) 512.

of his imprisonment is described in a historically plausible fiction; nor can the characterizations (which, as in the genuine Pauline Epistles, are added in a fairly incidental fashion) of those who send and those who receive greetings be read as ways of recommending the disciples of Paul. I confess that as far as I am concerned a clever forgery of this kind remains inconceivable, especially in a letter that is so very close to Paul, and would therefore presumably be the first to be seized on as inauthentic. Furthermore, there does not seem to be a parallel case of such a forgery in antiquity.[18]

If it follows that the letter is *neither Pauline nor post-Pauline*, then what is it? The boundaries between authenticity and inauthenticity can no longer be drawn with the same stringency as they were two decades ago. On the one hand, in genuine Pauline Epistles one always has to reckon with the interpretative glosses of an editor; indeed, some scholars even think that, with the possible exception of the Epistle to the Galatians, scarcely a single Pauline epistle has survived in its original form; almost all of them are compounded of passages from different letters.[19] On the other hand, the problem of

---

18. Speyer, *Fälschung* (note 15 above) 82 does indeed assert that even in the case of minor details, historically accurate information was manufactured in order to give the appearance of authenticity: "the more exact the information, the more false it is." However, the only instances provided are of precise personal descriptions, as for example in the spurious Acts of the Apostles and similar works, which are on a completely different level. This is the case as well for the precise details of time or place, which are adduced by G. Jachmann, "Gefälschte Daten," *Klio* 35 (1942) 60-88; W. Hartke, *Römische Kinderkaiser*, Berlin 1951, 27, 32f.; W. Speyer, "Bücherfunde in der Glaubenswerbung der Antike," *Hyp* 24 (1970) 56-62. Schenke, "Paulusschule" (note 17 above), 506f., shows precisely that the legends about Paul belonged to a completely different strand of tradition from the school whose perspectives were defined by the apostle's letters. So also N. Brox, "Lukas als Verfasser der Pastoralbriefe?", *JAC* 13 (1970) 73, n51, does certainly refer to secondary literature; really comparable texts, however, seem to be lacking; cf. id. *Verfasserangaben* (note 16 above), 60f. and "Notizen" (note 16 above), 84f., where the contradiction between the long list of those who send greetings and the picture of the lonely dying apostle in 2 Tim. 4:10f., 16 is emphasized. This section from 2 Tim. does indeed pose a problem; but it is worth asking whether the author may not still have genuine fragments at his disposal. Furthermore, a recommendation of disciples who remained faithful to Paul would be easier to believe in the case of 2 Tim., and the celebrated cloak and the parchments could themselves help build up the image of the humble apostle who needs nothing more than something to cover himself with (1 Tim. 6:8), but who at the same time longs for the sacred scripture (2 Tim. 3:15; cf. P. Trummer, "Mantel und Schriften (2 Tim. 4.13)" *BZ* 18 (1974) 193-207, especially 199, 204).
19. Thus Schenke, "Paulusschule,"

forgery presents itself in a different light when one is dealing with
an authoritative sacred text which must be "interpreted" for a new
situation. There is a whole range of intermediate stages from the
Targum, which translates a canonical text into another language
but at the same time interprets it, to the disciple of Paul, who interprets for a new situation what the apostle had written in earlier
letters by writing a new one.[20]

In fact, we do something similar when we preach. We could
indeed say: "So Jesus tells us: love your neighbor, even your insuf-
ferable employer, your grumbling colleague . . . ," or: "What does
Paul tell us? Christ is the end of the law, the end of all self-righteous
judgments, which yet day after day we enact . . . ," and no one unfamiliar with the text could distinguish the words of Jesus or of the
apostle from the interpretation. It goes without saying that the character of the reinterpretation is changed when (at a time when the
dubious nature of the forgery is thoroughly recognized) the genu-
ineness of the epistle is obtrusively emphasized (2 Thess. 3:17).

Could the Epistle to the Colossians be *an authentic Pauline epistle, heavily edited,* perhaps under the influence of the later Epistle
to the Ephesians? This has often been suggested. Goodspeed and
Knox think that Onesimus, perhaps identical with the later Bishop
of Ephesus of the same name, edited the Pauline corpus and wrote
the Epistle to the Ephesians as an introduction to it. According to
Knox, the Epistle to Philemon would actually have been directed
to Archippus in Laodicea as the master of Onesimus, via Philemon,
known to Paul in Colossae, and would therefore have been identical

---

509-14 (on Gal. 5:16). I have to confess that, with the possible exception
of 2 Cor. I am not convinced by the
partition hypotheses. On Phil. cf., for
the most recent discussion, Müller,
Prophetie (note 11 above) 207-10.
20. Cf. Brox, *Verfasserangaben,* 117-
19.
21. E. J. Goodspeed, *New Solutions
to New Testament Problems,* Chicago
1927; id., *The Meaning of Ephesians,*
Chicago 1933; id., *The Key to Ephesians,* Chicago 1956; J. Knox, *Philemon among the Letters of Paul,* Chicago 1935, summarized (and criti-
cized) in Moule, 14-18. For a further
critique cf. Lohse, 186f.; Ernst, 125f.;

Houlden, 126 (could Ephesians have
been written by a Gentile Christian?);
Stuhlmacher, *Philemon,* 20; on the
identification with the bishop, ibid. 57.
Against Knox's thesis, the following
points should be taken into account:
1. Nothing in Philemon suggests this
sort of possibility. 2. The warm and
personal style would scarcely be expected, if Philemon were merely a go-
between. 3. Philemon is the "beloved"
one, but hence also probably the one
who is called to "love" (vv. 2, 5, 7.
9). 4. The "ministry" mentioned in
Col. 4:17 is "received in the Lord,"
and thus can scarcely mean merely the
setting free of Onesimus.

with "the letter from Laodicea." [21] That could indeed explain the relationship between Ephesians and Colossians, but not the special characteristics of Colossians, unless one assumed that Onesimus had edited this letter more heavily than other parts of the collection. Benoit [22] has recently suggested that Colossians should be understood as a genuine Pauline writing; it would have been reworked by one of Paul's co-workers with reference to the Epistle to the Ephesians, which was composed by another disciple of Paul at the same time.

The trouble with all such solutions presented in terms of revision is the fact that the style and, to a large degree, the theological differences color the whole epistle. As a consequence, the very most which could be attributed to Paul would be the conclusion, 4:2-18, where, in the nature of things, no theological arguments and few opportunities for variation in style present themselves, and possibly also the household rules in 3:18—4:1, which are also traditional.[23] In fact, however, typical characteristics of the style of Colossians are found in these passages as well.

Colossians, like Philemon, Philippians, and 2 Corinthians, is written by "Paul and Timothy" (cf. 1 Thess. 1:1; the position in 1 Cor. 1:1, along with 4:17; 16:10, is different). Certainly Phil. 2:19 (cf. 1 Thess. 3:2, 6) shows that Paul is the actual author. Nevertheless, the joint authorship is taken seriously to the extent that those who are named alongside Paul appear either in the opening verses or else in the list of those who send greetings (cf. Rom. 16:21 with 1:1!), but never in both. In 2 Cor. 1:19, Paul has expressly attested to partnership with Timothy and Silvanus in the proclamation. If Paul were normally the actual writer and preacher

• would not Timothy, "of the same spirit" with Paul "as no other" (Phil. 2:20), have undertaken the task as soon as the conditions of the imprisonment made it impossible for Paul to do so?

• Would he not then also have composed, in the name of them both, a letter which Paul could neither write nor dictate?

• Would he not have left the apostle to write, if at all possible, at least the closing greeting?

• Would he not, in the letter, have extolled yet more unrestrainedly the significance of the apostle's ministry and sufferings than Paul himself would have done?

---

22. *Hymne*, 254.
23. Sanders, *JBL* 85, 45 joins 3:12-17

to this, but has to admit that 3:15 then forms an exception.

- Would he not have made it even more clear, by using the expression "I, Paul" 1:23), that this concerned only the apostle, and not his own participation in the work?

- Would he not have been steeped to a large extent in Paul's style and train of thought, but also have been glad to include traditional elements such as the hymn and its liturgical introduction, or the household rules?

Certainly it is not possible to prove or disprove either this or the other viewpoints; but the argument outlined above can account for the affinity with and differences from the Pauline Epistles, as also for the many personal notes and greetings. The letter does thus also remain pseudonymous if only because of 1:23); nevertheless it would represent a transition that would make more intelligible the further development, perhaps as far as the Pastorals.[24]

3. The Date and Place of Composition

In this case, could the Epistle to the Colossians have been written *at the same time as the Epistle to Philemon?* Tychicus would then not be mentioned as the bearer of the letter in Colossians, nor Philemon and Apphia as recipients of the private letter in Philemon. A reference to the Colossian philosophy would scarcely be expected in a private letter. Yet according to Philemon 22, Paul hopes soon to be set free, and even before then to make use of the services of Onesimus, as he is obviously doing at the time of writing (v. 13). This presupposes relatively liberal prison conditions. It is, accordingly, more conceivable that Philemon has returned his slave in accordance with the apostle's wish, and that the letter was written shortly afterwards. In both cases the Epistle to Philemon could perhaps be the "letter from Laodicea" (not that "to the Laodiceans"!). Philemon and Apphia must then have dwelt there; yet Onesimus, according to Col. 4:9, lived in Colossae, unless the expression is intended to designate the region within the Lycus Valley in the wider sense, or Onesimus's place of origin. Archippus, who is active in both communities (Col. 4:13), seems, according to Col. 4:17, to have been a Laodicean. The fact that Philemon and Apphia are not mentioned in Colossians is self-evident, if they lived in Laodicea.

---

24. Cf. note 1 to 4:7-18. W.-H. Ollrog, *Paulus und seine Mitarbeiter* §7.2 (to appear in WMANT) also, as I subsequently learned, thinks of Timothy as the author; his work provides a detailed argument in support of this position (especially on the person of Timothy, in note 70).

On the other hand, the fact that greetings are to be conveyed to the Laodiceans causes no difficulties at all, if Colossians were written a few weeks after Philemon. It would be a great deal more difficult to understand if both letters had been composed at the same time. One would then have to suppose that the house-church mentioned in Philemon 2 is not identical with the whole community, and that Paul did not append greetings to everyone, so that Philemon would not need to read the private letter to them all, if he had not been able to comply with Paul's wish. Moreover, one would also have to suppose that the fellow worker who wrote Colossians had no such scruples, since he would not have been able to conceive that Philemon had not followed the apostle's instructions in every respect.

This means that we can explain the situation more easily if Colossians were written shortly after Philemon. After the case of Onesimus had been satisfactorily settled and the former slave had been sent back to Paul, the exchange of letters could be proposed without any difficulties and greetings could be conveyed to the whole community. If Timothy's authorship is incapable of proof but at most can only be shown to be probable, then the identity of the Epistle to Philemon with that "from Laodicea" is still less capable of proof. Nevertheless, our hypothesis would explain why Philemon, an epistle which is not exactly suitable for a collection of letters, should have survived, without there being a trace of the other letter which was supposed to have been sent from Laodicea to Colossae.

If Colossians were written at about the same time as Philemon, the Ephesian imprisonment remains the most probable situation for

25. Cf. Stuhlmacher, *Philemon*, 21f.; Houlden, 139 and, already, Petrus Lombardus (259A); detailed argument is provided in G. S. Duncan, *St. Paul's Ephesian Ministry*, London 1929, esp. 66-94, 111-15, 145-61, 270f., 298f. This is attested to as well by the Marcionite Prologues (for the text see W. G. Kümmel, *The New Testament*, 1970². These are genuine documents from the Marcionite church shortly after the death of its head (id., *Introduction to the New Testament*). According to Haenchen, *Acts* and *New Testament Apocrypha* 2, 130f., they are spurious. The fact that the collection is not mentioned (or is it in 1:4, as Ernst, 156?) is not a decisive argument against this setting. More difficult is the fact that neither Mark (Col. 4:10) nor Luke (Col. 4:14; Philemon 24) are found in the Pauline Epistles of about the same period. This would be easier to account for in the case of Colossians being dated to a Caesarean (or Roman) imprisonment (cf. Acts 12:12, 25). On the other hand, Tychicus comes from Asia Minor (Acts 20:4) and is linked with Ephesus in 2 Tim. 4:12.

it.[25] This is all the more so since Onesimus's being returned to Paul and being sent again to Colossae. The comings and goings of Epaphras, Tychicus, and Mark, also create the presumption that the place of imprisonment was relatively close to the two communities in the Lycus Valley. If a fellow worker is the author then ideas that differ from those of the main Pauline Epistles no longer argue against a date in more or less the same period.[26] The similarity with the situation in Galatia could even argue for a certain historical proximity, although the differences should not be overlooked (v. 127f.). The presence of Luke causes no problem, unless one accepts that he wrote Acts (or at least the section concerning Ephesus), and would accordingly have had to mention this imprisonment and much else besides.

Our present Epistle is perhaps attested as early as 1 Clement 49:2, and probably in Justin (cf. p. 247). The text tradition there, however, is not always reliable, so that the resemblances to the text of Colossians could also go back to a copyist or, indeed, to a commonly-used formula. It is certain that the Epistle was included in Marcion's canon around 150.[27]

---

26. Against Ernst, 151.
27. A. von Harnack, *Markion: Das Evangelium vom fremden Gott*, Leipzig 1924[2], 51. Col. is attested to in all three witnesses (Tertullian, Adamantius, Epiphanius), ibid. 43°, 45°, 50f.°, 54°, 56f.°, 64°. Formulations from Colossians perhaps also make their effect felt in 1 Clem. 49:2; Ign. *Trall.* 5:2; *Pol.* 12:2 (cf. further *Odes Sol.* 16:18).

Commentary

The Opening Address (1:1-8)

Assurance of Grace (1:1-2)

Bibliography: Berger, K., "Apostelbrief and apostolische Rede/Zum Formular frühchristlicher Briefe," ZNW 65 (1974) 190-231.

1 Paul, an apostle of Christ Jesus by the will of God, and Timothy our brother, 2 To the saints and faithful brethren in Christ at Colossae: Grace to you and peace from God our Father.

Analysis

The opening address of this letter corresponds to those of the Pauline Epistles.[1] The letter is to be read during the service (4:16); for this reason, the first two verses are not merely an address, but an assurance of the presence of God. And indeed they do differ in this respect from the formulae found in both Jewish and Hellenistic letters; they come closer to the Old Testament and Jewish benedictions. The combination of (light,) grace, and peace occurs also in Ethiopic Enoch 5:7 (Greek text); that of mercy and peace occurs frequently (ibid. 5:5f.; cf. 1:8) [2] and in Wisdom 3:9; 4:15 grace and mercy are imputed to the chosen (or the "saints"),[3] while mercy and peace are combined in the opening address of a letter to the "brethren" in s. Baruch 78:2. "Grace" is what the believer finds with God, especially in his revelation. For Paul, the expression comprehensively designates the salvation of the era brought in through Christ. Thus the expression "grace" is associated with the traditional

---

1. Cf. Stuhlmacher, *Philemon*, 29.
2. Tobit 7:12 (S); Sir. 50:23f.; 3 Macc. 2:19f.; Jub. 12:29; 22:8-10; 1QS 2:1-4; cf. Num. 6:25f.; Isa.

54:10; 1QM 12:3; s.Bar. 78:2. On the whole question, cf. Berger, "Apostelbrief," 191ff. along with note 10.
3. Χάρις and ἔλεος (ὁσίοις 3:9 v.l.).

wish for peace, and transforms a customary greeting into an assurance of blessing.

Interpretation

[1] As in most of the Pauline Epistles (but not 1 Thess. 1:1; Phil. 1:1), Paul is designated an *apostle*. Apostles could as the addition of the genitive "your" or "of the congregation" shows, be called delegates of one or more congregations (Phil. 2:25; 2 Cor. 8:23). However, when Paul speaks in 1 Cor. 15:7 of "all the apostles," without any such addition, he is referring to a fixed group of witnesses to the Easter event; this group is obviously not identical with the twelve (1 Cor. 15:5), but it does presumably include them.[4] It is in this sense that Paul is an "apostle of Christ Jesus," and he bitterly defends his calling against others. This shows that the fixed, titular usage must be pre-Pauline.[5] Moreover, Paul can talk of the "superlative apostles" (2 Cor. 11:5; 12:11), by which he can hardly mean the original apostles, but rather apostles who are charismatic, and allegedly sent by the Spirit.[6]

The problem with the derivation of the title is that whereas the Greek word is certainly known as a technical naval term, though hardly ever in the sense of "envoy," the Jewish concept, by contrast, denotes—not a missionary—but one empowered with a temporary commission (1 Kings 14:6).[7] That can certainly account for the designation of one delegated by the community, but not for the designation of an apostle in the typically Pauline sense. Yet empowering and sending forth to proclaim are linked together in the case of the Old Testament prophets, even if the titular designation does not appear. The combination of God's appearing, of sending forth, and of proclaiming is particularly striking in the case of Moses.[8] The very fact of the divine appearance makes it almost impossible

---

4. Otherwise they would probably be mentioned at Gal. 1:18f. Furthermore, the later concept of the twelve apostles can be more easily understood in this way. It is certainly to this category that Peter belongs (Gal. 1:19a; 2:8). 5. M. Hengel, "Die Ursprünge der christlichen Mission," *NTS* 18 (1971/2) 32. 6. Cf. also Rev. 2:2. Itinerant apostles of this kind are positively mentioned for the first time in Did. 11.

7. שָׁלִיחַ = ἀπόστολος   3(1) Kings 14:6 (Á) LXX. 8. Exod. 3:14-16: ὤπται (cf. ὤφθη), ἀπέσταλκεν. He is called שָׁלִיחַ of God in Ex. R. 3:14; 5:12; b.Bab.Mez. 86b (v. B. Gerhardsson, *Die Boten Gottes und die Apostel Christi*, 1962 (SEÅ 27), 112). Secular usage (John 13:16) is attested to by Greek papyri of the fifth to eighth centuries A.D. (v. F. Agnew, "On the Origin of the Term Apostolos," *CBQ* 38(1976) 49-53).

for the person to whom this appearance is manifested to keep it to one's self.[9]

In Gal. 1:15 the sending of Paul is seen as parallel to that of the prophets (cf. Jer. 1:5; Isa. 49:1); thus the appearance of Christ in the New Testament corresponds to the appearance of God in the Old. Perhaps the Jewish usage of "one who is empowered" (even if the development of a distinctive institution came about only after A.D. 70, and always included only temporary and not specifically religious commissions), facilitated the transition from the verb "to send" to the substantive "one who is sent–apostle"; for even in the first years of the Jerusalem community, the twelve were considered as those "empowered by Jesus." *empowered to heal forces etc.*

In any case, the combination of "sending" and "proclaiming the gospel" had already been established (Isa. 61:1), and was taken up in the Jesus narratives and in Paul's writings (Luke 4:16-21; 1:19; 1 Cor. 1:17; also Rom. 10:14f.). So if the prototypical apostle for the post-Easter community is Jesus himself, who was sent forth in fulfillment of the whole prophetic mission, in order to proclaim the gospel, then the disciples of Jesus are conscious after Easter that they have been called and sent forth by the Risen One, as happened with the prophets of the Old Testament, through an appearance of God.[10] It is for this reason that the "will of God" is particularly mentioned in 1/2 Cor. 1:1 (cf. Gal. 1:1, 15); Col. 1:1.

Timothy appears alongside Paul, as at 2 Cor. 1:1; Phil. 1:1; 1 Thess. 1:1; Philemon 1. For the apostle, particularly, it is important that he should stand with the brethren in the community; that is, that he should not speak simply as a person of authority or of special dignity. Timothy was won over by Paul in (Derbe or) Lystra on the first missionary journey, and accompanied him from then on (Acts 16:1). At all events according to 1 Thess. 3:2, 6 he travels from Athens to Thessalonica and back, proclaims the gospel in Corinth along with Paul (2 Cor. 1:19), journeys several times to and fro between Asia Minor and Corinth (1 Cor. 4:17; 16:10), and is sent to Philippi by the imprisoned apostle (Phil. 2:19). According to Acts 20:4, he was one of those companions of Paul who were involved in the collecting of alms for the poor on the journey from Greece to Palestine. In all instances, apart from the letter to Phile-

9. H. Conzelmann, *History of Primitive Christianity*, New York, Abingdon, 1973, 39f.

10. F. Hahn, *Der Apostolat im Urchristentum*, KD 20 (1974) 54-77.

mon, the reason for his being mentioned is obvious—he is already known to the congregations.[11] Is that supposed to hold in the case of the recipients of the letter to Philemon as well? As a "brother," Timothy is ranked equally with those who received the letter.[12] It is only from his fellowship with the apostle, from whom he receives his legitimation, that he derives his authority to write to them.

[2] The wording of the reference to the recipients corresponds above all to that in Phil. 1:1 ("to the saints in Christ Jesus").[13] What is new here is the addition "to the faithful brethren." However, in Colossians it is frequently to be observed that customary phrases are supplemented by synonyms,[14] and the designation of Timothy as "a child (of the apostle) beloved and faithful in the Lord," serves at least as a start to such a process.

Since the article is not repeated, "holy" should correctly be taken as an adjective; but since Paul always speaks of the believers as "saints" in a substantival sense, it should rather be considered as careless usage. "Saints" is, then, to a certain extent a title of respect for them, while "brethren" unites them with Paul.[15] On the combination of "grace" and "peace" see the Analysis at the beginning of this chapter. Whereas "grace" denotes the act of divine love, which bridges the gulf between God and his people, "peace" describes the new relationship thus brought about. "From" is always used to introduce the sender of a letter in Hellenistic letters;[16] perhaps underlying Paul's variation on this stylistic form is the idea that God himself is the real author. The reference to God alone here—without Christ being introduced as well—is just as lacking in parallel in the Pauline letters as is the indication of the place without use of the participle.[17]

11. Ludwig, *Verfasser*, 62.
12. E. E. Ellis, "Paul and His Co-workers," *NTS* 17 (1970/1) 448f. and id., "Spiritual Gifts in the Pauline Community," *NTS* 20 (1973/4) 139, even goes so far as to think that the recipients were Paul's fellow-workers and therefore instructed to see that the letter be read in public worship (4:16). However, in his letters Paul frequently addresses the community as ἀδελφοί.
13. The reading Ἰησοῦ in A,D etc. is certainly a secondary assimilation to

such formulae; cf. 1:28. Again in Rom. 1:7 the term "saints" is used instead of "community" (Meyer, 168f.).
14. Ludwig, *Verfasser*, 64.
15. Calvin, 124. "Holy brethren" is unPauline (only 1 Thess. 5:27 v.l.).
16. Ἀπό or παρά (Berger, "Apostelbrief," 202).
17. Most of the manuscripts insert "Christ" according to the usual Pauline formula. The indication of the place, as well as the whole usage with ἀπό can also be lacking (1 Thess. 1:1f.).

Summary

The first two verses are not merely an address. They are an assurance of blessing, which brings about a new situation. For this very reason, emphasis is laid both upon the legitimation of the one who sends the letter, and at the same time upon the faithful listening of those called to be "saints," belonging to him as "brethren." Only when commissioned by God can such a letter be properly written, and only in faithful obedience can it be rightly read and heard. Thus in the opening address of the letter, sanctity and brotherhood grounded in the faith are imputed to the reader. Just as with Paul righteousness is not our own righteousness, but a righteousness which is imputed to us, a righteousness which is alien to us, so it is here in the case of one's sanctity.[18]

Thanksgiving (1:3-8)

Bibliography: Friedrich, G., "Lohmeyers These über 'Das paulinische Briefpräskript' kritisch beleuchtet" ZNW 46 (1955) 272-274; Schubert, P. *Form and Function of the Pauline Thanksgivings,* 1939 (BZNW 20); White, J. L. *Form and Function of the Greek Letter. A Study of the Letter Body in the Non-Literary Papyri and in Paul the Apostle,* 1972 (SBLDS 2)

3 We always thank God, the Father of our Lord Jesus Christ, when we pray for you, 4 because we have heard of your faith in Christ Jesus and of the love which you have for all the saints, 5 because of the hope laid up for you in heaven. Of this you have heard before in the word of the truth, the gospel 6 which has come to you, as indeed in the whole world it is bearing fruit and growing—so among yourselves, from the day you heard and understood the grace of God in truth, 7 as you learned it from Epaphras our beloved fellow servant. He is a faithful minister of Christ on your behalf 8 and has made known to us your love in the Spirit.

Analysis

These verses form a separated section; for from v 9 onwards the thanksgiving passes over into intercession, and accordingly the present or past tense gives way to the future. Certainly a similar phenomenon can be observed at Rom. 1:9f.; 1 Cor. 1:8; Phil. 1:4-6, 9-11.

---

18. Conzelmann, 178.

However, where Paul mentions his intercession for the community, the reference comes right at the start of the expression of thanks, and this prayer includes the thanksgivings, just as it does the entreaty for the future (so also 1 Thess. 1:2, and especially Philemon 4–6). Here, however, this entreaty is not given expression until v 9 (which also takes up again the intercession of v 3), and is stressed by the addition of "to pray." The expression of thanks is, then, clearly distinguished from the intercession. It consists of one single main verb, standing at the beginning, from which hangs a cluster of nine clauses, strung together by participles, relative pronouns or "as." (This appears less complex in the translation, where it is broken down into three sentences.) What we have, then, are loose associations, so that it is possible to pass from one clause to the next, without getting a synoptic view of the structure of the whole sentence.[1]

Interpretation

[3] Expressions of thanks at the beginning of letters are also to be found in Hellenistic letters,[2] though not in official documents. Such expressions of thanks bear the stamp of religious experience, as they do in Paul's case, and as can be established in the case of Epictetus in Hellenism, and for Philo in Judaism. The expression of thanks is clearly related to the community addressed in the letter.[3] As in Philemon 4–7; 1 Thess. 1:2-10; Phil. 1:3-8, the thanksgiving is expressed in very personal terms. The plural is found also in 1 Thess. 1:2. God is presented as "the Father of our Lord Jesus Christ."[4] The import of this is that it is God who has become present in Jesus Christ, and that, conversely, it is in Christ that God himself is found. It is not merely the community that is praised, but God's goodness, which the apostle sees at work not only in his own life, but also in others.[5] The idea that thanksgiving is offered "al-

1. Bujard, *Untersuchungen*, 79f.; participles and relative clauses carrying on from one another are characteristic of Colossians (ibid. 59-70). For a penetrating study of the difference in style between this passage and Paul, cf. ibid. 73f., 79-86.
2. Instances are given in Lohse, 12f.; for Judaism cf. 2 Macc. 1:10f.
3. Schubert, *Form*, 179-85.
4. Cf. 2 Cor. 1:3, although there it is true the formula is " . . . God and Fa-

ther. . . ." καί is certainly well attested here in Col. 1:3 by ℵAℵ but these same witnesses have also been assimilated to the usual Pauline formula in v 2 as well. ℵ gives the reading θεῷ καὶ πατρί, at 1:12 as well (v. ad loc.) but not at 3:17. This phrase is found in all three verses only in miniscules and in Ambrosiaster and Theodoret. It is, then, not characteristic of Colossians. B lacks "Christ."
5. Calvin, 124.

ways" for them is hardly limited by the addition of the clause "when
we pray for you." [6] Official and private spheres, liturgical and secular life, are inseparable in the apostle's case.[7]

[4] What Paul has heard of the life of the community, perhaps
through Epaphras (4:12), he renders by means of the triad of faith,
hope, and love.[8] It must be said that he does this in such a way that
the last of the three is introduced as the foundation of the first two.
In 1 Thess. 5:8 faith and love stand close together, and hope is mentioned later; in Philemon 5 and Gal. 5:6 only faith and love are
mentioned. Strictly speaking, "in Christ" signifies faith as living in
the realm of the power of Jesus Christ; but since Colossians often
uses "in" where Paul has other prepositions (v. note 14 of the Introduction), it could well be faith in Jesus Christ that is meant. One can
"hear" of such faith, that is, its effect is such that one can give a
report of it. At the same time, it is noted that faith lives inasmuch as
it points away from the individual to the one who is the real source
of all action, Jesus Christ.

Next to faith comes love. It remains the form in which faith mani-
fests itself. The two are really inseparable, for faith is always lived
as much with the lips as with the heart (Rom. 10:9), as much with
the hands and the feet as with the brain. The only difference is that
faith describes life from the perspective of its orientation toward its
source of energy in Christ. Love, on the other hand, describes that
same life from the point of view of its effect on other people, and
that universally on "all the saints"—in other words, on all those who
belong to the community of Christ.[9]

[5] If faith, love, and hope basically include all modes of time—by
faith being based on the past that consists of the life, death, and

6. Cf. v 9; cf. also 1 Cor. 1:4; 2
Thess. 1:3; Rom. 1:10; 1 Thess. 1:2;
similar to Col 1:3 is Philemon 4.
7. Friedrich, "Lohmeyers These" emphasizes how unliturgical the opening
verses are in comparison with the
phrases used at the end. They correspond not to the prayer used in worship, but to the form of the secular
letter, although it must be said that
this form is not merely repeated but
taken over in an enriched version.

8. Cf. 1 Cor. 13:13; 1 Thess. 1:3;
Pol. 3:3; it probably represents primitive Christian tradition, and in any
case it was not simply created as an
anti-Gnostic device (with Lohse, 16).
Caird, 167 further refers to Rom.
5:1-5; Gal. 5:5f.; Eph. 4:2-5; 1
Thess. 3:8; Heb. 6:10-12; 10:22-24;
1 Peter 1:3-8, 21f.
9. πᾶς, it is true, is found frequently
in Colossians as a purely plerophoric
usage (v. p. 18).

resurrection of Jesus, love permeating totally the community's present period, and hope being set toward the future—then this is at least no longer emphasized here. Just as faith is above all directed toward the present, heavenly Christ (cf. p. 84f.), so hope describes what is laid up in heaven. The hope by which one hopes has been reinterpreted as the hope which is hoped, and one wonders whether word and object designated by it do not go their separate ways since there is no longer a temporal dimension involved.[10] However, only the certainty and objectivity of the salvation guaranteed by God alone are really meant here; the idea that what is future is already present in God is also familiar from Jewish apocalyptic.[11] It is in this sense that Paul can speak of the eternal dwelling in heaven (2 Cor. 5:1). Only later will it emerge why it is particularly in this Epistle that the world "above" is especially emphasized (v. p. 133). More important is the fact that faith is grounded in hope, and not the other way round.[12]

Such statements as these are dangerous because the conviction that salvation is something objectively existent in the beyond, becomes the foundation of faith. At the same time, however, this does preclude the subjectivity of a faith based only on itself, resting on the experience of one's own soul's stirrings; and, along with this, it does understand hope as an effective act which actually generates faith and love.[13] The expression "in heaven"[14] thus captures the beyondness of salvation. Human beings, dwelling on an earth that has become heavenless, are told that they derive their life from the fact that the whole meaning of life lies neither in one's self, nor in humanity, nor in nature, but in the one who is encountered in (though he is also beyond) them both. The Colossians have already heard of this hope "before." One could understand this to mean "before the end," so that the proclamation of the gospel would

10. Petrus Lombardus, 260A; 261A; Zwingli, 220; Lohse, 17; Bornkamm, "Hoffnung," 58-62.
11. H. W. Kuhn, Enderwartung und gegenwärtiges Heil, 1966 (SUNT 4) 181-8; Ernst, 157: 2 Esdr. 7:14,77; s.Bar. 14:12; 24:1.
12. R. Bultmann, TDNT 532f. Meyer, 170 holds that this applies only to "love." Bengel, 810 links the ideas thus: "We give thanks . . . because of the hope. . . ." Schleiermacher, Pre-

digten I 203; II 209 accounts for hope being made the basis of what is said here by referring to the small size and the humility of the community at that time.
13. Calvin, 125.
14. The Greek text has the plural "heavens." This is merely a Semitism, but it expresses the fulness better than does the singular, which is more usually found in English.

be understood as the anticipation of the one who is to come. However, this is improbable, since the temporal component is not stressed and vv 7f. point in a different direction. The reference here, as in 1 John 1:1; 2:7, 13f., 24; 3:11, is probably to the beginning of the proclamation.[15] In both these Epistles the readers are thus summoned to return to the gospel in the face of false teaching.

It is for this reason that the gospel is also immediately characterized as a "word of the truth." It is "the truth of the gospel" which Paul defends as well in Gal. 2:5 against all distortions. "Truth" is not, as in the Greek or Western tradition, the result necessarily arrived at by empirical proof or logical deduction, in which what is expressed is in agreement with what exists. Truth, and this is a view which derives from the Old Testament, is the free act of those who fulfill what may be expected of them. The opposite would not be deception but disappointment. Truth is reliability,[16] so that it is an epithet attributable to a doorpost that is standing straight, water that does not dry up, a vine that bears fruit. It retains, then, its character of mystery; it can never be deduced with necessity, but only received as a gift; as when our partner remains devoted to us, when the post, the water, the vine serve our purpose. So the "word of the truth" is the word of God, on which one can rely (Ps. 119:43; Test. Gad 3:1). Thus God's truth is spoken of above all when he goes out from himself and discloses himself to his creatures. So the people of Qumran, in contrast to the children of the world, are the "men of truth," and the apocalyptic book is "a record of truth" (Dan. 10:21). So also the content of truth is designated in v 6 as God's grace; yet there, as in Colossians, the transition to another concept of truth becomes apparent, that is, to a concept according to which the marking off of the true doctrine from the false is the main function of truth.

[6] The triumphal march of the gospel, which is already "in the whole world" (by which is meant the Roman Empire) becomes more and more important for the followers of Paul. Indeed, Paul in

---

15. So Lohse, 18; Lohmeyer, 26 (cf. Meyer, 171): before their conversion; Moule, 50: before the spread of the false teaching. De Wette, 19 and de Boor, 167 both interpret eschatologically.

16. For the interpretation of truth as "reliability," cf. R. Bultmann, "Untersuchungen zum Johannesevangelium," ZNW 27 (1928) 128 n25.

Rom. 1:16 and 15:16 takes over eschatological promises like Ps.
98:2f. and Isa. 66:20; in the writings of his disciples this leads to the
schema of revelation (v. p. 107).

Monotheism already existed in Hellenism, in philosophy as respect
for nature, and in popular thought as belief in fate or destiny. In the
mystery religions, the gods did indeed retain their names; in fact,
however, there was only one God who was revered, and who could
be invoked under various names. It was this world that the one God
of Judaism had entered, a God of whom it was forbidden to make
any image. This belief had attracted many people of the time, even
if they were not completely converted to the Jewish faith. Paul's
message led, as was probably inevitable, to a rivalry with the Jewish mission. This situation was aggravated a good deal further
when, after the destruction of Jerusalem (and thus after the death
of Paul), Israel could only preserve its identity, historically, through
consistent obedience to the law. In contrast to this, the apostle's
proclamation signified on the one hand liberation from the law, that
is, from the preliminary conditions to be met by the individual. For
many people these conditions made entry into the Jewish faith
impossible, since they could only be satisfied in the exclusive community of Israel, and not in the world of the Roman Empire. On the
other hand, the apostle's proclamation signified, with its clear orientation towards Jesus Christ, liberation from an image of God which
had degenerated into a mere abstraction. As far as the gospel was
concerned, there was no longer any need to uproot oneself from
one's Greek or Roman world to change to a way of life which, with
its laws of diet and purification, made it practically impossible to
have any social intercourse with one's non-Jewish neighbors, or to
a historical setting in which one had no part. On the other hand,
the gospel was more than an abstraction which made no demands;
Jesus Christ wished to become Lord over his community, in the
very place in which they lived.

The sequence of words "bearing fruit and growing" (v. on v 10)
is not altogether logical; but in the figurative sense of the phrase, it
is the idea of bearing fruit which is the decisive notion. The phrase
could be influenced by the usage in Gen. 1:22, 28 etc. (cf. **Mark**

4:8), although there admittedly it is not metaphorical. Just as a tree
without fruit and growth would no longer be a tree, so a gospel
which bore no fruit would cease to be a gospel.

With the phrase "so among yourselves," the author returns to the
specific situation of the community. The alternating emphasis between universal and local community is characteristic of the whole
Epistle. By means of "heard and understood" much more emphasis
is laid on the objective acceptance of the message than on the subjective experience of it. Once more, the reliability of what they
have heard is emphasized, though in the sense of correct as opposed
to incorrect understanding. "To come to the knowledge of the truth"
in the Pastoral Epistles denotes the act of becoming a Christian (cf.
Heb. 10:26; 2 John 1; Col. 2:2f.).

[7] Epaphras is designated first of all as a "fellow servant." Abraham, Moses, David, and others, especially the prophets, are servants
of God. So also are those to whom God entrusts his secret(s)
(1QpHab. 7:5; Rev. 1:1; 10:7; 22:6), and through whom he makes
known his will (1QS 1:3 etc.). Hence learning is also spoken of here;
it appears relatively seldom in Paul but more frequently in the
Pastoral Epistles. The apocalyptic terminology of perceiving the
revealed mystery, and the demarcation of the true from the false
teaching, conceived more in terms of Greek thought, are linked together. Epaphras is further described as a "minister of Christ on our
behalf" [17]. His close relationship to the apostle is thus brought into
special prominence; his authority is that of the apostle, and for this
reason Christ becomes the real subject of his ministry. If one ob-
serves how in 1:23 Paul is seen as *the* apostle for the whole world,
it does indeed become obvious that his authority begins to be transferred to those who represent him.

[8] Nevertheless the human aspect of this is not forgotten. The
bond of love between the community and the apostle is not unimportant, although immediately this love is further described as spir-

---

17. This is undoubtedly the more difficult reading as compared with "for
you." It is supported by p⁴⁶ and the
majority of the witnesses of the Hesy-
chianic group. Or should it be understood as "in our place"? Perhaps underlying this usage there is a fixed
division of labor, according to which
Paul carried out the mission in the
central area of a town, while his fellow workers operated in the surrounding region (Ernst, 159).

itual.[18] The section then concludes with a renewed reference to the favorable state of the community.

In contrast to the Pauline Epistles, the *Spirit* plays hardly any role in our present letter. Many statements which Paul always or very frequently associates with the Spirit are found here without any such reference. In consequence, a different point of reference, most often "Christ," appears instead.[19] Apart from the anthropological, but also unPauline, usage in 2:5 (v. ad loc.), our present verse is the only one in which the substantive "Spirit" occurs, and even so it is without the article. In the comparable phrases in Rom. 15:30 and 14:17 (cf. 5:5), the Spirit is clearly designated as the subject of love or as the power of the joy in which one shows obedience. In Col. 1:8, on the contrary, the point presumably is only that a spiritual love is to be distinguished from one that is purely worldly. That at any rate is so for the use of the adjective in 1:9 and 3:16.

The background to such a distinction is a dualistic understanding of the world, which distinguishes between a wisdom that comes from above and one which is earthly-psychic-demonic (compare 1:9 with James 3:15).[20] This understanding of the world, however, is scarcely still operative here; the addition is probably only intended to set limits vis-à-vis a neutral or secular view of the world. Thus all the verses have now been mentioned in which there is any reference at all to the Spirit. This paucity of allusion is related to the fact that reference to the Spirit is extremely difficult to control by the use of objective criteria. Appeal is made to the Spirit in every kind of sectarian movement for which Christ has become incidental

---

18. Literally "in spirit" (cf. note 14 to Introduction); but as early as Theophylact (1212B) and Calvin, 126, it is rightly translated by "spiritual love," while Severian (317, on 1:9) sets "spiritual" in contrast to "worldly."
19. Schweizer, "Christus." Cf. the "word" (1:5) with 1 Thess. 1:5 ("not only in word, but also . . . in the Holy Spirit"), and "in truth" (1:6) and (endurance and patience) "with joy" (1:11) with 1 Thess. 1:6 ("with joy inspired by the Holy Spirit"); again, compare the combination of indicative and imperative in "walk in Christ Jesus" (2:6) with Gal. 5:25

(walk in the Spirit"), the "bearing fruit" and "growing" (1:6, 10) with Rom. 15:13; 7:4-6; Gal. 5:22 (in "power . . .", "newness . . .", or as "fruit of the Spirit"), and the "circumcision of Christ" (2:11) with that "in the Spirit" (Rom. 2:29; cf. also baptism "in one Spirit," 1 Cor. 12:13). The theme of an "upper" world (or world "above"), although also familiar to Paul, is yet described by him as living in the Spirit (and no longer in the flesh; Gal. 4:26-9; Phil. 3:3, 14); Col. 3:1, 17 is altogether different in this respect.
20. E. Schweizer, *TDNT* IX 663.

or nothing more than a cipher for something altogether different. In Christology, by contrast, the criteria for distinguishing between true and false teaching are more readily available. In the case of the Spirit, one has to take account of the content of what the Spirit says; but this means that one must refer back to theological and Christological propositions. Of course, even with a correct Christology, there is no guarantee that the truth can be possessed forever. This can be seen *in nuce* from precisely this Epistle, where knowledge of Christ is characterized so emphatically as something that must be lived out in an ethical way (cf. on v 10).

Summary

The author has learned from Paul to take seriously the thanksgiving formulas characteristic of Hellenistic letters. It may well be asked whether faith and love in actual fact were so characteristic of the community, in view of the attempt to come to terms with the Colossian philosophy and in view of the catalog of vices (a catalog which is clearly not superfluous as a warning!). All the same, the letter begins with thanksgiving, not with rebuke and complaint. The writer is justified in starting in this way because he knows of the "hope laid up for you in heaven." The sanctity of the community lies in the salvation that God has prepared for it, and which gives it its sense of direction.

The community lives "in Christ." Christ is, then, not merely a concept that serves to characterize its special nature as a Christian as distinct from a wordly community. It lives—whatever its character may be—in him, just as, conversely, "the world is in the power of the evil one" (1 John 5:19). Christ is the place in which the community lives, the atmosphere in which it thrives, and which does indeed permeate it. This has come about because the community has heard the trustworthy word, a word which brings forth fruit and increases, which carries experience with it, and which therefore never atrophies. So also its faith can live only as love.

Laying the Foundation (1:9—2:23)

Intercessions (1:9-11)

9 And so, from the day we heard of it, we have not ceased to pray for you, asking that you may be filled with the knowledge of his will

in all spiritual wisdom and understanding, 10 to lead a life worthy
of the Lord, fully pleasing to him, bearing fruit in every good work
and increasing in the knowledge of God. 11 May you be strengthened with all power, according to his glorious might, for all endurance and patience with joy.

Analysis

The letter proceeds to the intercessions already mentioned in v 3.
Verse 12 seems to return again to the thanksgiving. Purely from a
structural point of view, one could in fact identify three sentences
in vv 10-12, each beginning with a prepositional phrase ("in every
good work," "with all power," "with joy"), and issuing in a phrase
defining the objective "for the knowledge of God," "for endurance,"
"for a share in the inheritance").[1] However, the first of these phrases
defining the objective is to be found only in the manuscripts of the
𝔎 group, while the last phrase, unlike the first two, is not related
to a participle in the plural, and has thus assembled a completely
different function. What vv 12-14 in fact do is introduce the hymn;
hence the participle ("giving thanks") cannot be considered as a
continuation of vv 9-11, (in other words as a description of the author's activity), but must be understood as a summons to those who
receive the letter (v. note 1 to 1:12-14). The content of the intercession is expressed by a final clause ("that you may be filled with
the knowledge . . .") upon which an infinitive consequentially depends ("to lead a life"); this in turn is more closely described by
means of participles ("bearing fruit," "increasing," "strengthened
with all power"). The repetition of expressions or phrases that have
already been used is a feature that is to be observed especially clearly in this passage; so also is the addition of the adjective "all" or
"each,"[2] intended to express full assurance.

---

1. Meyer, 175.
2. Προσεύχεσθαι vv 3, 9; ἀκοῦσαι vv
4, 9; καρποφορεῖν καὶ αὐξάνειν 6,
10; ἐπιγνῶναι, ἐπίγνωσις vv 6, 9,
10; cf. Bujard, *Untersuchungen*, 86-8;
πᾶς 5 times in vv 9-11 (ibid. 159f.)
The summons to thankfulness (v 3) is
repeated in v 12; 3:17 (ibid. 99). A
really novel suggestion is found in Lamarche, "Structure," 454f, He detects,

in a chiastic arrangement; Thanksgiving (3a), Supplication (3b), News
(4a)/News (4b-8), Supplication (9-
11), Thanksgiving (12-20); however,
4a/b is surely not to be wrenched
apart, and the combination of thanksgiving and supplication is frequent
(Philemon 4; 1 Thess. 1:2; Rom. 1:8-
10), so that this structure is hardly
determinative.

Interpretation

[9] The introduction to the intercession is Pauline, but the follow-) ing formulation clearly refers back to vv 3ff.[3] Again (as in v 3) it is the continuity of the prayer, and thus the personal commitment of the apostle, that is stressed.[4] Although the content of the being "filled" is set in the accusative, there is no need for a rendering different from that given above (". . . with the knowledge of his will . . .").[5] The cognitive process is given extraordinary prominence; alongside "knowledge" is found "wisdom" and "understanding." This dual expression is attested in Jewish as well as Greco-Roman thought; [6] certainly the accumulation of terms is typical of Colossians. The importance of this aspect of faith is brought into special prominence, but so also is the open-minded nature of the knowledge (cf. pp. 108 and 117). The essential point, however, is that the content of this knowledge is described as the "will of God" (Rom. 2:18; Luke 12:47f.), and its consequence as leading "a life worthy of the Lord." It is, then, a question of knowledge in the Old Testament-Jewish sense; not of the ascertaining of a fact to which one eventually makes one's actions conform, but of insight into the demands of the Lord who expects obedience. This knowledge gives direct motivation, for one's actions.[7] For the more precise designation of this wisdom as spiritual, cf. p. 38.

---

3. Διὰ τοῦτο καί 1 Thess. 2:13; 3:5; Rom. 13:6; but this introductory formula is also found at Matt. 24:44; Luke 11:49; John 12:18; cf. Bujard, *Untersuchungen*, 88.

4. The addition καὶ αἰτούμενοι is lacking in manuscripts B and K; however, Colossians is fond of this sort of duplication by means of synonyms.

5. Masson, 93: "to come to maturity with regard to . . ."; but alongside the genitive (Rom. 15:14), the accusative is also found (Phil. 1:11; Acts 2:28; the accusative is also linked with other verbs of filling in Exod. 31:3; 35:31; 2 Chron. 5:14; Mic. 3:8; Rev. 17:3).

6. Deut. 4:6; Dan. 2:20 etc.; these two, with φρόνησις as the third virtue, are the supreme ἀρεταί of the human understanding in Aristotle, *Eth. Nic.* 113 (1103a, 5-8; cf. Lohse, 26). "In all . . ." could be taken with the

verb "walk" in v 10, but in that case there would be three rather detailed definitions all juxtaposed.

7. This is different from what is found in Aristotle, *Eth. Nic.* 1.1 (1095a, 6), where γνῶσις stands in opposition to πρᾶξις Here it is a matter of the transformation of the whole person in contrast to mere intellectual knowledge (Calvin, 156 on 3:10), although in this the word interpreted by the Spirit provides the sole access to such knowledge (id. 127 on 1:9). There is an abundance of instances in the Qumran texts, e.g.: ". . . to lead them with knowledge and to teach them insights into the mysteries . . . that they may walk perfectly" (1QS 9:18f., v. further Lohse, 25). Θέλημα αὐτοῦ is not, of course, the decree of redemption (as Chrysostom and others, cited in Meyer, 174).

[10] Phil. 1:10 also expresses the content of the knowledge in a final clause, though its form is different, corresponding to Pauline usage.[8] The idea that they should "lead a life worthy of the Lord" is not to be found in Paul (cf. also p. 122), but it is closely related to 1 Thess. 2:12; Phil. 1:27. "Pleasing to him" is probably to be understood as in Luke 2:14; [9] 1QS 8:6; 1QS 4:32f.; 11:9 as referring to what is well-pleasing to God (1 Thess. 4:1; Rom. 8:8; cf. 1 Cor. 7:32; 2 Cor. 5:9), although "to him" is not expressed in the Greek text. He, who by means of his revelation and gift presents us with the possibility of living the right way, is at the same time the norm of this life (cf. p. 124). Paul expresses this above all by reference to the Spirit (Gal. 5:16; Rom. 8:4); here it is transferred to Christ (cf. on v 8).[10]

The expression "every good work" is indeed also found in 2 Cor. 9:8, but is not typical of Paul. He speaks only of the works of the law in plural, since the work of the believer always includes the whole of one's life in its entirety. The expression occurs more frequently in the Pastoral Epistles (1 Tim. 5:10; 2 Tim. 2:21; Titus 1:16; 3:1, and often, in the plural). For the image of "bearing fruit and increasing" cf. on v 6. Whether this should lead one to think of an internal growth or of a missionary operation, directed outwards, cannot be said for certain.[11] The two ideas do indeed go together (3:12-17/4:5f.). On "knowledge" see the comments on v 9 above; and on the repetition of expressions already employed, see note 2 to this section. Both the additional descriptive phrases ("in every good work" and "through (in) the knowledge of God") must be related to the twofold expression "bearing fruit and increasing."

---

8. Εἰς τό (on this cf. note 14 to Introduction) is lacking in Col. 1:10.
9. Εὐδοκία (used in an absolute sense). At Qumran, by contrast, it is "his (God's) good pleasure" that is spoken of; however, Philo frequently uses the expression in an absolute way (e.g. *Spec. Leg.* I 300). In secular usage it is found in the inscription of Priene, "Goodwill towards the masses" (Dibelius, 7f.).
10. Cf. note 19 to 1:3-8 and E. Schweizer, *TDNT* VI, 429; VII, 131-132.
11. Martin, NCB, 52; P. Zingg, *Das Wachsen der Kirche* (Orbis Biblicus et Orientalis 3, Fribourg 1974) 283-5 (frequently in an apologetic or polemical context, ibid. 282). Theodoret 586A thinks of missionary propagation, which is the logical consequence of the fruit of faith. Calvin (125 on v 6) warns against basing faith on visible missionary success and lays emphasis on the promises of God. There is in fact no trace here of a spirit of penitence and of one's own wretchedness, or of a fear of "perfectionism" (de Boor, 170f.).

The knowledge of God is then the basis from which fruit and)
increase become possible.

Admittedly the construction here is no longer strictly logical or
grammatical, since the participles ought really to be in the accusative.[12] Here again Paul would have spoken of the power of the Spirit;
yet fruitfulness and increase are expressed primarily in terms of the
gospel (v 6), and only secondarily of those who are called by it.
In a way then the *extra nos*, the anchoring of faith outside our-   ✗ ⁿ
selves, is yet more strongly brought into prominence, since v 6
does not refer to the Spirit, which cannot always easily be distinguished from the phenomenon of individual inspiration, but refers
instead to what can be objectively described, that is the course of
the gospel throughout the world. At the same time, it is also maintained in v 10 that personal commitment is still essential within this
movement brought about by God and embracing the whole world.
Thus what Paul fuses together in his concept of the Spirit is developed here in two separate expressions.

[11] The reference to God's action is underlined in v 11 by means
of a threefold reference to his "power."[13] The accumulation of
words of similar value attempts to hint at the fullness of God's power,   ⌐
which surpasses anything that humans can express in words. God
should remain God, and not simply be appropriated by his creatures. Thus also the logical relationship involved in the construction cannot and should not be subjected to precise analysis. Paul
can likewise speak of life which comes by virtue of the power of
God; but in his case this is unequivocal and, from internal necessity,
bound up with its being manifest within the weakness of his life
and ministry as an apostle. In the same way, in the case of Jesus, the
power of the resurrection is also shown in the very one who is
crucified.[14] The mention of God's glory may derive from the fact
that power and glory often stand together. Thus the writer takes up
a concept which circumscribes God's absolute transcendence and
his Being beyond space and time (cf. p. 176f).

Thus again what is emphasized is the believer's whole capacity

---

12. Lohse, 28 n45.
13. Κατὰ τὸ κράτος; so LXX, Luke,
Acts, the Catholic Epistles and Revelation, but not Paul. δυναμοῦν is
is lacking in Paul, although he does
use ἐνδυναμοῦν .

14. 2 Cor. 13:4; cf. 4:7: it is only
when the treasure is set in earthen ves-
sels that God's power does not become
confused with rhetorical accomplishment or personal powers of attraction.

having its origin in God. Perhaps what the author is thinking of is the experience of baptism.[15] But at all events this power should take effect as perseverance in the specific situation of the believer's life. The Greek terms literally describe the "remaining beneath (something)" under what is inflicted upon a person, and the "long breath" which can hold out in face of failure or opposition. It is impossible to say whether the writer is thinking more of adverse circumstances or even suffering on the one hand, of difficulties and enmity with fellow workers on the other; or whether he is thinking rather of the perseverance of the eschatological hope. Probably the two are combined together; for vv 5 and 23 speak of the hope which has come to them through the message of the gospel. This hope is also expressed in the following verses, although in such a way that it actually denotes the life that is now present. Probably the sentence is to be understood in the sense that this kind of perseverance should be experienced "with joy." As a rule, indeed, the joy of the eschatological fulfillment is contrasted with the suffering of the present moment; yet this also leads to the paradox of joy in the midst of suffering, around which "the effulgence of God's majesty is woven."[16]

Summary

The strong emphasis on spiritual knowledge is particularly reminiscent of Gnostic thought; so also is the remarkable accumulation of expressions intended to hint at God's being which transcends the world, and for which every concept is inadequate. However, the idea of this knowledge being knowledge of the will of God is completely different to anything found in Gnosticism; neither is it understood in the apocalyptic sense, as insight into God's plan for the course of world history, or even for cosmic renewal, but as an understanding of the ethical demands made by God. It is very defi-

15. Thus Schnackenburg, EKK I, 42, and those cited in note 21 there; also Zwingli, 220.

16. Lohmeyer, 37, referring to Strack-Billerbeck II, 274, n1: "The glory of God descends upon him on whom suffering comes"; cf. III, 243. Calvin, 127 calls to mind Isa. 30:15 ("In quietness and in trust shall be your strength"). On the combination of suffering and hope, cf. 1 Thess. 1:6 (with reference to the Spirit, v. note 19 to 1:3-8); Phil. 2:17f.; Luke 6:21; Acts 5:41; Heb. 10:34; 1 Peter 1:3-8; 4:13. Lohse, 33 (as Chrysostom II, 2[311] and Theophylact 1216A on 1:12 already before him) takes "with joy" with what follows; this is possible, since the phrase stands at the end of the sentence.

nitely *not* the case then, that God is given into the grasp of the
person who possesses knowledge; whether in the sense of Gnosticism, where knowledge denotes deliverance, or in the sense of
apocalyptic, where knowledge leads to informed cognizance about
the future. Here, by contrast, the individual is set in a position of
responsibility before god.

Yet at the same time one is promised that all the power necessary
for undertaking this responsibility is again given by God himself;
so that intercession and thanksgiving form the language in which
the person summoned and supported by God is directed aright.
For this reason life in faith always remains open to further progress.
This life is indeed "endurance" and holding out under the hope
already laid up in heaven. As such, it is directed towards tasks to
be done in this world, that is, towards the "good work"; and it is
incorporated into the community of the church, which is continually refashioned in the course of the apostle's intercession. Hence
it is in this very section, so emphatically oriented towards the
"good work," that God remains in the full sense of being the only
God; so that one can never take refuge behind one's work, but remains constantly dependent upon God. Only thus does life take on
meaning, for the very reason that this meaning lies not in one's life's
achievemet but in the Lord who makes life become ministry. Thus
weariness and resignation are overcome, while confidence for the
"remaining beneath" and the "long breath" is given, so that "joy"
can accompany life in its entirety.

The Hymn and its Setting (1:12-23)

Bibliography: For the relevant literature up to 1963, see Gabathuler,
Jesus Christus; and up to 1969, see Schweizer, EKK I; and up to 1975,
see ib., *Forschung.* Especially important are: Norden, E., *Agnostos Theos.*
(Darmstadt, 1956), 250-4; Käsemann, *Taufliturgie;* Hegermann, *Schöpfungsmittler,* 88-202; Lyonnet, *RSR* 48, 93-100; Schenke, *ZTK* 61, 391-
403; Feuillet, *Christ,* 163-273; Deichgräber, *Gotteshymnus;* Kehl, *Christushymnus;* Wengst, *Formeln;* Schnackenburg, EKK I; Lähnemann, *Kolosserbrief;* Reumann, *Humanität,* Zeilinger, *Der Erstgeborene;* Benoit,
hymne; Burger, *Schöpfung;* and also the commentaries.

Analysis

The theme of the true knowledge of God has already been mentioned in vv 9-11; it is taken up again in 2:2f., and is developed in

the attempt to come to terms with the Colossian philosophy. Verses 12-29 are interpolated before this; obviously the intention is first of all to recall what the community has, before its baptism (?), acknowledged as the basis of its life.[1] Verses 15-20 clearly stand apart from the setting of 12-14 and 21-23. Typical characteristics of the style of Colossians are completely lacking in vv 15-20, except for the interpretative genitive "of the church" in v 18a, which has only been added later by the author, as part of his redactional process.[2] In vv 12-14, by contrast, these stylistic characteristics are found in great abundance, even though the author is taking over traditional,

---

1. Schnackenburg EKK I, 44f.
2. Ludwig, *Verfasser*, 75f. The participial construction (especially favored by the author of the letter) in v 20 does indeed probably belong to the hymn, but is not particularly remarkable.
3. With Wengst, *Formeln*, 172 (cf. Deichgräber, *Gotteshymnus*, 78-82) against Käsemann, "Baptismal Liturgy," 152-4 (37-9); Eckart, "Beobachtungen," 106; D. M. Stanley, *Christ's Resurrection in Pauline Soteriology*, AnBib 13 (1961) 203; Vawter, *CBQ* 33, 74, who find the tradition already taken over in vv 12-14 or (9-12) 13f. The argument based purely on content could conceivably be strengthened by the consideration that the author of the letter was influenced by the liturgy in vv 12-14, with which he was familiar. But in fact the various marks of style here—participial constructions, dependent relative clauses, piling up of genitives, circumstantial clauses introduced by *en*, and appended interpretive additions—are all so typical of the author of the letter that the provenance of vv 12-14 from him can hardly be doubted. Thus there are clear limits set to a division of verses arrived at by purely structuralist criteria. G. Giavini, "La struttura letteraria dell' inno cristologico de Col. 1," *RivB* 15 (1967) 317-20 finds the following pattern: C 12-14, B 15, A 16/a Christ (16b)/A' 16c, 17, B' 18 (a)b, C' 19-20a, so that Christ forms

the center (in 16b), from which the themes of creation are developed, of superiority of the first-born and of reconciliation, in this sequence backwards (in 16a, 15, 12-14) as well as forward (in 16c-17, 18b, 19-20a). However, since vv 15-20 clearly derive from a different hand than that responsible for vv 12-14, the only question worth raising is whether the author of these verses would have understood the hymn according to the pattern outlined above and would have supplied the missing section C. This it must be said is improbable in the extreme. The proposal put forward by Lamarche ("Structure," 454-60) merits consideration; he suggests that the theme is to be seen in vv 21-3 (A: transformation through Christ [21f.], B: admonition [23a], C: proclamation of the gospel [23b]), and that this is developed in 1:24—2:15 (C' in 1:24—2:3, B' in 2:4-8, A' in 2:9-15). However it has to be said that 2:4, 8 are so clearly orientated toward 2:16-23 that one would in fact do better to see the structure of the text from the point of view of the content; that is, to understand 1:23b as a transition to the new theme (1:24ff.) and 2:9-15 as the theologically defined basis of the polemic conducted by means of the Christological statement. The fact that 1:21-23 is obviously a commentary provided on the hymn is a point that Lamarche would not of course be concerned to dispute.

common Christian language; indeed, it is perhaps for this very reason that he is less tied to the model of his teacher, Paul, and thus his own style is more markedly present. In addition, vv 12f. constitute a statement about God, and the relative pronoun "in whom" does not easily form the transition to what is predicted about Christ and thus connect up with v 15. Further, the fact that vv 21-23 pick up the context of vv 12-14 proves that this section is a text deriving from the author of the letter.[3] The hymn (vv 15-20) is then introduced by means of a renewed expression of thanks. That would correspond to the original context, which presupposes an introduction such as "praised be Jesus Christ." It can be shown that vv 21-27 present a kind of commentary on vv 15-20, since (apart from the differences of style) expressions from the hymn, or notions such as that of the restoration of peace or the cosmic activity of Christ, are taken up here but interpreted in a different way. For the structure of each particular passage, reference should be made to what is said in the relevant sections.

(a) Introduction (1:12-14)

12   giving thanks to the Father, who has qualified us to share in the inheritance of the saints in light.   13   He has delivered us from the dominion of darkness and transferred us to the kingdom of his beloved Son,   14   in whom we have redemption, the forgiveness of sins.

Analysis

One must take the beginning of v 12 to refer to the Colossians, as parallel to the three participles in vv 10f., and hardly, as in v 9, to refer to the person from whom the letter comes.[4] Also, the use of the second person plural[5] makes the sentence part of the section

---

4. The order of words εὐχαριστοῦμεν προσευχόμενοι in v 3, the exact opposite in its form to what we have here, certainly does not provide a decisive counter-argument against allowing the subject of the verb in v 12 to be the same as that in v 9; just as the apostle can give thanks in the course of his entreaty, so also he can entreat in the course of his thanksgiving. However, v 9 is rather a long way removed from v 12, and since participles are often used in the sense of imperatives (BDF 486.2; other references are given in Lohse, 32f. nl.), here it will have to be interpreted as a summons to the Colossians (so also Martin NCB, 53 and, much earlier, Gomarus, 549a). One's conclusions here would of course be different if one were to follow Lamarche's analysis (note 2 to 1:9-11).

5. The second person plural form is probably to be retained, with ℵ B, as the more difficult reading.

addressed to the community. The life to which the community is called is in fact that which the apostle prays about in vv 9-11. The change to the first person plural in v 13 is also to be observed in 2:13, and quite frequently in Paul as well (e.g. 1 Thess. 5:5; Rom. 6:14f.; 12:1-6). The first person plural is good style here, since a general confessional statement concerning the basis of the faith is much more markedly in evidence than in v 12 (where the terminology of conversion reminds the readers of their beginnings and this confessional statement is binding both on those who receive the letter and also on the person who sends it.

An extended relative clause leads, in v 13, from God the Father, to whom thanksgiving is due, to Jesus Christ, who is designated, again by means of a relative clause, as the locus of redemption (v 14). At this point, then, the hymn is joined by yet another relative connecting particle. The opening with the relative pronoun in v 13 has thus been assimilated to the style of the hymn that follows; yet it is God, not Christ, who is denoted here. The terminology is decidedly unPauline. "The Father" [6] is found only at Rom. 6:4; there however it simply describes God as the Father of Jesus Christ. The expressions for "share" and "inheritance" are alien to Paul, who also uses the word translated here by the verb "to transfer" only in the proverbial usage "to remove mountains" (1 Cor. 13:2). "Dominion" in Paul denotes, in the singular, full power that is given to a person, or the authorities who are thus empowered; it is found only at 1 Cor. 15:24, along with other expressions, in a plural sense, denoting a demonical power, and not, as here, the whole power of darkness conceived of as something coherent. "Kingdom of his . . . Son" does not occur in Paul, even if it is presupposed in 1 Cor. 15:24; likewise lacking in Paul is the strongly Semitizing usage "his beloved Son," and the more or less equivalent designation "beloved Son" (Mark 1:11 etc.; 2 Peter 1:17). Since in Egyptian texts Pharaoh is called "beloved son" and "the very image of Horus," [7] it might be supposed that the expression stems from an original introductory for-

---

6. On the textual variants cf. note 4 to 1:3-8. The expression is not found in the Qumran texts either (Lohse, 34f.).

7. H. Wildberger, "Das Abbild Gottes, Gen. 1.26-30," *TZ* 21 (1965) 485, cf. 500; v. note 21 to 1:15-20; cf. further the inscription on the Rosetta Stone:

". . . living image of Zeus, son of Helios" (H. Kleinknecht, *TWNT*, 390). Yet in Zech. 12:10 as well, "beloved" and "first-born" stand in parallelismus membrorum (Kehl, *Christushymnus*, 53). On the Semitism "son of his love" cf. BDF 165 and p. 252 below.

mula to the hymn: Praised be God, and the Son of his love, who . . .
(or something similar).

Again, Paul does not speak of "forgiveness of sins," and in his
thought (apart from the fragment taken over from tradition in Rom.
3:24) "redemption" denotes deliverance from death.[8] Conversely,
examples of the verb to "enable" or "empower" (RSV "qualify") are
very seldom to be found outside the New Testament, and then only
in the passive; in 2 Cor. 3:6, on the other hand, the verb is likewise
used in the aorist active. It must be said that the expressions used
do also differ from the rest of Colossians. 1:3 and 3:17 point to the
thanksgiving to "God the Father." 4:11 speaks of the "kingdom of
God;" "dominion" is used in 1:16; 2:10, 15, as in 1 Cor. 15:24, alongside other terms, while redemption, forgiveness, sins, darkness, and
light do not occur again. Undoubtedly, then, traditional language is
used; and indeed, the terminology points to a very definite sphere,
one which also appears in the Qumran documents and in sermons
aimed at conversion.

Interpretation

[12] The summons to thankfulness resumes the theme of v 3, and
is also repeated in 3:17 (cf. note 2 to 1:9-11). The absolute usage of
Father is most unusual,[9] while the verb linked with it is equally in-
frequent. When Paul uses this verb in 2 Cor. 3:6, in place of "to
call," most probably he wants to emphasize the fact that God,
through his act of calling (note the aorist!), makes fit for his service
those who are themselves unfit (1 Cor. 15:9; 2 Cor. 2:16; 3:5).[10]
Probably it is this particular emphasis that the author of Colossians

8. Martin, "Reconciliation," 108. If
one were to translate πάρεσις τῶν . . .
ἁμαρτημάτων in Rom. 3:25 by "forgiveness," one would have a real parallel in a completely different and indeed pre-Pauline, traditional formulation. Ἄφεσις ἁμαρτιῶν (always without τῶν) is attested to in the Synoptic
Gospels and in Acts. Cf. note 39 to
2:8-15.
9. "The Father" and "the Son" are set
in relation to each other in Mark 13:32;
Matt. 11:27 (cf. 28:19) and 1 Cor.
15:24, 28, and also, as the context
makes clear, in Luke 9:26; Acts 1:4,
7; 2:33; Rom. 6:4; Eph. 2:18. It is

in contrast to other fathers that God
is described in this way in Eph. 3:14;
Heb. 12:9. Not until John's Gospel
(and also 1, 2 John) does the absolute usage "the Father" achieve a
prominent position. Outside the New
Testament it is found in Did. 1:5;
Barn. 12:8; 14:6; 1 Clem. 19:2; 2
Clem. 8:4; 10:1; Ign. *Eph.* esp. 3:2;
4:2. Jesus' cry "Abba, Father" was also
taken over in the liturgy of the Pauline communities.
10. According to Chrysostom (II 2
[312]) a king can indeed bestow positions of responsibility, but never the
ability to exercise such.

is still trying to convey; hence he follows Paul's exceptional usage. What is said about the "inheritance," which falls to a person is rooted in the Old Testament account of God graciously allotting the land of Canaan to Israel. However, this idea has long since been transferred, in an eschatological way, to the hereditary portion, which at some point in the future is supposed to be allotted to the believer (Dan. 12:13; Eth. Enoch 37:4; 39:8; 48:7; 58:5; cf. p. 225). "Share" and "inheritance" or "lot" are often used synonymously in the LXX and in the Qumran texts, or else juxtaposed by means of "and."[11] "Lot of darkness" and "lot (or "dominion") of Belial" are interchangeable terms in the Qumran texts (1QS 2:5–8:19; 1QM 1:11-13), so that the idea of a share appertaining to Belial in fact corresponds fully to that of "the dominion of darkness" in Col. 1:13. The same ideas characterize the insertion, strongly influenced by Qumran concepts, in 2 Cor. 6:14-18.[12] The same terminology is found especially in Acts 26:18, where turning "from darkness to light and from the power of Satan to God" leads to "forgiveness of sins" and to "a place (lot) among those who are sanctified." The call to make a decision between darkness and light is expressed just as emphatically not only in the Qumran texts and in the Testaments of the Twelve Patriarchs,[13] but in Joseph and Asenath, 8:9; 15:12, as well.

Thus, then, in Col. 1:12-14, as in all these passages, the actual terminology of conversion is found; this speaks of the power of God, which makes fit for service those who are unfit and brings them out of darkness into light. It also has repercussions in later passages

---

11. W. Foerster, *TDNT* III, 760-2; μερίς is found alongside κλῆρος in Deut. 10:9; 18:1, and alongside κληρονομία in Sir. 45:22; it is found in connection with (τῆς) κληρονομίας in Ps. 15:5; Sir. 24:12, and as a textual variant for this in Deut. 9:26. חֵלֶק is found in the Qumran texts only in the Damascus Document 20:10, 13 (possibly also freely translated in 26, DJD I, 102), and not therefore "often" (as Lohse, 35 asserts to be the case); נַחֲלָה is found in 1QS 4:15f. etc. Perhaps "inheritance" emphasizes still more strongly the sense of this being a gift (Chrysostom II 3[312]).
12. On this see J. Gnilka, "2 Kor.

6.14–7.1 im Lichte der Qumranschriften und der Zwölf-Patriarchen-Testamente" in: *Neutestamentliche Aufsätze (Festschrift J. Schmid)*, Regensburg (1963) 86-99. Cf. below p. 191.
13. Correspondingly φῶς, σκότος, ἐξουσία, ἄφεσις (τῶν) ἁμαρτιῶν, κλῆρος, ἐν τοῖς ἁγιασμένοις/ἁγίοις are found in both Acts 26:18 and Col. 1:12-14; cf. H. Conzelmann, *TDNT* VII, 431-3.
14. Post-Pauline, if the argument of G. Friedrich, "1 Thess. 5.1-11 der apologetische Einschub eines Späteren," *ZTK* 70 (1973) 288-315, is to be accepted.

(1 Thess. 5:4f.;[14] Eph. 5:8; 1 Peter 2:9; 1 Clem. 59:2; 2 Clem. 1:4-8; Barn. 14:5f.) [15] Bearing this in mind, one can understand the sharp distinction made between darkness and light and world and community, in Col. 1:12f. One could even ask whether the saints in whose inheritance the community has been given power to share, may not denote the angels.[16] At any rate, in view of the parallel with v 13, one would have to think of the inheritance as a state that has already been attained, so that the community here as at Qumran, would, as it were, already be living in heaven. That is, however, improbable, first because the term "saints" in 1:2, 4, 22, 26 (!); 3:12 always describes the members of the community, and second, because this is the case as well with the parallel formulation at Acts 26:18. Here, then, it is conceived of in context of the church, which does of course represent something as remarkable as heaven on earth, and is indeed bathed in God's light.[17]

[13] Verse 13 makes a further, and still more emphatic, reference to what God has done in the past, an act which is valid once and for all. The world is experienced as a "dominion;" the background to this usage, noted in connection with v 12, indicates that what the verse is speaking of is a change of sovereignty, that is, uprooting oneself from one sphere and moving into another.[18] The believers have not only come to an ethical decision of their own free will; they have also been set free from a power which has been holding sway over them. In 2 Cor. 6:15 it is true Belial and Christ are mentioned alongside each other; but it must be remembered that in Acts 26:18, and Col. 1:13, the expression "dominion" is used only for the realm of darkness (cf. Isa. 9:1; 60:2 etc.), while the realm of light is more precisely defined by "God," "the inheritance of the saints (or of

15. H. Conzelmann, TDNT VII 422 and n164.
16. Lohmeyer, 39; Lohse, 36; Martin NCB, 54; Schnackenburg, Herrschaft, 209-11; id. EKK I, 42f. Cf. 1QS 11:7f.; 1QM 12:1ff.; 13:4; 1QH 3:21ff. Caird, 171, thinks of Jewish Christians.
17. Presumably the apposition is as often to be connected, almost like an adjective, with "the inheritance of the saints" (Schnackenburg, EKK I, 42f.). It is not merely an ideal prolepsis (Meyer, 179); yet I am in complete

agreement with R. Schnackenburg (in a remark made in conversation) that this does not provide a basis for a triumphal view of the church (v. on v 13).
18. This same phrase is used in Jos. Ant. 9.235 to describe the "transferring to the empire" of the king of Assyria. Plato, Resp. VII (518A) speaks of the transition from light to darkness and vice-versa, as also happens to the soul when it is taken above to view heavenly truth and then returns again to the material world.

those who are sanctified)," "forgiveness of sins" and "faith in me (Jesus Christ)" or "the kingdom of his beloved son."[19] It is then a matter of being set free from slavery for service; for a service that bears the stamp of freedom as a result of living face to face with God or Christ and of the forgiveness of sins. It is also a matter of being transferred to the kingdom of the Son.

Underlying this idea is the promise made to David of the coming kingdom of the Son of God (2 Sam. 7:16; Ps. 2:7; 4QFlor. 1:11; 4QPatr. 4; Luke 1:33); admittedly, the promised "son" was identified more and more with Israel (instead of the Messiah; thus in Pss. Sol. 17f.; Jub. 1:24f.; 4QFlor. 1:7f., and presumably 14-19, where the "anointed one" of Ps. 2:2 is put in the plural, seems to be taken to refer to Israel; and in 4QDib. Ham. 3:4-8 God has called Israel, "my first-born son").[20] In 1 Cor. 15:24-28, Paul, in a much more reserved way, characterizes the kingdom of the Son as a preliminary period before the end, and sees explicitly in the Son the one who is subordinate to the Father, and who subordinates himself once and for always.[21] However, the fact that this is deeply rooted in the Davidic tradition clearly indicates that in Col. 1:12f. as well, what is meant is not simply a kingdom of light in a transcendent world, but, as in 1 Cor. 15, the sphere in which Christ reigns. The future nature of the "inheritance" is affirmed as well (3:1-4).[22]

Both passages, then, are interested in the functions of Christ within the time span of this world, not in the spatial limits set on the sphere of his sovereignty. Paul emphasizes the character of this

19. Cf. already Bengel, 811. In the Qumran texts as well, the מַלְכוּת (βασιλεία kingdom) of God (1QM 6:6; 12:7) of the Son of David (4QPatr. 4), or of Israel (1QSb 5:21; 1QM 19:8) is set over against the מֶמְשָׁלָה| (ἐξ-ουσία, power) of darkness (Lohse, 37). In Rev. 12:10 the two expressions are, it must be said, synonymous (Abbott, 208). In the Qumran writings, as generally in Jewish apocalyptic, "lot" and "inheritance" can likewise designate something that one has already taken possession of, such as the title to something still set in the future (Kuhn, Enderwartung, 72-5).
20. RB 68 (1961), 202f.; cf. E. Schweizer, "The Concept of the Da-

vidic Son of God," in: L. E. Keck and J. L. Martyn, eds., Studies in Luke-Acts, Nashville, Abingdon (1966) 190. The title παντοκράτωρ(2 Sam. 7:8) is also at home in this tradition. It appears in 2 Cor. 6:18 and often in Rev. 21. In a similar way the kingdom of Christ in Rev. 20:4 refers to the period of 1000 years before the end; that of the Son of Man (Matt. 13:41) pertains to the time before the judgment. On the contrary, the final state after the parousia (or in eternity is intended in Matt. 16:28; Luke 1:33; 22:30; 2 Tim. 4:1, 18; 2 Peter 1:11.
22. Lohse, NTS 11, 209 against Conzelmann, 181; in agreement with him, cf. p. 179.

reign of Christ as a battle; hence what he has in mind, above all, are the "powers," although the community is obviously involved as well. Col. 1:12f., by contrast, lays special emphasis on being set free from sin for a new life of obedience; hence it is the community with which it is primarily concerned. The perspective of 1 Cor. 15:24-27 is not taken up in Colossians until 2:10, while the universal reconciliation extolled in the hymn (1:20) represents yet another outlook. Thus the spatial concepts are not central as far as the content is concerned, but they have already set their stamp on the whole mode of expression (v. p. 173 and 178f.). "Son of his love" is a Semitic formulation and means little more than "beloved Son"; although presumably in Greek greater stress is laid on "love," as for example in the expression "men with whom he (God) is pleased" (Luke 2:14). This is especially likely since usually only the distinctively active characteristic of the person mentioned is described by the genitive (lit. "judges of unrighteousness" Luke 18:6, etc., cf. note 7 to 1:12-14).

[14] What has been said in a pictorial and spatial manner is now interpreted in terms of "redemption" and "forgiveness of sins" (cf. note 39 to 2:8-15).[23] On the one hand, these terms describe only the negative aspect of being set free; in this respect it differs from the Pauline formulation of the "righteousness of God," which overtakes a person, permeates one's life and has one's faith as its correlative. On the other hand particular and positive emphasis is laid, in conjunction with the dualistic terminology of 1:12f., on God's objective action, that is the abolition of alienation from him.

Summary

What the writer really has in mind here is probably the primary experience of faith, or baptism, as the liberating act of God (described in the aorist). It is difficult to prove that the precise terminology of a baptismal liturgy is used, but this seems likely, since there is a clear affinity with statements about the call of God or the conversion to him. The whole paragraph is headed by the summons to thanksgiving. This may well be related to the original introduction to the hymn. In its present context, the thanksgiving for this

---

23. The connection is, as often in Col., to be understood as ongoing, and not in the pregnant sense of life ἐν Χριστῷ (cf. Introduction, note 14).

fundamental act of deliverance in Jesus Christ is set at the end of
the apostle's intercessions for the community. This thanksgiving is
the real purpose of the way of life described in vv 10f. What God's
power accomplishes in them culminates in their being able to offer
thanks. This deliverance is experienced so intensely that it has to be
portrayed in terms of two mutually exclusive spheres.

However, no longer, as for instance in Rom. 1:3f., is the sphere
of the present life in the world separated from the sphere of life
after the resurrection. The dividing line between darkness and light
cuts right through the world, and the differences are evaluated meta-
physically. These differences, then, can no longer be described
merely in terms of temptation and suffering on the one side, and of
fulfilment and a total lack of suffering on the other. The reason for
these two spheres being brought together can perhaps only be
understood in a situation where taking the step of faith in Jesus
Christ, and the undergoing of baptism brings release from the fear
of demonic powers or from people who bring pressure to bear on
one. Where to take this step of faith can be at the expense of one's
career, one's civil rights and even, in the end, of one's life.

Nevertheless, these statements are repeated to a community that
has long since been baptized; the transition from darkness to light
is then accomplished not merely in a dramatic way once and for all,
but constantly anew. The text then does not assert that anything
like a transformation of human nature takes place; what occurs is
a change of lord. This Lord, however, asserts himself in a whole
host of decisions, experiences, actions, and thoughts.

In the last resort, redemption may mean

• liberation from oneself;

• liberation from engaging oneself in a cause beneath whose
weight one's family is crushed;

• liberation from an affectionate but dominating paternalism
which never allows a child to grow up and be independent; or

• liberation from an insistence upon freedom, as opposed to an
unduly strict ethic of achievement, that causes others to break down
under pressure of work.

If redemption really means all this, then it can only happen in such

a way that the allegiance to the Lord becomes effective again and
again in the many concrete questions of life.

(b) The Hymn (1:15-20)

15 He is the image of the invisible God, the first-born of all creation; 16 for in him all things were created, in heaven and on
earth, visible and invisible, whether thrones or dominions or principalities or authorities—all things were created through him and
for him. 17 He is before all things, and in him all things hold together. 18 He is the head of the body, the church; he is the beginning, the firstborn from the dead, that in everything he might be preeminent. 19 For in him all the fulness of God was pleased to dwell,
20 and through him to reconcile to himself all things, whether on
earth or in heaven, making peace by the blood of his cross.

Analysis

It is no longer a matter for dispute that we have in these verses a
hymn which has been taken over by the author.[1] The prerequisites

1. On this point v. Schweizer, *Neo-testamentica*, 293-301 and the further bibliography in Lohse, 41 n64. The parallelism between 1:15/18b and the causal ὅτι-clauses was worked out by Bengel (812 on 1:18b, and systematically by Schleiermacher, *TSK* V/I, 502f. For the various different reconstructions, see the surveys given in Gabathuler, *Jesus Christus*, 11-124; Feuillet, *Christ*, 163-273; Benoit, *hymne* 238 (where a summary list is provided); Burger, *Schöpfung*, 9-11, 15f.; cf. in addition von Allmen, *RHPR* 48, 38-41; Deichgräber, *Gotteshymnus*, 143-55; R. G. Hamerton-Kelly, *Pre-Existence, Wisdom and the Son of Man*, London, C.U.P., 1973 (MSSNTS 21), 171; Martin, *Lord*, 40-4 and NCB pp. 61-6, essentially as above. Kehl points out that vv 15, 16a, c and 18b, 19, 20a both have almost the same number of syllables, while vv 17, 18a (with τῆς ἐκκλησίας as the transition to the second strophe, v. 42f.) are to be understood as a connecting strophe. Lohse, 44 takes only the references to the church in v 18a and the blood of the cross in v 20

to be secondary glosses; Schenke, ZTK 61, 221f., who discusses only vv 18b-20, brackets out the phrase concerning the blood of the cross and the two εἴτε-clauses. Pöhlmann, *ZNW* 64, 56, obtains four strophes (vv 15-16a/16b-d/16e-18a/18b, c, 19, 20a) by deleting τῆς ἐκκλησίας and the ἵνα-clause and by taking v 20 to end with εἰς αὐτόν (for further bibliography, v. *ad loc.*, 53 n2). Gibbs, *Creation*, 99, leaves the question open. On E. Bammel's proposed solution cf. Houlden, 157-62. For further publications since 1970 see Schweizer, "Forschung," 181-6. More recently Caird, 174f. has posited Pauline authorship and holds a supposedly earlier function for the hymn to be completely irrelevant (but cf. below, p. 299). D. v. Allmen, "Überlieferung und dichterische Schöpfung in paulinischen Hymnen" in: *Hit-Müvészet*, Bern (1975) 22f., counts 1:15, 16a-c/16d-18a as the first double strophe; the second would be incomplete, since the author hints at it rather than cites it (v. note 6 below).

for this are present, as far as form is concerned; there is a certain
rhythm in the construction both as a whole and in detail. There
is also a portrayal of Christ, self-contained and surpassing anything
that might be expected in the context; and again, there is the customary opening by means of the relative pronoun.[2] More importantly, the distinctive characteristics of the style of the author of the
Epistle are not found here, although they otherwise appear throughout the letter, while a plethora of unusual concepts also appear.[3]
Above all, however, one cannot help but notice the theological difference between the hymn itself and the commentary which the
author of the Epistle provides.

The parallel between v 15 and v 18b is the obvious starting point,
as far as *form* is concerned. Both verses, from the point of view of
style, begin with the relative pronoun. "First-born of all creation"
and "first-born from the dead" correspond, as do the predicates
"image" and "beginning" in the first half-lines; in Philo "image"
and "beginning" are predicates of wisdom and can be directly juxtaposed.[4] The two parallel sets of expressions are then followed
(although not directly in the second instance unless v 18c is bracketed out), by an explanatory clause, which says of the universe, or
the fullness (? of the universe) that it was created or was pleased
to dwell "in him." In both cases (but this time in the first strophe
not immediately following, if one retains v 16b), this explanatory
clause is continued in what is said about Christ as the origin and

---

2. Rom. 4:25; Phil. 2:6; 1 Tim. 3:16;
Heb. 1:3 (on this v. E. Grässer,
"Hebr. 1.1-4," in: *EKK Vorarbeiten
Heft* 3 (1971) 65f.); cf. the participles in Rom. 1:3f. "Hymn" is meant in
the widest sense of the word and can
include dogmatic, confessional, liturgical, polemic or (best of all, as Gabathuler, *Jesus Christus*, 23f.) doxolog-
ical intent (Benoit, *hymne*, 230f.).
3. A list of these unusual concepts is
given in Masson, 106 (10-12 expressions) in Lohse, 41f.; cf. above p. 45.
4. *Leg. All. I* 43; cf. *Conf. Ling.* 146f.
and *Rer. Div. Her.* 230f., where the
Logos, as the "image" and archetype
is the one set over us, and is distin-

guished from man created "according
to the image" (whereby man as *nous*
is again to be distinguished from man
formed from clay, *Leg. All.* II 4f.).
The underlying idea here is he who
is the "image of God" becomes the
beginning of a new succession of those
who bear his stamp (cf. below, note
22 and also note 45). On Logos as
"beginning" == Glory, Son, Wisdom,
Angel, God, Lord in Just. *Dial.* 61:1;
62:4 (cf. also the reference to the
Image in 62:1) cf. Hegermann, *Schöpfungsmittler*, 77; on the passages in
Philo concerning the image, ibid., 85,
96-8.

purpose of the creation or redemption of the universe, through
whom and for whom the universe was brought into being.[5]

Finally, the references to heaven and earth in v 16 and v 20 also
correspond; although they are not, in fact, introduced at the same
point in the strophe, and it is only in v 20 that the two terms are
differentiated by means of "whether . . . or." In addition one may
note the parenthesis in vv 17, 18a, which does not follow the pattern
of being linked by a relative particle, but reintroduces Christ by
means of "and he. . . ." [6] From the point of view of form, this yields
the following structure:

15   He is the image of the invisible God, the first-born of all creation;
   16   for in him all things were created, in heaven
      and on earth, visible and invisible;
         all things were created throungh him and for him.
         17   He is before all things,
            and in him all things hold together.
         18   He is the head of the body
               (the church).

He is the beginning, the first-born from the dead.
  19   For in him all the fullness of God was pleased to dwell
    20   and through him to reconcile to himself all things,
      making peace, whether on earth
      or in heaven.

see p 129

---

5. These clauses ("for in him all
things were created"/"all things were
created through him and for him")
are arranged chiastically in 16a/e
(Pöhlmann, ZNW 64, 57). With Pöhlmann and Kehl, *Christushymnus*, 34,
one can detect material that has been
added in v 16, even if one differs from
them in regarding (only) the enumeration of the powers as redactional:
16a and e include the reference to
heaven and earth. In v 20a the prepositional expressions enclose the clause
about the reconciliation of the universe. Thus, for the sake of the parallelism with v 16, "for him" will likewise be taken to refer to Christ and
not to God (v. Schnackenburg's consideration of this point, *Herrschaft*
(note 16 to 1:12-14) 218).

6. As far as form is concerned, the
relative clauses has already been
abandoned with the use of τὰ πάντα
. . . (at the end of v 16), although
if need be this short clause could
still be taken as dependent on ὅτι.
Hence Gabathuler, *Jesus Christus*,
128f. (likewise P. Lamarche, "La
primauté du Christ. Col. 1:12-20."
As Seign 46(1974), 59-64, id.
"Structure," 455f.) makes this clause
the beginning of the second strophe. In
that case, however, the parallel v 20a
would be the beginning of a no longer
extant second half of the second
strophe; and this beginning would
have been appended by the author of
Colossians as directly dependent on
v 19. This is possible, but it is not an
idea that commends itself.

Clearly one cannot reckon with any certainty on a hymn of this kind being structured precisely according to formally symmetrical rules.[7]

[18a] However, the expressions tentatively bracketed out are suspicious on grounds of their *content* as well. It is in the interpretation of the body in terms of the church (v. 18a) that this is clearest, for the strophe does not begin until v 18b, which speaks of redemption.[8] The discussion previously was only concerned with the cosmos, so the "body," of which Christ is the head, must be the universe. The contrast between "body" and "head," which is not found in this way in Paul, also belongs quite naturally in the prevalent Greek view of the Universe-God.

From Plato onwards, the concept of the universe as a divine body is found frequently. In Orphic hymns and in Philo, as well as in the form of a comparison in Cornutus and Dio Chrysostom, the definition of Zeus, the Logos (?), heaven or ether as "head" of this body can also certainly be proved to have existed before the time of Colossians.[9] Further, it should be observed that v 18a does not speak of "his (Christ's) body" or "the body in Christ," as New Testament usage would require, if the church were meant by this (cf. 1:24,

---

7. Nevertheless, there is an instance of this in 1 Tim. 3:16; against this, however, cf. Phil. 2:6-11.

8. To attach v 18a to the second strophe (a suggestion still found in S. Schulz, *Komposition und Herkunft der johanneischen Reden*, 1960[BWANT 81] 61) is impossible on stylistic grounds. In fact Chrysostom had already (III 2f. [320]) realized that "head of the fullness" was actually to be expected, and offered the solution that the church here represents the whole of humanity. Quite out of the question as well is the idea that the entire first strophe should be connected (in the sense that the writer of the letter is responsible for this connection) with the new creation (Zeilinger, *Der Erstgeborene*, 188f.; 204f.; Burger, *Schöpfung*, 66 (cf. pp. 61f. below); against this, v. Schweizer, "Forschung," 183f.). Equally impossible is the interpretation of v 18a in terms of a pre-existent church (Houl-

den, 171; cf. Gibbs, *Creation*, 105f.) or in terms of the pre-existent One defined already as the head of the future church.

9. E. Schweizer, TDNT VII 1037; 1054, (cf. below, note 37 to 2:16-23). Why should one say (like Ernst 169) that there are no convincing parallels? In Philo it is not quite certain whether the head of the world body is the Logos (*Quaest. in Ex.* 2.117, which could be a Christian revision [a view now also found in Kehl, *Christushymnus*, 96f.]) or (certainly) heaven (*Som.* I 144). The Orphic declaration about Zeus as head, for which the evidence in Aristobulus is not beyond doubt (N. Walter, *Der Thoraausleger Aristobulos*, 1964(TU 86), 112f.), is also attested in Pseud.-Aristot. *Mund.* 7 (A.D. 100 ?), and is probably echoed in Jos. *Ap.* II 190 (v. below, note 47). On the cosmos as a divine body, cf. note 37.

2:19). Hence should anyone want to ascribe the addition of "the church" to the author of the hymn, they must reckon with the following improbable points:

(1) the person who composed the hymn has carried out a systematic reinterpretation of the Pauline image by speaking of "head" and "body";

(2) he speaks not of Christ's body, but of "the body";

(3) he does already mention the church in the strophe dealing with the creation and preservation of the cosmos, but omits this where it would be expected, in the second strophe which describes redemption, so that it only appears in the commentary with the "and you . . ." (v 21);

(4) he writes in the style of the author of the letter, with loosely attached explanations. The first three points are exactly what one would expect if in the hymn the body stands for the cosmos; this is also the case with the fourth point, if "church" has been added by the writer of the letter.

[20] If then it has been established that in this passage the turning of a cosmic expression into one relating to the church goes back to the author of this letter, then there is a close parallel to this process evident in the mention of the "blood of the cross." This phrase is certainly set in its proper place, in the second strophe, which deals with reconciliation. However, from the first line of this strophe onwards, the reconciliation of the universe is ascribed to the Risen One, and to the fulness dwelling in him. In the author's commentary, on the other hand, the same verb, rarely found otherwise (v. p. 89), is resumed; now, however, it refers to humanity as the object of this reconciliation, and it also refers to the death of Jesus (vv 21f.). This reinterpretation of an expression relating to the cosmos in terms of one relating to the church reveals precisely the same hand at work as does the addition of the church in v 18a. That is the theology of the author of Colossians, which is evident in vv 21f. as well as in vv 12-14.[10]

To this same theology belongs the typically Pauline reference to the cross, which likewise appears in 2:14 (cf. note 81 below). Hence if one wants to ascribe this reference to the cross to the author of

---

10. Paul does also exhibit certain relevant analogies. In Rom. 4:17 he interprets the cosmic formula of the one who calls the dead to life, and calls into existence that which does not exist, in terms of the justification of the sinner.

the hymn one again has to reckon with the following improbable points:

(1) the author of the hymn was likewise a disciple of Paul;

(2) for some reason or other, he allows the cross to be subordinate to the resurrection;

(3) he does not mention humankind, which otherwise appears throughout as the object of this reconciliation (e.g., Rom. 5:10f.; 2 Cor. 5:15-21; cf. Rom. 15:5);

(4) he repeats "through him" [11] in a way which is grammatically almost impossible.

Conversely it can be shown that the writer of the letter is happy to combine, in a new way, expressions which are used by Paul. It can also be seen, from elsewhere in the letter, that at the end of an interpolation the writer picks up the thread by repeating what has come before it. Thus we have on the one hand the striking concept of the redemption of the universe and its connection with the resurrection, and on the other hand, competing with this former view, the reference to the blood of the cross. The theological tension between the two must go back to the reinterpretation effected by the author of the letter.

[16] It is not so easy to reach a decision in the case of the two further instances. The enumeration of the powers in v 16 is peculiar. The contrast between "visible and invisible" and the expression "thrones or dominions" are both equally unPauline. This could, of course, suggest the author of the hymn [12] just as much as the writer of the letter. Both within the New Testament and outside it, the elements ("elemental spirits") never appear in such series of angelic powers; there is, then, surely no reference to them here. It is equally unlikely that the powers mentioned here are identical with the angels worshiped by the Colossians (v. p. 159f.). It does, however, seem that the typically Jewish enumeration of the powers contradicts the Hellenistic summing up of the whole cosmos as "visible and invisible," since in the Jewish enumeration only the invisible is men-

---

11. The omission of this in BD°etc. is a later attempt to alleviate the difficulty.

12. So Lohse, 43. Ὁρατός is moreover a hapax legomenon in the New Testament. For Jewish and Christian parallels to the enumeration of the spiritual

powers v. note 17 to 1:24-9.

Pöhlmann, ZNW 64, 66, asks whether the author of the letter has introduced the four angelic powers in place of works of creation that were originally mentioned here.

tioned.[13] So then, the reinterpretation of "visible and invisible" in terms of a Jewish way of thought, and, at the same time, the relating of this to the community's fears of the "principalities or authorities" (cf. 2:10) must go back to the author of the letter. He thus manages to establish a connection between the hymn and the specific situation in Colossae. For the writer of the letter (as distinct from the hymn) it is important that the "principalities or authorities" are actually subjugated, not reconciled. For him it is Christ who, as "preeminent" (1:18c) or "the head," disarms them and goes ahead of them in his triumphal procession (2:15). Thus the essential point for Christ's preeminent position is indeed expressed in v 18c.[14] The hymn, by making "the head of the body" a predicate of Christ, emphasizes his unity with the world, which is gathered up and—according to the second strophe—redeemed in him. The author of the letter, however, interprets this as predominance over the powers. The difference need not necessarily indicate separate layers of composition. All the same, the arguments concerning both form and content come together here, and lead us to suppose that what we have are two additions from the person interpreting the hymn.

This analysis, in particular the separating of the theology of the cross from the hymn, has recently been disputed. Instead it has been conjectured that the hymn grew precisely from the central Christian statement about the reconciliation on the cross; that is, it developed, so to speak, from the second strophe backwards,[15] just as the Old Testament doctrine of creation was fashioned as a consequence of the credal confession of God's historical act of redemption (cf. note 83 below). It is certainly the case that allusion is made in the New Testament to the position of Christ as mediator in creation, in order to describe the dimensions of the one whom the community extols as its savior.

All the same, it remains an open question what exactly is meant

---

13. Otherwise one might, with Houlden, 163 (cf. below, pp. 284) take "thrones" and powers to refer to political authorities. Against this, however, v. note 76 to this section.

14. Πρωτεύειν is found only here in the New Testament. Sir. 24:6 possibly provides relevant parallel (Glasson, NT 11, 154f.), but this is not at all certain. Ernst, 175 does in addition also hold "of the invisible God" (v 15) and the reference to heaven and earth in v 20 to be redactional.

15. Ernst, 177 (on 175, ibid., he discusses the question of whether the reference to the cross could be original); ib., Pleroma, 90f. (where he thinks of the redemption that takes place in the resurrection); Wengst, Formeln, 177-9; Lähnemann, Kolosserbrief, 41.

in these parallels by salvation. From the Jewish and New Testament parallels (v. pp. 73ff.), it is precisely statements about resurrection or exaltation and about a peace concluded with nature that one would expect. If one refers in particular to the Jewish Day of Atonement (v. note 54 below), it can be established that the parallels which are adduced appear only in the framework of the hymn and not in the hymn itself; but it is clear that the theme of creation scarcely belongs there originally. Alternatively, one might suppose that only the first strophe, for which there are many Hellenistic-Jewish parallels, is traditional, whereas the second was composed (by Paul) to suit it; but in that case one must not only assume that the first strophe (in vv 16?, 18a) was in fact supplemented, but also that the second strophe was subsequently revised again (on the basis of Ephesians, which came into existence at about the same time). For otherwise it would be impossible to account for the clause about the preeminence of Christ (v 18c), and the reference to the blood of the cross, with the clumsy repetition of "through him." [16] Yet this whole hypothesis is altogether improbable; it does not properly account for the way the concept of the head of the body of Christ in v 18a originated.

Another attempt to reconstruct the process of composition also thinks in terms of three layers. According to this view, the original text contained only the following: "He is the image, the first-born of all creation; for in him all things were created, visible and invisible. He is the beginning, the first-born from the dead. For in him, all the fulness was pleased to dwell, whether on earth or in heaven." Everything else would then have been added by the writer of the letter, apart from the interpretation in terms of the church (vv 18 and 24!), and the reference to the blood of the cross (v 20), which would be glosses added by a later reader. The same three layers would also be detected in 2:9-15.[17] This is a suggestion worth considering; it would have the advantage that the "fulness" could sim-

---

16. So Benoit, *hymne,* 248-50; for an attempt to deal with this argument, v. Schweizer, "Forschung," 184-6. The similar suggestion advanced by J. Jervell (*IMAGO DEI. Gen. 1.26 im Spätjudentum, in der Gnosis und in den paulinischen Briefen,* 1960 [FRLANT 58] p. 211) is rejected by Ahrens, *Diskussion,* 243f.

17. Burger, *Schöpfung,* esp. 56-9, 98-101, 108-111; on the interpretation of the "fulness" in terms of the universe v. ibid. 48f.; on the glossator's corrections in 1:22-4, v. ibid. 74-8. Also according to Burger the first strophe has the function of serving as the basis for the second (ibid. 52).

ply refer to the universe, which having originated from Christ, finally flows back into Christ, and which would be identified with the "visible and invisible," earth and heaven.

However, there is another answer that could be given to the question of why the text as we have it now shows no break between the first and second strophes (v. pp. 84f.). According to this view, both the writer of the letter and the supposed glossator are followers of Paul. The cross would have been introduced by the former at 1:20, whereas it would have been interpreted (cosmically) by the latter at 2:14. But this shows how difficult it is for these two layers to be separated. Not every logical tension in a hymn needs to be explained in the same literary-historical way—at least as long as these tensions do not too obviously protrude. And it is always precarious to assume that any redaction has been carried out after a letter has been written. Therefore, this radical (and original) solution is scarcely compelling.

In the first strophe, then, Christ is extolled as he in whom, through whom, and for whom the whole creation has come about. The connecting strophe supplements this by saying that the permanence of the cosmos is secured by Christ who has been preordained and set as its head. In the second strophe he is celebrated as the Risen One, in whom, through whom, and for whom, by means of the presence of the divine "fulness," the reconciliation of the world has come about. It is impossible to say whether the additions in vv 16b and 18c really belong here or not; it actually makes little difference, although without them the theological expression is more refined.

(1) The original hymn: (a) First strophe (1:15-18a)

Interpretation

[15] Before the relative clause (literally: "who is the image . . . ," just as in v 18b "who is the beginning . . .") there must have been an introduction; presumably this was a call to praise, which might well have contained the title "son" (v 34f.). The first predicate of Christ is "image of the invisible God." That appears to belong simply to the context of the question of how God can be perceived; and that seems all the more likely since 2 Cor. 4:4 (cf. 2 Cor. 3:18) points in the same direction: in the apostle's preaching, the glory of Christ shines forth as the glory of "the image of God."[18] Yet that

is not enough; for the one who is thus described here is not the earthly Jesus, but the preexistent mediator in creation.[19] How can he be the "image of God"? Certainly image is not exclusively the making visible of the invisible;[20] that is still less so in the platonic sense, where the image as a concretion, a becoming incarnate, necessarily denotes a limitation of the heavenly "idea" as well.[21]

In Wisdom of Solomon 7:25f., it is the full presence of God in his wisdom that is described:

> For she is a breath of the power of God,
> and a pure emanation of the glory of the Almighty;
> therefore nothing defiled gains entrance into her.
> For she is a reflection of eternal light,
> a spotless mirror of the working of God,
> and an image of his goodness.

Reflection, glory, mirror, come close to what is said in 2 Cor. 3:18-

18. 2 Cor. 3:18 I understand in the sense that the apostle, like a mirror, reflects for his hearers the brilliance and glory of Christ (this agrees with J. Dupont, Gnosis, Louvain 3rd edn. 1960, 119f.), and in this process he, like his hearers who accept his message, is changed into "the same image" (E. Schweizer, "2 Cor. 3.12-18," GPM 26[1971] 89).

19. Kehl, Christushymnus, 99 (cf. 77f.) emphasizes the fact that the preexistence follows only from the confession of Christ's activity in creation, and is not taken over in a mechanical way from wisdom expressions. Caird (176-80) takes v 15 to refer to the earthly Jesus. Cf. notes 112, 669-72 in the 2nd Ger. ed. of this commentary.

20. The expression "invisible" is not found before the Hellenistic period; it is not especially striking, since God thus becomes associated with the world, in which there is indeed both visible and invisible.

21. It is in this way that Plutarch, a little later, can justify the adoration of the Persian king. God appears in him as he appears in the sun, although certainly without becoming one with him. The king is (merely) his εἰκών (Them. 27(I 125C); on this further, v. Schweizer EKK I, 11, note 12).

22. Wisdom is "image," "beginning," "vision of God" = "the archetype" (also Som. I 232) of the earthly wisdom which is its "copy" (Leg. All. I 43); in this respect it is equal to the incorporeal idea (Som. I 79) and subordinated to the 'original pattern' (δεῖγμα), e.i. God, but also εἰκών and παράδειγμα of the others (μιμήματα , Leg. All. III 96; II 4). Where Philo is not speaking in technical terms of wisdom as the "image of God," he can, it is true, also unreflectingly understand "image" as "copy"; thus he speaks of the sensual as a copy of the spiritual (Plant. 50), and of man as a copy of God (Op. Mund. 71.146; Omn. Prob. Lib. 62; cf. Migr. Abr. 40; Ebr. 133; Abr. 3; Spec. Leg. 1, 171; II 237 Decal.' 101; Det. Pot. Ins. 87; Praem. Poen. 29. 114; Vit. Mos. II 65). Further passages from Philo are cited in note 4 to this section and note 9 to 2:16-23. Cf. E. Schweizer, TDNT IX, 476.

4.6 and Heb. 1:3. Undoubtedly, then, the idea is not of a gradual transition from God to the world, by which, through an increasing concretizing (and thus limiting) God becomes world. It is precisely in Philo that the invisibility of the Logos is portrayed as the "image" of God.[22] It is only as an image of the image of God that the world becomes visible.

How can one speak of an invisible image? Obviously only on the assumption that the function of the image is not, or at least not primarily, that of making the invisible perceptible for man. What then? As early as Wis. 7:25f. the image is described in dynamic terminology as "emanation"; it represents the active power and goodness of God, that is, his creative and redemptive work. According to 2 Cor. 3:18, the image coins others after its own form. In Philo we also find a movement which leads from the prototype, God, to the copy, the Logos, and causes Logos in turn to become the imprint for the world. The Logos, as image of God, becomes the organ through which God carries out the creative fashioning of the world.[23] For Philo himself this is not an unbroken succession of emanations; his belief in the creation serves to correct views such as these.

That is all the more so for Paul, Colossians and Hebrews. If the author, or perhaps the hymn itself, stresses so emphatically that Christ is set over all other dominions, then it is exactly the notion of emanations, that he intends to avert.[24] Yet it is already said of

23. Instances are given in Schweizer, EKK I, 12, notes 18-20: *Leg. All.* III 96; *Op Mund.* 24f.; etc. (cf. note 29 to this section).

24. This point is stressed by Kehl, *Christushymnus* (n. 19 above).

25. In the Greek, the instrumental dative appears; however, ‎בְּ can be rendered equally by ἐν or διά (Ps. 103:24, LXX: "You have created everything in wisdom"). According to Job 28:23-7 wisdom is like God's architectural plan or blueprint, in which the world to be created is already contained. Thus also the Rabbis explain that God has created the world "in wisdom" (Targum Neofiti I on Gen. 1:1, ed. A. Diez Macho, *Textos y Estudios* 7, Madrid 1968), be-

cause in Prov. 8:22 wisdom is designated as "beginning" ("in which," according to Gen. 1:1, God created heaven and earth; Strack-Billerbeck II, 356f.). Philo hence understands wisdom as the "place" of the world (*Op. Mund.* 16-20; cf. *Som.* I 62-5; E. Schweizer, *TDNT* VII, 1054-1055; L. Wächter, "Der Einfluss platonischen Denkes auf rabbinische Schöpfungsspekulationen," *ZRGG* 14 (1962) 42-50). On the repercussions of this, v. note 12 to C II Christology. Burney, *JTS* 27, 175-7, even wishes to understand vv 15-18 as a meditation on the first words of the Bible. True, ‎בְּ can be rendered by ἐν, διά and εἰς, and רֵאשִׁית by πρὸ πάντων, τὰ πάντα, κεφαλή, or ἀρχή. However, the Hellenistic-

wisdom, that God created the world through her (Prov. 2:19). She
is God's "master workman" (Prov. 8:30).[25] The fact that God can
be known from his creation was taken for granted by Judaism from
the Old Testament onwards; from there it was taken over naturally
by the Christian community as well, and was in no sense called into
question. However, that did not in the least detract from the distinction between creator and creature, and the following expression sets
Christ clearly on the side of the creator.

"Image" is not, as for most present-day readers, something which
is identical merely in outline and appearance with the object that
has been copied, but which otherwise differs completely from it (as,
for instance, a photograph instead of a living person). Already in
Greek religious usage, the image always bears the character of that
which it represented; that is, the person represented became present
in the image.[26] The fact that Christ participates in the act of creation serves to distinguish him from a created being, and it is for
this very reason that, as the "image of the invisible God," he is God's
revelation. The creation cannot, then, really be recognized as the
work of the creator except in Christ (cf. p. 71f.). But this means
that Christ is designated "image of God" here in a sense different
from 3:10 which speaks of the new person in Christ who is being
renewed "after the image" of the creator. The schema of Christ as
second Adam plays hardly any part in Colossians.[27] The concept
"image" in the hymn could be rendered in modern terminology by
"representative" or "manifestation of God."

Jewish character of the hymn is obvious enough, and ἀρχή does not appear until the second strophe. The
very most that would be possible is
that such speculations lay in the background to the hymn, and that this
was no longer consciously realized;
however, Hellenistic-Jewish instances
provide a much more obvious background. It is still doubtful as far as I
am concerned whether already in the
pre-Christian period wisdom and Son
of Man were connected together (as
Lohse, 48, argues, appealing to Eth.
En. 42:1f.; 49:1, 3; cf. F. Christ,
Jesus Sophia, 1970 (ATANT 57), 54-
6, 70, 141-3, 147f., 153), quite apart
from the uncertain dating of the Simi-
litudes of Enoch. In Eth. En. 48:10
(52:4), traits of the Messiah may have
been transferred secondarily to the Son
of Man (K. Müller, "Menschensohn
und Messias," BZ 16(1972) 169-71);
in the probably original literary stratum (ibid. 165-7), wisdom is only that
which reveals the Son of Man (48:7).
26. H. Kleinknecht, TDNT II, 389-
390; likewise in the New Testament
throughout (G. Kittel, ibid., II, 395).
Cf. below pp. 248f. and Lightfoot, 143
(with patristic references).
27. Where wisdom appears as the
image of God. Gen. 1:26 is not involved, and vice-versa (Jervell, [note
16 above], 50).

More difficult is the expression "first-born of all creation." [28] In view of what has been said, this cannot mean that Christ is the first member of creation; instead it must be understood in a comparative sense—earlier than . . . before all . . . ,[29] so that the expression approximates the Rabbinic description of God as the "pretemporal one of the world." [30] Certainly this contrast, which was brought into sharp focus as a consequence of the Arian controversy (cf. pp. 250f.), may not have experienced at this earlier stage at all. The continuation of the sentence (vv 16b-17) and the parallel with the "first-born from the dead" at least indicate that the "first born" brings about the formation and re-formation of all that come after him. He is not merely the first but passive object of God's activity, but simultaneously he is the acting subject who extends God's activity to the creatures that follow him.

Thus again it is not Adam whom the writer has in mind; moreover, Adam is seldom given the epithet "first-born." As early as the Old Testament itself, this expression does not necessarily indicate an elder brother, but only the special position of one who is beloved

28. Cf. A. Hockel, *Christus der Erstgeborene. Zur Geschichte der Exegese von Kol. 1.15* (Düsseldorf 1965); a survey is given on 31-3. On the absence of the article cf. A. T. Robertson, *A Grammar of the Greek New Testament in the Light of Historical Research*, 1914, 772. BDF 275.3 understands it in the sense of "every created thing."

29. Cf. πρῶτός μου, John 1:15, 30; πρωτότοκος ἐγὼ ἦ|σύ, 2 Sam. 19:44 LXX (A. W. Argyle, "Colossians 1:15," *ExpTim* 66 (1954/5) 61f. and 318f.; cf. H. G. Mescham, ibid., 124f.). Whereas Aristobulus (Eus. *Praep. Ev.* XIII, 12.11, and on this v. Walter, *Aristobulos* [note 9 above] 66f.) notes only that wisdom "is before heaven and earth," Sir. 1:4 explains that "wisdom was created before all things"; Sir. 24:9 affirms that it is "from eternity" and thus that it "will not cease to exist"; Prov. 8:22 declares that Yahweh "created (wisdom) at the beginning of his work," so that it was already there at the creation (8:27-30;

also Wis. 9:1f., 9; Sir. 24:3[?]). According to Philo *Fug. Inv.* 109, God is the Father and Wisdom the Mother through whom everything has come into being (likewise *Det. Pot. Ins.* 54; *Ebr.* 30f.); cf. *Leg. All.* II, 49; *Rev. Div. Her.* 199, and the Logos as the organ of God (*Cher.* 127).

30. Strack-Billerbeck III, 626. The fact that God is called "primogenitus totius mundi" (Chr. Schöttgen, *Horae Hebraicae I,* Leipzig 1933, 922) does not mean much, since the rabbi to whom this is attributed comes from the thirteenth century (ibid. II, 742, 791). More to the point, in fact, would be Sir. 24:3 (cf. 5), where Latin witnesses read "primogenita ante omnen creaturam" (Glasson, *NT* 11, 155f.), although this, it is true, could have been formulated under the influence of Col. 1:15 (cf. note 23 to C II Christology and p. 251).

31. W. Michaelis, *TDNT* VI, 875 and 876 n30; pp. 873-874; Strack-Billerbeck III, 626; for Adam is 'the first formed' v. Wis. 7:1; 10:1.

by his father.[31] Hence it may be asked to what extent the messianic
title "the first-born" (Ps. 89:28) has already begun to exercise some
influence.[32] It does at least suit the position of the son who is subordinate to the Father but is clearly set over the world, and who
belongs completely to the Father. Rom. 8:29 already points to the
combination of "image" and "first-born" as predicates of Christ.

Thus two points are affirmed: first, that Christ is the one who
causes those who believe to be made like his image and to follow
him as brothers and sisters; second, that as such he clearly accomplishes the will of God as the one prior and superior to all.[33] Heb.
1:6 points in a similar direction. There the title is interpreted, by
means of the words of a psalm, to indicate the superiority of Christ
to the angels of nature, and it is developed in v 10 by means of the
reference to Christ's activity in creation (!). In Rev. 1:5, Christ is
extolled as "the faithful witness, the first-born of the dead, and the
ruler of kings on earth," and in 3:14 as "the faithful and true witness,
the beginning of God's creation."

According to Philo, the Logos is the "first-born," the (messianic)
scion promised in Zech. 6:12, the eldest son of God, indistinguish-
able from his "image"; the son who acts in imitation of the Father,
according to the "archetypal prototypes" or "models" (of the thing
to be created) and brings the creation to fulfilment. That is certainly
not the direct paradigm for Col. 1:15, not least because Colossians
and Philo do not use the same word,[34] but it does indicate the background against which these verses are to be understood.[35]

The first line, then, exalts Christ, according to the pattern of the
Logos in Hellenistic-Jewish writings, as he in whom the basically
inaccessible God does, as creator, actively fashion the world, and

32. A. Schlatter, *Gottes Gerichtigkeit*,
Stuttgart 1935, 283; *Mi.Hb.* 12th
ed., 113; Kehl, *Christushymnus*, 87f.
Philo *Agr.* 51; *Conf. Ling.* 146; *Som.*
I, 215.
33. P. van der Osten-Sacken, *Römer
8 als Beispiel paulinischer Soteriolo-
gie*, 1975 (FRLANT 112) 281.
34. Hockel, *Christus* (note 28 above)
41f. In the case of Philo, it is always
(apart from one passage) πρωτόγονος:
Conf. Ling. 62f.; 146; *Agr.* 51; *Som.*
I, 215; cf. *Deus Imm.* 31f. (and note
22 above). There is further discussion

in F. W. Eltester, *Eikon im Neuen
Testament*, 1958 (BZNW 23), 39;
H. Wilms, *EIKON. Eine begriffsge-
schichtliche Untersuchung zum Pla-
tonismus I: Philon von Alexandria*,
Münster (1935) 80.
35. This ultimately has its roots in
Plato's description of the visible world
as the "image of the spiritual," as the
"perceptible God" and the "uniquely
born" (*Tim.* 92C; cf. 34A); in Judaism, however, this is God's "word," not
the world; in the New Testament it is
Christ.

thus turns himself toward humans who had been unable to see
him. As the present tense of the verb shows, it is the exalted one,
confronting the community that sings his praise, who is extolled as
"image" and "first-born." Thus what Christ means in an enduring
sense for the community is not recounted in terms of salvation history, but is expressed in a song of praise: it is he, the one through
whom God can now, for the first time, be perceived in his creation
and thus can become intelligible.

[16] This is expressed in the all-formula which was widely used at
that time; "all things" is spoken of no less than four times, and "all"
is mentioned on three further occasions (not counting v 18).[36] In
the reasons given for what is said in these verses, God's activity
must therefore necessarily be spoken of in the past tense. Christ is,
then, not merely a symbol or cipher for an essence of God which
remains eternally the same, and which may be described and
learned; rather it is he who allows God to be known as the one who
is active, who enters into the world and has an effect upon it.
Nevertheless, the translation here should be "in him," and not, as
would be possible from biblical usage, "through him"; for at the end
of v 16 "through him" and "for him" are distinguished from "in him,"
and v 19 resumes the "in him" simply in its particular, local sense.
Also v 17 is scarcely to be understood in a merely instrumental way.

Underlying this "in him" is the Hellenistic-Jewish view of the
Logos as the "place" within which the world exists, and underlying
that in turn is the Stoic concept of the world as a body filled and
surrounded by God.[37] This refers not only to the Platonic world of
ideas, even if one ascribes the more precise description as "visible
and invisible" only to the redactor. Rather, the operative idea is
one widespread in Greek thought from the Stoa onwards, of God
as the one who comprises everything, so that Christ represents the

36. Pöhlmann, ZNW 64, 57f.; Jewish
and Hellenistic parallels are given on
58-74; for Aramaic analogies, v. P.
Stuhlmacher, "Erwägungen zum Problem von Gegenwart und Zukunft in
der paulinischen Eschatologie," ZTK
64 (1967) 442, n42. As distinct from
Rom. 11:36, the formula here refers to
Christ; cf. however, for Paul, 1 Cor.
8:6 (R. Kerst, '1 Kor. 8.6—ein vor-
paulinisches Taufbekenntnis?', ZNW
66 [1975] 135) and note 56 below and
also p. 200.

37. E. Schweizer, TDNT VII, 1029-
1030 (Plato); 1032 (Aristotle); 1035
(early Stoicism); 1037-1038 (first
century B.C. and A.D.), 1038 (Seneca); 1043-1044 (articles on Stoicism), plus note 25 above and note
37 to 2:16-23.

sphere in which the world was created and is preserved. Indeed, the Stoic expressions were later understood as expressions about the creative action of God (cf. note 9 to Excursus on 2:8). All the more then in Judaism, with its belief in the creation, the original Stoic idea of fusing together of God and world [38] was completely ruled out of the question. Further, in Col. 1:16 the verb joined with the descriptive phrase "in him" is one which is dynamic, not static. And at the same time, the "in him" is interpreted by means of "through him," which indicates the origin in the act of creation,[39] and "for him," which points to the consummation in the action of God which is to come. It is for this reason that we have the perfect tense here in place of the aorist. What happened in God's act of creation, is still valid, as v 17b makes clear.

The formulation "for him" is an innovation, vis-à-vis the Jewish Wisdom literature. The strongly eschatological orientation of the New Testament community thus takes effect; therefore one has to interpret this alongside the reference to the beginning "through him" and the continuation" in him," as an indication of the final purpose,[40] and not only of the model for which everything was created.[41] This means that the world cannot be understood in the

---

38. It has, it is true, from the Stoic expressions (H. Sasse, *TDNT* III, 876-877; E. Schweizer, *TDNT* VII, 1037-1038) intruded in one place, Sir. 43:27.

39. Yet "from him" is lacking (as in 1 Cor. 8:6); Christ is (apart from Heb. 1:10) not the creator but the mediator in creation. Prat, *théologie* I, 347, recalls the idea of the Logos as the "place" of the future cosmos (cf. note 12 to C II Christology) and distinguishes effective ("through"), exemplary ("in"), and purposive ("to") cause. Alting, 394a, by contrast, understands "in," with reference to the Hebrew, as purely instrumental.

40. Similarly Sir. 24:9 (note 29 to this section). Philo, *Cher.* 125, sets alongside "by which," "from which," and "through which," only the question "why"; yet in *Spec. Leg.* I 208, εἰς ἕν denotes the purpose lying behind the conflagration and reconstruction of the world (cf. note 7 to Excur-

sus: The Colossian Philosophy [2.8]). Anaximander is supposed to have affirmed that everything originates from (the infinite) and disappears into this (Diels I, 85.1ff.; the account of this comes only from the 6th century A.D.!). "Ad quod" is found in Seneca *Ep.* 65:8, and the Rabbis speak (in the 3rd century A.D. of the world having been created for the Messiah (Strack-Billerbeck III, 626).

41. Thus, more or less, in M.Ant 4:23: ὦ φύσις |, ἐκ σοῦ πάντα|, ἐν σοὶ πάντα ;, εἰς σὲ πάντα;, which only describes "the self-contained harmony" (Lohse, 51; cf. Kehl, *Christushymnus*, 100f.). To be compared here are Oppian (2/3 century A.D., ed. F. S. Lehrs, *Poetae Buccolici et Didactici*, Paris 1831, Halieutica I, 409: Ζεῦ πάτερ, ἐς δὲ σὲ πάντα καὶ ἐκ σέθεν ἐρρίζονται) and furthermore (although they can scarcely be dated) the magical papyri referred to in Lohse, 49, n120, and Lohmeyer, 59, notes 1 and 3.

Stoic sense as the continuously available presence of God; it can only be understood with reference to God's activity, which extends from the creation to the consummation.

Further, "heaven" is also expressly included in the creation. There is then, no highest place, no ether as a section of the world, a sphere in which divine perfection and sheer luck would simply be present. Also, heaven is only heaven through what God has done. Again, the invisible realm, the world of the angels, has been created by him. This is expressed by the hymnic prayers of the Diaspora Synagogue, as they appear in the Greek Bible.[42] This, then, is the reason for the first strophe. However, if this action of God takes place in Christ, then at the same time the writer affirms that this action of God embraced by Christ is to be understood as an act of grace, directed toward the salvation of humanity.

[17] It is only from this point onwards that the writer can speak of the preservation of the creation; this he does in three short lines which form a link. Again, the dependence of the world on what God has done in Christ is expressed in terms of Christ's position temporarily before [43] and spatially above the world (as "head"). Only thus can he be praised as the one who holds the world together and keeps it from breaking into pieces.[44] Elsewhere, of course, the New Testament is more interested in the world passing away than in it being preserved. Even here it is not simply the preservation of the world that is guaranteed; what is expressed is Christ's lordship over this world. It is Christ who is spoken of by means of the emphatic "he," which calls to mind the extremely expressive "I"

---

42. 1 Chron. 29:11f.; Esth. 4:17b-d (an addition); Neh. 9:(=2 Ezra 19.) 6; Gr.En. 9:5f.: Pöhlmann, ZNW 64, 71f.

43. The temporal predisposition is characteristic of Old Testament thought; cf. note 29 above. Since πρό, except in the phrase "above all" (James 5:15; 1 Peter 4:8), always has a temporal connotation, one should scarcely read into it here an intensification of the idea, in the sense of lordship over everything (as does Wagenführer, Bedeutung, 59f.). The present tense of the verb which appears here is a feature which this verse shares

with John 8:58: "Before Abraham was, I am."

44. Συνέστηκεν is lacking in the LXX, but is found in Pseud.-Aristot., Mund. 6 (397b: "everything exists from God and through God") and in Philo, Rer. Div. Her. 281 (that which is made up of the elements). Sir. 43:26 is rather closer as far as content is concerned, but uses different terminology: ἐν λόγῳ αὐτοῦ (God's) σύγκειται τὰ πάντα; similarly Wis. 1:7 of the Spirit; cf. further Philo, Fug. Inv. 112; Jos. Ap. II 190. On the emphatic αὐτός, cf. Lightfoot, 153f.

used of Yahweh in the Old Testament, or Jesus in the New. Hence whereas it may be said that the world in its past, from which it originates, in its present, in which it now exists, and in its goal, to which it is moving, can only derive its existence from God's good gift, it must also be said that this gift of God bears the name of Jesus Christ.

[18] The fact that *the* body, not his body, is spoken of shows that the expression used is a fixed and universally recognized formula. Within Pauline usage, Christ never even appears as head; in 1 Cor. 12:21, the head is one among many members. However, Zeus, the heavens, the spirit, perhaps even the Logos, are indeed familiar as "head" of the world body (v. note 9 above). As far as the usage of "head" is concerned, both in the Old Testament and in Paul (1 Cor. 11:3) the emphasis falls, of course, not on the organic connection or similarity of substance, but on the preeminent position of the Lord.[45] Hence, in the hymn, it is Jesus Christ, in whom "all things" are held together, who is understood as the one in whom God's creative activity has taken place and in whom God's consummating activity will take place; and therefore it is he who also remains as Lord over the world, between the creation and the consummation.

Conclusion

The essential point is the fact that creation becomes a theme to be considered. The creation is indeed presupposed throughout the New Testament, but is seldom expressed in a thematic way. Still more significant is the fact that this happens here in a predominantly Christological context. A comparison with Acts 17:22-31 shows in what different ways the Pauline proclamation has been understood. In the Areopagus Speech as well, the Hellenistic-Jewish tradition is dominant. There also, the train of thought starts from the creation, and the idea of being "in him" is given special prominence. In Acts, however, this idea relates to God, in whom we live; and the Lukan Paul can obviously speak of God in the same way as can Greek piety (v 23), enlightenment (vv 24b, 25a) and poetry (v 28), in

---

45. Deut. 28:13; 1 Chron. 5:12; cf. Gen. 49:3 etc. It is linked with the image of the body in Test. Zeb. 9.4; Philo, *Praem. Poen.* 125 (cf. 114); Jos. *Bell.* 3.54. According to Philo, *Quaest. in Gen.* 2:9, man is the ἀρχική τις κεφαλή , which includes the destruction of the rest of creation. idea that man's destruction involves tion.

agreement with Jewish statements about creation. Also in Acts the doctrine of Christ became the dividing line. But in Acts 17, Christology is simply added to a doctrine of God to which Jews, enlightened Greeks, and Christians can all agree. The Christological addition consists in a reference to the resurrection and the judgment in Acts 17:30-32. Col. 1:15-18a, by contrast knows that even God's creative activity can only be understood in relation to Christ. A God who did not bear the countenance of Christ would not really be God.

However, this means that God can truly be recognized only in his turning toward us, that is, in his movement of love. There would seem to be the obvious danger that God could thus be reduced to a mere symbol for everything that is humanly considered to be love (as, similarly, the God Eros represents the human phenomenon of love). However, this danger is averted by the fact that Christ is praised as the one who, from the beginning, indeed from before creation, is the "image" and "first-born," the expression of God's love set in motion, a love which is finally directed toward us. God cannot be perceived as secluded in himself, but only in his becoming an image, that is, in his action toward the son and, via the son, toward the world.

This action of his, however, is absolutely prior to the world, so that all love within the world is only an emanation of his love which was there before the world began, which existed between God and his "image," between Father and "first-born" son.[46] The hymn affirms that the world is not meaningless as regards its origin and its goal, but that it has been borne by God's good purpose. Christ becomes Lord by giving meaning to the whole of life.

(b) Second Strophe (1:18b-20)

[18] The second strophe again begins with a relative clause and with predicates used of Christ, parallel to those found in v 15. The "beginning" of the way of God, according to Prov. 8:22, is wisdom, and the connection with "image" is evident in Philo (v. note 4 above). One should not then merely translate by "might" or "power," but actually think in terms of the "beginning" which gives birth to

46. On this v. E. Jüngel, The Doctrine of the Trinity: God's Being Is in Becoming, Edinburgh/London (1976);

v. also W. Kasper, Jesus the Christ, London (1976), 82f.

the ongoing event; and one should also think of the effective presence of God, which as a creative power produces a further development out of itself. This is elucidated by the addition "first-born from
the dead." [47] Rev. 1:5 calls Christ "first-born of the dead," [48] which
serves to emphasize the fact that he is the first of a succession of
others.[49] Col. 1:18, on the other hand, stresses his separation from
the sphere of the dead.

This serves to distinguish the original event, as the basic cause
which sets everything in motion, more emphatically from the resurrection of the others which results from it. Just as Christ, by virtue
of being the "image" of God is the "first-born of all creation,"
because all things were created in him, through him and for him,
so, correspondingly, he is first-born from the dead, because the new
creation of life from death should take place in him, through him
and for him. This is not, of course, said in so many words; instead,
the reconciliation of the universe (v 20) is spoken of. But the point
of this, in the sense of the hymn, is presumably to describe precisely
this new eschatological creation.

This way of joining the first and second strophes corresponds to
what is found in Jewish expressions. Creation and the making of
peace are linked together at an early stage.[50] However, it is precisely
in the earliest instances that the main concern seems to be with
effecting peace in nature, an idea which in Judaism of course includes the angels who rule over nature.[51] Again, where the themes

47. So also Calvin, 131. Ἀρχή also
denotes "beginning" in the passage,
which fits the first strophe well, in Jos.
Ap. II, 190: ὁ θεὸς ἔχει τὰ σύμ-
παντα . . . , ἀρχὴ καὶ μέσα καὶ τέλος
οὗτος τῶν πάντων .
48. So also p⁴⁶ ℵ* here. The parallel to v 15 would thus be still more obvious; a subsequent insertion of the
ἐκ would be conceivable in parallel to
the phrase, which appears about 44
times, about the resurrection ἐκ νεκρῶν. However, since νεκρῶν in this
phrase is always found without the
article, except for two verses which
derive from traditional material (1
Thess. 1:10?; Eph. 5:14; cf. further,
with ἀπό, Matt. 14:2; 27:64; 28:7),
one must reckon rather with the influ-

ence of this tradition on the author of
the hymn and explain the subsequent omission of the ἐκ as a remini-
scence of v 15 (and Rev. 1:5).
49. So also Rom. 8:29, "the first-born
among many brethren"; 1 Cor. 15:20,
"the first fruits of those who have
fallen asleep"; Acts 26:23, "the first
to rise from the dead"; cf. Heb. 2:14f.
50. S. Nu. 6:26 §42 (R. Hananya,
ca. A.D. 70; Strack-Billerbeck I, 216
with n1).
51. On the whole question, cf.
Schweizer, "Versöhnung," 487-94.
Even if one were to think only of the
making of peace "in the circle above
and below," that is, amongst angels
and men (J. J. Meuzelaar, *Der Leib
des Messias*, Amsterdam 1961, 107f.),

of creation and temple cult are found together, the concept of the
stone in the temple (as the basis of the covenant) is central within
the early witnesses; this stone both includes the outflow pipes for
the waters flooding over the earth and also wards off a renewed
bursting forth of the primeval flood.[52]

In the Eighteen Benedictions, the first three petitions give praise
for the creation, the resurrection, and the dominion of "the awful
name" of God; it is only after this that the theme of forgiveness of
sins also comes in. Yet in the Musaph prayer for New Year's Day,
the only prayers used are this first part (1-3) and, after readings
from Scriptures, further concluding praise and blessing (16-18).[53]
Also in Philo's explanation of the New Year Festival, creation and
the making of peace between the elements of nature are closely
linked. In Jewish writings before A.D. 70, then, there seems to be no
mention at the New Year of reconciliation in the sense of forgiveness of sins.[54] On the Day of Atonement, on the other hand, only
forgiveness of sins is mentioned, and hardly anything is said about
the creation.[55] Moreover, the two festivals are separated from each
other by a ten-day period set aside for repentance.

In the New Testament, creation and the resurrection of the dead
are formally linked in Rom. 4:17; in 2 Cor. 4:6, creation and the

this would still not be identical with
the "community of belief" of the
church, which unites Jews and Gentiles (ibid. 110, 116). The Jewish
parallels, like the wording in Col. 1:
15-18 according to which everything
was created and reconciled through
Christ, clearly go beyond this concept.
52. P. Schäfer, "Tempel und Schöpfung," *Kairos* 16 (1974) 122-33. The
Prayer of Manasses (Ode 12 in LXX
= Const.Ap. 22:12) praises the Creator, whose terrible and blessed name
stops up the deeps.
53. Strack-Billerbeck IV, 211-14 and
I, 158 (RH 4.5).
54. Lohmeyer, 43-6, wishes to understand the hymn from the perspective
of the Day of Atonement; however,
the citation, "To make peace between
what is above and what is below"
(Lohmeyer, 44) does not appear in
the place that he mentions. The closest approximation to it is bBer. 16b =

Strack-Billerbeck I, 420) "in the family above and below"); yet the text
here is not concerned with either the
New Year or the Day of Atonement.
In Gen.R. 3 (on 1:4; 3d), which Lohmeyer cites, the discussion is concerned only with the making of peace
between light and darkness and day
and night (in other words in nature!);
and it is likewise doubtful whether one
should take it to refer to the Day of
Atonement, since while the formulation in Gen. 1:5, "one (instead of
"the first") day" could point to this,
it could also indicate the Sabbath or
the first day of offering sacrifice in
Num. 7:12, quite apart from the relatively late date of the text (H. Strack,
*Introduction to the Talmud and Mid-
rash*, 1931, 217f.).
55. Sir. 50:22 describes rather actions
in history, to which παντοκράτωρ (vv 14
and 17 LXX) can also be taken to
refer.

new creation are joined together in the illumination brought about
by the glory of God; in 1 Cor. 8:6 creation and new creation are
perhaps bound together in baptism,[56] and according to the traditional baptismal formula of Eph. 5:14, it is precisely resurrection
from the dead that baptism signifies. In Heb. 1:3 the text of the
wisdom (creation-) predicates of Christ clearly run over into what
is said about his exaltation at the right hand of God, even if there
is an intervening clause, which may well only be redactional anyway,
concerning purification from sins.[57]

1 Tim. 3:16 makes absolutely no mention of the death of Jesus,
and the restoration of the world to its proper place is brought about
by the triumphal march of the Lord, on his journey to heaven and
through all the nations. In Phil. 2:6-11, the song about preexistence
leads on from the theme of obedient self-abasement to that of glory.
John 1:1-18 is indeed familiar with the creation statement promulgated about the Logos, and the statement about incarnation (in
"glory"),[58] but knows nothing of reconciliation on the cross.[59] Thus
the statement about the reconciliation of (the elements of) nature
by means of the resurrection of Christ is thoroughly stylized.

[19] First, however, the discussion concerns the indwelling of the
"fulness" in Christ. Either God should be supplied as the subject
unexpressed,[60] or else "fulness" is to be taken as the subject. In the
first case, however, one would have to translate: "He (God) resolved
that in him (admittedly already anticipated) all the fulness should

56. Cf. Kerst. "1 Kor. 8.6" (note 36
above) 130-9. If ἡμεῖς δι᾿ αὐτοῦ
were really taken to refer not to one's
status as a created being but to the
new creation of the community, then
this formula would also progress, from
the soteriology (of Baptism), secondarily into the cosmology (ibid. 136f.).
57. Grässer, "Hebr. 1.1-4" (note 2
above), 66; G. Theissen, *Untersuchungen zum Hebräerbrief*, 1969 (SNT
2), 50.
58. However, this statement is most
likely redactional; but for a different
view, v. H. Zimmermann, "Christushymnus und johanneischer Prolog," in
*Neues Testament und Kirche (Fest-
schr. R. Schnackenburg)*, Freiburg

1975, 258. M. Rissi, "Die Logosleider
im Prolog des vierten Evangeliums,"
TZ 31 (1975) 321-26, thinks of two
songs (vv 1f., 3b-5, 10-12b/14, 16f.).
However one analyzes the passage,
there is at any rate no reference at all
to Jesus' death, although the section is
concerned with the breach between
the Logos on the one hand and the
world and its salvation on the other.
59. In Rev. 3:14, "beginning of the
creation" and "true witness" do indeed
stand together; yet 1:5 shows that
"first-born of the dead" is an interchangeable concept for the latter.
60. Thus e.g. G. Delling, *TDNT* VI,
303; Gibbs, *Creation*, 100.

dwell, and should reconcile through him." If it is difficult to supply an unexpressed subject of this kind in a hymn concentrated fully upon Christ, it is all the more difficult to propose that a different subject should be assumed for the infinitive "to dwell" than for the infinitive "to reconcile." If one still allowed that "all the fullness" should be the subject, then by supplying the subject "God," one would merely achieve an easier transition to the masculine form of the participle "making peace." In that case, however, it is much simpler to accept that "all the fulness" is the subject throughout, and that the masculine participle is found as a consequence and that it is used as a designation of God.[61]

As early as Ps. 68(67):17; "it has pleased God to dwell upon it (Sinai)" Zion can appear in place of Sinai, Ps. 132(131):13f. In the Targums, the Logos and the Shekinah (Presence) replace God: "it has pleased Yahweh's Word to cause his Shekinah to dwell upon it"; "Has it really pleased Yahweh to cause his Shekinah to dwell amongst men?"[62] The idea that God himself has chosen a place where his name should dwell belongs to the deuteronomistic theology; Zion is also described in Isa. 8:18; 49:20 as the place in which God or the people of the final days dwell.[63] Thus the miracle mentioned in Ps. 68:17 consists in the fact that it pleases God to fill heaven and earth, and it pleases him to speak with Moses from out of the ark of the covenant.[64] Without doubt, then, the miracle should be expressed thus, that he who fills all things is at the same time able to restrict himself and makes his dwelling where he becomes accessible to people.

But how then is the expression "fulness," which occurs only here in the New Testament without the genitive, to be understood? It can designate the full content, the full measure, the sum total or completion, a great amount or a being full. The Gnostic documents offer no further help, since God does not belong to the Pleroma, while the redeemer forsakes the Pleroma and does not take it up

---

61. Mark 13:14 offers an analogous instance; cf. further BDF §134.3; 296. So also Münderlein, NTS 8, 266.
62. Ps. 67:17 LXX: εὐδόκησεν ὁ θεὸς κατοικεῖν ἐν αὐτῷ, and Ps. 131: 13f. LXX: ἐξελέξατο . . . εἰς κατοικίαν . . . ὧδε κατοικήσω. The Targum of Ps. 68:17 and 1 Kings 8:27 is cited in

Schweizer, Neotestamentica, 294 n3; the second passage is also cited in G. Delling, TDNT VI, 303.
63. These and other references are given in Lohse, 58.
64. R. Meir on Jer. 23:24; cited by G. Delling, TDNT, VI, 290.

panthein

into himself.[65] Certainly in the Hermetic writings, where the complete unity of the cosmos is affirmed, God can also be designated as the fulness which includes the whole universe in itself.[66] But the expressions in the Wisdom literature and Philo stand much nearer Colossians than does this pantheism. In the Old Testament, indeed, God is he who fills everything (Jer. 23:24). The most that could be meant by that, however, is the divine act of filling, and that does not yield good sense.[67] Philo's expressions go further on this point; according to these, God "has filled (the Logos) through and through with incorporeal powers," so that the Logos is "full to overflowing with him (God)."[68] Presumably by this one ought to understand God as the fulness (in the sense of sum total) of all powers, so that the idea expressed here is that in Christ dwells everything which is alive in God as the power of creation and recreation.

Or, in more concrete terms, in this second strophe the whole fulness of the power of grace is to be seen as that which makes life out of death possible. This could also explain the striking occurrence of the same term in the Prologue to John's Gospel, in which of course the same Hellenistic Jewish background of wisdom or logos speculation is operative ("from his fulness have we all received grace upon grace," John 1:16). In the Prologue to John as well this is the correlative to activity in creation. The only difference is that in John 1:16, the writer speaks of the "fulness" of Christ, not the

65. Schweizer, EKK I, 21; Lohse, 57. Furthermore, the formulation with πᾶν τό shows that there is no strictly technical usage here, in the sense of an already established designation of God (Hegermann, *Schöpfungsmittler*, 105). On this whole question, cf. Ernst, *Pleroma*, 72-94.

66. Corp. Herm. XVI.3 (ca. A.D. 3?); cf. Lohse, 57.

67. Further references are given in G. Delling, *TDNT* VI, 288-290. Kehl, *Christushymnus*, 116-24, points to the fact that the fulness of God's being has been dwelling in Christ from eternity; thus the idea here can only be of God's active presence in salvation (so also Zeilinger, *Der Erstgeborene*, 166). Ernst, 199ff. (on 2:10) mentions Ps. 104(103):24; here as well, however,

it is only the verb that is found: "the earth is full of your possession (or 'creation')," whereas those verses which have the substantive (Jer. 8:16; 29:2; Ps. 24(23):1) do not describe God's proximity to the world. Whether syncretistic openness vis-à-vis the "fulness" of the religions plays any part (Ernst, 218f., Excursus) is very doubtful. A (Gnostic) system of intermediate links between God and world (Martin, *Lord* 75 on 2:9) is at any rate not presupposed. Gibbs, *Creation*, 107f., understands it thus: Christ's eschatological power leads the creation to its consummation; Benoit, *hymne*, 252 things of a concept combining God and creation.

68. *Som.* I, 62; 75 (Hegermann, *Schöpfungsmittler*, 108).

"fulness" of God becoming effective in Christ, and he also refers to "grace" directly.[69] This idea of the fulness of Christ is in any case how the writer of Colossians has understood it, according to Col. 2:10. The verbal form denotes "to take up residence" rather than the continuous "to dwell." If it is possible to be this precise, the idea is really of the exaltation of Christ as the event in which this fulness of the powers of God, which waken the dead, took up residence in him.[70]

[20] The consequence of this indwelling of God's fulness is described as the reconciliation of the universe. It is not explicitly stated at what point in time that has happened or should happen; but the two verbs "take up residence" and "reconcile," which are closely connected with one another by means of "and," must be understood to be contemporaneous. Thus then the reconciliation had already been brought to completion by the resurrection, although this does not rule out the possibility that it has also taken place "for him"; in other words, that its final consummation is still awaited. This statement is unique.[71]

Altogether different is the way that John 1:1-18 speaks of the world rejecting the Logos, so that salvation pertains only to those who are able to see his glory. If 2 Cor. 5:19 (cf. John 3:16, etc.) uses the expression "world" in the declaration of reconciliation, then surely it is the world of people that is meant by this.[72] And if Rom.

---

69. M. D. Hooker, "The Johannine Prologue and the Messianic Secret," *NTS* 21 (1974/5), 54-6, recalls Exod. 33:19, according to which Yahweh, "full of grace and faithfulness" (34:6), causes "all (his) glory" to pass before Moses. Cf. also note 17 above.

70. Cf. the "authority" given to the Exalted One in Matt. 28:18 (John 5:27; 17:2; Rev. 12:10; in Acts 2:33 he is given the Spirit), the establishing 'in power" in Rom. 1:4, and the exaltation over everything in Phil. 2:9-11.

71. Eph. 1:10 has probably been influenced by this verse in Colossians. Kehl, *Christushymnus*, 159f., proposes that ἀπο-καταλλάξαι(for which there is no evidence before Col. 1:20; v. F. Büchsel, *TDNT* I, 258) should be understood in the sense that it is being used to remedy the ἀλλάξαι of Rom.1:23 (that is, the exchanging of the glory of God for idols in the form of creatures). However, in the first place this would only be intelligible if the formulation in Rom. 1:23 would have been known to the author of the hymn; and secondly in this case it would be not the creatures, still less the universe, that would have to be reconciled, but people, whom the creatures worship. To take εἰς αὐτόν to refer to God (as suggested in Houlden, 173) is ruled out on account of the parallel with v 16d.

8:17-21 also speaks of a setting free of the whole creation, then it is surely only to be understood as an event which is still pending, and which is closely connected with the reconciliation of humanity, as a consequence of this. Moreover, for Paul it is always God, not Christ, who reconciles. Phil. 2:9-11 does indeed include things in heaven, earth, and under the earth, but as subordinate not reconciled powers. Col. 1:20 does then presuppose that the division in nature was experienced as a decisive problem.

This is decidedly the case in the Hellenistic world of the time, and the witnesses collected in the Excursus on 2:8 are plentiful at the time of our letter. The stability of the world has become problematic. The struggle of the elements of nature against one another expresses itself in catastrophes and threatens to lead to a complete breakdown of the universe. The fragile nature of the world and its order is experienced everywhere, and the individual seems like a prisoner of nature, a nature at war with itself. The same Hellenistic author frequently affirms two ideas, namely, that the world is supported by the Logos in an equilibrium which is admittedly unstable and which could at any time fall victim to catastrophe, and furthermore that real stability can only be attained through a return to unity. While the first strophe of the hymn has taken up the problem of the world's existence, a problem not otherwise known in the New Testament, the second strophe proclaims the world's reunification and final stabilization.

This stabilization is designated as "making peace." The verb occurs only once in the New Testament, just as the expression "peacemaker" occurs only once in Philo (*Spec. Leg.* 192.)[73] By means of this Philo explains the trumpet of the New Year Festival as being the signal for the cessation of war, a cessation which God as founder and protector of peace, inaugurates; peace, that is, between the parts of the universe that are fighting against each other within the world of nature. For the Hellenistic Jew Philo as well,

---

72. The fact that in 2 Cor. 5:19 καινὴ κτίσις also appears could lead one to assume that there is in the background a formulation still more markedly cosmic in its orientation; but בְּרִיָה (חֲדָשָׁה) ([new] creation) in Rabbinic thought denotes merely the individual person; only in Damasc. 4:21

does it probably mean the creation (v. W. Foerster, *TDNT* III, 1016, 1023 with note 159).
73. Lyonnet, *RSR* 48, 93-100. Only the adjective in Matt. 5:9 can be compared. All the relevant instances are given in the Excursus to 2:8.

then, the struggle of nature and its stabilization is a central problem, although very closely juxtaposed with this are statements about how God's Logos holds nature in steady equilibrium. The answer given by the hymn here is of course different from that provided by Philo. The verb is in the aorist, and thus denotes the making of a peace that has been concluded once and for all.

In this respect the statement approximates those Stoic, Pythagorean, and Plutarchian statements, which expect the final return of unity from the period after the universal conflagration, or else postpone it to a transcendence that belongs to the world above. No longer does peace have to be restored afresh year by year in the cult; it is secured in Jesus Christ once for all time. However, the background here in Colossians, just as in these texts, is the feeling, widespread throughout the Hellenistic world, of living in a world that is breaking up, in which the struggle of everything against everything else characterizes the whole of nature.

This peace extends over earth and heaven; it is, then, all embracing, as the further definition,[74] which probably indeed belongs to the hymn, expresses it. The more detailed designations "in heaven" and "on earth" affirm not that earth is reconciled to heaven, but that everything in heaven and everything on earth is reconciled (to Christ or God). This is intelligible only if it is conceived of in cosmic rather than anthropological terms; that is, if the phrase belongs to the hymn. The idea expressed in the last line of the hymn is this: the elements which fill the whole universe are engaged in struggles with each other (in Jewish terms the hymn speaks of the universe as "heaven and earth"). The hymn supposes that angels, that is "divine powers,"[75] stand behind the elements and move them. These invisible powers also belong to the universe, according to v 16. But just as reconciliation on earth includes not only people but first and foremost the elements, so likewise in heaven. Everything is reconciled, both those (angels) who move and those (elements) that are moved. What the writer of the letter gives as his interpretation is borne out by vv 23f.

---

74. Otherwise it would hardly be appended by the author of the letter with the awkward resumption of δι' αὐτοῦ
75. Instances are given in Schweizer,

Beiträge (v. note 85 below) 85f., and W. Grundmann, *TDNT* II, 288-289; 295-299.

(2) The Interpretation Given by the Writer of the Letter

[16] For both Jews and Christians of the first century A.D. it is taken for granted that nature is animated, and that it is ruled by all manner of angels or powers. The world of nature is not simply encountered as an object, but is experienced (in a way parallel to a certain extent to our modern conceptions) as a power that challenges, oppresses, and controls man. The writer of this letter is interested less in the harmony of the world, as it is brought about in Christ, than in the subjection of all other powers, which he now enumerates. Admittedly only the last two designations appear again later (2:10). Since grouping by fours is not typical of Paul either, it could go back to the usage of the Colossians, a usage which the author employs more extensively within the hymn, where it suits the style, than he does later.[76]

[18] The same interest is evident in the emphasis on the predominance of Christ "in everything"; in fact, in the second strophe of the original hymn in particular, it is not this, but the reconciliation of the universe that is the main concern. However, the writer of the letter does also give his interpretation in 2:10, 15,[77] in the sense of Christ being preeminent over the subjugated powers. More remarkable is the interpretation of the "body" in terms of the church (v. above p. 58f.). As distinct from the whole of the hymn itself, the discussion no longer relates to the creation and reconciliation of the universe, but simply to one section of the human race instead. The new coinage vis-à-vis Paul (cf. pp. 163f.) can thus be traced back to the fact that the cosmic expression of the hymn was concerned with the world body.

---

76. Θρόνοι is also found in Test. Lev. 3:8 (alongside ἐξουσίαι), and in Sl. En. 20.1 (alongside "dominions, principalities, authorities" etc. [nine legions!], cf. O. Schmitz, *TDNT* III, 166-167); "authorities" comes also in Eth. En. 61:10 (for further discussion, v. W. Foerster, *TDNT* III, 1096-1097).

77. The interpretation of O'Brien (*RTR* 33, 45-53; more cautiously also Schnackenburg, *Herrschaft* [v. note 16 to 1:12-14] 218f.), in terms of a conclusion of peace forcibly imposed, which could lead to a harmonization with Colossians 2:14f. is impossible in view of what the text says (cf. below p. 354f.). Also the tension with 1:21f. may not be resolved by distinguishing between v 20a, as having a timeless reference, and v 22a, as something definitively brought about already (against Lähnemann, *Kolosserbrief*, 43).

In this connection, one may ask whether the concept of a God embracing the universe already belonged to the background of Pauline usage, and for this very reason could so readily be transferred here from the cosmological to the ecclesiological sphere;[78] or whether, conversely, it was only the writer of the letter who first brought the expression of the hymn (understood in light of the widespread cosmological concept of the world as "body") into conjunction with the Pauline expression and interpreted it in that sense.[79] At all events, this change was bound to happen, because for the writer of the letter Christ is indeed "head" over the universe and over the powers of the world, but only the church is "his body."[80]

The theological formulation is thus completely changed. The function of Christology is no longer to express the fact that God's activity in creation can be recognized alone in Christ (that is, that God's activity is only properly understood when we see it as the movement of his love toward us). Its function now is above all to recognize the fact that Christ as lord over all powers is acknowledged as head only where the church turns in faith toward him, and by this very act becomes "his body," filled by him with life (2:19).

[20] The same interest is betrayed once more in the way that the reference to "the blood of his cross" is introduced. The hymn speaks

78. So K. M. Fischer, *Tendenz und Absicht des Epheserbriefes*, Berlin 1973, 48-78, esp. 71-8. The instances need to be sifted. Macrobius is writing c. A.D. 400, and the magical papyri can scarcely be dated; on *Quaest. in Ex.* and *Orph. Fr.* 21a cf. note 9 above. Undoubtedly prior to Colossians are only the instances not mentioned by Fischer concerned with the ether or heaven as head of the world body. To these can be added the similar statement about Zeus, which is scarcely open to question, and the comparisons (v. above p. 58f).

79. So E. Schweizer, *TDNT* VII, 1071-1073; cf. id., "Menschensohn und eschatologischer Mensch im Frühjudentum," in: *Jesus und der Menschensohn, Festschr. A. Vögtle*, ed. R. Pesch and R. Schnackenburg, Freiburg 1975,

113-6. If this explanation is accepted and the parallel of the "vine," "in" which the branches live (John 15:1ff.) is taken seriously, then it has to be assumed that the hymn in Col. 1:18a goes back directly (or else prompted by the Pauline discussion of the body of Christ) to the purely Hellenistic concept of the world body, whose head is the ether (or Zeus or Logos), whereas the author of the letter gives his interpretation in the sense of the Pauline theologoumenon. However, even if conversely the view of the universe-God is seen as the root of the Pauline usage, it has to be accepted that the hymn has gone back beyond Paul to the Hellenistic view.

80. Käsemann, *Baptismal Liturgy*, 167f. (50f.).

of the resurrection as the beginning of the new creation. Now with
Paul one would certainly expect the resurrection to be understood
also as the divine acceptance of Jesus' death, although one would
scarcely expect this to be expressed by the formula "the blood of
the cross."[81] Thus it appears here in a strange way, added to the
assertion that the indwelling of the whole fulness of God in the
Risen One has brought about worldwide reconciliation. The second
statement, that peace has been brought about through the blood of
the cross clearly stands in contrast to that. This, however, is the
position of the author of the letter for whom peace is to be found
precisely in this suffering of Christ, which takes place on the human
plane and which awakens faith. And it was through this suffering
that Christ gained the church as the community of his people.

Conclusion

An astonishing feature has been observed long ago, namely, that
in the second strophe the hymn speaks of the reconciliation of the
universe, although the first makes it clear that ever since creation
the universe has been established and protected in Christ. Nowhere
is anything said about a discrepancy between the two. In addition
then it must be asked whether one can speak at all about a reconciliation of the universe. Does not reconciliation necessarily demand
the deliberate response of that which allows itself to be reconciled?
Ought not reconciliation be limited ot human beings who believe?
Neither question can be answered unless the character of hymnic
language is made clear.

In the hymn, the speaking or singing is done by the community
of those who worship. We must not speak explicitly of faith or
confession since it is in the very act of singing the hymn that they
express themselves. Neither the belief of the community, as it sings
the hymn, nor the non-belief of others can be advanced as the essen-

---

81. Paul does take over the expression,
"blood" of Christ in a traditional formulation in Rom. 3:25 and in 5:9;
however, apart from the eucharistic
texts (and perhaps John 19:34), it is
characteristic only of Heb., 1 Peter, 1
John, and Rev. "Blood of the cross" is
unique in the New Testament; yet the
reference to the cross is characteristic
of Paul, and it will be from him that
the writer has taken it up here. Colossians otherwise never refers to Christ's
"blood" (although in 1:14 the word
has intruded in some miniscules from
Eph. 1:17).

tial theme here. The real theme is the demeanor of the one who is
sung of in the hymn, a demeanor that at most can only be mirrored
in that of those who sing. The person addressed in hymnic language
is God or Christ. The point therefore is not to impart information
which would be unfamiliar to the person addressed.

Narrative elements may become part of this language, not however, in order to offer details as information, but to convey the reaction (thankfulness, joy, and so on) which has been evoked by the
acts which are narrated. Hence also the account is not given as a
complete logical whole, but emphasis is laid on those facts which are
decisive for this reaction, those, that is, which are still effective at
the present time as well. However, to go into detail is altogether
unnecessary, because the real concern is the encounter with the one
who does not need to be told anything more at all. Again, the
object of their praise can only be his goodness or faithfulness, which
has been demonstrated in many acts, too numerous to list.[82]

One should not, then, expect any mention of a discrepancy that
has arisen between the first and second strophes. Indeed, there is no
narrative at all; instead, he who is exalted and enthroned at present
vis-à-vis the community is praised as the image of God and as the
beginning (that is, he in whom God again and again gives himself
to the community), and, also as the firstborn of the creation and new
creation (that is, as he to whom the community, as created and
recreated, owes its existence). Since the community lives in the
sphere both of creation and of redemption, it praises Christ simultaneously as creator and redeemer.[83] So strong is the concentration
on him as present with the community in his *exaltation*, that absolutely nothing at all is said anywhere of his appearing on earth. The
most that can be argued is that this is presupposed in the phrase
"of the dead." That does indeed go further than Phil. 2:7f. ("the

---

82. Compare the pure songs of praise
in Rev. 4:8; 5:13 with those which are
supplemented by subordinate clauses
which give the reason for the praise
(4:11; 5:9f.); instead of those one may
find a predicate (the Lamb "who was
slain," 5:12).

83. An analogy is provided to a certain
extent by the juxtaposition of the New
Year Festival and the Day of Atonement (cf. above p. 75). In Israel the

experience of redemption led to the
statement of the creation (v. G. von
Rad, *Old Testament Theology* I, 1962,
136-9: "Creation is part of the aeti-
ology of Israel!" (ibid. 138); cf. Isa.
51:9f. (the primeval flood moves in
the Red Sea); Ps. 106(105):9; 114
(113):3 (ibid. 178); the two are juxtaposed in Ps. 102(101):14-29. Thus
nature and history cannot be rigidly
separated (ibid. II, p. 341).

form of a servant ... in human form"), and 1 Tim. 3:16 ("was manifested in the flesh").

Instead of the idea of turning to humanity in the Incarnation, the
idea is instead introduced of God turning to humanity in Christ, an
act that is already accomplished as creation and is fully realized as
new creation in the resurrection. Still less should one expect anything to be said of those who are neither able nor willing to join in
the song here. It is Christ who is the theme; there is no limit to the
safekeeping and salvation brought about by his love. How then
could any restrictions be placed on this within the community's
hymn of thanksgiving?

If then the first strophe corresponds quite well to the religious-
historical parallels in the wisdom sayings of Hellenistic Judaism, the
second in corresponding style describes the newly attained world
of peace (v. p. 74), that is, the new creation inaugurated in the
resurrection of Jesus Christ from the dead, the reconciliation of the
universe. As in John 1:14 and Heb. 1:3, so also here the main theme
is provided by a Christological statement which does indeed presuppose the incarnation, resurrection, and exaltation at the right
hand of God. The positive rôle of creation, indeed, in Col. 1:20, the
actual reconciliation of creation, is thus the exact opposite of what
the Gnostics would have preached.[84]

In the second half, then, (as also in John 1:14 and Heb. 1:3, at
the end) common Christian idiom can be detected even more
markedly. In Col. 1:20 there is also the further theme of the reconciliation of the universe, a theme that plays a considerable rôle in
Hellenism, but which has also, at least in Philo, infiltrated into the
Hellenistic Jewish sphere. In the hymnic language of worship a
radical concentration on Christology is thus brought about. Here
everything else may and indeed must simply keep silent. Both the
past (the state of non-peace) and the future (for those who are
still "dead" are embraced by Christ who is present, and both are
therefore sanctified. Such a concentration on Christ must have its
place in the life of the community. It is found above all in the cele-
bration of the sacraments.[85]

It must be pointed out that the whole thing would be falsified, if

---

84. E. Schweizer, *TDNT* VII, 1075,   *zur Theologie des NT*, Zürich 1970,
note 474.   144f. and "Forschung," 186-8.
85. On this v. E. Schweizer, *Beiträge*

? should a song contradict our theology

what is expressed in the singing of the hymn were to be taken over
directly as doctrine.[86] For in this case the Lord who is praised in
the hymn would become a possession which could be placed at
our disposal. The invisible God is praised in the hymn as the one who
(according to the first strophe) approaches us again and again in
Christ, who is his "image." If, however, this becomes just a doctrinal
statement, it would make his invisibility disappear without the need
being felt to rehearse again the miracle of the encounter with
Christ and of being grasped by his love. There would then be the
idea of a visible nature of God which those who possessed the correct doctrine would have at their disposal. So everything that the
hymn said would be understood as an illusion that would blur the
view of the realities.

The way in which the hymn praises what, according to the second
strophe, is an unlimited power of reconciliation, would then become
a doctrinal statement about universalism which would have Christ
and his activity at its disposal. The goodness promised in the hymn
would then no longer be the free goodness of the one who gives
himself to us. The prodigal son who, having returned home, extols
the father's countless goodness, would have turned this occasion
for praise into the exact opposite had he transmitted it to his brother
as doctrine; for the brother, now likewise having the guarantee that
he would subsequently receive full forgiveness—and more—from
his father, would want to squander his inheritance.

Only the person who really knows of the invisibility of God (v 15)
and of the "dominion of darkness" (v 13); only the person who
knows of the world in its unreconciled and restless state, can properly sing of the one who contains everything so that it is secure "in
him," and who therefore remains the goal toward which everything
exists. The world can then be neither idolized (as in world-famous)
nor cursed (as in worldliness). It finds its place "in him." Something of this "foolish" joy comes alive in worship in the Gregorian
chants, and in the wild melodies of African churches, but also in
the songs of praise on the death of strict Jews in the Warsaw Ghet-

---

86. On this cf. pp. 291f. and (earlier)
Ahrens, *Diskussion,* 278. I must therefore maintain (more strongly than does
Ernst, 179f.) the tension between the
theological statements of the hymn on
the one hand and the interpretation
given by the writer of the letter on the
other, although I think that they both
must have their place together in the
worship of the community, but in different places—the one in the song of
praise, the other in the teaching.

to and in the persecuted Huguenots' psalms of praise. Like a strong, secure tenor voice in a choir, the voice of the one who sings in this hymn will carry its hearers and readers along with it.

Human love can only serve as a feeble analogy for what the hymn sees, as it were, through God's eyes. Thus a husband can still see in his wife, now ill and disfigured with age, the one with whom he has shared so many experiences, ever since he first loved her when she was a young maiden. So also a mother can already see in her difficult son, as he is entering the stage of puberty, the person he will one day become. Only faith has the knowledge that goes beyond all these present anxieties and realizes that what God's love sees in the world is indeed reality, since his love is stronger than everything that seeks to contradict it. Therefore the community's song of praise is absolutely right in viewing the world in light of what God has created—"and God saw everything that he had made, and behold, it was very good" (Gen. 1:31)—and will one day create —"Then I saw a new heaven and a new earth" (Rev. 21:1).

The writer of the letter, on the contrary, is *bound* to reinterpret the hymn because he is lifting it out of the situation of the community's worship, and transporting it to a completely different sphere of usage, that is, to the sphere of promise and of warning to others. With his emphasis on the pre-eminence of Christ over the powers, which were presumably an important factor in Colossae, he does indeed emphasize the fact that the hymn cannot be apprehended without letting the lordship of the one who is sung about become real in one's own particular situation. The reference to Christ's lordship over the church, and to the price paid for this on the cross, serves to draw the listeners into the community, to summon them to the act of faith, an act that must be repeated over and over again. The community has previously been described in vv 12-14 as the sphere of light in contrast to the sphere of darkness. This, however, is a theme that must be considered in context of vv 21-23.

c) Commentary on the Hymn: Application to the Reader (1:21-23)

21   And you, who once were estranged and hostile in mind, doing evil deeds,   22   he has now reconciled in his body of flesh by his death, in order to present you holy and blameless and irreproach-

able before him 23 provided that you continue in the faith,
stable and steadfast, not shifting from the hope of the gospel which
you heard, which has been preached to every creature under heaven,
and of which I, Paul, became a minister.

Analysis

With this repeated declaration of reconciliation, the writer takes
up again the verb of v 20. This is a verb which, in the whole of the
Bible, is found only here and in Eph. 2:16, itself dependent upon this
passage. There is no evidence at all of it having been used before
the writing of the Epistle to Colossians (v. note 71 to 1:15-20). However, the expression "and you" is set in advance of this and is decisive
for the writer of the letter's reinterpretation.[1] By means of this,
reconciliation is understood anew as the reconciliation of those who
believe. Here the dominant theme is the transition from "darkness"
to "light," which has been indicated in advance in vv 12-14, but is
not even so much as hinted at anywhere in the hymn itself.

That this transition is the main theme is shown not only by the
more extensive description of "you" in v 21, but above all by the
stylistic flourish "now" (however); this latter is in a gramatically
impossible way, placed before the verb in v 22, in order to distinguish the new situation of the converts from their former state
(1:26f.; 3:7.; Rom. 6:22; 11:30; cf. 16:26; 1 Cor. 6:11; Gal. 1:23).
The further designation "in his body of flesh by his death" corresponds to the addition that has already been inserted in v 20.
Essentially, however, it is the addition of a final clause, which is
limited again by the condition of v 23, that emphasizes the open-
endedness of the declarations made in the hymn, that is, their correlation with the community's response of faith and hope. The expressly cosmic terminology appearing at the end again shows that
vv 21-23 are indeed an interpretation of the hymn. At the same time,
it is by means of this terminology that the writer is able to find a

---

1. Luke 1:76 forms a parallel of a sort
(Lohmeyer, 69 n1); yet there also
one probably has to reckon with a new
literary layer, in which the transmitted
hymn was applied to the specific event
of the circumcision of the Baptist (H.
Schürmann, *Das Lukasevangelium I,*
Leipzig 1970 *[HTKNT]* 88f.). In Col.
2:13 as well, the "and you . . ." set at
the start is again brought in in a grammatically incorrect way; further, the
nun de in 1:26 breaks off the relative
clause of vv 25f. and starts up afresh.
This seems to belong to the style of
the writer of the letter.

point of connection for the theme of the apostle's missionary charge (vv 24-29).

Interpretation

[21] As in 3:7f., it is the "once" of those who are addressed that is portrayed. This first of all is designated, by means of an expression found in the New Testament only here and in Eph. 2:12, 4:18, as "estrangement," that is, as spatial separation from God.[2] It is then further described as enmity against God.[3] Certainly, what is meant by this is not only their spiritual state, but the entire orientation (in an objective sense) of their lives (cf. Rom. 5:10). Also, it is not particular moral aberrations that are being discussed; this is made clear by the reference to their thought. The form of this is unPauline, but the content corresponds to the apostle's own usage. The writer in fact affirms that what is usually called sin is not simply the sum-total of wrong actions or attitudes, but is basically a false orientation of one's entire life. From this vantage point, Paul himself set his blamelessness as to righteousness under the law on the side of this former separation and hostility (Phil. 3:6f.), since his hundred-percent moral perfection was directed not toward God but toward his own concern to remain blameless. In Col. 1:21, this earlier situation is made more specific by means of the reference to "evil deeds."

So then, disposition and works are in no way opposites; so also according to Rom. 8:4-7 the demands of the law are indeed fulfilled by those who set their minds spiritually, but not by others. From the Old Testament onwards, no practising Jew could speak of a pure disposition that did not express itself in specific action.[4] The difference now is that the writer has to insist that it is not that

---

2. So also Acts 2:39 (cf. 22:21); Eph. 2:12f., 17; in all these verses there are echoes of Isa. 57:19. At Qumran, God's 'bringing near' and the "coming near" of the member denote entry into the community (Lohse, 63, note 6). Chrysostom IV. 1 (325) sees in this estrangement stress being laid on human guilt.

3. Since it is their "mind" (διάνοια, never in Paul, who uses φρονεῖν [Rom.8:5-7]) that is spoken of, the expression is to be interpreted in an active sense as "hostile," not passively as "hated." The interpretation "hostile to the thought (of God)" is already rejected by Erasmus, 503.

4. "The soul governed by the evil spirit is enslaved in lusts and evil works" (Test. A. 6:5; Lohse, 64). Calvin, 133 also precludes an interpretation that restricts the meaning of the text to inferiores concupiscentiae (baser lusts).

individual evil acts can be evaluated, and then all offences added up, but that each individual act betrays the basic direction of one's whole life, so that even a morally praiseworthy life can be sinful, and, conversely, a moral offence can have positive effect.

[22] As in vv 12-14 the actual terminology of conversion is used, so in v 22 as well the period after baptism is sharply distinguished from that before baptism by means of the "now." The hymn is again resumed, by means of the verb used here, but is now related to the community that is addressed. It is for that reason as well that the reconciliation with God is linked simply and exclusively to the death of Jesus. The further description is striking: the reconciliation takes place "in his body of flesh by his death." [5] In English one has to translate this by something like "in his body that is dying for you." "Body of flesh" (cf. note 27 on 2:8-15) is an innovation compared with Paul, but is attested in e.g. Sir. 23:17; Eth. Enoch 102:5 (Greek); 1 QpHab 9:2. Thus the body of Jesus put to death on the cross should, for the sake of clarity, be distinguished from the body of Christ, which the community represents. This emphasizes that the involvement of Jesus (as far as "death") has also penetrated into the corporeal sphere; for otherwise the designation "by his death" was completely sufficient in itself.

However, this addition can only be understood if the author is playing with the double meaning of "body" as the designation of the crucified body of Jesus, and of the community as the body of Christ. He has indeed already in v 18a set Christ in relation to the community, and he will, in v 24, repeat the point that the body of Christ is the community. For him at least then, the question of being reconciled in the body of Christ (= in the community) is closely related to the question of being reconciled in the body (of flesh) of Christ (= in the crucified one or through the crucified one). If he has understood his master aright, then this means that for Paul as well the expression about the change of lordship "through the (crucified) body of Christ" (Rom. 7:4) is closely connected with the ex-

---

5. "Death" should not be taken to refer to the experience of baptism on account of the fact that (in BC etc.) autou is lacking (against Zeilinger, Der Erstgeborene, 141); in fact αὐτοῦ is probably only missing because it comes already after σαρκός. For the idea of the "flesh," cf. p. 162. The fact that Marcion gives an interpretation (without "flesh") in terms of the church as the body of Christ (Tertullian, Marc. V, 19:6 [722.18-23]) is characteristic.

pression about being immersed "into the one body (of Christ),"
that is, the community (1 Cor. 12:13 cf. 27).

Yet it is the involvement of Jesus, that is, the price which has been
paid with his death for this reconciliation, that is strongly emphasized; the idea then is not just that of the body of Christ as constantly present in the sacrament or in the community.

In this connection it may be observed that in the whole of the New
Testament it is always the individual person, not God, who needs to
be reconciled. It is certainly not a matter of a calculated business
payment intended to assuage an angry God. Above all, the plethora
of different images shows to what a limited extent Paul can be tied
down to one particular idea. Only in Romans are various other metaphors found alongside the typical Pauline image of justification
(3:24-26 et. al.). Thus we have the image of

— substitution, already intelligible within the whole context of
  human trade and intercourse (4:25; 5:6-11; 14:15);
— atonement, presupposing a legal situation (3:25);
— the sin-offering, with its special orientation in the cult (8:3); [6]
— reconciliation, relating to a breach of an association (5:10f.);
— ransom, recalling a situation of imprisonment or slavery (3:24;
  7:4);
— an exemplar, purely ethical in nature (15:3-5);
— the prototype, where the person following him shares in his
  experience (6:4-6).[7]

2 Corinthians 5:14 shows to what a limited degree the sense of
the individual images should be forced to its logical conclusion. The
fact that "one has died for all" does not mean that all these therefore no longer have to die, but exactly the opposite, that "therefore
all have died." The concepts of substitution and of an exemplar
are thus combined in the same sentence. This clearly shows that in
Colossians 1:22 the intention is not to establish a compensatory
theory but to describe the solidarity of God with the person, which

6. Περὶ ἁμαρτίας is a frequent technical usage in Leviticus in this sense.
In the parallel passage in Gal. 4:4f.,
v 5 is elucidated by 3:13; thus both
passages speak of ransom from the
curse of the law.
7. E. Schweizer, *Jesus*. London (SCM,
1971), 95. Thus although I find extremely dubious the reconstruction,
based on completely uncertain hypotheses, of four primitive Christian Chris-
tologies in Schillebeeckx, *Jesus*, 404-
38, yet he is certainly right in saying
that the concept of atonement is only
one of several possibilities.

goes as far as physical death itself. This act of Christ is so all-embracing that it is by means of it that the past has become a subordinate clause. It is for this reason that what is described here is "not
what we are, but the purpose for which we have been made." [8]

The clause attached here shows of course that it is not merely a
theoretical proclamation of impunity that can be meant by this.
Already in 2 Cor. 5:18 reconciliation and "ministry (of reconciliation)" are directly juxtaposed. Paul never speaks of his conversion,
but only of his calling. Thus for Paul reconciliation can have no
other consequence than that God commissions a person for a new
ministry. Hence it is that this very ministry participates throughout
in the ambiguous (to human eyes) and humble nature of the ministry of the crucified one (2 Cor. 6:3-10). The "presenting" is expressed by means of an aorist tense, since what is described is an
act whose consequences are once and for all. In legal parlance, the
word signifies being arraigned before judgment; traces of that idea
may still be found in 1:28 and likewise in Jude 24.[9] In Col. 1:22
however, the idea is rather on the analogy of mediatory usage, that
is, where the text speaks of going in before God during the course
of one's priestly duty.[10]

At any rate, the real goal of Christ's reconciling activity again
turns out to be Christ himself. It is to *him* that the members of the
community should be reconciled. It is he who gives sense and purpose to all that happens. Thus it is for this reason that reconciliation and ministry belong so inseparably together. And it is in exactly this way that one is given a share in real salvation; salvation, in
other words, which is not only expressed as a theoretical declaration
concerning the person, but into which we are brought with all our
actions, thoughts, and feelings. In this reconciliation, God takes
hold of us, together with our actions, and gives his approval to us
and to what we do. And what we do should be "blameless and irre-
proachable," specifically "before him," that is, in his eyes. So even if

---

8. Lohmeyer, 69 on v 21 and Conzelmann, 187.
9. Στῆσαι κατενώπιον τῆς δόξης αὐτοῦ
ἀμώμους. Κατενώπιον is otherwise
found only in Eph. 1:4, likewise connected with (ἁγίους καὶ) ἀμώμους.
Presumably then there are more or
less fixed expressions underlying these
phrases.
10. Deut. 10:8; 18:5, 7; 21:5; Rom.

12:1; cf. Eph. 1:4 and further references in Lohse, 65 note 23; on ἐνώπιον
. . . cf. Rom. 14:22; 2 Cor. 4:2 (in an
eschatological sense, however, in 5:10;
Jude 24). Calvin, 134 sees in this the
importance and incomplete nature of
sanctification before the final judgment. Both interpretations are found
in Beza, 406b.15-29 and Calov, 810a.

it would be better to take "before him" with the verb rather than
with the adjective, the point still holds that God alone possesses the
measure by which holy and unholy can be distinguished.[11] People
should "be such that *he* could find no fault with them nor reproach
them."

[23] The conditional clause makes it quite clear that the indicative
and imperative belong together (v. p. 122). What has been settled
once and for all by God is valid for as long as the community lives in
faith and hope (v. p. 33). That means that everything that concerns God has been done, and is valid once and for all. The community has a share in this, inasmuch as it lives on this basis. When
the community ceases to live on this basis, what comes to an end is
not God's reconciliation, but the life that derives from this reconciliation. In just the same way, music or love exist not only when
they are heard or experienced, but even when they are rejected or
repulsed. However, they have no existence among those who are
completely unmusical or among those who have shut themselves off
completely from love, even though music or love surround them.
One presumably has to translate "continue in the faith," since the
verb is often used in this construction with the dative. Otherwise
one would have to take it as an instrumental dative and translate
"established by the faith" (cf. 2:7).

One may ask to what extent "faith" is understood already at this
stage as making a decision for Christ, a decision which only subsequently leads to a distinctly ethical characterization (cf. pp. 33
and 124). In that case the designation here would refer to the basis
by which this new life is given its distinctive stamp; yet in any case,
as with Paul, these both still belong closely together. The fact that
a person is rooted in God is taken seriously both in Paul (1 Cor.
3:11f., cf. Eph. 2:20; 2 Tim. 2:19) and in the Synoptic tradition
(Matt. 7:24-27), since both derive from Old Testament songs of
praise about the work of God in "founding" or "establishing." [12]
Here, however, in addition to this, mention is also made of the perseverance, the steadfastness indeed, by which "they do not allow
themselves to be shifted from their hope." In face of the oft-repeated

---

11. This is stressed still more strongly
if one links the phrase "before him"
closely with the adjectives, a connection that is obviously correct in Eph.
1:4. Cf. p. 111.

12. Ps. 8:4; 24(23):2; 102(101):26;
Isa. 48:13; 51:13, 16; Lohse, 66 note
33.

attempts to accommodate the Christian proclamation to every kind
of understanding of the world, it becomes more and more important
to remain steadfast in the apostolic proclamation.[13]

It must of course be said that the proscribing of the danger of
heresy leads straight to the danger of orthodoxy. And the case is
similar in warning of the danger of a faith which threatens to give
up the essential content with which it has been provided, that of
the crucified and risen Jesus Christ. This leads to the danger of a
faith which clings to statements of truth that have been correctly
represented but which fails to realize that at a different time, in
changed circumstances, it must be relived. Certainly the nature of
faith as basically open-minded is maintained by this usage of
"hope"; but the idea here is rather that of the hope already laid up
in heaven (v. p. 34), that is, of the transcendence of God. Nevertheless, faith still remains a state of being stretched out towards that
other world, which alone provides the means for this world to
receive its ultimate seriousness and its ultimate joy.

The final phase does indeed govern the following section. There
the gospel appears as the decisive event, just as in 1:4f. it is described as the basis of faith and hope. Likewise also in that passage
(1:6), there is a description of the gospel resounding throughout
the whole world. All the same, this is even more important here,
because the cosmic language (suggested, no doubt, by the hymn)
comes through more clearly. Although what is meant by "creation"
is humanity, and in no sense the whole of nature, as it is in the
hymn.[14] In this way the event of the Pauline mission to the Gentiles, (as the addition expressly states here) moves directly into the
spotlight of the salvation event, without it being made clear whether
or in what way this is to be distinguished from the event of the crucifixion and resurrection of Jesus Christ.

Thus it can be seen that Colossians stands in a line of development
that can be ascertained otherwise as well (v. p. 108). The commission to proclaim the gospel throughout the world is pictured in al-

13. Cf. the warning against "going
ahead" in 2 John 9.
14. W. Foerster, *TDNT* III, 1038. The
expression "to preach the gospel to the
whole creation" is found again in the
New Testament only in Mark 16:15,
also specifically in the context of the
world mission. Even if the presence of
the article here (א) is thought to be
secondary, one must still translate by
"the whole creation" and not "every
creature" (contra RSV). The absence of
the article has probably come about
through the influence of v 15.

most rapturous Deutero-Isaianic language in Mark 13:10; 14:9;
Matt. 28:19; (Mark) 16:15 as well, and by Paul himself in Rom.
15:15-21 (cf. 1:5, 8, 14-16; 1 Cor. 1:2; 1 Thess. 1:8). However,
whereas with Paul what is emphasized above all is that the nations
of the world should be brought to obedience to Christ, the emphasis here is rather on reaching to the furthermost corner of the whole
(creation that is "under heaven." This is bound up with the schema
of revelation, which from 1:26 (v. ad loc.) onwards does indeed govern what is said. Finally, a striking feature is the very emphatic "I,
Paul," especially since the apostle is associated, by means of the
expression "minister" which is never used in the Pauline Epistles),
with the event of the mission that is spreading throughout the
world.[15]

Summary

What, then, is the theological significance of the fact that the author has, in his letter, taken over the hymn and provided a commentary on it? It is this: the hymn has thus become an address to the
community to which the letter is directed. It is they, and no longer
the exalted Christ, who are addressed by the hymn. Whether they
assent to this or not remains an open question; for the writer of the
letter inserts the hymn because he wants to speak to the community
about something they do not already conform to in their thought
and activity. Hence what was contained within the act of singing
the hymn must now be given expression in their lives; and it is to
that that they are now summoned.

Still more important is the fact that the imparting of faith, the
teaching, and the summons are all turned into a warning with ethical implications. Thus the boundless praise of Christ in the hymn
can no longer remain the exclusive theme; it must now be explicitly

15. Cf. note 11 to Introduction. In 1
Cor. 3:5, Paul wishes consciously to
set himself on the same level as Apollos, and only subsequently to specify
his own function as that of planting as
distinct from Apollos's job of watering;
and here he can designate himself
along with Apollos as διάκονος. In 2
Cor. 3:6; 11:23 he can, in the comparison with the opponents, take over
their terminology for himself as well.
Even there, however, he does not say
that he is "a minister of the gospel" or
even, as in Col. 1:24 of "the church"
(Lohse, NTS 11, 210). In fact, the
closest approximation in Paul would
be the phrase λατρεύω . . . ἐν τῷ εὐαγ-
γελίῳ in Rom. 1:9. The expansions in
some manuscripts by means of ἀπόστολος (and κῆρυξ) show that the unusual
nature of the expression was certainly
felt.

said what this means in the situation of those who receive the letter. There is thus, in v 16b, c, an enumeration of what is included in this unlimited lordship of Christ. Indeed, it is made clear, by means of this enumeration in specific terms, that the "thrones, dominions, principalities, and authorities" no longer play the same rôle in Colossae as they did hitherto. The will of this Lord, to exercise his pre-eminence in everything (v 19), now includes the life of those who are addressed. Therefore the writer can no longer speak without reference to time, but must instead say explicitly "now."

Above all, the readers are now addressed as a community which stands in a much closer and in fact different relationship to Christ than does the rest of humanity or even the whole realm of nature. The writer has already hinted at this figuratively by saying that the community is the "body" of Christ ("of Christ" is the correction given by the author), only because Christ has died for them.

What this means is enlarged upon in the attached commentary, in a similar way to what we have seen already in the introduction in vv 12-14. This interpretation could give rise to the misunderstanding that the divine church now simply takes the place of the divine universe; and that the song of praise about this church, which has been brought to perfection and which is governed and beloved by God, takes the place of the stirring Stoic song of praise about the universe to which exactly the same epithets apply.[16] When this song of praise, which could only take effect in faith, became a form of teaching to be transmitted, God would be at one's disposal; now no longer in the understanding of the sage, who perceives God in creation, but in the power of the custodian of ecclesiastical secrets, doctrine, and sacraments. So this would be worse than the Stoic universalism, because it would thus say that the presence of God is open not to all but only to a few; and yet the idea of having God at one's disposal would not be avoided.

However what is said does in fact demand a change in the way of thinking and acting. This change has its basis in the involvement of Jesus Christ himself, in his human existence, and especially in his death. Hence this change is not the consequence of an event in the natural world such as happens for example with a forest disappearing when it is swept away by an avalanche. It is for this rea-

16. Cleanthes fr. 537 (von Arnim I, 121.23-123.5).

son that the verbs "preach" and "hear" replace the purely objective statements about "founding" and "reconciling." Likewise the personal pronoun "you" replaces the substantive "everything." This is, then, an event that takes place on a personal level between the individual and God.

Hence the change from alienation, as it is now expressed, has to be affirmed in a constantly renewed orientation to the achievement of Christ.[17] It was in the singing of the hymn that this new orientation actually came about. Now, however, the point has to be made that this does not, of course, come about *only* in the singing of the hymn, but that from this moment onward it must force its way into everyday life.

This becomes clear, in exemplary fashion, in the apostle's existence, through which his Lord will become effective throughout the whole universe. The authority of Christ, which is permeating the whole world, is no mysterious power of nature, but the authority of the word and life of the apostle, who performs his ministry in the shadow of his Lord who died on the cross; thus he drags himself, sweating and shivering, hungering and thirsting, beaten and abused, through the length and breadth of the Roman Empire. This certainly no longer sounds so sublimely lyrical as do the expressions of the community's jubilant song. But here an analogy may help: just as children press themselves against the knotholes in the fence outside a football ground so as to be able to see at least something of the game taking place on the other side, so the community may learn to peer again and again through knotholes such as these and thus gain a glimpse, certainly not of the whole but at least a bit here and there, of the great activity of God which traverses the earth in the person of the apostle.

World Mission as Revelation of the Mystery (1:24-29)

Bibliography: On v 24: E. Güttgemanns, *Der leidene Apostel und sein Herr*, 1966 (FRLANT 90); E. Kamlah, "Wie beurteilt Paulus sein Leiden?" *ZNW* 54 (1963), 217-232; Kremer, *Leiden*. On v 26: G. Bornkamm, *TDNT* IV, 802-828; N. A. Dahl, "Formgeschichtliche Beobachtungen zur Christusverkündigung in der Gemeindepredigt," in *Neutestamentliche Studien für R. Bultmann*, 1954 (BZNW 21) 3-9.

17. This is emphasized by the terminology of conversion, which is dominant both in vv 12-14 and in vv 21-3.

24 Now I rejoice in my sufferings for your sake, and in my flesh I complete what is lacking in Christ's afflictions for the sake of his body, that is, the church, 25 of which I became a minister according to the divine office which was given to me for you, to make the word of God fully known, 26 the mystery hidden for ages and generations but now made manifest to his saints, 27 To them God chose to make known how great among the Gentiles are the riches of the glory of this mystery, which is Christ in you, the hope of glory. 28 Him we proclaim, warning every man and teaching every man in all wisdom, that we may present every man mature in Christ. 29 For this I toil, striving with all the energy which he mightily inspires within me.

Analysis

Here, as in the final short sentence of v 23, the apostle speaks in the first person singular [1] about his commission in general, and similarly, in 2:1-5, of this in relation to Colossae.[2] By means of an appended relative clause, characterizing Paul as a minister of the gospel, the interpretative commentary on the hymn proceeds, in v 23, to a new theme. This is expressed in ecclesiological terms first of all, by means of the clause concerning the suffering endured by the apostle on behalf of the church; hence the appended relative clause (v 25a), parallel in every way to the end of v 23, characterizes Paul as a minister of the church. Next it is developed in the schema of revelation: the "mystery," hitherto hidden, is now manifest to the nations. The phrase "but now" in v 26, which marks the new beginning, interrupts the sentence and is in turn qualified by four interdependent relative clauses [3] and a final clause governed by them (v 28b), concerning the content of this secret, Christ, and the form of the apostolic proclamation.

Interpretation

[24] Exaggerated formulations are in fact more characteristic of Paul than they are of Colossians;[4] yet what is said here goes further

---

1. The plural does appear once in v 28, since the idea is of the apostolic proclamation taking place everywhere; Paul is fitted into this again in v 29 by means of the first person singular.
2. Ludwig, *Verfasser*, 83.
3. On the interruption of the sentence,

cf. note 1 to 1:21-3; on the infinitive clause without the article in v 25 and the relative clauses loosely dependent on one another, cf. note 14 to Introduction.
4. Bujard, *Untersuchungen*, 116.

than anything that we can find in Paul. Certainly Paul sees his sufferings as a necessary element of his apostolic activity (Rom. 8:30f.; 1 Cor. 4:9-13; 2 Cor. 11:23-33; 12:9f.; 13:4; Gal. 6:17); certainly he can connect the theme of the revelation of the gospel, shining forth, and that of the apostolic ministry of suffering (2 Cor. 4:4-6,[5] 7-18; 5:18-21[6]/6:1-11; cf. 1 Thess. 1:5f.; 3:3f.; Acts 14:22); certainly he can speak of his ministry for the gospel in an almost rapturous manner (Rom. 15:15-21).[7] Yet it is alien to him to say that anything of this sort was endured for the sake of the church.

Nevertheless, there are points of contact. Acts 9:16 does indeed say that sufferings are linked with the apostolic ministry. This corresponds to the way the prophets were thought of in the Judaism of that time. It is this idea that Paul has taken up, especially through his understanding of his ministry in light of Jeremiah and Deutero-Isaiah;[8] and the offer to let himself be cut off from God for the sake of his people (Rom. 9:3) comes close to the idea of a representative suffering. Admittedly it is only Jesus' death that takes effect in Paul's suffering (2 Cor. 4:10, Phil. 3:10). That is, he makes a basic distinction between Christ's suffering and his own afflictions as an apostle.[9]

Above all, 2 Cor. 1:3-11 makes it clear in what sense this happens for the sake of the community: first, in the sense that Paul himself needs consolation in his suffering and thus learns how to console. Second, that he learns what it means to believe in the God who raises again from the dead; and third, that he thus grows into a fellowship of intercession and thanksgiving with his community. In addition, 2 Cor. 11:23, 27-29 (as Col. 1:29) recalls the trouble and distress which involvement for the community brings with it. To this can be added the fact that according to 2 Cor. 4:7-15, it is only the messenger's weaknesses that allow the power of Christ and the glory of God to shine forth without them being overshadowed by human brilliance.

---

5. Here the key words are εὐαγγέλιον and δοῦλος.

6. Here the key word is διακονία; cf. διάκονοι in 11:23.

7. Alongside εὐαγγέλιον, the reference to the χάρις ἡ δοθεῖσά μοι recalls the phrase in Col. 1:25.

8. Cf. Kamlah, "Leiden" 217-32; K. Rengstorf TDNT I, 439-440; T. Holtz, "Zum Selbstverständnis des Apostels

Paulus," TLZ 91 (1966), 321-30; M. Hengel, "Die Ursprünge der christlichen Mission," NTS 18 (1971/2), 20-2; Isa. 66:20 is also to be compared with Rom. 15:16. Chr. Wolff, Jeremia im Frühjudentum und Urchristentum, 1976 (TU 118), 142, rejects the idea of influence from Jeremiah.

9. Kamlah, "Leiden," 228f.; cf. Güttgemanns, Apostel, 94-126.

Joy in suffering is spoken of quite often (1 Peter 1:6; cf. note 16 to 1:9-11); behind this stands experience of the various levels on which a person exists. That is, in the midst of real pain there is a deep level, in which the union with Christ becomes reality, something that is even stronger than any suffering. The exalted one's victorious march through the world takes place not in a triumphal advance (such that those who belong to him appear as those who hold possession, and give generously from the riches of their power) but in suffering and this fact belongs to the essence of the Lord who is proclaimed in this epistle (2 Cor. 13:3).

However, whereas the sufferings in Col. 1:24 are designated as being endured "for your sake," this is to be understood in light of the following clause. The decisive question in this case is that of the meaning of "Christ's afflictions." This expression is never used in the New Testament for the Passion, nor for Jesus' experience of suffering in general. The disciple's "affliction" or "being afflicted" can be designated as participation in the "sufferings of Christ" or as bearing the "death of Jesus" (2 Cor. 1:4-6; 4:8-10);[11] but the expression characteristically changes as soon as the discussion relates to the sufferings endured by Christ himself. The usage here, then, forbids the interpretation of Christ's sufferings as endured for the sake of humanity—that is, as his Passion.

Of course, the usual exegesis,[12] almost without exception, makes a clear distinction. On the one hand there is the suffering of Jesus, which brings about reconciliation, that is, the cosmic event of the death of Jesus.[13] On the other hand there is the suffering which is still lacking, that is, suffering which is connected with the proclama-

10. Παθήματα in the case of Paul, except for those instances where it means "passions," always denotes the "sufferings of Christ," in which the apostle has a share (Rom. 8:17f.; 2 Cor. 1:5-7; Phil. 3:10; similarly 1 Peter 4:13; 5:1?); otherwise it refers either to the sufferings of Jesus (Heb 2:9f.; 1 Peter 1:11) or else to those of the community (2 Tim. 3:11; Heb. 10:32; 1 Peter 5:9).

11. It is for this reason that H. Schlier, *TDNT* III, 143-144, affirms that θλίψεις and παθήματα are identical; similarly W. Michaelis *TDNT* V, 933.

12. The fact that Col. 1:24 does not appear in either the Apostolic Fathers or the Apologists shows how difficult the verse had already been found to be by that time (Kremer, *Leiden Christi*, 5f.). From Chrysostom (IV 2 [326f.]) onwards it is emphasized that the expression betrays the humility of the apostle, who would like to point away from his own suffering (ibid. 10-20); Photius even interprets ὑστέρημα (in comparison to the afflictions of Christ!) in this sense (631.24; earlier on it is interpreted differently; v. Kremer, 25-9).

13. So Bultmann, *Theology*, 303; ibid., 148.

tion,[14] or in particular with the Gentile mission [15] and the further growth of the community.[16] Where special emphasis was laid on the similarity between the apostle's sufferings and Jesus' passion (and that was mainly the case in Catholic exegesis) the gentitive was understood as strictly subjective. Christ in his passion endures expiatory sufferings, which have, objectively, brought about redemption; however, he also suffers in the task of leading people to this redemption. But these are sufferings that he can no longer personally take upon himself, even though he would have wished to.[17]

Another interpretation runs basically along the same lines: Christ denotes "body of Christ." The idea thus expressed would be that Christ himself continues to suffer in his church; this makes clear the cooperation between Christ and Christians.[18] In that case the further phrase "for his body" is to be interpreted in the sense that every member of the body can fulfill certain tasks, which are to the advantage of the whole church. True, the question of whether these afflictions are merely exemplary or fully expiatory is thus given a confusing and contradictory answer.[19] However, it is impossible that the author of Colossians, immediately following his emphatic references

---

14. This interpretation is given from Theodore of Mopsuestia (279.21-280. 20; ibid. 21f.) onwards; e.g., Knabenbauer (Kremer, 106), von Soden, 35 (ibid. 128), Bultmann, *Theology*, 303 (ibid. 150). Zwingli explains: not what is lacking, but what is still to be added (222). Lightfoot, 164 also makes the traditional distinction between satisfactory and edificatory suffering, while Schlatter distinguishes between the suffering involved in the work of reconciliation and that involved in its consequences (Kremer, 138f.); Käsemann points to the tension between sacramental thought, according to which everything has already been brought to fulfillment, and the charismatic outlook, which above all sees the tasks that are still waiting to be done (ibid. 151).

15. From Theodoret, 604B onwards, this explanation is offered, e.g., by Ch. K. von Hoffman; Masson, 111 (Kremer, 141, 149).

16. Percy, *Probleme*, 132f. Calvin,

136f. rejects the idea of expiatory sufferings on the part of the apostle, since his task is the building up and not the reconciliation of the church.

17. Chrysostom (IV, 2 [326f.]); Gomarus 549a on 1:13; also, however, Kremer himself (*Leiden Christi*, 189-91), without citing any evidence from Paul (191, n4).

18. So e.g. Pelagius (Kremer, 40; but understanding Christ as a genitive of quality: ibid. 55); also Augustine, who does, however, add that the sufferings of the believers are like the tax which they paid to their "head" (in Ps. 61:4 [C. Chr. SL 39, 774.11-26], Kremer, 42-7); Gregory the Great points as does Augustine, in Ps. 86:5 (1202.26; 1203.31-3)—to Acts 9:4, by which Paul is designated as God's "unicorn" (Job 39:11) which is prepared to endure sufferings (in Job 2(25) and 39 (30-33) = PL 75, 612AB; 76, 590B-592A).

19. Thomas Aquinas (Kremer, 63-70).

to the reconciliation achieved once and for all in the death of Christ
(1:12-14, 20, 21f.), should explain, in the same breath, that in fact
this has not yet been fully accomplished.

Hense the expression "Christ's afflictions" has been taken to refer
to the sufferings of the apostle, or of members of the community in
general. They are called "Christ's afflictions" because the persecution is directed against Christ,[20] or because the afflictions are experienced in the body of Christ,[21] for the sake of Christ,[22] "in Christ," [23]
or more precisely, in a sphere that is characterized by him.[24] This
interpretation was indeed linked at an early stage with the view that
God has appointed a specific measure of suffering for the church,[25]
and this was then more and more strongly connected with apocalyptic ideas.[26]

One has to start from the phrase "to complete what is lacking" in
someone.[27] This implies in the first place that one must take seriously
the composite, as distinct from the simple, form of the verb.[28] Paul
suffers in solidarity "in place of" or "for the sake of" others. This
raises the question of whether it is instead of/for the benefit of
Christ, or instead of/for the benefit of the community. The preposition prefixed to the verb here can be used with the same meaning
as the different preposition that appears in the phrase "for the sake
of his body," [29] so it might be used to make the meaning of the verb

---

20. Ambrosiaster, 176.4-7 (Kremer, 38).

21. Thus first of all probably Severian (289.3f.; 632.1-3), a disciple of Diodorus in the 4th century A.D. (Kremer, 20f.).

22. J. Leclerc (Kremer, 116).

23. M. Luther (Kremer, 111).

24. The reasons for this view have been given above all by A. Deissmann, and it is a tradition that has frequently been carried on (Kremer, 99-105).

25. Thus Thomas Aquinas in the sense of meritorious suffering (Kremer, 64f.; cf. this commentary p. 278); M. Flacius Illyricus and M. Chemnitz (Kremer, 113); Wikenhauser (ibid. 100); similarly Calvin (136), who does, however, set alongside this the required conformity of the believer to Christ and the help afforded the church by the apostolic sufferings.

26. Bengel, 813 (Kremer, 118f.); the parousia can even be accelerated (J. Schneider and H. Windisch; Kremer, 133, 135f.); recently also R. J. Bauckham, "Colossians 1:24 Again: The Apocalyptic Motif," *EvQ* 47 (1975), 168-70.

27. Ἀναπληροῦν τὸ ὑστέρημά τινος; 1 Cor. 16:7; 2 Cor. 9:12; 11:9; Phil. 2:30; Corp. Herm. 13:1; Test. B. 11:5 (βS¹); 1 Clem. 38:2; cf. Jos. *Ant.* 5.214 (U. Wilckens, *TDNT* VIII, 593).

28. This holds for all the parallels that are to be found (Kremer, 159f.), although it is true that this still does not decide the questions of whether the prefix ἀντ᾽ means "in place of" or "for the benefit of."

29. Mark 10:45 ἀντὶ πολλῶν = 14:24 ὑπὲρ πολλῶν.

explicit. "In my sufferings" definitely describes the suffering of the apostle. "Afflictions," however, are never in the New Testament ascribed to Jesus. So if the expression "Christ's afflictions" were supposed to mean Jesus' passion, one would expect the two terms to be exactly the other way round: "in my afflictions I complete the sufferings of Christ which are still outstanding." [30]

Thus, what is suggested by the subject matter is also confirmed by the choice of vocabulary. Indeed, from the parallel in 2 Cor. 1:4-7, one can understand "Christ's afflictions" only as the sufferings endured in the community for the sake of Christ, or "in Christ." [31] Further, Phil. 3:10 cannot be adduced as an instance that proves the opposite. [32] The passage in Philippians does indeed go no further than what is actually said in 2 Cor. 1:5, that the apostle has been led into sharing in Christ's "sufferings." Participation in or solidarity with Christ's sufferings is certainly an idea that is expressed in Paul's writings, but the idea is, of course, also linked, in Phil. 3:10 and in Rom. 6:3-11; 8:17; 2 Cor. 4:10-14, with participation in or solidarity with his resurrection or glorification. When Gal. 6:17 speaks of the "marks of Jesus" visible on the body of the apostle, without making any reference to the resurrection, then the point is surely that Paul is thinking simply of the wounds he has endured in his ministry for Christ, although these do, of course, link him with Jesus' suffering. This kind of parallelism between the apostle's afflictions and Christ's suffering is undoubtedly what is also presupposed in Col. 1:24-28. [33]

But how then is it possible to speak of a lack? The sentence departs from normal usage in that the genitive (of the afflictions) definitely does not denote the person who suffers a lack. The genitive of the thing, rather than the person, is also found in the Old Testament; but what it describes is not that which shows a lack but that which is lacking. [34] If one understands the sentence thus, then

30. So 2 Cor. 1:4f., where Paul understands his "afflictions" as "Christ's sufferings" borne by him.
31. W. Michaelis, *TDNT* V, 933.
32. So F. Hauck, *TDNT* III, 806.
33. Cf. πληροῦν 1:25; 2:10; παραστῆσαι 1:28, 22 (Lähnemann, *Kolosserbrief*, 45).
34. U. Wilckens, *TDNT* VIII, 595; instances of the addition of that which is lacking, expressed in the genitive or dative, are given by Wilckens, ibid.

593. Still less does it mean "remainder" (Percy, *Probleme*, 129). The combination "lack of Christ's afflictions (to be endured) in my flesh" is rightly rejected, ibid., 130. Even if an appendage of this sort would be grammatically possible in Colossians, the idea that a fixed measure of suffering is assigned to the apostle Paul is not readily intelligible; hense the addition has to be taken, as in normal usage, to refer to the verb.

the point is not that the "afflictions of Christ" are only endured in a way that still lacks something, that is, that they are not yet complete; but that "Christ's afflictions" are (for some reason or other) still outstanding. The idea of a precisely predetermined measure of such sufferings is scarcely present here, even though apocalyptic language is evident from v 25 onwards.[35] Paul stresses the necessity of sufferings, most always, in fact, with reference to his own; yet he does not have a specific number in mind.

Probably there is a variety of different notions involved in this. On the one hand, the sufferings of the community are understood simply as something that is necessary and imposed by God's will, before the glory that is to come. On the other hand, Paul has meditated on the meaning of these sufferings, especially those he has endured as an apostle. What applies to all the members of the community applies particularly to him. As the one who proclaims Jesus Christ, he does, as it were, represent his Lord, and therefore shares in his weakness, in which alone God's glory takes effect on earth. At the same time, it is only the suffering which the apostle takes upon himself that really allows his message to become credible. In Col. 1:24, these two motifs are connected together: the apostle represents Christ in the world, and he brings Christ's work to fulfilment by his authentic proclamation of him as the redeemer of the community.[36]

If what has been said above is taken into account, that 1:20-22 makes it impossible to think of any supplement to the atoning work of Christ as still incomplete, then this verse must be understood thus: the apostle rejoices in his sufferings, which are endured for the sake of the community. That is, his proclamation thus becomes credible; it stands out in clear contours and thus displays its power. In this way Paul, for the sake of the body of Christ, the church, fulfils what may still be lacking. He does this not only in his words, but in his flesh, that is, in his own actual, physical existence. This can only mean the undergoing of "Christ's afflictions," of difficulties

35. Lohse, 70 n14, uses the presence of apocalyptic terminology as the basis for understanding the verse in this way (cf. also F. Hauck, TDNT III, 806; A. Oepke, TDNT IV, 1098; G. H. P. Thompson, "Ephesians III.13 and 2 Timothy II:10 in the Light of Colossians I:24," ExpTim 71 [1959/60] 187f.). However, there is no real evidence for this (Kremer, 198f.). In Mark 13:19f., 24 (Lohse, 70) it is unclear whether the days pass away more swiftly (s. Bar. 20:1f.) or whether a prescribed period of days (but not directly of suffering) is reduced (Barn. 4:3).

36. Conzelmann, 187f.

undertaken for the sake of Christ; and these difficulties alone allow the proclamation to become effective in such a way as to let faith attain its fulness among the Colossians and among the other communities throughout the world.[37] The idea that his life is thus compared to that of Jesus is certainly contained as well in the range of words used, and provides an accompanying theme.

[25] What is said at the end of v 23 is again taken up by means of the key word "minister." Paul never describes himself as a minister of the church (cf. note 15 to 1:21-23). The expression "office" is just as unusual; Paul, in this connection, always speaks of the grace of God given to him; however, 1 Cor. 9:17 bears a close relationship to what is said here.[38] The nuance given here is probably dependent on the fact that the term "office" includes the idea of a plan which is inclusive and can be handed on.[39] Arrangements and decrees made by the authorities are designated thus.[40] What it is rather surprising to find is the direct address "for you"; however, the Colossians are, as in v 27, seen as an example of Gentile nations in general. Rom. 15:19 also speaks of the bringing to fulness (RSV "fully preached")[41] of the gospel; probably, then, in similar fashion to what is found in Romans, "word" is to be understood as the event of proclamation. The aorist here designates not the continual ministry that strengthens and improves the community, but a definite conclusion by means of which an objective is attained.[42]

Therefore, "all the Gentile nations" refers here specifically to those in what was at that time known as the Mediterranean sphere, who,

37. So also W. Schmithals, *Das kirchliche Apostelamt*, 1961 (FRLANT 61), 39f. In this respect persecution is specifically to be thought of, but so also are illness and concern for the community (cf. A. Oepke, *TDNT* IV, 1097-1098, who does, however, think of Christ as "universal man").

38. Οἰκονομίαν πεπίστευμαι otherwise found in Rom. 12:3, 6; 1 Cor. 3:10; Gal. 2:9; cf. Eph. 3:2, (7); 2 Tim. 1:9.

39. In Eph. 1:10; 3:9 it is God's plan for the history of salvation that is meant by this; but in Col. 1:25 this is not the case (with Lohse, 72f. n37 against Lohmeyer, 80). Chrysostom

(IV, 2 [327]) does indeed know various meanings of οἰκονομία, but expounds Col. 1:25-7 as a picture of carefully planned education (IV, 3f. [328-32]).

40. O. Michel, *TDNT* V, 152; cf. Jos. *Ant.* 2:89 of the provisions, shown to be needed by Joseph's dreams and undertaken nationally, for the coming years of hunger (ibid. 151).

41. Cf. Col. 4:17 πληροῦν (but present!) τὴν διακονίαν.

42. So also the aorist is used in Rom. 15:19, according to which the gospel has been fully preached in the area stretching from Jerusalem to Illyricum.

as a whole, had still to be reached by the gospel.[43] If one takes "word" to mean the content, that is the promise of acceptance given to the world by God, then it has, once and for all, been promulgated and thus concluded in Christ. If, however, one takes it to mean the promulgation of this promise, its actual coming into being, then it is still going on.[44] The specification, by means of "to you," of the purpose to which this is directed clearly interprets it in the second of these two senses, and guards against the misunderstanding that the content of the word would still need to be supplied.

[26] Precisely because the more specific ideas put forward here are unexpected,[45] they obviously matter a very great deal to the author. In fact, what we have here is a popular schema of revelation[46] (attested also in Rom. 16:25f.; Eph. 3:3-10; and in part in 1 Tim. 3:16; 2 Tim. 1:9; Titus 1:2f.; cf. 1 Peter 1:20), which obviously had its origins within the Pauline school. The schema was according to the following pattern: the "mystery" (Rom., 1 Tim., Eph.), kept secret (Rom.) or hidden (Col., Eph.) for "long ages" (Rom., Eph., 2 Tim., Titus)[47] "but now" (Rom., Eph., 2 Tim.) is "disclosed" (Rom., Eph., 1 Tim., Titus)[48] and "made known" (Rom., Eph.)[49] to the "nations" at the "command" of God[50] (Rom., Eph., 1 Tim.). There is also the further point that the "gospel" is referred to, in the immediate context (Rom., Eph., 2 Tim.) and Paul's apostleship is emphasized (Rom., Eph., 2 Tim., Titus); moreover, the hymn of 1 Tim. 3:16 speaks in cosmic categories.

The beginning of this process is indeed found already in Paul in

---

43. It is not, of course, 100 percent of the population that is to be thought of; a city like Corinth, in fact, stands for the whole of Achaia (1 Cor. 16:15; 2 Cor. 1:1; 9:2; 1 Thess. 1:7f.), since the gospel will go out from there and take hold of the whole surrounding country.

44. "A word has thus been issued, that goes now on and on. . . ." (A. Pötzsch, Gesangbuch der evang.-ref. Schweiz, 1952, note 364).

45. Masson, 112.

46. Dahl, "Beobachtungen," 4f. As far as rabbinic parallels are concerned, Strack-Billerbeck on Rom. 16:25 cite b. Shab. 88b (III, 319f.); more rele-vant than this, however, is the passage concerning the Torah, the "treasure . . . preserved throughout 974 genera-tions (before the creation of the world)" and "given flesh and blood" on Sinai (Strack-Billerbeck II, 354, with parallels).

47. Αἰῶνες, αἰώνιος.

48. Φανεροῦν (in Ephesians, ἀποκα-λύπτειν; in Romans, both).

49. Γνωρίζειν (three times in Ephe-sians). The schema is, of course, also taken over in Gnosticism (e.g., Basil-ides, Hipp. Ref. VII, 25.3 [203.5-8]).

50. In Romans and Titus: ἐπιταγή; in 2 Timothy: πρόθεσις; in Ephesians: οἰκονομία.

1 Cor. 2:7-10 where the subject under discussion is the "mystery," which has been "hidden," decreed "before the ages," and is now revealed. Yet there the whole argument is concentrated on the folly of the "wisdom of God," that is, the message of the cross, while the opening for the nations and the course of the gospel through the world is not given special prominence.[51] In contrast to the "but now" of the revelation which has taken place, one must interpret the first phrase as in the translation above ("hidden for ages and generations") and not in the sense of concealing from the powers of the "aeons" (the actual word in the Greek text) and "generations." This idea might well fit 1 Cor. 2:8, but it would not hold for the remaining parallels for the schema of revelation. In this way, the basic inaccessibility of God, and thus the special position of the "saints," the fact that they are different from the world, is given extraordinary prominence. Thus, as in Rom. 16:26 and 1 Tim. 3:16, only members of the community can be meant, and not some group such as angels [52] or charismatics.[53] Eph. 3:5 perhaps [54] interprets in the sense of "to the holy (!) apostles," and the Pastorals make the call to apostleship with the proclamation (to all nations), more clearly the central emphasis.

[27] Again emphasis is laid on communicating the knowledge and at the same time on the freedom of the divine will. That emphasis is achieved above all by means of the genitives dependent on each other; they bring into prominence the fulness (which surpasses every possible mode of human expression) or the revealed mystery, that is, of the glorious presence of God.[55] Is this accumulation of words required because the theme is no longer, as in the case of Paul, the eschatological orientation of God's righteousness, but

---

51. Examples of the apocalyptic background (Dan. 2:28: "there is a God in heaven who reveals mysteries, and he has made known . . . what will be in the latter days" etc.) and the Qumran background (1 QpHab. 7:4-6: "God has made known all the secrets of the words of his servants the prophets; for there is another vision for a time; it hastens to the end . . ." etc.) are given in Lohse, 74f.
52. So Lohmeyer, 82 ("his saints," characteristic of Colossians, cf. 3:16);

Bieder, 94. Cf. this commentary, p. 51.
53. Those mentioned by Lohse, 75 n54 (Käsemann, Asting, etc.).
54. If ms. B is not original.
55. Πλοῦτος and δόξα of God are found together in Gen. 31:16 and frequently (Lohse, 75 n62). Δόξα, familiar in classical Greek only in the sense of "opinion" or "renown," has taken on a new sense from the Old Testament כָּבוֹד , and partly also from the later concept of the שְׁכִינָה , the "presence" of God.

rather (in a schema which could thus also be employed elsewhere), the unveiling of a hitherto unknown mystery?

"Among the nations"[56] seems to be attached in a rather strange way. One might therefore suppose that the emphasis does not fall on this phrase,[57] although otherwise (from the schema that is used) one would naturally expect that it did. However, the phrase is again resumed in the definition given to the content of the revealed mystery: "Christ in you." But this means that the Christ now dwelling among the nations becomes the real theme. The "in you" is, then, no longer a purely arbitrary usage, but characterizes Christ as the subject both of the revelation that draws the whole world into its domain and of the response of faith which comes about as a consequence of this.

One will then have to remember also the view that, for Greek speakers, the term "Christ" expresses nothing in itself.[58] By means of the addition here, then, what is described is the attribute of Christ as a saving figure. Thus the mission to the nations is brought into the category of a, indeed *the*, decisive saving act of God. Christ is he in whom God has forced his way into the world of the nations and won them for himself (1 Tim. 3:16). It is for this reason as well that nothing more is said of mysteries, or of anything such as a disclosure about the coming to an end of the final events, or of descriptions of heaven, all of which frequently occur in apocalyptic texts. Instead, the theme is one single individual, who embraces everything in himself, that is Christ himself.[59]

The fact that it is precisely at this point that there is further mention of the "hope of glory," or (according to what is said in 1:5), the "foretaste of glory," serves to characterize this procession of Christ through the nations as being on the one hand an event belonging to the final epoch, a foretaste of the kingdom of God, and on the other

56. This is how the phrase has to be translated (cf. 1 Tim. 3:16).
57. Lohse, 75 n63.
58. Without the background provided by the Old Testament, it denotes nothing more than "the one anointed with oil"; cf. the misunderstanding of it as a proper name in Suet. *Claud.* 25 ("impulsore Chresto"). Scott, 34 interprets "mystically": "Christ in you" (so also Gomarus, 558a, amongst others).
59. G. Bornkamm, *TDNT* IV, 814-

816. So also Mark 4:11 (ibid. 818), whereas Matt. 13:11; Luke 8:10 again introduce the plural in accordance with apocalyptic usage. The fact that the secret is one single thing, that is the (crucified!) Christ, is also emphasized in 1 Cor. 2:6-10. Whether one takes ὅς (א CDetc.), according to BDF 132.2 (addendum), or ὅ (p46 BD, etc.) to refer to πλοῦτος or (preferably) to μυστήριον in fact, makes scarcely any difference.

hand as something not yet foreclosed, but proceeding to a goal yet to be achieved. So then it is precisely this unveiled mystery itself which is in no sense simply available to humans (cf. p. 117). In a certain sense then, Christ, who traverses the Gentile world in what his messengers bear as the afflictions of Christ, and which as yet have not reached their fulfilment, takes the place of what in Paul is the function of the Spirit, which stands as the "earnest" and "first-fruits" of the coming fulfilment (Rom. 8:28, 2 Cor. 1:22; 5:5; cf. pp. 36f.).

[28] With v 28, the description of the apostolic proclamation is again resumed. The "we" style probably serves to indicate the proclamation taking place everywhere, before v 29 goes on to mention the special involvement of Paul himself. Of course, what the writer has in mind here is nothing other than the Pauline mission, since neither the twelve nor any other apostles appear at all. However, this "we" also probably includes Paul's fellow workers, to whom indeed Colossae was indebted as well for its call to faith. A striking feature is the further description of this apostolic proclamation as "warning" and "teaching." Indeed the verb ("to proclaim"), to which these are subordinated, still designates the proclamation of Christ in all the world, a proclamation which is characteristic of the Pauline understanding of his commission.[60] Yet the activity of teaching recedes to the background with Paul,[61] and does not resume a central position again until the Pastorals.

To this must be added the fact that the teaching is qualified as "warning,"[62] that is, being seen simply as an ethical summons, and not as a saving proclamation. Warning does certainly have a place in Paul's ministry as well (1 Cor. 4:14). It is, however, a continuation of his proclamation of the gospel to provide, where the specific situation demands it, an accompaniment of warning for the transition toward putting the gospel into practice. What we call the work of a minister, that is keeping the community company in the concrete problems which demand proof of a life lived from the gospel, thus becomes the central task in Colossians, specifically in the very

---

60. 1 Cor. 2:1; 9:14; with a different expression in Gal. 3:1; frequently, however, the verb used is either κηρύσσειν or εὐαγγελίζεσθαι.
61. Used of Paul himself only in 1

Cor. 4:17; cf. the substantive in Rom. 6:17 (?); 16:17 (1 Cor. 14:6).
62. Νουθετεῖν, which in fact literally means: "to adjust the sense" (cf. our "to bring someone to his senses").

context which speaks of the saving event of the worldwide proclamation of the gospel. Thus the weight of the apostolic message, a
message basic for the foundation of the church, is shifted onto the
activity of providing advisory accompaniment. This is certainly
bound up with the message, but comes about of necessity only as a
consequence of it. In the case of Paul, it usually falls to the responsibility of the members of the community.[63] So what seems to be in
view here is more the consolidating task of the fellow workers (with
their stronger local connection), than the spiritual care of the community. This impression is yet more strongly enforced by the fact
that "every man" is mentioned three times [64] as the object; in other
words, the welfare which falls to the share of the individual is given
special prominence. It is certainly possible, even if it is not especially probable, that all the writer would mean by this would be the
undifferentiated treatment in the sense of 3:11.

Again, as what follows shows, wisdom is to be understood in a
very strong sense as a practical and ethical direction for life (cf.
p. 44). "Every man" should be presented as perfect (not merely
"mature") in Christ.[65] 4:12 is also to be understood in the same
way.[66] Underlying this is the recollection of the call to be perfect
before one's God (Deut. 18:13), that was taken up especially at
Qumran.[67] It is possible that the expression derives from the usage
of the Colossian philosophy, just as at 1 Cor. 2:6 it could be a term
used by his opponents and taken over by Paul.

But no special connection with initiation into the mysteries can
be proved, at least for the time of Colossians.[68] The passage in Philo
which sees in the perfect one a person standing between God and

---

63. The gift of "teaching" and "warning" (παρακαλεῖν) is found in Rom.
12:3, 7f. alongside that given to the
apostle (1 Cor. 12:28); "warning"
(νουθετεῖν) is a task for the leaders
of the community, and indeed for
every member of the community (1
Thess. 5:12, 14; Rom. 15:14).
64. The deletion of the second mention of "every man" in D°G should
probably be viewed as a correction
intended to alleviate the sense. The
frequency of the usage of this phrase
shows that there are no "hopeless
cases" (de Boor, 205).

65. The same verb as in 1:22; it can
denote both being installed into office
and being presented before God's
judgment (cf. p. 93).
66. Masson, 114 ("spiritual coming of
age"); τέλειος does indeed also stand
in contrast to παιδία and νηπιάζειν (1
Cor. 14:20). G. Delling TDNT VIII,
76 holds that the two meanings merge
into one another.
67. Ibid., 73.
68. Ibid., 69; Lohse, 78 differs on
this point.

humanity is, in fact, in complete agreement with what is said elsewhere in his works about excellent men, or indeed of people in
general,[69] and is thus not typical of the language of the mysteries.
Certainly such perfection consists less in infallibility, even if it is
understood in a more or less moral sense, than in the complete and
undivided way in which a person, with all one's positive and negative attributes, is orientated toward God or toward Christ.[70] The
further designation "in Christ" affirms that this perfection is not
simply measured by the standard of a general ethical doctrine of
value, but is defined by the one who (namely, Christ) often does
not correspond to this standard. Yet this formula is so frequent in
this epistle, that it carries no greater weight than does our adjective
"Christian."

[29] From a general statement about the apostle's task, the last
verse proceeds to Paul's personal participation, by means of which
the theme of v 24 is again resumed. Both aspects are given equal
emphasis: all the trouble and activity[71] that the apostle allows his
ministry to involve him in, and also the source of all this, lies completely in the power of Christ. This is not transcendent in the sense
that it takes effect in another world; it does indeed come to the
apostle from beyond, from the transcendent, but it takes effect in the
concrete situation of his life and work on earth.

Summary

The section describes the apostolic ministry. It does this in such
a way that it includes in v 28 the ministry which is given to every
member of the community to perform. This understanding of the
ministry is indicated by the plural formulation, but above all by
the fact that the ministry is extended to include the real pastoral
function of protecting the community. On the one hand, the unique
nature of the apostolic task—that receives a quality belonging very
clearly to the sphere of salvation history—is strongly emphasized.
Only the portrayal of the prophetic commission in the case of Jeremiah or in Second Isaiah provides a start at least for this develop-

69. *Som.* II, 230; 234; *Virt.* 9; *Op.*
Mund. 135.
70. G. Delling *TDNT* VIII, 76; cf. 73-
77. It is excellently paraphrased by

Zwingli, 223: "Be steadfast to me as
I am steadfast to you."
71. Ἀγών is contention, not war; cf.
pp. 104f.

ment. In the apostle's proclamation, that which was "for ages" sealed
is now opened up. Therefore this ministry is also specifically characterized by means of "Christ's afflictions," as they are endured by
Paul in a way which, eschatologically, surpasses the prophet's suffering. They take place for the sake of the community, for it is only
thus that the message can reach them and at the same time also
become credible.

The apostle's commission and his life have become one; so also
then have his proclamation and his suffering. Everything is directed
toward those whom the God who has become manifest wishes to
attain. As far as content is concerned, the breakthrough of the gospel, that is, the message of God's gracious and positive response to
his people, is mentioned as going beyond the borders of Israel out
into the world of the nations. On the other hand, however, this ministry is described especially with regard to its activity in pointing
to the right way, and to the transfer of the message of the gospel
into all the concrete problems of life. Thus the ministry is described
not in its unique nature but in its continuing proclamation.

Thus the problem of the relation between saving event and proclamation of the saving event is presented. This, expressed in an
exaggerated fashion, appears in the formulation of v 24, where the
distinction between satisfactory and edificatory suffering has given
rise to hundreds of years of theological work. However, it appears
also in the gulf between the statement (formulated in terms of the
pathos of saving-history) about the unique unveiling of the mystery
in v 26 and the practical pastoral description of the continual ministry in v 28. If, however, God has promised himself to humanity
once and for all in Jesus Christ, then this holds good exclusively for
the activity of Jesus Christ himself. Whether he (in his situation on
earth) makes the promise to a people directly, or whether he sets it
on its proper course through the agency of his disciples, as at the
commissioning,[72] whether he offers bread directly to an individual,
or does this at the Feeding of the 5000 by means of his disciples, in
no way affects the issue here. In that case, however, his going out
to the nations in the mission of his disciples after Easter is essentially
no different from the way in which he goes out to those in Galilee
during his earthly activity. Hence one can understand that this going

---

72. "He who hears you, hears me"
(Luke 10:16).

out to the Gentiles has become almost a constitutent part of the confessions of faith.[73]

Certainly Christ in his active role may be distinguished from the means through which he acts. The means involved can be a word, a gesture, a meal, even suffering silently endured by Jesus or by a messenger whom he sends. But in every case the distinctive feature is the activity of Christ himself, not the particular means, although obviously this activity can never reach and heal the person unless it is mediated. Where it is understood strictly as the activity of Christ himself, the specific form it takes, for instance, in the apostle's involvement, must also be taken seriously as opening (or perhaps closing) the heart of the hearer for Christ's coming. The means (the gesture, the bread, the disciples) is not identical with Christ; for it is always an open question whether it really brings Christ with itself or actually hinders it. Also, from the point of view of those who receive this, it is clear that an event of this kind, which transforms the world, cannot merely be accepted intellectually. Rather, its intention is to bring about a change in the people who receive the message, to fashion them afresh and to direct their lives toward God.

For the relation between saving event and proclamation, there may perhaps be an analogy, albeit unsatisfactory in some respects, with the fundamental promise by which a man pledges himself to a woman forever, and the expressions of love that follow from this promise. These might consist of words or gestures or deeds, or even be mediated by means of letters or friends. But they would never be what they are without the past and future provided by the promise that has been made once and for all. It thus also becomes clear that the gesture or deed, letter or friend, are never identical with the actual person who is in love; rather, he enlists them in order to express his love. They might indeed mediate this, but they could also make it counterfeit, when they no longer bear the stamp of his love.

73. At any rate in the hymn in 1 Tim. 3:16 the preaching of the gospel among the nations is set alongside the incarnation and exaltation of Christ, and its progress through the world runs parallel to that of the Resurrected One through the heavenly regions. Reconciliation and the ministry of reconciliation belong together according to 2 Cor. 5:18f., and the apostle's capacity as a witness also belongs to the confession of faith in 1 Cor. 15:5; Acts 2:32; 3:15; 5:32; 10:39; 13:31.

The Apostle's Involvement for the Community (2:1-5)

1   For I want you to know how greatly I strive for you, and for those at Laodicea, and for all who have not seen my face,   2   that their hearts may be encouraged as they are knit together in love, to have all the riches of assured understanding and the knowledge of God's mystery, of Christ   3   in whom are hid all the treasures of wisdom and knowledge.   4   I say this in order that no one may delude you with beguiling speech.   5   For though I am absent in body, yet I am with you in spirit, rejoicing to see your good order and the firmness of your faith in Christ.

Analysis

The section belongs with 1:24-29 (v. note 3 on 1:12-23); what was said there in general terms concerning the apostle's ministry is here given particular personal reference to Paul's relations with the Colossians. The purpose of his ministry is again described as the knowledge of the mystery of God, that is, of Christ. Only in the last two sentences does the point emerge that this knowledge might be endangered; thus the writer effects a transition to the section dealing with the philosophy that has taken root in Colossae.

Interpretation

[1] It is by means of a Pauline formula (1 Cor. 11:3) that the transition is provided to a still more direct and personal portrayal of the apostle's ministry for the very people who are addressed. The catchword here is "striving"—it has appeared already in 1:29, and is now related to the specific situation of the community. For no mention can be made of the apostle's own work without the purely human aspects being taken seriously: that is, he strives for them with all his power, and they have not seen him face to face. The course of the gospel through the whole world makes Christ become Lord of the world; and this takes place in a number of very specific encounters, accompanied by all their needs, difficulties, pains, and pleasures. The fact that Laodicea is also mentioned among the communities for which the apostle carries on his struggle may indicate that the peril spoken of in the next section concerns other communities as well.[1]

---

1. In later manuscripts Hierapolis has also been added on the basis of 4:13 though very rarely.

[2] The purpose of the apostle's involvement is to provide encouragement. The word can indicate warning as well as consolation. Underlying this is the insight that real comfort can only be given when a person is taken seriously to such an extent that the person is given a warning, that is, the writer expects something from that person.

Correspondingly, one can only properly be warned when the possibility is left open for one to be encouraged as well. It is for this reason that their "hearts" are also mentioned. In the Old Testament the heart denotes the person's own self, especially with reference to deliberate decisions. The fact that the writer speaks no longer of "your" hearts, but "their" hearts could indicate that he has forgotten the specific situation the letter is intended for. However, he is only thinking (if the phrase be taken in the sense of "all your hearts") of the wider circle of communities extending beyond Colossae. They are thus addressed as people who open themselves freely to the encouragement and accept it within the context of what they are doing.

The participle is again left hanging, in a way which is both loose and grammatically incorrect.[2] It is presumably to be translated "knit together" (as above) since it is to be rendered thus in 2:19; while in 3:14 love is also designated, although admittedly by means of a different expression, as that which binds everything together.[3] Yet the alternative meaning of this word—"instructed"—may suggest that this binding together takes place through the apostle's actual teaching. Whereas 1:28 explains that the apostle would like to make everyone "mature in Christ," the reference here is to "love," which alone, according to 3:14, brings perfect unity. There, insight into and understanding of the divine mystery are to be seen as the real purpose, as distinct from love which is the means to this end. What is perhaps indicated by this is that the community's outward appearance of unity, dictated by love, is not yet the final goal, if full knowledge of Christ is still lacking, since this unity is endangered by the "philosophy" mentioned in v 8.

As in 1:9-11 and 2:7, the superabundance of such knowledge is

---

2. To refer to καρδίαι it would have to be feminine; to refer to αὐτῶν it would have to be in the genitive, as in fact is the case in ℵ. Continuation by means of nominative participles is however characteristic of Colossians (Bujard, *Untersuchungen*, 59-63).

3. Lohse, 80f; G. Delling, *TDNT*, VII, 764.

indicated by means of the synonyms amassed here.[4] It is, however, worth noting that this only happens in the context of perception, above all in connection with the schema of insight into the divine mystery now revealed. It is here, as the author sees it, that the fundamental transcendence of God, which humans can never gain mastery of, must be absolutely upheld. Paul himself speaks of the event of the Spirit (1 Cor. 2:6-16). This emphasizes even more strongly that perceiving describes a process in which the individual remains continually dependent upon God's action and that thus all proclamation takes place "in secret" (1 Cor. 2:7).

In other words, this proclamation also remains something of a secret; it is not merely the communicating of a mystery that has been revealed. The difference cannot be emphasized too strongly. According to Col. 2:2 as well, such perception should continually arise afresh. Indeed, the very plurality of expressions bears witness to its open-ended nature. Nevertheless, it becomes clear that the reference to the Spirit is no longer sufficient (cf. note 19 to 1:3-8). The expression translated here by "assured" has the meaning, outside the Bible, of "certainty," and that meaning strongly reverberates here, since it is perception that is under discussion. However, the idea of fulness belongs so strongly to the stem of the word that the (as it literally means) "plerophoric" surpassing of the riches of this perception must be brought out in the translation.

"God's mystery" is again defined by means of "Christ."[5] This serve to stress Christ's unique and completely comprehensive position. It was said in 1:27 that he is the Christ who is proclaimed among the nations. That qualification is now omitted, since the intention here is simply to show that the person who possesses Christ no longer has need of anything else.

[3] Again, as in v 2, the fulness of knowledge is emphasized by means of two juxtaposed synonyms, by the word "treasures" which precedes and qualifies them, and by the addition of "all." The main point, however, is that these treasures of wisdom remain "hidden" in the very act of their being disclosed; that is, they elude all human

---

4. On this point, cf. Bujard *Untersuchungen*, 147-50.
5. All other readings want to refine this terse formulation (v. Lohse, 81f.).

Hilary (*De Trinitate* 9.62 = PL 10, 331A) resolves the matter in such a way that "the God Christ" represents the mystery.

efforts to grasp them. It is God alone who can freely bestow them,
and it is only in the obedience of faith that they can be received.
Thus Christ remains, as it were, the subject of all our knowing."
This knowing is never finished once and for all. Revelation can only
occur when one hears again and again afresh. Indeed, the point thus
articulated is that Christ is sufficient, and that there are no other
mysteries important for salvation besides or in addition to him. On
the one hand it is the case, then, that the whole relevation of God
takes place once and for all in Christ, and one need no longer seek
knowledge anywhere else, as some of those in Colossae were obviously trying to do. On the other hand, however, one can never appropriate such knowledge once and for all; rather, one must discover
it again and again afresh, by allowing it to be given by Christ.

[4] There is now, for the first time, an explicit reference to the way
in which the community is endangered.[7] A warning is given, by
means of a concept found only here in the Bible, of gross rhetoric.
It is the same opposition as in 1 Cor. 2:7; to those who do not know
about the "hidden wisdom of God," which can only be spoken of in
secret; or who (according to Col. 2:2f.) do not know about the hidden secrets of wisdom and knowledge, that is, of "God's mystery,"
Christ. Those people are, indeed, delivered up to "plausible words
of wisdom" (1 Cor. 2:4), the art of persuasion (Col. 2:4, literally).
   Thus the theme portrayed in the previous verse is again resumed.
There is a knowledge to which we can only surrender ourselves,
because God always remains the subject of the process of perception, and never lets himself be debased into becoming a mere object
that we can possess, and take hold of in our own hands. The person
who is not prepared to engage with him as a partner in discussion,
but is content merely with one's own ideas, is defenseless in face of
anyone practicing the art of persuasion; for in that case the starting

6. Barth, *Dogmatics* II/I, 252; cf. I/2,
10f. The language is biblical. In Prov.
2:3-6 θησαυροί, σοφία, γνῶσις are
found, as also are σύνεσις, ἐπίγνωσις
θεοῦ (Col. 2:2); in Sir. 1:25 there
appears θησαυροὶ σοφίας, and in Isa.
45:3 θησαυροὶ . . . ἀπόκρυφοι, which
mediate the knowledge of God; in
Eth. En. 46:3 we find "the Son of

Man, who . . . reveals all the treasures
of that which is hidden."
7. Whether one translates as in RSV
or whether one understands ἵνα simply as a characterization of the imperative and renders τοῦτο λέγω by
"What I mean . . ." (thus Moule, 87)
in fact makes scarcely any difference.

point for the whole discussion is wrong. If Christ is the central focus of all knowledge, this means that we have not conquered reality by approaching it from the categories at our disposal. It also means that reality is opened up to us because God, as our creator, does not want to shut himself off from us, but rather to give himself to us. When, in debate with others, one has to formulate the truth of one's belief, the simple appeal to the Spirit and its power is not enough, because others claim to possess the Spirit as well.

In this situation a paradox appears: the person who is aware that the life deriving from faith cannot simply be transmitted and taken over in precise formulations must yet make clear, by means of precise formulations, at what point and for what reasons one's own position differs from that of others. These, however, are necessarily Christological propositions because what matters is that the content of what is said should be unequivocal as far as Christology is concerned; and not (as in 1 Cor. 2) whether or not these formulations are accessible to human wisdom.

[5] In v 5 it is hardly the Holy Spirit that is to be thought of, as indeed is probably the case in 1 Cor. 5:3.[8] Certainly, it is not always clear whether Paul himself is thinking simply of the spirit naturally belonging to everyone,[9] or of the Spirit of God, for the simple reason that the spirit of the believer is shaped completely by means of the Spirit of God. In 1 Cor. 14:14, the spirit given to the spiritual person, and clearly distinguished from his mind, is nevertheless designated as "his spirit." However, the fact that Col. 2f. speaks of being absent (literally) "in the flesh," and not "in the body," as in the parallel formula in 1 Cor. 5:3, leads one to believe that here in Colossians the emphasis lies elsewhere.

No longer does the Spirit of God mediate a physical presence, which would be impossible for Paul; the spiritual presence of the apostle, that is, his psychic reaction to the joy about the news that has come from Colossae (and the letter contains information about this joy) stands in contrast to his purely bodily absence.[10] This

---

8. E. Schweizer, *TDNT* VI, 435-436; it has to be said that the "authority of Jesus" is distinguished from this spirit in 1 Cor. 5.

9. 1 Cor. 7:34: the woman should be holy "in body and spirit"; according to 2 Cor. 7:1 (scarcely Pauline; cf. note 12 to 1:12-14), the spirit, like the flesh, can be defiled.

10. With E. Schweiger, *TDNT* VI, 435f. Greek parallels in Karlsson, *Eranos* 54 (1956), 138f.

interpretation gains in probability mainly because nowhere else in Colossians does the Spirit of God assume theological importance otherwise (v. p. 24f.). Paul uses both "flesh" and "spirit" in a purely anthropological sense (2 Cor. 7:1) or else (in the majority of cases) as theologically important concepts, and in this case the "flesh" stands in sharp contrast to the Spirit of God. In addition it should be noted that 1 Cor. 5:3 describes an extraordinary act of Paul, in which he associates himself, by means of God's Spirit, with the community, in order to pronounce judgment on the wrongdoer. In Col. 2:5, however, the discussion relates to his perpetual participation in the fortunes of the community, that is, to his joy at the community's well-ordered situation and firmness in the faith.[11] Certainly no trace of the military aspect of this image is to be found here.[12] The point is simply to distinguish the good standing of the community, in contrast to the danger with which the "philosophy" might threaten them. It is difficult to decide whether this is mere *captatio benevolentiae*, or whether the community as a whole is still unaffected by the philosophy, and that this is only engaging the attention of a few of its members.[13]

Summary

The discussion here relates, in an almost exuberant way, to knowledge and wisdom. We know what it can mean when a doctor locates the source of an illness, or when a mechanic realizes where the cause of a car's trouble lies. We know as well what worldly wisdom can encompass; for example, the wisdom of old age, in which the experience gained along the byways and at the critical turning points of life's journey is brought together; or again the wisdom of youth, of those who have discovered what really matters, and have found a way in life that makes them happy. And now it is explained that the fulness of this knowledge and wisdom is already provided for us entire and complete in Christ.

Admittedly this fulness cannot simply be carried away like goods from a supermarket. It cannot be supplied by mere persuasion or

---

11. On this reading v. *BDF* 471.5.
12. So Lohmeyer, 95 and already Chrysostom V 3 (334). Still less is the forming of a contrast to the Gnostic usage of στερέωμα for "firmament" to be thought of (H. Chadwick, "All Things to All Men" (1 Cor. IX, 22), *NTS* 1 [1954/5] 272).
13. Cf. the Excursus: The Colossian Philosophy; Hooker, "Teachers" (esp. 315-9, 329-31), and on this, Schweizer, "Forschung," 173.

you must have xx to have ... even ... possibly ... accessibly to such knowledge

simple argumentation that is accessible to anyone. The reason this fulness of wisdom and knowledge possesses its secretive character is that it is contained within the Christ who is still alive and wants constantly to encounter anew the person who believes in him. It does not proceed from a Christ who is dead and can be dissected and whose form can thus be acquired as knowledge. It is for this reason that the fulness cannot simply be communicated by means of teaching. It is for this reason as well that the apostle has to struggle for his community. Indeed, it is only by means of his complete personal involvement that he is able to reach those who must, again by their own personal involvement, open themselves to the message brought by him, in order that they may find constantly renewed consolation for their hearts. Thus it is not a question here of individualistic piety. What provides comfort for the heart is the love which draws people together into the community; and correct knowledge thrives only in that fulfillment of life which looks beyond itself to the other person as well, in other words, to the community.

The Confrontation with the Colossian Philosophy (2:6-23)

Bibliography: Bornkamm, G., "Die Häresie des Kolosserbriefes," *TLZ* 73 (1948) 11-20 (= *Das Ende des Gesetzes* (München 1952) 139-56; Delling, G., *TDNT* 670-86; Dibelius-Greeven, 27-9, 38-40; Hegermann, *Schöpfungsmittler*, 161-66; Hooker, *Teachers;* Kehl, *Christushymnus,* esp. 70-4, 152-6; Kern, W., "Die antizipierte Entideologisierung oder die 'Weltelemente' des Galater- und Kolosserbriefes heute," *ZKT* 96 (1974) 185-216; Kramer, A. W., *Stoicheia tou kosmou,* Diss. Leiden 1961; Lohse, 146-50; Schenke, *ZTK* 61, 391-408; Schlier, H., *Der Briefe an die Galater,* 1949 *(KEK* 7) 116-19; Schweizer, "Background," id. "Elemente," id., "Versöhnung," id., "Forschung," 173-80.

Analysis

Whereas the apostle has thus far spoken of his ministry, he now addresses, directly and for the first time in the imperative, those to whom he is writing. True, an imperative form did appear in v 4; but this was directed at those attempting to lead the community astray. In this way the writer touched on the theme which the rest of the chapter deals with explicitly. This passage as a whole can be divided into the following sections:

• the basic foundation in vv 6f.

- the Christology, in vv 8-15, set in contrast to the Colossian philosophy (this refers to the salvation the community has already experienced, which is expressed in the second person plural preterite); and
- the actual defense against the false claims in vv 16-23.

This last section can be further subdivided into the imperative in vv 16-19, arising from the presentation of the Christology, and the question in vv 20-23, prompted by the further brief reference to the baptism that they have undergone.

Thus the central point of the letter is reached. Up to 2:5, the foundation has been laid by means of what is actually said about Christ and by reference to the apostle's proclamation (which has reached as far as Colossae). With 3:1 the exhortation begins. This is still set against the background of the danger that is presently threatening the community. Even so, it goes far beyond the specific cause that has occasioned it.

(a) From Indicative to Imperative (2:6f.)

6   As therefore you received Christ Jesus the Lord, so live in him,
7   rooted and built up in him and established in the faith, just as you were taught, abounding in thanksgiving.

Interpretation

[6] By means of the "therefore," the dispute with the false teaching is explicitly joined to what is said about Christ as the content of the revealed mystery and about the apostle's proclamation. This is likewise the case for 2:16, and again for the exhortation following from it in 3:1, 5, 12.[1] Both points are vital: first, that only through the Christology can the threat of being enticed by the philosophy be met, and the inference be drawn for practical conduct in the whole sphere of their life; and second, that it is this very existence in the present perilous situation and in the everyday life of the community that represents the real object of the letter. The sentence is an excellent example of the intimate connection between indicative and imperative (Gal. 5:25; Rom. 15:7; Phil. 2:5; Col. 2:20; 3:1-4).[2] The

---

1. Cf. Lohmeyer, 96. It has to be said that 3:5, 12 are scarcely directed against the Colossian philosophy (Schweizer, "Forschung," 166).

2. Cf. the Excursus in W. Schrage, EKK on 1 Cor. 5:7.

statement in the indicative refers back to their having "received," that is, to their having heard the message about Christ. The verb is used, for the taking over of tradition, in the New Testament only in Mark 7:4 of the special tradition of the Pharisees, by Paul nine times (including 2 Thess. 3:6) and similarly in Heb. 12:28.[3] The mention of the "tradition" corresponds to this usage.[4]

The crucial point, however, is that it is not just any kind of phrase that can express the content of this message; instead, the content is specified as "Christ Jesus the Lord." True, this is merely the concentrated form of an expression found already in the cry "Jesus (is) Lord" (1 Cor. 12:3; Rom. 10:9), the only difference being that "Christ" has now been added.[5] However, it is made quite clear that with the proclamation of this expression Christ himself enters the plan. Thus the writer emphatically circumscribes the way in which Jesus Christ is superior to everything else which could lay claim to the Colossians' commitment, and prepares the way for the Christological statement in vv 9f.

Apart from the formula "Father of our Lord Jesus Christ," taken over in the thanksgiving, and the phrase "in the Lord," also characteristic of Paul [6] in the list of greetings, the title "the Lord" occurs only in the exhortation (1:10 and 3:16—4:1) thus differing from Paul's usage. Here also the usage is specifically exhortatory, as the summons to "live in him" immediately makes clear in this verse. As distinct from 1:10, the "Lord" does now denote the sphere in which one is to live this way of life. That the writer speaks thus shows that the change is brought about in terms not merely of a

---

3. Παραδέχεσθαι, by contrast, is found in Mark 4:20; Acts 15:4; 16:21; 22:18.

4. Παράδοσις in Mark 7:3-13 and parallels; 1 Cor. 11:2; Gal. 1:14; 2 Thess. 2:15; 3:6; παραδιδόναι in Mark 7:13; Luke 1:2; Acts 6:14; 7:42; 16:4; Rom. 6:17; 1 Cor. 11:2, 23; 15:3; 2 Peter 2:21; Jude 3. As indeed Mark 7:3-13 shows, both terms describe the handing on of tradition, e.g. that of the law from the revelation at Sinai through Moses, Joshua, the elders and the prophets up until the synagogue (Ab.1.1. = Strack-Billerbeck IV, 447). K. Wegenast, Das Verständnis der Tradition bei Paulus und in den Deuteropaulinen, 1962 (WMANT 8), 128-30, thinks of the taking over of teaching, as happened in the mystery religions and in Gnosticism.

5. The closest approximations to the expression here are provided by Phil. 2:11 and 2 Cor. 4:5, where the absence of the article goes back to the predicative usage; otherwise, for a parallel usage where the article is found, cf. Eph. 3:11 (for an analysis of the usage, cf. W. Kramer, Christ, Lord, Son of God, London, SCM, 1966 SBT (first series) 50, §66c).

6. Seven times in Rom. 16!

correct grasp of what has been transmitted, but of the sovereignty
of the living Lord in the whole life of the community. Thus the
close connection between the two statements is clear. The point of
the summons to the community is that they should allow the one
who has already come to them in the proclamation to become alive,
and that they should return to him, again and again anew, in everyday decisions and actions. Belief and action are not to be separated;
the faith of the community is fulfilled in what it does.

[7] Both the indicative, asserting the fact that the community is
deeply rooted in Christ, and the imperative, calling them to be built
up and established further, are expressed by means of the following
three participles. The images of planting and building merge into
one another; [7] they are indeed rather vague as shown by the fact
that they are combined with the call to live (in Christ). What the
exhortation obviously presupposes is the fact that the community is
deeply rooted in Christ. This is expressed in the perfect, whereas
the following two verbs are in the present, that is, they affirm that
living in the Lord should take place as the building up and establishing of the community.[8]

This happens by virtue of their faith, which is specified in more
detail by means of the reference to what they have been taught.
Certainly one must not at this stage draw a sharp distinction between faith as the way a person acts and faith as the content of a
confessional formula which is believed and thought to be true (v.
p. 95). Yet what this precise formulation brings to mind is the fact
that faith can only be understood as faith in . . . , that is, as a faith
directed toward a definite object, transmitted by means of the proclamation. It cannot be understood simply as some sort of human
confidence directed toward any kind of objective whatever.

However, this object of faith has been specified as "Jesus Christ,
the Lord," that is, as a living partner whose wish is always to become

7. 1 Cor. 3:9; cf. 6:10f.; Pseud.-Philo,
Antiquitates Biblicae, ed. K. Kisch, In-
diana 1949; 12:8f. (vine and house of
God), and J. Pfammater, *Die Kirche
als Bau*, 1960 (AnGr 110), 19-21; for
the community as a plant cf. 1QH
6.15f. (likewise cosmically understood!); Ps. Sol. 14:3f.; cf. moreover
the "living stones" in 1 Peter 2:5; but

in secular Greek usage ῥιζοῦν is also
used of buildings (Ch. Maurer, *TDNT*,
VI, 990.).
8. A contrary view on this point is
expressed by Ph. Vielhauer, *Oiko-
dome. Das Bild vom Bau in der
christlichen Literatur vom NT bis
Clemens Alex.*, Karlsruhe 1940 (Diss.
Heidelberg), 102-5.

an active participant in dialogue. For this very reason, returning to Christ will not consist simply in intellectually recalling something which had once been communicated but rather in letting oneself be moved, newly orientated and directed in one's entire activity by what has been communicated. Thus one overflows (RSV "abounds") in thanksgiving.

Conclusion

These two verses lay the foundation for the ensuing rebuff of the Colossian philosophy. By referring to the fact that the community has "received" Christ, the writer draws together everything that has thus far been said, for example in the hymn and its interpretation, or even in the description of the apostle's proclamation. Yet it is exactly this receiving of Christ that must be continually relived in the walking (RSV "living") in him (v 6). It is not much use knowing about the pure fresh air of the forest, if you are still stuck in chaotic town traffic and do not take the chance to wander off to where the breeze of the forest will surround and permeate you. The image of being rooted, built up, and established provides a link between the foundation that has been laid once and for all and the ever-continuing event of faith. A tree with good deep roots can withstand being shaken by a storm; a building whose foundations go deep can be raised up to tremendous heights; a well-constructed edifice can survive severe battering. The fact that this life of faith can be definitely described as an overflowing of thanksgiving clearly shows how deep its roots lie in the indicative of the saving event. At the same time this indicative must be heard again and again anew as a summons to lead one's life on the basis of thankfulness of this kind.

Excursus: The Colossian Philosophy (2:8)

History of Research

The discussion about the philosophy permeating Colossae has swung back and forth between two extremes. Behind the "elemental spirits of the universe," some scholars saw angelic powers of Gnostic origin, that is, demons hostile to God. This understanding of the problem was precipitated more and more by the idea that Gnosticism had its roots in Judaism, even if it had taken over a great deal of

Iranian tradition. Thus a distinction could be drawn between (a) the leaders of this movement, with their roots in syncretistic mysteries and Persian worship of the elements, and (b) the Colossian Christians, who adhered to a Gnosticism with strong Jewish characteristics and lacking in polytheistic tendencies. Alternatively, it could be denied that there was any Gnostic influence whatever, and the most that might be involved would be an angel cult inspired by one of the mystery religions. Or else the emphasis could quite simply be laid on the stand taken against the worship of the creature instead of the creator, a danger dealt with already in Rom. 1:18-32.

Finally, from the lack of parallels in contemporary non-Christian religions, it could be denied that the "elements" had anything at all to do with spiritual powers. So at first it may have seemed that a consensus of opinion prevailed, at least in the point that it was a matter neither of a purely syncretistic nor a purely Jewish movement. But in recent scholarship the attempt has again been made to understand the philosophy completely in terms of the Phrygian Cybele cult. On this view, Christ would only have been brought in as an afterthought, in order to import the monotheism familiar from Judaism. The concept of the Pleroma would then have helped to classify all worship of gods in terms of one deity.

However, some scholars opted for the opposite extreme. For them it was merely a question of a purely Judaistic-legalistic teaching; in this teaching the elements of the universe (which would have been bound to lead to veneration of the creator) would have received exaggerated importance. Finally, it has been claimed that no false teaching at all had crept in; only concepts from various philosophies in vogue at that time had infiltrated.[1]

The Information Given in the Text

What are the data provided for us in the text? The "philosophy" threatening the Colossians is mentioned for the first time in 2:8; yet vv 9-15 begin by describing the significance of Christ in a positive way, and one may very well doubt whether this presupposes any reference at all to the philosophy being combatted. Methodologi-

---

1. All the instances mentioned here for the history of research on this subject are given in Schweizer, "Elemente," 147f. and id. "Forschung," 173-6 (for the period from 1970); cf. Weiss, CBQ 34, 294-314; and recently Caird, 163f. (who posits a Jewish-Stoic movement).

cally, to presuppose this is certainly problematic.[2] In any case, the key-words from v 8, "human tradition" and "elemental spirits of the universe," are also not taken up until the actual dispute with the philosophy in 2:16-23 (vv 20, 22). Thus all we know for certain is that the following played an important role at Colossae:

- precepts concerning food and drink and festivals (cf. on v 17; these precepts were not divine commands but merely secular— "human"—v 22; cf. on v 8);
- exercises in self-abasement, (probably consisting of fasting), perhaps sexual abstinence and worship of angels (cf. on v 18);
- the elements of the universe, which somehow held humanity captive within the "world" (v 20).

Perhaps there was even something along the lines of a mystery rite being carried on as well (cf. on v 18). The key phrase, elements (RSV "elemental spirits") of the universe, appears also in Gal. 4:3, 8-10, similarly connected with an observance of festivals (v. below p. 157).

It would be a remarkable coincidence if there were no connection at all between this usage and the Colossian notions, even if we can be sure that the Galatian false teaching was not simply the same as that at Colossae. Undoubtedly at Galatia circumcision was required, and Paul sees in this an insistence on the Mosaic law as a whole. But Ignatius (*Phld.* 6:1) also speaks of "Judaism," even though he has pagan legalism in mind; and when Paul in Gal. 4:3 associates himself with those whom he is addressing, he explicitly equates the pagan state of being bound to the elements ("elemental spirits") of the universe (that is, the condition of the Galatians before they were converted) with his own bondage to the Mosaic law. 4:8-10 even seems to suggest that the Galatians' renewed bondage to the elements ("elemental spirits") of the universe denotes a reversion to heathenism. Above all, not until 5:3 does the apostle make the Galatians aware that accepting circumcision must result in accepting the whole law. This, then, is a conclusion which the opponents in

2. Lamarche (v. note 3 to The Hymn and its Context: 1:12-23) even connects vv 9-15 with the section that is started in 1:21, and then begins a new section with 2:16. If moreover the circumcision mentioned in 2:11 was actually supposed to have been practiced as in Galatia, then the completely different reaction to it in Col. 2:17 would be all the more astounding (v. ad loc. but cf. on 2:11 below).

Galatia have not drawn. Obviously, therefore, what they have proclaimed is not simply the Mosaic law, but circumcision, observance
of months, seasons, and years, and the taking the elements of the
universe seriously.

Thus it appears possible that in Galatia as well the prevalent
world view was one with little more than Jewish trimmings, although
certainly the Jewish component was still significantly more in evidence here than at Colossae. (This could be argued provided that it
was not Paul who viewed what were basically heathen demands in
light of legalistic observance of the Jewish law so that he could
have identified the two much more closely than did the Galatian
Syncretism.)

Perspective from History of Religious Research

Whatever conclusion we reach on the above question, the concept
of the elements of the universe is in any case decisive. All the parallels that have been found thus far make mention only of the elements
earth, water, air, fire (and ether).[3] The simple designation "elements" (without "of the universe") does not include stars and astro-
logical spirits until the second century A.D.[4] Further, these elements
are never adduced in the New Testament lists of powers and authorities, not even in Colossians (1:16; 2:10). Our starting point must
be the fact that there is no contemporary evidence for the meaning
of "elemental spirits" or "stars." The power which they wield, by
binding men to the "world" through ascetic "regulations" (vv 20f.),
is, then, probably comparable to the power belonging to the commandments of the law, which are certainly not demons either.

What is the source of this power?[5] *Heraclitus* gave his definition
of God as the one who undergoes alteration, who is day/night, win-
ter/summer, war/peace, sateity/hunger (Diels I 165, 8-11), and thus
establishes necessity, war and strife as iron laws of all that happens
(ibid., 169, 3-5). The repercussions of this definition were felt for a

---

3. Blinzler, *Lexicalisches*, 439-41; this
is also the case in Valentinus (*Iren.
Haer.* I 1, 10 [5:4]-I 48). Cf. further
G. Münderlein, *Die Überwindung der
Mächte. Studien zu theologischen Vor-
stellungen des apokalyptischen Judentums und bei Paulus*, Diss. Zürich
(published by the author) 1971, 93f.,
110; he does however also include an-

gelic beings, since they likewise belong to the created order.
4. Delling, *TDNT* VII, 679-683. O.
Böcher, *Christus Exorcista. Dämonis-
mus und Taufe im NT*, 1972 (BWANT
96), 20-32, sees the elements as also
being the dwelling places of the demons.
5. All the instances for this section

long time, and from Heraclitus onward the idea of strife between
the members of the universe (the elements themselves, that is, as they
are called not later than Aristotle's account) and their being reconciled again in 'love,' characterizes the image of the world (*Empedocles*, ibid. I, 315, 21-316, 2; 322, 17-323, 10; 327, 6-10). "Mighty
strife amongst the members" thus becomes the principle of transi-
toriness (Aristotle, *Metaph.* 11.4 [1000ab]), "the destruction of
everything through everything," as "Hippocrates" formulates it, at
more or less the same time as the Epistle to the Colossians (Diels I,
183,8).

This Empedoclesian view of the "four roots of everything that
exists," that is, of the four elements, is the concept with which not
only Philo and Plutarch, but also Simon Magus and the Rabbis,
attempted to come to terms in New Testament times.[6] Thus this
view must far and away have dominated the spirit of the age. The
stability of the world, constantly threatened by natural catastrophe,
is preserved only in the equilibrium of fear and that only with difficulty. Hence the Stoics speak of the universal conflagration (or
even of the universal flood), that is, of a coming total destruction
which will indeed lead to a new "coming into being of the world."[7]

It is precisely in this connection that Philo speaks of God as the
"author and protector of peace." With the trumpet of the New Year
Festival he sounds the cessation of war and institutes peace between
the "parts (or members, cf. note 5 on 3:5-11) of everything that is"
(*Spec. Leg.* 11.192), the "elements" as he elsewhere calls them
(1.208, 210). According to *Vit. Mos.* 11. 117-133, the high priest,
who effects reconciliation and with whom the universe enters into

---

are collected in Schweizer, "Versöhnung," 494-9. Wengst, "Versöhnung,"
15f., thinks that the angels are at least
representatives of the elements"; this
is very improbable, since the elements
never appear in the New Testament
lists of powers. Pagan worship of the
elements, against which Aristides,
Apol. 4f. conducts a polemic, also remains improbable. It is most likely true
that the elements (as something held
in dread) also take on something of a
powerful nature; but this is altogether
different from that of the angels or
the authorities mentioned in 1:16.

6. Schweizer, "Elemente," 153-5. On
Empedocles cf. W. K. C. Guthrie,
A History of Greek Philosophy II,
Cambridge 1965, 122-265, esp. 140-
57.
7. So e.g. in von Arnim II, 190.36-9
and I, p. 32.3-13, 19-23; Sen. *Quaest.
Nat.* III, 28:6; on the precarious
equilibrium and balance cf. Pythago-
reans (Diels I, 449.9-16); Plut. *Is. et
Os.* 49; 55 (II, 371AB; 373D); Philo
Spec. Leg. I, 208; II, 190f.: *Aet.
Mund.* 112; 116 (where, in 111, Her-
aclitus is cited).

the temple, is the one who establishes and guarantees the "harmony of everything that is," the union of the upper and lower world (cf. *Rer. Div. Her.* 151-153; 199-201 [compared with *Som.* 11.235]; *Spec. Leg.* 1 96f.; *Quaest. in Ex.* 2, 68, 118). However, technical concepts employed by the Pythagoreans and Stoics are not the only terms found in this connection in Philo's writings. Most important of all, he uses "author of peace" as a designation of God, in connection with the New Year Festival, and this is just as much a hapax legomenon for him as is the corresponding verb in Col. 1:20 for the New Testament.

Attempts to Find a Solution to the Problem

1. The Hymn

In the writings of the Pythagoreans in the first century B.C., in those of "Hippocrates" and of Philo in the first century A.D., and of Plutarch at the turn of the second century, there is, then, a predominant feeling of being in a fragmenting world constantly threatened with decline because of the eternal conflict of the elements with one another. The first answer to this problem is that given by Philo, who starts from the unified conception of the world provided by the Stoa and above all, by the Old Testament belief in creation.[8] Again and again God's faithfulness brings to an end the conflict among the elements and thus keeps the world alive. This is the answer given by the hymn, which, like Philo, is interested in the existence of the world (the same verb in both, v. note 44 to 1:15-20), the only difference is that in the hymn the reconciliation is accomplished once

---

[8.] Statements such as those about Zeus as the originator of everything (Chrysippus, von Arnim II, 315.3-11) are understood by Philo (*Aet Mund.* 8) in the sense of the Old Testament belief in creation. This is all the more the case with the statements about the Logos as the active principle over against passive matter, and its identification with "God" (which may be due to the author who reports these sentences) in Zeno and Cleanthes: von Arnim I, 24.7; 110.27; II, 111.10; 322.18; 335.25; III, 263.23. Plut. *Is et Os.* 45; 67 (II, 369A; 377F); cf.

Comm. Not. 34 (1076C) which speaks of the δημιουργός of the ὕλη. In his account of various Stoics, Diog. Laert. VII, 135 (von Arnim I, 180.2. 5-7) speaks of the σπερματικὸς λόγος which produces everything (out of the στοιχεῖον), and in Pseud.-Aristot. *Mund.* 6 (399a, 30-b22) the (military) trumpet-signal appears at the creation. On the whole question cf. M. Pohlenz, *Dia Stoa. Geschichte einer geistigen Bewegung I*, Göttingen 1954, 67-9, 75. For the equating of the cosmos with God, cf. above note 38 to 1:15-20.

and for all in Christ, and does not have to be brought about again every New Year.

2. *The Colossian Philosophy*

From the perspective of a more markedly Platonic-Aristotelian conception of the world, one must look for the unimpaired world in transcendence (or, in Jewish terms, in eschatology). This is the second answer given to the problem of the threatened world. Aristotle rebuked Empedocles because the "strife" that breaks up this world yet brings the four elements back again to their original purity. In other words it is actually "love," while, conversely, love in Empedocles' view, leads to compounding, and thus to the present impure, constantly threatened world (*Gen. Corr.* 2, 6 (33b-334a); *Metaph.* 1.4 (958a); 114 (1000b)). Typically, Hippolytus (*Ref.* VII. 29.9, 11, 13) takes over this reversal of concepts in his treatise about Marcion. The real unimpaired world can only be the world to come, or (as it is already described in the pre-Aristotelian Pythagoreans) the world "above" (Aristotle, *Metaph.* 1 8 [990a]).

Philo can also speak in this way; the key-words "ether" (as the uppermost element), "heaven" and "above" are found in *Spec. Leg.* 1 207; and, according to him, the soul in its ascent gives back to each of the four earthly elements what properly belongs to them (*Rer. Div. Haer.* 281-3; cf. Jos. *Bell.* 6, 47). This idea is bound up with the fact that from Empedocles onward the dominant view was that a person is driven into the calamitous circuit of the elements, pursued from one to another, and that the person can only escape from this by rigid asceticism.[9] Plutarch was fascinated by Empedocles to such an extent that he wrote ten books about him (and this only a short while after the Epistle to the Colossians was written). Plutarch depicts the sublunary world, characterized by the struggle between the elements (*Is. et Os.* 63 [11 376D]); from this world the souls ascend, after death, first of all to the moon. If the souls are still weighed down by what is earthly, and are not yet pure enough, then they are pursued back down into the elements. Otherwise they become semi-divine demons which appear to humans as redeemers (or saviors), descend below to the shrines of oracles,

9. Diels I, 358.3-8 (cited of Plutarch II, 361C and 607C!); 362.9(?); 363.9f.; 368.15, 28. On Empedocles cf. Guthrie, *History* (note 6 above), esp. 157, 163, 250-65; on the Pythagoreans, ibid. I, 1962, 146-340; on Alexander Polyhistor ibid. 201 n3.

and cooperate in initiation into the mysteries. Philo identifies them
explicitly with the angels of the Bible. Souls that are fully purified
finally ascend to the ether and enter into blessedness.[10] These
Empedoclesian-Pythagorean ideas, according to Hippolytus' account
(ca. A.D. 200), misled Marcion into discarding belief in creation and
renouncing meat and sexual intercourse, because he wished thus to
escape from the raging strife and from being hurled back into the
elements.[11]

All the above-mentioned motifs are found concentrated in a
Pythagorean text of the first century B.C. (Diels I, 448.33-451.19).
The universe has come into being from the four elements, the
immortal, divine, upper element is the ether. Essentially, the balance is held in tension between light and darkness, warm and cold,
dry and moist (cf. note 17 to 3:5-11). If one outweighs the other,
then this leads to a change of day and night or of the various seasons. In all this, the earthly sphere remains unstable, unhealthy, and
mortal, in contrast to the pure, immortal, and divine world above.
It is this world above into which the immortal souls are led by
Hermes, away from earth and sea up into the highest (element),
provided they are pure; otherwise they are fettered again by the
Erinyes. Hence the whole atmosphere is full of souls (= demons or
heroes; in Jewish terminology, angels). So one must pay honor to
the gods and, in the afternoon at least, to the heroes (angels) as
well. One must undertake purificatory baths and forego certain
foods and kinds of meat,[12] as well as sexual intercourse.

However, this means that all the distinctive themes evident in Col.
2:16-23 are also found in this text, which was certainly written earlier than Colossians. (The sole exception is Sabbath observance; but
according to Ign. Magn. 9:1, cf. Phld. 6:1, this also seems to belong

10. Fac. Lun. 28-30 (II, 943C-E).
The demons (according to Philo, Gig.
6; 16; Som. I, 140f. = angels!) are
σωτῆρες. In Def. Orac. 10 (II, 415BC)
the scale of progression of the elements
earth-water-air-fire is equated with the
transformation of the ascending souls
(men-heroes-demons-partakers of divinity (θειότης); ed. Bernardakis,
Leipzig 1879, and ed. F. C. Babbit
(Loeb), London 1st edn. 1936, 2nd
edn. 1957, without indications of var-

iants; cf. below note 10 to 2:8-15). An
explanation in terms of natural science
is given in Cic. Tusc. I, 42f. (18f.);
cf. Sext. Emp. Math. 9.71.
11. Ref. VII, 29.13-23; 30.1-4. The
repercussions are still evident in com-
pilers of the 6th century A.D. (Diels
I, 289.8-19; 293.12-17).
12. Wine is also often mentioned,
e.g. Diels I, 479.13, cf. 21f.; 480.28.
Similarly in Apul. Met. XI.23.

to the "Judaism of the uncircumcised!"). These distinctive aspects are:

- the importance of the "elements of the universe"
- the flight from the "world" to the realm "above"
- the foregoing of certain things to eat (and drink)
- the worship of angels
- abstinence from sexual intercourse (Col. 2:21 ?)
- baptism (Col. 2:12), and
- the concept of the ascent to heaven, which is perhaps experienced in anticipation by means of mysteries (Col. 2:18 ?)

Moreover, the concepts thus mentioned are precisely those that led to the completely different answer provided by the hymn (Col. 1:15-20).

This, then, seems to be the background to the philosophy at Colossae. Those who represented it could probably join in the words of the hymn in 1:15-20; but the difference between them and the person who wrote the hymn lay in their different conceptions of the world. This meant that they had to seek the unimpaired world "above," and to consider asceticism as a means to their being set loose from the world and ascending to the exalted Christ. There was, demonstrably, a Jewish Pythagoreanism as early as the first century B.C.,[13] and Philo complains about the infiltration of syncretistic-heathen cults into Jewish families (Spec. Leg. I, 315f.). The Colossian "philosophy" does then seem to have been an actual philosophy; it seems that it may also have included some kind of mystery rite. It did not doubt the unimpaired and redeemed world brought about through Christ; it was only that it wanted to ensure the soul's ascent to the upper world.

3. The Author

A third answer is given by the author of the letter. He is at one with the Pythagoreans and Platonists in that he sees the decisive act of salvation not in the world being preserved but in the saving of the community from the snares of this world. However, he thinks in

13. M. Hengel, *Judaism and Hellenism*, SCM 1974, I, 166f. and II, 108 n392 (cf. also I, 164f. and II, 106 n377 on Euseb. *Praep. Ev.* XIII, 12.9); Walter, *Aristobulos* (note 9 to 1:15-20), 65f.; 66 n2; 158-62 on Philo.

Moreover Grotius (680a, 683a; on 2:16, 21) had already thought in terms of Pythagoreans (which is the only possibility that de Wette, 49 excludes!).

categories of sin and forgiveness, and can thus explain that everything which is decisive has already happened—the community already lives "above," having risen together with Christ. It is for this
reason as well that his call to them can only be to ethical testing
of their faith in the world, not to ascetic separation from it. This
becomes clear in 3:1—4:1.

(b) Christ, Lord Over the Powers, Salvation of the Community (2:8-15)

8 See to it that no one makes a prey of you by philosophy and empty
deceit, according to human tradition, according to the elemental
spirits of the universe, and not according to Christ. 9 For in him
the whole fulness of deity dwells bodily, 10 and you have come
to fulness of life in him, who is the head of all rule and authority.
11 In him also you were circumcised with a circumcision made
without hands, by putting off the body of flesh in the circumcision of
Christ; 12 and you were buried with him in baptism, in which you
were also raised with him through faith in the working of God, who
raised him from the dead. 13 And you, who were dead in trespasses and the uncircumcision of your flesh, God made alive together with him, having forgiven us all our trespasses, 14 having
canceled the bond which stood against us with its legal demands;
this he set aside, nailing it to the cross. 15 He disarmed the principalities and powers and made a public example of them, triumphing
over them in him.

Analysis

With v 8 the warning about the philosophy clearly begins. True,
this had been articulated already in v 4, so that one could take vv
4-8 to be a warning, and separate off these verses from the reference
to the apostle's ministry (1:24—2:3) and from the Christological
exposition (2:9-15; v note 3 to 1:12-23). Yet 2:5 also refers to the
theme of the apostle's involvement, and 2:1-4 is in fact itself a cau-
tionary admonition addressed to the community. On the other hand,
the rebuff of the philosophy (a theme found in 2:16-23) clearly
begins at 2:8, so that one should rather think of the new section as
beginning here, with v 8.

The demarcation vis-à-vis Christ made at the end of the verse
introduces the positive presentation of the Christology. This presentation, prefaced by "for" as the basis for the warning, describes,

by means of interdependent clauses and participles, the superiority
of Christ on the one hand and the new life belonging to those baptized in him on the other. The toing and froing between what is said
about Christ (vv 9, 10b) and what is said about the community is
not arranged in terms of cause and effect; the statement about baptism is merely appended: ". . . in him also you" (v 11a).

The construction begins afresh in v 13, by means of "and you," [1]
set rather abruptly at the start of the sentence, and by the transition
to God as subject. Conversely, the description of God's saving act
in Christ is now linked (by means of five participles loosely attached to one another [2]) to an expression concerning the forgiveness
of sins vouchsafed to the community, although it must be said that
this construction is twice interrupted by means of a finite verb introduced by "and . . . ." The former usage points to the style of the
writer of the letter, while the latter is altogether untypical of a
hymn. Hence the assumption that fragments of a hymn, cited verbatim, are to be found in vv (13c) 14f. [3] is scarcely plausible. Further, the alternation between "with him" (v 13b) and "in him" (v
15), or between "you" (v 13b) and "us" (vv 13c, 14) can be observed already in vv 12f., and is characteristic of the Epistle to the
Colossians.[4] Indeed, three words ("bond," "nail to," "disarm")
which occur in these two verses are otherwise not found at all in
the New Testament. A further three ("cancel," "against," "make a
public example") are not used by Paul, while "triumph" is found
only once, in 2 Cor. 2:14.

Undoubtedly, then, what is used here is an unfamiliar image
which probably stems from Christian tradition. The question, however, is whether this tradition had already been firmly fixed. Only
the reference to the "legal demands" argues that it had, because it

1. Cf. similarly 1:21 (on this v. note 1
to 1:21-3) and 2:8. "You" is repeated
in the Greek later in the verse; the
omission of this in DGP, etc. is a secondary refinement; the change to
ἡμᾶς (p⁴⁶B etc.) in fact represents an
accommodation to ἡμῖν (conversely LP, etc. read ὑμῖν for ἡμῖν).
2. Cf. note 14 to Introduction and Bujard, *Untersuchungen*, 63; this usage
is characteristic of Colossians.
3. Lohse, 106; Schenke, *Christologie*,
222; this idea is also considered in

Ernst, 206. Wengst, *Formeln*, 184f.,
asks whether τοῖς δόγμασιν and the
ὅ -clause have only been subsequently introduced by the author into an
existing tradition. According to Burger, *Schöpfung*, 108, it would be the
closing words of a liturgical text that
we have cited here: Cancelling the
bond, nailing it to the cross, he set
forth the principalities and powers,
presenting them in his triumphal procession."

4. Bujard, *Untersuchungen*, 80-6.

could in this case be explained as a clumsy addition inserted by the writer of the letter. Yet this explanation may not suffice; if the writer is really thought capable of such clumsiness, then the whole construction may go back to him as well. At any rate the combination of forgiveness of sins (1:14, 1:20-22) and subordination (not reconciliation!) of the powers (1:16b, c, 18c, added by the redactor) theologically suits his viewpoint well. Little more can be said, then, except that what we have here is traditional imagery used in abundant measure.

Interpretation

[8] Introducing the warning by "see to it" is normal usage. The community should open their eyes and see where danger is threatening. The construction is striking, but does not point to one single figure as the seducer, since the participle with the article stands in place of a relative clause.[5] Hence one must translate: "that there is no one who. . . ." Even the remarkable order of the clause, with "you" set at the start, is not impossible.[6] The seduction is actually described, literally, as "trapping,"[7] and the philosophy as "empty deceit."

In the Hellenistic world even religious communities offered their teaching as philosophy; yet this was done vis-à-vis non-believers, as especially in the mission of Hellenistic Judaism.[8] In Colossae, then, the point at issue is a movement which understands itself as a philosophy; however, in using the term "philosophy" one should not rule out the religious character, as found for example in the case of the Pythagoreans and in the newly awakening Platonism. This philosophy is devalued here as "human tradition." This is what happens in Mark 7:8 as well, vis-à-vis the Pharisaic tradition, which at the same time (in very similar fashion to Col. 2:22) is charac-

---

5. BDF 412.4 (with appendage). Cf. Gal. 1:7. In spite of the rarity of this word, ὁ συλαγωγῶν is not therefore to be understood as a technical term (the Seducer").
6. Ibid. 474, 5c; ℵ‚AD alleviate the difficulty.
7. Heliodorus 10.35 (307): abduction of a daughter.
8. 4 Macc. 5:11; Philo Leg. Gaj. 156; Mut. Nom. 223; the Mosaic commandments = τὰ τῆς ἱερᾶς φιλοσοφ-

ίας . . . δόγματα: Vit. Cont. 26; for Pharisees, Sadducees, and Essenes as three schools of philosophy v. Jos. Bell. 2, 119; Ant. 18.11. In actual Hellenism, conversely, philosophy is presented as something like an initiation into the mysteries (G. Bornkamm, TDNT IV, 808-810); yet no direct equating of the two appears until Theon in the second century and Stobaeus in the fifth century A.D. (Lohse, 95).

terized, in the words of Isa. 29:13, as "a commandment of men." [9]
Obviously the application of this warning given by the prophet concerning human traditions has become current in the community (cf.
also Titus 1:14). *man made ideas 1?*

The contrast between the elements of the universe and Christ is
appended in a rather loose way ("according to the . . . . . not according to Christ"). Whereas in the first part of this ("according to
human tradition") the preposition correctly introduces the norm
according to which the philosophy is conceived, the second part
("according to the elements . . .") specifies the foundation on which
this is based. The letter thus contests the divine origin of the philosophy; human tradition stands in contrast to the "mystery of God,"
which has already been interpreted in v 2 in a strictly Christological
fashion. The content of the philosophy is human and worldly, a doctrine about the "elements," not about "Christ."

[9] Verse 9 resumes 1:19, but interprets it in a twofold way. First,
the "fulness" (cf. pp. 76f.) is defined more precisely by means of the
genitive "of deity." The idea is in fact parallel to Philo's statement
that the Logos is brimful of God (*Som.* 1:75). Indeed, the usage of
the abstract noun "deity," which occurs only here in the Bible, is
striking. There is a frequently-quoted passage from Plutarch, which
comes very close indeed to the position of the Colossian philosophy.
According to this the ascending souls become heroes, then demons
(or "saviors"; in Jewish terms, that is, "angels"), while a few become
partakers of "divinity" (v. note 10 to Excursus on the Colossian Phi-

9. Both passages are concerned with
food laws, and the argument in Col.
2:22a is related to Mark 7:19 (K.
Berger, *Die Gesetzauslegung Jesu*, I,
1972 (WMANT 40), 471).

10) Θεότης ("deity") has to be distinguished (as it is by Meyer, 238;
Lohse, 100; Anwander, *BZ* 9 (1965),
278) from θεότης ("divinity in the
sense that something has the quality
of the divine," H. Kleinknecht, *TDNT*,
III, 123), although the two words are
often confused. Thus E. Stauffer,
TDNT III, 120 n1, cites the passage
from Plutarch as though it were θειότης that stood there; likewise Meyer,
238; Abbott, 248; Lohse, 100 n45; Pr.-

Bauer, 708 s.v. Luc. Icaromenipp. 9 is
also thus cited by Meyer, Abbott,
Stauffer, Pr.-Bauer, Pass, Liddell-Scott
s.v., but, in fact, according to the critical Loeb edition it distinguishes the
one "God" from beings of second and
third "divinity." Plut. *Pyth. Or.* 8 (II,
398A) declares that everything is (in
the case of votive offerings) filled with
"divinity" (= divine spirit); *Is. et Os.*
(II, 359D), by contrast, speaks of
kings who ascribe to themselves the
rank of "deity." For this passage in
Colossians, Aug. *Civ.D.* 7.1 (C. Chr.
SL 47, 185, 1) even introduces a new
expression "deitas" in order to signal
the difference.

losophy, 2:8). Yet this passage is, as a rule, cited wrongly, as though it read "deity" not "divinity." [10] However, since the two expressions sound almost the same in Greek it is nevertheless possible, although in no sense certain, that the usage does go back to the Colossian philosophy, for which transformation into "deity" was the highest object to aim for. At any rate, the verse maintains that the "whole" fulness of deity is to be found in Christ and that they therefore have no need of anything else.

Secondly, this indwelling is described as "bodily." But the word, in the sense of "actual, real," is also set in contrast with all that is merely apparent. As distinct from 1:19, the *present* tense of the verb is found here; yet 1:19 does also mention the fact that the whole divine fulness *has* been pleased to dwell in the Resurrected One. The present tense of the verb here clearly also relates to the Resurrected One who is now present as the Exalted One in the community. However, the writer of the letter has already inserted a reference to Jesus' crucifixion at 1:20; he is, then, consciously thinking of the continuity of God's dwelling in the Incarnate as well as the Exalted One. This is presumably the case here as well, and he perhaps chooses the adverb "bodily," because he is also thinking of the presence of God in the body of Jesus.

According to Paul's view, the person who is raised does indeed possess a body (1 Cor. 15:35-44), even if it is not a "body of flesh," as Col. 1:22 says the Crucified One has (cf. 2:11), but rather a completely different body, beyond human comprehension. Yet these Pauline passages make it possible for the disciple of Paul to

---

11. So also Moule, 93f. The following meanings would be conceivable: (a) as an organism, as a whole (fulness); (b) imprinting its own self in the "body of Christ" (in the church; so Masson, 124f.); (c) in essence (v. p. 254). However, (a) and (b) could scarcely be expressed simply by σωματικῶς on its own; (c) is found in the writings of the Church Fathers, who already presuppose the formulation arising from the Christological discussion in the 3rd and 4th centuries. At the time of the Epistle to the Colossians "essence" could only be understood as above, in contrast to "appearance," that is, as "reality, effec-tive existence." Examples of the relatively rare adjective are found in Ptolemaeus, *Tetrabiblos*, Basel 1553, p. 52 and p. 132, in this sense of the word; for the substantive cf. this commentary pp. 157f. The idea of the indwelling of Christ in the church as his body is very far removed from this present passage; all the more so is the equating of Christians with Christ (A. Anwander, "Zu Kol. 2.9," *BZ* 9 (1965), 278). Also, there are scarcely "echoes to be heard of the great theme of the growing body and the redemption of the universe" (thus Ernst, *Pleroma*, 103).

take as his starting point the full bodily presence of God in the Incarnate and Crucified One, and thus also to praise the One now
exalted as he in whom this presence of God is available for the community. The importance of this lies in the fact that it can thus be
seen that the "deity" of Jesus Christ is to be conceived of not in the
category of substance but in the category of God's activity.

It is the fulness of the divine power(s) (1:19 !), of the "working
of God" (as the immediate following formulation in v 12 expresses
it), which has become present in the Christ event, in the death and
resurrection of Jesus, and which thus still encounters the community in the one who has reached his fulness. Therefore this fulness
cannot be limited, in spatial terms, to a heaven which one will only
attain to (perhaps!) after death, as the Colossian philosophy taught.
In all this it should not be forgotten that it is God himself who
works in Christ; in other words it is not merely a power that proceeds from God and is to be distinguished from his being (as it may
be in the case of his influence on a prophet). God is God precisely
in his acts.[12]

[10] The implication of the Christological expression becomes
clear: the community is fulfilled in him. Paul uses this formula
merely as the expression of a wish (Rom. 15:13, Phil. 1:10f.; 4:19),[13]
whereas here it is itself the assurance that the community has already found in him everything that matters[14] Presumably the point
at issue between the Colossians, influenced by the philosophy, and
the writer of the letter is precisely this, whether the fulness is in
fact attained when one is united in faith with Christ, or whether
this only follows on the soul's ascent after death. It is possible that
the Colossians spoke of the "fulness" which they would like to attain, and that Col. 1:10 wishes to make the point that they are indeed
already in community with this "fulness." [15] Yet the obvious mean-

---

12. Certainly it is not merely a moral
and religious indwelling of God in
Christ that is to be thought of here
(v. p. 287f.); however, it is also not
permissible (with Meyer, 238) to separate off this statement as metaphysical
from that in 1:19 as historical (v. p.
252f.). Ernst, *Pleroma*, 100, interprets
the phrase as "fullness, which is divine," and not "whole, full deity."

13. Lohmeyer, 106.
14. So also the Prologue to the Fourth
Gospel (1:16): "from his πλήρωμα we
have all received grace upon grace."
15. So e.g. Dibelius-Greeven, 29; similarly Dupont, *Gnosis* (note 18 to 1:15-
20), 422. Ernst, 201 interprets: participation in the new creation.

ing is also the more probable: "you are filled to the brim" through him (as the giver of all fulness).[16]

By means of a loosely attached relative clause,[17] Christ is introduced as "head" of all might and authority. Thus the Old Testament and Pauline understanding (cf. note 45 on 1:15-20) of the "head" in the sense of preeminent authority is taken over, without the powers being designated as his "body" (cf. pp. 82f.). This is precisely what the author cannot say, since for him it is only the church that is the body of Christ.

[11] Again by means of a loosely attached relative clause, the situation of the community is described. "Circumcision" has been carried out, but not "with hands." This usage of the word is Hellenistic; yet the adjective "made without hands" in its purely Greek sense merely denotes something which has grown naturally in contrast to something which has been artificially constructed (e.g., a lake, path, hill).[18] In the Old Testament the idols manufactured by humans[19] are contrasted with the living God. This later leads to the idea that God does not dwell in a temple made with hands, but in the temple of the universe formed by nature,[20] or even that laws

16. G. Delling, TDNT VI, 292.
17. Cf. note 14 to Introduction; p[46]BDG read "which is" (neuter singular) instead of "who is" (masculine singular) as in 1:24; 2:17? (cf.: 22f.); 3:14 (after a feminine!); it is true that ὅ ἐστιν is a favorite flourish in Colossians (cf. note 13 to Introduction), but in 2:10 this is all but impossible (BDF, 132.2 [appendage]).
18. Hdt. 2.149; Xenop. An. IV, 3:5; Jos. Ant. 15:324; on this further v. E. Lohse TDNT IX, 436. Jos. Ant. 4:55 does indeed speak of a fire brought about by God; but "made with hands" does not stand in contrast to this: the contrast is provided by blazes summoned forth by natural gas or storms.
19. Lev. 26:1; Isa. 46:1 (also Isa. 16:12 of a pagan sanctuary); Philo Vit. Mos. I, 303; II, 165; 168 (as opposed to God, the governor of the universe); this theme is found in Jos. Ap. 2.188-92 in express contrast to the real God and the virtues serving him.

20. Philo Vit. Mos. II, 88, basing his argument on Isa. 66:1; in building the temple one uses the same materials as does God in the construction of the universe; yet Philo can also say of the first man that it is the cosmos, and not dwellings made with hands, that has become his house (Op. Mund. 142). Devaluing the temple, by contrast, the expression is found in Pseud.-Philo, Ant. (note 7 to 2:6-7) 22:5, of the altar; cf. Sib. 14:62; cf. 4:6, 11; Pseud.-Heracl. ep. 4:2 (Fragmenta Pseudepigraphorum quae supersunt Graeca, ed. A. M. Denis, Leiden, 1970, 157): God is not χειρόκμητος; Pseud.-Euripedes (ibid. 171) and Jos. Ant. 8.227-9. Mostly, however, from 1 Kings 8:23-53 onwards it is God's dwelling in heaven and in the temple that is emphasized (Philo Spec. Leg. I, 66f.; 2 Macc. 14:35; 3 Macc. 2:9; cf. Ps. 50:8-13; Jos. Ant. 7:371; 8:107f., 114, 117, 125f.; Bell. 5:458f.).

and forms of government made by hand are in opposition to those of the universe.[21]

The background to all this is to be found in Stoic expressions.[22] In the New Testament the word is used in the polemic against temple piety.[23] Here it is associated with a different tradition. In the Old Testament, the statement that "man looks on the outward appearance, but the Lord looks on the heart" (1 Sam. 16:7), leads to the demand for circumcision of the heart (Lev. 26:41; Deut. 10:16; Jer. 4:4), that is, a circumcision "made without hands."

Here, however, the expression is no longer used to indicate the contrast between circumcised and uncircumcised. Instead the point is the ethical distinction between fulfilling cultic regulations in an external sense and being completely obedient to God's commandments so one's innermost self is involved. The necessity of external circumcision is thus presupposed throughout (Ezek. 44:7, 9). It is only in the LXX of Jer. 9:25 that the uncircumcision of the flesh in the case of the heathen stands in contrast to the uncircumcision of the heart in the case of the Israelites.

This ethical understanding is so dominant in Philo's world that he has to emphasize that the external ritual is not thus invalidated.[24] At Qumran, it is interpreted eschatologically. The circumcision of the foreskin of the inclination and of stubbornness becomes the basis of the external covenant (1QS 5:5; cf. 1 Qp Hab. 11:13). Thus circumcision of the heart is understood as an eschatological act of God, as a gift of the Holy Spirit, (Jub. 1:23), and is taken up in this way in Rom. 2:29 and Odes Sol. 11:1-3.[25]

Paul uses the image in expressly polemic fashion in opposition to Jewish legalism by drawing a contrast between piety characterized

21. Philo Vit. Mos. II, 51; Mut. Nom. 26 (if it is to be read thus).

22. Zeno fr. 264f. (von Arnim, 61.25-62.7); cf. Eur. Herc. Fur. 1345 (frequently reiterated up until 1 Clem. 52:1); Apul. Met. 5.1; in Latin authors: Cic. Nat. Deor. I, 8:20 in contrast to "eternal"; Seneca, ep. 41:3: only that which is not made by human hands arouses religious feelings.

23. Acts 7:48; 17:24; Heb. 9:11, 24; for later sources that are relevant cf. also Barn. 4:11; 6:15f.; 16; cf. further the "heavenly dwelling" (= the new

body) in 2 Cor. 5:1 and John 2:21 along with Mark 14:58.

24. Spec. Leg. I 6; 304f.; Migr. Abr. 89; 92; likewise R. Aqiba (ob. A.D. 135), cited by R. Meyer, TDNT VI, 80.2f.

25. On this v. E. Käsemann, An die Römer, 1973 (HNT 8a) 69f. In Col. 2:11 the reference to the Spirit is lacking; v. above note 19 to 1:3-8 (against Käsemann, ibid., 70: "the circumcision of Christ effected by the Spirit"). Cf. E. Schweizer, Matthäus und seine gemeinde, 1974 (SBS 1971), 90-2.

by the spirit on the one hand and the letter on the other (cf. also
Phil. 3:3). In Col. 2:11 the circumcision of Christ is indeed understood as an eschatological fulfillment; but there is no longer any
trace of a contrast that could almost be termed dualistic. It seems
rather to be the case that circumcision of Christ accomplishes for
the "uncircumcision of the flesh" (v 13) what the circumcision of
the flesh (as "a shadow of what is to come," v 17)? has accomplished only for Israel. Thus it is again the ethical contrast that is
introduced.

Therefore it is very doubtful that what we have here is a polemic
against a practice introduced by the Colossian philosophy.[26] In the
context, only the full validity of the redemption brought about
through Christ should be set over against this philosophy. As one
cannot find direct polemic against the propositions of the Colossian
philosophy in the metaphors used in vv 14f., it is equally impossible
to find it in the traditional metaphors of circumcision effected in an
ethical way; although these latter are never otherwise in the New

26. So Lohse, 101f., who thinks of the removing of clothes on the occasion of initiation into the mysteries. True, there is no direct evidence for this; but according to Apul. Met. 11:23f. (cf. note 29 to 2:16-23), the initiand puts on first a coarse and then a fine robe, which is brightly painted and is called an Olympic stole. A survey of the interpretations of this verse by English-speaking commentators is given in Martin, Lord, 84f. To him it is to be granted that for Paul baptism as a consummating intensification of circumcision would certainly be out of the question. But his fellow worker, who could at all events write Col. 2:17, connects the view represented in 2:17 with the Jewish tradition, also taken over by Paul, which sought to understand the rite of circumcision as referring to the circumcision of the heart. The difference is that, in con-trast to Paul, Colossians lacks the se-vere criticism of a claim erected on the basis of the law.

27. It is impossible, with J. Moffatt (The New Testament, London 1913, 251), to supply from the alpha-priva-tive a "not" for this expression as well. Without v 13, according to which the now discarded "uncircumcision" is surely that of the Colossians, it would be possible to think of Christ's "putting off the body of flesh," that is his death, by holding that the geni-tive applies to both expressions (C. A. A. Scott, Christianity according to St. Paul, Cambridge 1932, 36; Käsemann, "Baptismal Liturgy" 162 [45f.]; Moule, 95f.; Schenke "Christologie," 223; cf. Col. 1:22). Benoit, RB 63, 20, emphasizes the fact that according to 2 Cor. 5:21 (cf. Rom. 8:3), Christ has been made sin; hence it is his cru-cified body that is to be thought of in Col. 2:11. Yet even apart from v 13, it would scarcely be conceivable that the readers could have understood the death of Jesus as his "circum-cision." Very obviously relevant, by contrast, is the idea that the "foreskin" to be put off is sin, "desires and stub-bornness" (Deut. 10:16f.; 1QS 5:5) or disobedience to God's command-ment (Rom. 2:25; cf. Sir. 23:17 LXX: "a whorish person in his body of flesh"). On "flesh" cf. p. 162.

Testament linked directly with baptism. The understanding of circumcision as "putting off the body of flesh" [27] or "uncircumcision"
(v 13) also shows that the discussion here is not polemical.

Both phrases are indeed to be understood in a spiritualized sense,
as the parallelism with "trespasses" in v 13 suggests. Since "sense of
the flesh" (2:18, RSV "sensuous mind") is clearly evaluated negatively
in ethical terms, and putting off the old man (3:9 RSV "old nature")
means setting aside every possible kind of vice, the "body of flesh"
must be meant in the sense of body of sin (Rom. 6:6, RSV "sinful
body"). Indeed an interpretation of this verse from Romans is
given here, as v 12 immediately shows. Naturally in this respect the
author is not likely to forget that the Colossian philosophy looks for
redemption only when the soul, separated from the body after
death, ascends to heaven, so that their redemption is still uncertain.

This picture of redemption in the Colossian philosophy might have
suggested to the author the Hellenistic image, attested for example
in Philo, of the discarding of the body by the soul (that loves God);
but here at any rate it is conceived of in a purely ethical manner.
So then this image has scarcely anything to do with circumcision
carried out in Colossae, by means of mysteries. It simply relates to
the writer of the letter's particular concern to describe the redemption as already accomplished, and the making of their dwelling
"above" as something that has already happened, although all this
is of course ethically still to be brought to fulfillment.

The circumcision of Christ is then the circumcision which belongs
to Christ, which is given by him, which brings forgiveness of sins
and thus makes it possible for people to live ethically in a new way.
The idea that the comparison with circumcision was used because
children were already baptized [28] is improbable, since the fact that
circumcision is limited to the male offspring would not suit the
purpose.

[12] The fact that this verse is dependent on Rom. 6:4 or on baptismal tradition already present in Paul [29] is indicated particularly

28. J. Jeremias, *Infant Baptism in the
First Four Centuries* London 1960,
39f.
29. In favor of this would be the fact
that the expression only appears in
the fundamental statement in Rom.
6:4 and not in Paul's interpretation of

this in vv 3 and 5ff. (cf. also 1 Cor.
15:4). Moule, 96, points to the parallel, as far as the content is concerned,
in Mark 8:34. A synopsis of Col. 2:11-
13, 20; 3:1f. and Rom. 6 is given in
D. von Allmen, "Pour une synopse
paulinienne," *Bib* 57 (1976), 98f.

by the fact that both verses speak not of dying or being crucified with Christ (Rom. 6; 8:6), but of "being buried with him." It is difficult to decide what the background to this phrase is; whether on the one hand it is a comparison between being baptized in water and being laid in the earth (cf. Matt. 12:40: as Jonah "in the belly of the whale," so also the Son of man "in the heart of the earth"); or whether on the other hand emphasis is laid on Jesus' burial (Mark 15:42-7; 1 Cor. 15:4),[30] and the intention is to express the completeness of his death or even to counter the hypothesis that his death was only apparent.

In striking contrast to Paul,[31] the concept here (expressed by means of a participle) is followed by the finite verb, "you were raised." Paul in Corinth is faced with a misunderstanding natural enough 'for Hellenists. It is a view that thinks of the blessedness and the unimpaired nature of the resurrection life as if it has already begun with baptism (1 Cor. 4:8). In opposing this, Paul maintains, in a striking transformation of the schema, that we were indeed buried with Christ in baptism, but that the resurrection is separated from this as being an event experienced only in the future.[32] Even 2 Tim. 2:11, where the opponents are entrenched in an identical

---

30. Calvin, 145, thinks of the consequences of dying with Christ, which are included by this choice of words. The intention can scarcely be to state emphatically that the "dying" takes place in the death of Jesus and in the conversion for which baptism represents only the subsequent confirmation as the believer's confession of faith (M. Barth, *Die Taufe ein Sakrament?* Zürich 1951, 312-18; cf. this present commentary p. 282); this would not be completely excluded, in the sense of 1QS 3:4-12; 5.13f., for the original tradition, even if it would not be likely. For Paul, however, it would be impossible (εἰς τὸν θάνατον comes as well in Rom. 6:4; cf. vv 3, 5-8).

31. Nevertheless, Rom. 6:11 can also use the formulation: "consider yourselves . . . alive to God in Christ Jesus," 2 Cor. 5:17 can speak of a "new creation," and Gal. 2:20 of Christ living in me, that is I who "have

died" (L. S. Thornton, *The Common Life in the Body of Christ*, Westminster, 2nd edn. 1946, 59f.).

32. Especially striking is 2 Cor. 4:14: "with Jesus (whose resurrection from the dead lies already in the past) he will raise us (in the future)." The phrase σὺν Χριστῷ (for bibliography on this v. W. Grundmann, *TDNT* VII, 766; Lohse, 104f. n76; also v. G. Otto, *Die mit* σύν *verbundenen Formulierungen im paulinischen Schrifttum*, Diss. Berlin 1952, reported on in *TLZ* 79 (1954), 125; P. Siber, *Mit Christus leben*, Zürich (1971) is essentially limited to the eschatological statements governed by apocalyptic (including those concerning an eschatological participation in being glorified on the basis of present participation in suffering) and to the baptismal expressions (bearing the stamp of this view or of the mystery religions). Cf. U. Wilckens, *Der Brief an die Römer* (EKK) on Rom. 6:2ff.

position (2:18!), still maintains this distinction ("if we have died
with him, we shall also live with him").

In Col. 2, by contrast, the concern is the exact opposite, that is to
counter the community's fear that because of the elements (RSV
"elemental spirits") obstructing the way to heaven they may not
be able to journey upwards and reach Christ. Therefore the writer
has to emphasize that all that matters has already taken place, and
that it is no longer possible for any "element" to block the approach
to the Exalted One.

Nevertheless, there are still indications that the writer is thinking
back to Paul's argument. Indeed, according to Col. 2:22, being buried with Christ certainly takes place in baptism, as in Rom. 6:4,[33]
while being raised with him, by contrast, takes place "through
faith in the power (RSV working) of God." [34] This at least approximates what is said in Rom. 6:4, that being raised finds its fulfillment
in leading a life that has become new. Above all, however, 3:1-4
explains that being raised from the dead means a continual directing
of one's attention to "the things that are above," and that the newness of the resurrection life is still hidden until the Parousia, when
Christ himself will be revealed as this life and we will be revealed
with him. In 2:12, however, the emphasis is different to what we
find in Paul, when it says that the new life has already broken in on
them through faith which trusts God to do everything.

It is difficult to decide what the antecedent of the relative pronoun is here. Does "being raised with" take place in baptism or in

---

33. Βαπτισμός p[46]BD° is the non-
technical usage of the word, which
stands above all for Jewish purification
practices (Mark 7:4; Heb. 9:10; of
baptism [by John the Baptist] only in
Jos. Ant. 18:117, although presumably
Heb. 6:2 also includes Christian baptism). Perhaps it is to be preferred
as the more difficult reading. Josephus
uses βαπτίζειν otherwise frequently for
"to drown" or "to dive in," also in a
passive sense of a ship sinking (Ant.
4:81 of dipping hyssop during purification ceremonies; 10:169 metaphorically), and once of the destruction of
a city (Bell. 4:137).
34. Scarcely: "faith created by God's
power" (Calov, 825b) or "faith living

as God's power" (so Lohmeyer, 112,
though not literally); it is rendered
correctly in Scott, 45; Lohse, 105f.
One may doubt whether Paul would
speak of "faith in the power of God;"
the only comparable phrase is in 2
Cor. 1:9 ("to rely on God who raises
the dead"). In Rom. 6 there is no reference at all to faith (R. Schnackenburg, Baptism in the Thought of St.
Paul, New York 1964, 71), apart from
the belief in the future resurrection
(v. 8). Is this the case because faith
precedes baptism (Rom. 1-5), however
much it then also, as "obedience of
faith" (1:5), characterizes life after
baptism (Rom. 12-14)?

Christ? Probably it should be understood in the former sense. This still serves to stress the actual moment at which they were raised from the dead, as something already accomplished. This then corresponds exactly to the beginning of the verse which speaks of being buried "with" Christ "in" baptism; to juxtapose "in (Christ)" and "brought to life with (Christ)" would scarcely be intelligible.[35]

Union with Jesus' death and resurrection should not be termed "mystical," since apart from anything else the emphasis in this context is not on human feelings and experience. Reality of sacramental grace [36] means, according to vv 13-15, that in the death and resurrection of Jesus something has happened which has significance for the world as a whole. This has been explicitly granted to the community in baptism in such a way that what has happened not only objectively provides the basis for, but also subjectively defines their subsequent life which is thus totally directed toward that grace (3:1).

[13] The following sentence explains what is actually meant by the resurrection life that they have already attained: it denotes being set free from uncircumcision, on the basis of forgiveness of sins.[37] As in 1:21, the explanation is introduced by means of a superfluous "and you," set at the start (cf. note 1 to 2:8-15). The period before baptism is designated as death. This is a traditional usage (cf. Luke 15:24-32: the lost son "was dead and is alive;" John 5:25; Eph. 5:14;

---

35. With G. R. Beasley-Murray, *Baptism in the New Testament,* London (1962), 153f., against Lohse, 104 n73 (likewise W. Grundmann, *TDNT* VII, p. 792 n122), who comes to the opposite conclusion because "in him" (v 11) has a Christological point of reference and in Eph. 2:6 the two prepositions are juxtaposed; for Col. however, this would still be the only verse in which this would be the case. Schnackenburg, *Baptism* (v. previous note) arrives at the same view because ἐν ᾧ (= Christ, v 11a) also still controls v 12a, while ἐν ᾧ (= Christ, v 12b) inaugurates the second train of thought in a way completely parallel to this.

36. Lohmeyer, 111 speaks of the new miracle of a "spiritual raising of the dead" in the person who is to be baptized (cf. p. 286f. of this commentary).

37. The expression, which is used in the LXX for "to give," denotes a "release" (H. Conzelmann, *TDNT* IX, 389). It is found, in relation to a trial, in Acts 3:14; 25:11, 16 (ibid. 393); above all it serves in Philo *Spec. Leg.* II, 39; Luke 7:42f. as a term proper to the context of legal obligation. The word could then have been suggested by the matter under discussion (Col. 2:14a). Paul, it is true, uses it only in the general sense, not of God's forgiveness of sins. Schnackenburg, *Baptism,* 69f. (v. note 34 above) emphasizes the fact that the forgiveness of sins precedes the making alive, and is not identical with it.

James 1:15; Rev. 3:1). The author uses it without considering that he has just understood baptism as burial (according to 2:20; 3:3 as dying).[38]

This unreflecting usage shows that his sole concern in this passage is with the awakening from death which they have already attained, that is, with the new life that they have already taken up. Only in consequence of this can baptism be understood also as dying to a false standard of living. The fatal character of life before baptism is defined by the use of "trespasses;"[39] to walk in the trespasses means to be dead even during one's life.

One may doubt whether the "uncircumcision of your flesh" is intended to recall the heathen's bodily state of uncircumcision. The "circumcision" in v 11 is certainly to be understood metaphorically; so likewise is "putting off the body of flesh." 1QS 5:5 does indeed speak of the foreskin of the inclination and 1QpHab 11:13 and Jub. 11:23 (cf. Deut. 10:16. Aq.) of the "foreskin of the heart," which is defined more precisely as ways of gluttony or as "sin." So the recollection that the Colossians are, as Gentile Christians, uncircumcised in the literal sense of the word, may indeed have led to this metaphor being used.[40] But since as such they were living in heathen vices (v. 3:5), the "uncircumcision of the flesh," which they do indeed in this literal sense still possess, is actually identical with the "trespasses" which caused their life to become death.[41] Yet this very

---

38. Or does 2:12 avoid the image of dying (with Christ) because baptism can be understood as the burial of the one long since dead, whereupon the raising from the dead follows? It would be different "in trespasses" and v 13b were secondary; then the being dead (v 13) could be taken to refer to the situation brought about through baptism (Burger, *Schöpfung*, 98-100).

39. Whereas Paul speaks a good 50 times of sin (cf. p. 165), of which the plural is used only in citations (Rom. 4:7; 11:27; 1 Thess. 2:16), formulas that are taken over (1 Cor. 15:3; Rom. 7:5?; Gal. 1:4?) and expressions that are influenced by these (1 Cor. 15:17), the word appears in Colossians only in 1:14 in an unPauline connection and in the plural. Paul makes use of παρά-

πτωμα(1) for the transgressions of the person who has been baptized (Gal. 6:1; alongside ἁμάρτημα in 1 Cor. 6:18; never with ἁμαρτία), (2) in traditional formulas (Rom. 4:25); also thus in 2 Cor. 5:19?) (3) in connection with the fall of Adam (Rom. 5:12-20), which is already designated thus in Wis. 10:1. In LXX the expression describes the individual transgressions as distinct from the otherwise dominant tendency to understand sin as a collective attitude (W. Michaelis *TDNT* VI, 170).

40. This would be still more likely if one were to read with D* ἐν τῇ ἀκροβυστίᾳ (p46etc.: ἐν τοῖς παραπτώμασιν); but even then this would still remain a symbol of spiritual alienation (Moule, 97).

death has been conquered by virtue of the fact that God has already made them alive "together with him."

From v 13 onwards God, who is mentioned at the end of v 12, is to be thought of as subject. The author can use "he" to refer in one phrase to God and in the next to Christ because he, like Paul, takes very seriously the idea that God is revealed only in the Christ event. While according to 1 Cor. 4:4f. the "Lord" (Jesus) will come as judge, so that everyone will receive their reward "from God," yet the Lord is seen as the one in whom God does indeed manifest himself (cf. also 2 Cor. 5:10 together with Rom. 14:10). The absolute subordination of Christ to God and his involvement in the activity of God (1 Cor. 15:28) is thus not annulled but underlined. Later, in the Pastorals and the Johannine Epistles, it is true that this is no longer so clearly affirmed. There, Christ is more and more emphatically made equal to God.

[14] The "bond" mentioned in v 14 is that issued privately by one's hand, and not attested to by a notary.[42] Philemon 19 provides a good example of this. The idea that man has put himself under obligation to the devil or the evil powers, and cannot discharge himself of this debt,[43] lies completely beyond the compass of this passage.

---

41. Cf. pp. 189f. This forms a starting point for Eph. 2:11-22, where the Christ event is seen as having a pivotal position as the abolition of the boundaries between what is called uncircumcision and what is called circumcision. On "flesh" cf. p. 162. Calvin, 146, considers both interpretations but comes down on the side of a literal understanding.

42. Lohmeyer, 115, n4; E. Lohse, *TDNT* IX, 435-436. In the case of the χειρόγραφον which the debtor himself writes, control by the official writers is omitted (O. Gradenwitz, *Einführung in die Papyruskunde*, Leipzig 1900, 38, 126; similarly L. Mitteis, *Reichsrecht und Volksrecht*, Leipzig 1891, 484). On the history of the exegesis of 2:14 cf. E. Best, *A Historical Study of the Exegesis of Col. 2:14*, Diss. Rome 1956.

43. Lohmeyer, 116f. From Irenaeus and Origen onwards the verse has been understood in this way, and the renunciation of the devil in the baptismal rite goes back to these ideas (cf. pp. 260ff.).

44. Strack-Billerbeck III, 628 (O. Kuss, *Auslegung und Verkündigung I*, Regensburg 1963, 302f.). The closest approximation is the prayer "Our Father, our King," which is cited from shortly after A.D. 100, although it is true that this does not prove that it already existed at that stage in complete form. There it says: "Wipe out (more precisely: smash to pieces) through your great mercy all the records of our debt." According to Ab. 3:16 (R. Aqiba, ob. A.D. 135), God collects the debt by means of his punishing angels just as a shopkeeper does by means of his collectors (Strack-Billerbeck I, 583).

The image used here occurs quite often in Jewish thought, without any such overtones.[44]

Nor is "to cancel" a striking image in this context; it goes back to the biblical expression of cancelling sins.[45] This image is then also resumed by means of "to take away, remove," which suggests the idea that this record of debt is set between man and God and prevents access in either direction. It is not clear what meaning is to be ascribed to the image of nailing to a cross. Records of debt, it is true, were crossed through with an X;[46] but this could have no possible relevance other than that the similarity of form may have evoked the altogether different image here.

Nor is the fact that public confessions of guilt were occasionally set up on stakes as praise to the gods and as a warning to others[47] relevant in this context. Perhaps the underlying idea, although rather unclearly expressed, is that the weight of human guilt fell upon Christ and was crucified with him;[48] that Christ has, as Paul formulates it, become the "curse" or "sin" for us (Gal. 3:13; 2 Cor. 5:21). Is it the custom of affixing to the cross a note of the executed person's crime that has led the writer to use this metaphor,[49] or is he merely calling to mind the proclamations of the authorities that were hung up?[50] At all events, it is clear that this remission of debt has only come about by virtue of Jesus' death on the cross.

What is meant by the reference to the regulations or "legal demands"? With what should one connect this expression? It is impossible to accept the solution offered by the Fathers, that redemption has taken place through the (credal-) dogmas,[51] since this

---

45. Ps. 51(50):3, 11; 109(108):14; Isa. 43:25; Jer. 18:23; 2 Macc. 12:42; Sir. 46:20. Judaism speaks of "to smash to pieces, to declare invalid, to sweep away" (Strack-Billerbeck III, 628).

46. Deissman, LAE 336f. In the Greek word there is no echo of the play on "cross," since this would be equivalent to a letter T rather than a letter X.

47. Carr, JTS 24, 493f.; however, χειρόγραφον seems to have been used only for documents.

48. Cf. O. A. Blanchette, "Does the cheirographon of Col. 2:14 represent Christ himself?" (CBQ 23[1961], 306-

12). The condemned person was not always fastened with nails, but this did often happen; in the case of Jesus it is presupposed in John 20:25 (and Luke 24:39?).

49. Dibelius-Greeven, 31. Ernst, 205 also thinks of an allusion to the inscription on the cross.

50. Conzelmann, 191.

51. Thus Oecumenius, 360C (against this, Erasmus, 890B), whereas Theodoret, 612B seems to think of Christian commandments. In both cases, τοῖς δόγμασιν is taken with ἐξαλείψας (cf. Severian, 323).

usage of the word only grew up centuries later. This term could be understood as:

- (written) regulations [52]
- the signature by which one obliges oneself to effect the regulations [53]
- the bond confronting us with its regulations
- the bond (issued) against us with its requirements.[54]

At any rate, the regulations have caused the offense stipulated in the documents.

From Paul's usage, one would take it for granted that the Old Testament law is referred to. Certainly in Rom. 7:8-13 Paul can speak of the "commandment" instead of the "law," perhaps under the influence of Gen. 2:16),[55] and he can even on one occasion use the word in the sense of an individual commandment of the law (Rom. 13:9);[56] but he always uses an expression different from that found in Col. 2:14. Whereas "law" is found more than a hundred times in Paul, in Colossians, by contrast, it does not occur at all; and "regulations" is never used for the law in Paul, nor is it found in the rest of the New Testament in relation to the Old Testament commandments.[57]

The verb from the same root is to be found in Col. 2:20 in the passing reference made to the regulations that emanate from the Colossian philosophy. Obviously v 16, which interprets vv 14f. does indeed obviously speak of this as well. Since the same expression

52. Thus E. Larsson, *Christus als Vorbild*, 1962 (ASNU 23), 85.
53. J. A. T. Robinson, *The Body* 4th edn 1957 (SBT 1st series 5), 43 n1.
54. Percy, *Probleme*, 88f. and note 43; Dibelius-Greeven, 132. It has to be said that "with its regulations" would then be anticipated or brought in later in the sentence in a remarkable way.
55. Cf. the explicit interpretation of ἐνετείλατο (Gen. 2:16) in Philo *Leg. All.* I, 90-5 (93: ἐντολή) and Jos. *Ant.* I, 43. It is true that Rom. 7 cannot simply be reduced, in terms of the history of salvation, to the commandment of Gen. 2 (thus, correctly, G. Schrenk, *TDNT* II, 550).
56. In 1 Cor. 7:19 it is the commandments also valid in the Christian com-

munity that Paul has in mind, and in 14:37 the commandment of the (earthly or exalted) "Lord," ἐντολή appears 9 times in Paul, but in Colossians only once and that in a different sense.
57. Apart from Eph. 2:15 (if the text is original, then it is dependent on Col. 2:14); the expression is used in connection with the emperor in Luke 2:1; Acts 17:7 (cf. Heb. 11:23 v. 1.); and of the Apostolic Decree in Acts 16:4.
58. Thus Plutarch speaks of Empedocles. and Iamblichus as anonymous Pythagoreans (Diels I, 357.7; 464.1; 466.31); for Jewish commandments v. 3 Macc. 1:3; Jos. *Ap.* 1:42; Philo *Gig.* 52 (cf. note 8 to this section).

seems to be the normal one for the Pythagorean rules,[58] the author probably chooses it because the requirements that have become important in Colossae are for him basically on the same level as the Old Testament commandments, although he never simply equates the two (cf. p. 156f.). He wishes to include everything which in the form of commandments or requirements could endanger the certainty of salvation.

[15] In a certain sense, v 14 is couched in expressly unmythical language: what we find opposed to Christ and his community are the regulations, all the taboos to which they are led by their fear of not being able after their deaths to escape from the "elemental spirits." This is also Paul's understanding of the situation in Gal. 4:3, 8-10. In v 14 the image used is that of the nailing of the bond to the cross. In v 15 the concept is clearer, but also decidedly more mythological: the powers are thought of as enemies who are disarmed.[59] In itself the middle form of the verb denotes "to undress, take off" (3:9!). In that case, however, one would have to accept first that Christ is the subject, and secondly that he would be conceived of as being "clothed" with the powers.[60] Since the middle quite frequently stands for the active,[61] and since God has been the subject from v 13 onwards, the verse should probably, in fact, be translated as above.

This is made the more likely by the following picture of a triumphal procession in which God makes the conquered powers march behind Christ in the same way as the Roman emperor made prisoners of war march behind the one whose triumph it was. Thus they are delivered up for public exhibition and derision. "In him" refers then to Christ and should not be rendered "in it," referring

---

59. One must not equate them with the "elements" (v. p. 60), as does W. Grundmann, *TDNT* VII, 793 n124, although legalism and "elements" belong together also in Gal. 4.9f. (v. p. 162f.; also Houlden, 166).

60. In that case it would be possible to recall Zech. 3:3f., according to which the high priest takes off the old garments and puts on glorious new ones (Lohmeyer, 119), or the body of flesh put off by Christ (2:11), that is the Adamic body tyrannized over by

the rulers of this aeon (Käsemann, "Baptismal Liturgy," 162 (45f.). Cf. p. 348.

61. BDF, 316.1. Used in an active sense in Ev. Nicodemi 2:7 (Acta Pilati 7, Descensus 23 = Tischendorf, *Evangelia apocrypha*, 329 = Hennecke I, 474): Christ disarmed Hades and Satan. Yet this text was to continue to expand up until the 5th cent. R. Leivestad, *Christ the Conqueror*, London 1954, 103 translates (with Lightfoot): remove, take off.

to the cross, though grammatically this would be possible. For what the writer has in mind is probably Christ's exaltation, that is his triumphal procession to heaven (1 Tim. 3:16).[62] It is scarcely the Gnostic myth that we have here. The powers have certainly already been dealt with on the cross. This is not something that happens only gradually in the course of the redeemer's ascent.[63] The idea that the Resurrected One should lead the prisoners with him was already there for the community to read in Ps. 68(67):19: this verse is actually cited subsequently in Eph. 4:8.[64]

Summary

Here we have a Christology presented in a quite specific situation characterized by the Colossian philosophy. It looks at first sight as though this Christology is concerned only with the glory of Christ. The section begins with the claim that the whole fulness of the essence of God is included in Christ, and hence that he is superior to every power and authority. Correspondingly the section concludes with the portrayal of the victor's triumphal procession, with his prisoners, already disarmed, bringing up the rear.

It is necessary for the author to say this in view of the Colossians' uncertainty. Yet more astonishing is the affirmation that the community has also already attained to fulness in him (v 10a) and is already raised from the dead (v 12). This also needs to be said to those who are afraid that they will not find the way "above." It needs to be said today as well to a world no longer convinced in any sense of the absolute and undisputed superiority of the church, but convinced rather of the superior position of every other kind of power.

62. So Schnackenburg, *Herrschaft*, 216f. It is true that the ascent to heaven is not mentioned (Ernst, 205); hence Leivestad, *Christ* (v. previous note), 104f.; G. Delling, *TDNT* III, 160, both think of the crucifixion. The same metaphor is found in 2 Cor. 2:14, where, however, Paul willingly lets himself be led by Christ (G. Delling ibid., 160 and Moule, 100).

63. So *Asc. Is.* 10:14; 11:23 (Christian, 2nd cent. A.D.?); altogether different are the ideas in Philo (*Rer. Div. Her.* 282) discussed on pp. 183f.; against Schenke's reconstruction of a

Gnostic fragment v. pp. 135f. and note 3 to this section.

64. The metaphorical language has been wildly developed in the Gnostic writings; J. Danielou, *The Theology of Jewish Christianity*, London 1964, 203f., draws attention to *Ev. Veritatis* 20:15-25, according to which the proclamation of the Father, the new, sublime teaching, is fastened to the cross and Christ takes off the "perishable rags" in order to come to those who in their oblivion have been "undressed." He also refers to Odes Sol. 23:5-9, where God's plan of salvation appears as a letter.

It needs to be said to a world for which heaven is locked away, a world in danger of becoming heavenless. And it needs to be said with complete assurance.

However, the problems do not simply disappear. For in what sense is the whole being of God to be found in Jesus Christ? Can one let oneself be informed about it, as for instance one may gather from the information on the wrapper on a bar of chocolate that a half pint of milk had been used to produce it? Or does one have to understand it in a sense analogous to what one might say of a piece of music, that "it encompasses the whole of the nineteenth century?" The first instance is an example of a fact that one accepts in a way which is purely objective and merely intellectual; the second might describe an experience that is purely subjective, and which another person may be completely unable to confirm.

Could we establish the presence of God in Christ simply on the basis of information we have been given, or, on the contrary, does it just depend on what we project onto him? The statement in v 9 is clearly meant to be an objective truth, which nevertheless only comes alive when v 10a also becomes true. This point has already been made in v 6 by the combination of indicative and imperative. Therefore it now also becomes crucial to discover what the basis is for the divine and superior status of Christ.

The author has already introduced a reference to the cross of Jesus in 1:20, 22; here he attempts to offer an interpretation which arises out of this event. It is in Christ that the victory has been gained; it is in the cross that Christ's lordship is grounded. This does, of course, leave open the question of whether this is anything more than a mythical formulation borrowed from Pauline tradition. But it is certainly more, for the new life is expressly interpreted as life deriving from the forgiveness of sins. Without doubt, then, something of this newness ought to make its presence felt.

Presumably this is what is hinted at by the expression (already understood in a spiritual sense), concerning circumcision, by which the uncircumcision of the flesh is removed. It is then spelled out in a very specific way in 3:5—4:1. However, this newness is not the possession of divinity in the Gnostic sense. Above all else it is liberation from the "legal demands," that is, from the very means humans use to establish their superiority.

Thus people are set free from the compelling need to succeed, to triumph, to set themselves up over others. People are set free from the compelling need that can force bosses and managers to terrorize their workers and employees; that can force trade union leaders to refuse to back down; that can lead workers to reject wage offers even when they are reasonable; the compelling need that can make a husband and wife torment each other, and so on. It is this funda-mental freedom that forms the main theme of vv 16-23.

(c) Christ, Freedom from Ascetic and Legal Demands (2:16-23)

16   Therefore let no one pass judgment on you in questions of food and drink or with regard to a festival or a new moon or a sabbath. 17   These are only a shadow of what is to come; but the substance belongs to Christ.   18   Let no one disqualify you, insisting on self-abasement and worship of angels, taking his stand on visions, puffed up without reason by his sensuous mind,   19   and not holding fast to the Head, from whom the whole body, nourished and knit together through its joints and ligaments, grows with a growth that is from God. 20   If with Christ you died to the elemental spirits of the universe, why do you live as if you still belonged to the world? Why do you submit to regulations,   21   "Do not handle, Do not taste, Do not touch"   22   (referring to things which all perish as they are used), according to human precepts and doctrines?   23   These have in-deed an appearance of wisdom in promoting rigor of devotion and self-abasement and severity to the body, but they are of no value in checking the indulgence of the flesh.

Analysis

Following the brief mention of the philosophy in v 8, the remarks about Christ were interpolated in vv 9-15; only now do we have the continuation of the warning. It is possible to view vv 16-19 as a polemic directed primarily against religious and cultic demands, and vv 20-23 as a polemic concerned more with ethical and ascetic requirements.[1] Yet v 16 does, in fact, speak of abstaining from food and drink, and v 23, conversely, of false worship. Vv 18f. are almost untranslatable, first because of the unusual terms which probably belong to the Colossian philosophy, and secondly because of the relative clauses and participles, loosely arranged side by side, a phenomenon normal enough in this Epistle! This is similarly the case

---

1. Thus Ludwig, Verfasser, 91. It can be said that 3:1-4 comes as a positive statement after 2:20-3 as 2:19 does after 2:16-18 (Lähnemann, Kolosser-brief, 135); but in fact 3:1-4 has a dif-ferent character as a transition section.

in vv 22f. In both sections there is a reference back to the Christ event, briefly in v 17, and quite clearly in v 20.

Interpretation

[16] Passing judgment is important for the philosophy, since it makes clear precisely which spheres are sacred and which are worldly or demonic. This is as much so for questions of food and drink as it is for sacred and nonsacred days: "incense here, demons there."[2] The sequence festival—new moon—Sabbath corresponds precisely to that of the Greek Bible (Hos. 2:13; Ezek. 45:17; in a different order in 1 Chron. 23:31; 2 Chron. 2:3; 31:3; Just. *Dial.* 8:4).[3] We do not know what grounds there were for the observance of these festivals in Colossae. It is possible that the worship of angels, who ruled over the stars and thus the calendar, had something to do with it.[4]

Probably the "Judaism" of the "uncircumcised," attested to by Ignatius, also kept the Sabbath festival (*Phld.* 6:1; *Magn.* 9:1). The abstention from food could go back to the Mosaic commandment concerning food. Nevertheless, the abstention from drink goes beyond the requirements of the Mosaic law; however, renunciation of wine is found in a number of Jewish movements. Abstention from meat and wine is attested to in Jewish,[5] Greek (cf. note 12 to the Excursus on the Colossian Philosophy) and Christian[6] sources. Among the motives that can give rise to it are protests against the culture in which one is living, the desire to restore ancient ideals or be liberated from materialism, fear of food polluted by being offered to idols or as a result of the transmigration of souls, and rational advice for a healthy life.[7]

2. Conzelmann, 192. It is characteristic that the concern in this is with practical conduct, not dogmatic teaching.
3. Gal. 4:10. Months (festive)—seasons—years.
4. According to the Kerygma Petrou (Hennecke II, 95: first half of 2nd cent. A.D.) 2a = Clem. Al. *Strom.* VI, 5:41, the Jewish cult is the worship of angels and archangels, the months and the moon; according to Elchasai (Hipp. *Ref.* IX, 16:2f.), the Sabbath is to be observed on account of the course of the stars. Cf. note 25 to C IV Ethics.

5. Num. 6:3; Judg. 13:4; Jer. 35:6; Amos 2:12; Philo *Vit. Cont.* 73f. (cf. 37); Test. R. 1:10; Luke 1:15; 7:33. Cf. Ep. Ar. 142: food, drink, touch (Ernst, 213); cf. further O. Böcher, *Dämonenfurcht und Dämonenabwehr. Ein Beitrag zur Vorgeschichte der christlichen Taufe*, 1970 (BWANT 90), 282-4; id., *Christus* (note 4 to Excursus: the Colossian Philosophy), 115-21, esp. 116.
6. Rom. 14:21 (linked with observance of various days, 14:5f.); Eus. *Hist. Eccl.* II, 23:5 of James.
7. Further details are given in Schwei-

[17] "Body" in Greek can designate the concrete substance or mass in contrast to the purely theoretical idea.[8] In Philo, the "shadow" has the same relation to the body as does the name to the object, the copy to the original.[9] The idea which Philo particularly develops, under Platonic influence, is that as a rule God can only be recognized in copies or shadows, and cannot be seen directly. Col. 2:17 proceeds much more from the general distinction between shadow and real object, which need not contain any contrast as such. Heb. 8:5; 10:1, on the other hand, follow the Platonic-Philonic view, and set the (earthly) shadow in contrast to the (heavenly) "type" or "image" (of earthly things). However, both Colossians and Hebrews conclusively provide a corrective to their respective emphases by means of their eschatological (the shadow is the type for the old era, while the object is the type for the era of salvation) and Christological interpretation (in Christ, reality has broken in).[10]

The attempt has clearly been made in these abstract formulations to overcome the problem of how one can both view the Old Testament positively and yet also limit its importance vis-à-vis the New. This is far removed from the answer given by Paul. He specifically maintains that the law is holy, the commandment holy, right and good, but yet emphasizes that sin uses this goodness to lead man to death (Rom. 7:12f.). Therefore for him Christ is "the end of the law" (Rom. 10:4), so that his community "no longer stands under the law" (Gal. 5:18), and those who still live by works of the law bring a curse on themselves (Gal. 3:10).

Paul, in speaking of the law, could never use the relatively innocuous image of the shadow of that which is to come. Even the concept of the heavenly and earthly Jerusalem (Gal. 4:25f.) does not include

---

zer, "Background" §5; cf. p. 167f. of this commentary.
8. E. Schweizer, *TDNT* VII, 1039-1040; cf. 1026.
9. *Decal.* 82; *Migr. Abr.* 12; *Conf. Ling.* 190; *Rer. Div. Her.* 72 (where Plato's Parable of the Cave, *Resp.* VII, 514A-515D, is clearly in the background); *Vit. Mos.* II, 74; *Poster. C.* 112; *Ebr.* 133. In *Leg. All.* III, 96, εἰκών and σκιά stand on the same level and denote the Logos as a copy of the παράδειγμα (= God) and again the Logos, for its own part, as ἀρχέτυπος and παράδειγμα of the created beings;

in ibid. 100-3, the shadow is set over against the First Cause, that is the Uncreated One and the clear vision. Cf. further Jos. *Bell.* 2:28, where the acknowledgment *de iure* is opposed to the state of affairs as it exists *de facto;* cf. also note 22 to 1:15-20.
10. S. Schulz, *TDNT* VII, 398. The "future things" (or "that which is to come") thus denote not the new world after the Parousia but the Christian present seen from the standpoint of the Old Testament (Lähnemann, *Kolosserbrief*, 136, n98).

the idea that the former is the heavenly "type" for the earthly or for
Sinai. It is Adam, not Moses, who is the "type" of Christ (Rom.
5:14). On the other hand, at Colossae it is also not a question of
mere indulgence, such as tolerating abstinence from meat and wine
or observance of festivals for the sake of those who are weak (Rom.
14:2-6, 21). For the question is bound up with anxious concern
about the cosmic elements, and this concern comes into conflict with
faith in Christ. Thus it would probably fall under the verdict of
Rom. 14:23, that whatever does not proceed from faith is sin (cf.
vv 20-23).

However, is the discussion here concerned with the law at all?
The word does not appear in the whole Epistle and the "legal demands," which v 14 speaks of, seem to stand nearer to Pythagorean
rules than to the Mosaic law, although a Jewish element is certainly
included. The situation differs in at least one respect from that in
Galatians. There circumcision is demanded as an indispensable pre-
requisite for salvation. Moreover, in Galatians the return to being
subject to rules dictated by the elements (RSV "elemental spirits")
of the universe (Gal. 4:3, 9) is clearly understood, at least by Paul,
as an imposing of the Mosaic law upon themselves.

At Colossae it is not disputed that Christ has reconciled the universe; circumcision is scarcely something that is insisted on, and
has perhaps not even been carried out. The movement flies the flag
not of the Mosaic law, but of a modern philosophy which intends,
by means of appropriate practices, to cleanse their souls and fit them
for the ascent to Christ, the Lord of all (cf. p. 133f.). Thus it is that
a fellow worker of Paul can take up the schema of shadow and
object and regard every kind of "requirement," whether of the Mosaic law or Hellenistic asceticism, as the preparatory stage which is
replaced by that which is perfect.

While we may thus have clarified the meaning, the construction
is still obscure. The formulation "but the body (is) of Christ" (as
it literally means) must be expanded to make the meaning clear.
The most plausible emendation is to suggest that a *nominative*
originally stood in place of the genitive: the accumulation of every
kind of requirement is "a shadow of what is to come, but the body
(= the object itself) is Christ." This corresponds precisely to the
usual contrast between shadow and substance (= object). It is easy
to understand how this corruption came about, since by changing

one single letter [11] of the original, the commonly-occurring phrase
"the body of Christ" was obtained.

If this emendation is not accepted, then one must interpret the
text thus: "the reality, however, belongs to Christ";[12] but it has to
be said that the phrase in the Greek would be a very terse way of
expressing this. Or else one could translate: "the body (= the reality), however, is the body of Christ."[13] But again it must be pointed
out that this presupposes that a word has been omitted. Or again, one
could take the phrase with the next verse: "with regard to the body
of Christ . . .";[14] but this fails to give good sense. However one understands this phrase grammatically, the meaning at least is clear.
The only point that is not altogether certain is whether it is Christ
or the church that is set as reality in contrast to the shadow.

[18] No one should, as the verb puts it, cheat the Colossians out of
their prize or "disqualify" them. "Taking pleasure in . . ." (RSV "insisting on") reproduces a Hebrew phrase, common enough in the
Old Testament; literally it means "wishing in. . . ." [15] This phrase is
taken up again in v 23 in the newly-coined phrase "desired worship"
("desired" in the sense of freely undertaken or self-chosen, suitable
for oneself; RSV has "promoting rigor of devotion"). The "humility"
(RSV "self-abasement") mentioned here is presumably a slogan being
bandied around in Colossae, for in 3:12, as in Phil. 2:3 and else-

---

11. Toῦ is lacking in ℵ cDEFGKL
Chr. Thdrt., etc.
12. 1 Cor. 3:23 is to be compared with
this. The fact that the church belongs
as a body to its head (Lohse, 117), or
that Christ has offered his body in sacrifice for the church, could play some
part and have led to this contracted
phrase. It is scarcely to be supposed
that it would have been noted, against
ascetic demands, that corporeality belongs to Christ (Lähnemann, *Kolosserbrief*, 137).
13. Lohmeyer, 123.
14. This is already mentioned by
Chrysostom VII, 1 (313 = Oecumenius 37C) as a possibility, but in X, 3
(369, on 4:4) he clearly thinks otherwise; cf. further ABP (?) in C.
Tischendorf, *Novum Testamentum
Graece II*, Leipzig 1872 *ad loc.*; also

Aug. Ep. 27 = CSEL 44; 373.12, who
appraises it positively.
15. Ps. 112 (111):1: "to find pleasure
in his commandments" (literally: "to
wish in his commandments"); similarly perhaps Test. A. 1:6; cf. G. Schrenk,
TDNT III, 45 and Alting, 398a with
reference to the Hebrew. Less probable is the understanding of the participle as an adverb: "Let no one willfully
(or frivolously) condemn you in matters . . ." (Dibelius-Greeven, 64). It
is true that on the occasion of a ship-
wreck someone shouted to a cynic:
"Here you are joking frivolously (θέλων)!" (Epict. *Diss.* II, 19.16 in A.
Friedrichsen, "θέλων Col. 2:18," *ZNW*
21 (1922), 136). A literal translation
"in that he attempts (to condemn
you)" (von Soden, 53) also fails to
yield good sense.

where, it is spoken of in an altogether positive way. It becomes suspect, however, when one boasts about it. Probably what is meant here is the sort of humility which one calls attention to by fasting.[16]

As in v 23, angel worship is linked with this; most likely, then, the two belonged together in the minds of the Colossians. The phrase as such could also be translated "the angels' worship";[17] the idea that humans participate in the angels' heavenly worship is not impossible. The angelic liturgy at Qumran [18] presumably has in mind a form of worship on earth, for which the heavenly worship provides the model, and for which the presence of the angels is entreated.[19] Where the idea expressed is that of visions and ecstatic heavenly journeys of the soul, then one also finds the concept of humans joining in the heavenly worship. However, the expression in v 23 must certainly denote an action on the part of a person (and one which the author repudiates), not an activity of the angels;[20] the author is, then, thinking of angel worship.

This is the more likely since, as Rev. 22:8f. shows, God, Christ,

16. Lev. 16:29, etc. Herm. v. III, 10:6; s. V 3:7 (W. Grundmann, *TDNT* VIII, 7, 26; Kehl, *ZKT* 91, 368; what is meant by this is scarcely that one remains conscious of one's origin from the "elements" (Philo *Som.* I, 212).

17. This is found quite frequently from Luther onward (Meyer, 263); more recently Francis, *ST* 16, 126-30; Carr, *JTS* 24, 499f. Cf. Rev. 4:4-11; 5:8-14; 11:16-19. Synge, 60 considers the conjecture ἀγγέλλων ("proclaiming," without τῶν).

18. Translated in J. Strugnell, *The Angelic Liturgy in Qumran, Congress Volume* Oxford 1959, 1960 (VTSup 7), 322f.

19. Ibid. 335, 320; admittedly 1QH 3:21f. speaks of the fact that the purified spirit of the person is given its position with the host of the holy ones and enters into fellowship with the community of the heavenly ones (cf. 3:20: "raised up to everlasting height"). It is true that what is meant by this is perhaps only predestination to heavenly life (H. Hübner, "Anthropologischer Dualismus in den Hoday-

oth?" *NTS* 18 [1971/2], 271-3). According to 1QSb 4:25f., the priest serves already "in the heavenly palace" (on this further v. Francis, *ST* 16, 127-9; Asc. Is. 7:37; 8:17; 9:28-34; Corp. Herm. I, 26; Kuhn, *Enderwartung* [note 29 to 1:1-8], 183-5, cf. 47-9). G. Thiessen, *Urchristliche Wundergeschichten*, 1974 (SNT 8), 276f., emphasizes the fact that present and future remain finally unconnected at Qumran because no one takes the place of Christ, who combines both in himself. Since the Old Testament cult was already carried out "before Yahweh," the earthly and heavenly habitations of God could easily coincide in the thought of the Qumran community, the priest becomes the angel of the countenance and the people become the temple (J. Maier, *Die Texte vom Toten Meer II*, Munich 1960, 77f.).

20. Francis, *ST* 16, 131, hence has to see in this an expression, bearing the stamp of the author of the letter, used for visionary heavenly ascents.

and the angles often form something akin to a heavenly triad[21] while angels and spirit (of God are frequently interchangeable,[22] and the angel is readily used in place of God himself.[23] Even Paul reckons with the presence of angels in worship (1 Cor. 11:10).[24] Above all, the practice of offering worship to souls as they ascend to heaven is attested to in the philosophy influenced by Pythagorean ideas (cf. note 10 to Excursus on the Colossian Philosophy; in Judaism these souls are identified with the angels, and in Hellenism with the "saviors" in the mysteries.

The addition "on entering into that which he . . ." or "what he on entering (has viewed)" (RSV "taking his stand on [visions]") is puzzling.[25] If the former rendering is followed, the writer would be specifying on what occasions fasting and angel worship took place;[26] if the latter, then he gives these as the content of what is seen in the vision.[27] Alternatively, one would have to connect the phrase with what follows by means of a difficult construction: "puffed up because of that which . . . ."[28] The expression is certainly used in the second century A.D. of entering (a sanctuary?) to receive an oracle; and this entering was connected with an initiation. The fact that Lucian in

21. Luke 9:26; 1 Thess. 3:13 (?); 1 Tim. 5:21; Rev. 3:5 (also the seven spirits in 1:4 are thought of as the seven archangels).
22. Examples are given in E. Schweizer, "Die sieben Geister der Apokalypse," in id., *Neotestamentica*, Zurich 1963, 195 n32; 199 n51; cf. 199f.
23. Jub. 18:9-14; 19:3, etc. In Rev. 18:4 (along with 5) the angel speaks in the first person that properly belongs to God (H. Kraft, *Die Offenbarung des Johannes*, 1974 (HNT 16a), 228).
24. Further discussion of this is given in Ellis, "Gifts" (note 12 to 1:1-2) 138-44.
25. The addition of μή or οὐχ in CG, etc. is a correction which is intended to dispute the fact that the visionary has really seen something. Since ancient manuscripts do not separate individual words from one another, it would be possible to suppose that κεν had inadvertently been written only once instead of in duplicated form (or

else to understand ἑώρα as a not properly suitable imperfect) and to interpret κενεμβατεύων as "on the occasion of his error." However, this would be formulated in a curious way, and the author has no need at all to deny the fact that the visionary has looked upon whatever it may have been. Lightfoot, 195 conjectures the form ἑώρᾳ, which can perhaps mean "by being suspended, balancing in the air."
26. However, can one "enter into" something seen in a visionary way? Perhaps; but the participle refers to the person passing judgment; it ought then to be in the past ("on the basis of his — already accomplished — entering into . . ."), cf. Lohse, 120f. n51.
27. For the obligation to fast as the content of an angelic vision v. 4 Ezra 5:13, 20; 6:31; it is found frequently as a preparation for receiving revelation (Francis, *ST* 16, 114-19).
28. Greek accusative; so Friedrichsen, *ZNW* 21 (note 15 above), 135f.

the case of his Isis initiation while on the way from the realm of death, or from there up to the world of the sun, "journeys through all the elements" could even indicate that one accomplished in advance, by means of certain rites, the soul's heavenly journey up through all the elements.[29] However, the linguistic parallels are uncertain.

Possibly all that is meant is investigations painstakingly researched:[30] "what he has seen by painstaking research" or "again and again painstakingly researching what he has seen."[31] But in either case, the writer would have had to specify what the person was investigating. This information could only be dispensed with if there were already a fixed meaning for the expression at Colossae, referring to one specific action. This is more readily conceivable in the case of the first of these explanations. So the most probable rendering is: "what he saw on entering (the world above)."

With this one could perhaps compare 2 Cor. 12:2 ("caught up to the third heaven") or Rev. 4:1f. ("and lo, in heaven an open door! and the first voice . . . 'Come up hither, and I will show you . . .'" cf. 17:3; 21:10); these, it must be said, are experiences of an ecstatic nature.[32] Most likely, then, the idea here is of a visionary experience

29. Examples are given in Dibelius-Greeven, 35. They remind the reader of the Isis initiation (Apul. *Met.* XI 23, 7 [A.D. 2nd cent.]; for critical comments on this v. H. Krämer, *Die Isisformel des Apuleius* (Met. XI 23, 7), *WuD* 12 (1973), 102f., who translates the introduction: "Hear, but believe (only), what is true" (but may one supply "only"?). A. D. Nock, "The Vocabulary of the New Testament," *JBL* 52 (1933), 131-9, draws attention to the fact that ἐμβατεύειν always follows μυεῖσθαι, and is not part of the same process (132). The detailed discussion of the instances in F. O. Francis ("The Background of EMBATEUEIN (Col. 2:18) in Legal Papyri and Oracle Inscriptions," in Francis-Meeks, *Conflict*, 197-207) shows that the mention of a preceding initiation is probably only incidental. The word means only "to come into (a possession)" or "to enter (an oracle)." So one has to be very careful

about taking it to refer to the mysteries. Carr, *JTS* 24, 498, interprets it from the perspective of classical Greek usage as a (sacred) presence in a specific place.
30. 2 Macc. 2:30 "Penetration and consideration from every angle and painstaking investigation"; cf. ἐμβαθύνειν (Codex H: ἐμβατεύειν) in Philo *Plant.* 80: "to penetrate (further into knowledge)." So S. Lyonnet, "L'epitre aux Colossiens (Col. 2, 18) et les mysteres d'Apollon Clarien," *Bib* 43 (1962), 423f., but as an allusion to the mysteries (433-5).
31. So H. Preisker, *TDNT* II, 535-536 with examples for both interpretations. More recent treatments of the subject are mentioned in Lohse, 119-21.
32. Francis, *ST* 16, 122-5 thinks of entry into the heavenly world, as it is described in apocalypses; but ἐμβατεύειν never appears in these (Lohse, 120 n49), though it is indeed used in LXX for the entry into the

(the setting being some sort of initiation) in which the Colossians did indeed experience entry into the heavenly sanctuary.

The following clause introduces the polemic. "Sense [33] of the flesh" (as it literally means; RSV "sensuous mind") is a concept expressed in Old Testament or Jewish terms. Flesh is not simply that which is material or corporeal. Nor is it evil; rather, it has been created by God, although admittedly it is restricted, mortal, susceptible to illness and temptation. So the flesh, as God's creation, can be completely permeated by the Holy Spirit. Conversely, the "spirit," that is human imagination, can be completely "flesh." This latter is the case when we no longer think of ourselves as creatures of God, but would ourselves like to be God, that is, "puff ourselves up" (Col. 2:18) [34] or "boast" (1 Cor. 1:29 and frequently; not in Colossians).

Strictly speaking, as in the Old Testament, it is not the flesh as such that is evil, but only putting one's trust in the flesh: "Cursed is the man who trusts in man and makes flesh his arm, but whose heart turns away from the Lord" (Jer. 17:5). Thus also according to Col. 2:18, "carnal" (RSV "sensuous") thought consists in putting one's trust in almost anything except Christ, and thereby becoming too self-confident. This can certainly lead to the flesh in which we trust becoming more and more the power that controls us. Thus one ends up being controlled by it, as though by a drug in which one seeks happiness. It is in this sense that the flesh can be spoken of as demanding its tribute, and as something which one must satiate (v 23).[35]

---

promised land (Josh. 19:49, Moule, 105). This meaning would suit as far as the content is concerned. Perhaps the customary phrase about "entry (into the sanctuary after the initiation)" has been combined with the biblical usage of the entering into the promised land and means for the Colossians the entry into heaven which they have already experienced in advance in a visionary manner (at baptism?). However, we know far too little to be certain about this.

33. Νοῦς; Rom. 8:7 φρόνημα).
34. The same verb appears in 1 Cor. 8:1, where it is not Judaistic righteousness through the law that is being at-

tacked but the arrogance of the knowledge which thinks it can understand God better than the piety of the "weak" could.
35. E. Schweizer, TDNT VII, 131-133; 136; but with E. Brandenburger, Fleisch und Geist, 1968 (WMANT 29), esp. 42-58, 223-8, the division into two spheres, which had already taken place in Judaism, is to be emphasized still more strongly as the background by which the statements of Paul, basically corresponding to the Old Testament, have been freshly fashioned (cf. Schweizer, "Menschensohn" (v. note 79 to 1:15-20) 110-12; on the division into two spheres in

[19] Whatever conclusion we come to on these points of detail, it is clear in any case that the community is in error in no longer holding fast to Christ as the "head." In theory the Colossians would be in complete agreement with this verdict. But their fear of being caught in the elements when their souls try to ascend, and of not reaching the Exalted Christ, shows that they did not completely trust his power. For this reason the writer inserts the reference to the fact that the *whole* body is cared for by Christ. Whereas in v 10 the writer has firmly maintained that Christ is Lord over all power and authority, now the other side of the coin is made clear, that is, the care and concern that the head shows for the body.

Here, as throughout the Epistle (where it is the author himself who is speaking), the "body" must denote not the cosmos,[36] which is certainly no longer growing in God's power, but rather the church (1:18, 24).[37] And again it becomes clear that while Christ is indeed head over the whole world, only the church is his body. This does, of course, involve the idea that Christ is lord over the church. This relationship of sovereignty must not then be falsely transformed into an ontic context.[38] This is what happens in Gnosticism, but it

---

Judaism, v. *TDNT* VII, 109 along with the references on line 20; 120; cf. p. 191f. of this commentary along with note 36 to 3:5-11. On the whole question raised in this note v. p. 147 of this commentary.).

36. Against Dibelius-Greeven, 36; a similar view is still expressed in Lohse, *NTS* 11, 206f.

37. As according to Col. 1 the believers (v 10) or the gospel (v 6) are still growing, by which is meant the (inward and outer) growth of the community. Fischer, *Tendenz* (note 78 to 1:15-20), 73 refers to a papyrus cited by Reitzenstein (P. Leid V); but what is quoted here is in fact a conglomeration of Pap. V (P. XIII, 762-77 in K. Preisendanz, *Papyri Graecae Magicae II*, Stuttgart 2nd edn 1974, 122) and Pap. W (P. XII 238-44 = A.D. 4th cent., ibid., 57). Αὔξων stands only at the end of the second mentioned of these and means nothing more than that "he makes everything to grow." Rather more to the point would be

P. XXI (ibid., 146, A.D. 2/3 cent.): ". . . Lord, . . . for whom heaven is the head and the air is the body, . . . who produces goodness and nourishes the terrestrial sphere and causes it to grow (and also the whole earth and the whole cosmos)." However, the source of these late utterances is the Egyptian teaching, an account of which was already given in the Augustan period by Diod. S. (I, 11:5; Diels II, 242:31f.), according to which Isis and Osiris preside throughout the whole cosmos (the "body" with its five "members" (note 5 to 3:5-11), that is, the elements, ibid. 11:6) and nourish everything (but not the world body!) and cause it to grow (cf. note 17 to 3:5-11). The passage from Philo (*Quaest.* in Ex. 2, 117) quoted by Lohse, 122 n66 says nothing of growth and has presumably been subjected to Christian revision (cf. note 9 to 1:15-20).

38. Conzelmann, 193.

is also what takes place in a triumphalist understanding of the church (cf. pp. 97f.). Yet it is precisely the knowledge of Christ's lordship over the church that signifies also knowledge of his power, help, and concern.

Attention here is concentrated on Christ to such an extent that the author uses the masculine relative pronoun even though "head" is feminine in Greek.[39] So also in the case of Paul it is the body of Christ, the church, which is the sphere of lordship and blessing into which people are called. Yet strictly speaking it is not the body that grows but rather the sum total of people called to membership in it. Thus this verse brings out a further shade of meaning when it equates the church with the body—the body defined as in process of growth (literally, the growth growing from God) and assisted by the head. This development is bound up with the fact that whereas Paul thinks primarily of the body of Christ in concrete terms, as the flock living together in the local community, the writer to the Colossians thinks of the universal church.

"Joints and ligaments" are probably just figures of speech,[40] and do not refer to those who hold office.[41] At no point are officers of the church appealed to in the attempt to come to terms with the danger threatening in Colossae, and 4:17 is not clear in this connection (v. ad loc.). Perhaps the idea here is of the part played by the apostle and his fellow workers in mediating the message. This mediating role is given special emphasis in this epistle (1:7-9; 1:23—2:1). These fellow workers have a function which historically is unique

39. The idea of the body "holding fast of the head" is impossible even within the metaphor. On the function of the head in the body cf. E. Schweizer, *TDNT* VII, 1029 n53; 1033; 1036; 1041.

40. W. Goossens, *L'eglise corps du Christ*, Paris 1949, 44f., thinks that this phrase combines together two common images and hence that they should not be worked out in detail.

41. Thus Masson, 133: "organes de liaison"; yet more markedly id., *L'epitre de St. Paul aux Ephesiens*, 1953 (CNT IX), pp. 195f. on Eph. 4:1-16 (and Col. 2:19, ibid., 198). Cf. note 27 to C IV Ethics and John of Damascus 896D: "teachers of the word." In Eph. 4:16 (but not, he informs me in an oral communication, in Col. 2:19) R. Schnackenburg, "Christus, Geist und Gemeinde (Eph. 4:1-16)," in *Christ and Spirit in the New Testament, Festschr. C. F. D. Moule*, Cambridge 1973, 290, likewise takes the same image to refer to those who hold office, whereas I, without denying that certain duties must have been arranged within the community, would also in Ephesians lay the emphasis on "each of us . . ." (v 7; v. note 24 ibid.); thus those mentioned in v 11 only provide examples of the gifts of grace and duties given to every member of the community and which, apart from the arrangement necessary on purely practical grounds, are basically all of equal value.

in the growth of the church;[42] but they do not on that account become officeholders as distinct from laity.[43]

[20] What in v 12 was termed being buried (with Christ) in baptism is now taken up, in a way that is similar to that in Rom. 6:4, 8, by means of "dying (with Christ)." In Romans as well this verb is used in a passage where the emphasis is laid on being separated from sin. In Paul, however, it is always used with the dative ("to die to sin" Rom. 6:2, 10 cf. Gal. 2:14; 6:14) whereas here the formula is (literally) "to die off from (away from) the elements of the universe." This clearly shows that it does not mean exactly the same as in Romans. For in Romans it is a matter of escaping from the domain of sin (in the singular!) an escape which signifies an unequivocal change, decisive for eternal salvation, from sin to God; whereas here it is a matter of being set free from all the various taboos which are enumerated in what follows.[44]

The fundamental act of putting off the "body of flesh" in baptism (v 11) has the consequence that one need no longer be afraid of the elements of the universe and the "regulations"[45] dependent on them, for the very reason that those who have been baptized are, in fact, no longer "living in the world." This shows that the "elemental spirits of the universe" and "universe" (or "world") must, in fact, be the same. It shows that the problem lay in getting away from the world and its elements and in reaching the upper sphere, in which Christ reigns. All these requirements obviously served the purpose of making this ascent possible after death (cf. pp. 131f.). It shows, further, that the author has learned from Paul to under-

---

42. Cf. the role of Paul's mission to the nations (v. on 1:23). In any case, one will have to translate by "supplied by (διά)" and not merely "equipped with" (with Moule, 107).

43. None of the words for "office" (τέλος, τιμή, ἀρχή, λειτουργία) is used for what we call office, although the last three are found for Jewish and Gentile holders of office, for Christ or the entire community; only the term διακονία is used, which also describes the duty of every member of the community. This shows how important is it for the New Testament that duties are indeed to be arranged properly but

are in no case to be separated into higher and lower grades of this kind (E. Schweizer, *Gemeinde und Gemeindeordnung*, ²1962 (ATANT), § 21).

44. Cf. note 39 to 2:8-15 and Rom. 6:7 "freed (literally, justified) from sin" (singular!); 7:6 "discharged from the law, dead to that which held us captive." This shows that the power of the "elements" occupies more or less the same place as the power of the law does in the case of Paul.

45. The same root as in v 14 (v. ad loc.).

46. H. Strathmann, *TDNT* VI, 535.

stand "life" as a conscious choice of place, of the sphere in which one feels at home and where one expects to find strength, direction, and meaning; a choice, that is, between the "world" and its elements on the one hand and "heaven" and the sovereignty of Christ on the other. Our home [46] is in heaven, from which we . . . await the Lord Jesus Christ (Phil. 3:20). The world is thus no longer the norm, authority, and source of all help and direction; it is simply the world, nothing more.[47]

It is characteristic, certainly, of Colossians that the eschatological formulation does not appear until 3:4, as distinct from Phil. 3:20, where it follows immediately. Since the Colossians are anxious that they may not, after their death, be able to ascend to that region above, the author stresses the other side of the matter: they have actually been transposed into that region above already, even if this fact is not yet clearly evident. They must therefore no longer allow regulations to be made [48] as though they were still living in the world. It is thus this very adherence to the ascetic regulations mentioned in v 21 that means they are slipping back into the world! This is not to deny that there is an asceticism which may be freely undertaken and necessary for the cause of the gospel (1:9; 2:1; 3:5; 4:13, 18).

[21] Three instances of these regulations are given. "To come near" can denote sexual intercourse,[49] as in 1 Cor. 7:1, although there it is true the woman is mentioned as the object. The verb is often used in this sense [50] and the opponents in Corinth proclaimed abstinence from sexual relations, while the false teachers in 1 Tim. 4:3 combined this with the prohibition of certain foods. If the verb had been used in Colossae as a slogan in this sense, then the readers would immediately have understood it as such; but whether they did so we do not know. Verse 22a rather suggests not (and thus differs from 1 Tim. 4:3). One would then have to take 22a to refer only to the last two prohibitions mentioned in 21.

In favor of this would be the fact that the first and third expres-

---

47. Conzelmann, 193; cf. pp. 172f. of this commentary.
48. BDF 314 (appendage).
49. So A. R. C. Leaney, "Colossians II.21-23," *ExpTim* 64 (1952/3), 92.
50. E.g., Gen. 20:6; Prov. 6:29; Jos. *Ant.* 1:163; Eur. *Phoen.* 945; Plat.

Leg. 8 (840A); Plut. *Alex.* 21:30 (I 676E); M. Ant. I, 17.13 (6); above all also in absolute usage: Aristot. *Pol.* 1335b, 40; related to foods, by contrast, in Diels I, 463.17, 19 (29ff.), of Pythagoreans.

sions of v 21 would in this case not say exactly the same thing.[51] This would be an advantage since they are not juxtaposed and cannot therefore be thought of merely as variants of each other for rhetorical effect. But is this explanation adequate? It is certain that the second expression is concerned with questions of food and drink (v 16) and the third even gives a warning against merely touching forbidden objects of this kind.

[22] However, as the following clause points out, foods are not powers which can fill them with dread; they are simply perishable provisions.[52] Only when one is already afraid that they contaminate the soul and thus hinder the ascent through the elements, do they become powers. By inserting the remark at this point, the writer intends to make both these themes explicit: first, that the things of this world (as for example foodstuffs) are meant to be used, and second that they have no power since they are transient.[53]

This rebuke certainly shows that the Colossian regulations were at any rate not merely hygenic rules,[54] nor a call to live according to nature,[55] nor moral admonitions.[56] Nor, however, does it seem that the Colossians practiced asceticism in the strict sense of the word, although "relentlessness (RSV "severity") to the body" points in this direction. It seems instead to have been an endeavor to protect the soul from encumbrances which bind it too much to the various elements of the universe, and could thus endanger its ascent. All these regulations are purely human, as a quotation from scripture (Jer. 29:13 LXX) affirms. This citation was also used in Mark 7:7.

51. Both expressions are found alongside each other with the same meaning in Exod. 19:12 (Lohse, 123 n73). De Wette, 54 concluded that it was sexual abstinence that was meant. Caird, 200 sees in this verse irony on the part of the apostle: finally one must touch absolutely nothing at all.
52. Conzelmann, 193. Ἅτινά ἐστιν introduces a polemical observation on the part of the author in vv 17, 23 as well.
53. This is the argument presented, probably in traditional fashion, in 1 Cor. 6:13 as well, with reference to foods; they belong to the sphere of the stomach, whereas sexual inter-

course affects the body. Mark 7:19 even speaks of the toilet (a word which Oecumenius does indeed insert into Col. 2:22). Paul in this connection would probably refer to the fact that these foodstuffs derive their character from creation and to the express commendation that God gives them (1 Cor. 10:26, 30f.; Rom. 14:20; cf. 1 Tim. 4:4f.).
54. As Diels I, 476.7-13; Pauly-W. Suppl. VII, 62f.
55. As Philo (H. Lewy, Sobria Ebrietas, Giessen 1929, 71 with n3; but cf. 6 n3).
56. As Diels I, 475.26-31; Philostrat. Vit. Ap. I 8; Philo Vit. Cont. 74.

It was probably also employed in other attempts to come to terms with food regulations as well.[57]

[23] The following verse is almost impossible to translate. The opening words show it to be a polemical observation on the part of the author. That being so, "to be reputed" (RSV "have . . . an appearance") must be understood in opposition to "really to be."[58] This sort of apparent wisdom is made manifest, then, in worship undertaken of one's own free will,[59] and in exercises aimed at achieving humility, as for instance the discipline of fasting or the self-denial involved in ruthlessly punishing one's body; so at least v 21 paraphrases the idea. The rest of the sentence is difficult. Literally it means: "not in some esteem for the satisfaction of the flesh." Since it is only here that the article is found with "flesh," its satisfaction is certainly evaluated in a negative sense.[60] In fact, in the opinion of the writer of the letter it is precisely these regulations concerning abstinence that are conducive to the satisfaction and not to the mortification of the flesh, with the result that (as has been said above) they cause those who submit to them to fall back into the world.

This is a good Pauline concept. The apostle's exemplary way of life, by virtue of which he was blameless in righteousness under the law, was, in fact, a "confidence in the flesh." But how is one supposed to take the first part of the verse? Does one have to under-

57. Grammatically, the phrase ("according to human precepts and doctrines") ought at least according to the sense to be connected with δογματίζεσθε; the content has then been anticipated in a vivid mode of expression.
58. Λόγος is found in contrast to ἀλήθεια; in Diod. S. XIII 4.1; XIV, 1.2; in contrast to ἔργον; in Polystrat. S. 33 (according to Pr.-Bauer s.v.1a); cf. Demosth. Or. 20:18 (462): "It has a certain reputation," which turns out, however, to be a "lie" (cited in Moule, 108, where, however, the reference is given incorrectly).
59. Perhaps indeed this is intended in a critical sense: "worship chosen by oneself." In favor of this are the parallel formulations which thus designate a person who would like to be a phi-losopher (or guest of honor or teacher [so Herm. s. IX, 22:2]), but is not one. However, similar combinations also occur which stress the voluntary nature of what is taken on (examples of both are given in Pr.-Bauer s.v.). Since the other expressions are evaluated positively (1:9; 3:16, etc.; 3:12), and are only disqualified by being characterized as "appearance," it is better to understand this phrase in the sense of an additional accomplishment voluntarily undertaken.
60. In favor of this view is Philo Vit. Cont. 35:37: the Therapeutae love σοφία (Col. 2:23) and δόγματα (2:14, 20), use the simplest possible food to help combat πλησμονή; and keep the Sabbath (ibid. 30; Col. 2:16).

stand everything from the end of v 22 as a parenthesis, and then connect the two parts thus: "for the use but not for the satisfaction of the flesh, by ascribing honor to it (taking it too seriously)"? However, since the first half of the sentence contains an "on the one hand," one must, of course, look for the contrast (which is often merely assumed in Greek) in the second half of the sentence. The whole expression would then be dependent on the beginning of v 23.[61]

But what then is the meaning of the three words that follow "not" ("in some esteem"; RSV "of no value") for the whole phrase? It could be understood as

— "without any (Christian) concern" [62]
— "bringing no honor for the fulfilling of the flesh" [63]
— "(but) no real value against the indulgence of the flesh" [64] or
— "of no real value (except) for the satisfaction of the flesh." [65]

The last is the most likely, but it is impossible to be certain.

Conclusion

The whole section is waging war against taboos. This is indeed a very modern theme. In fact, the basic attitude in Colossae is strikingly similar to that which is being combatted at the present, although both the motivation and the actual way this takes effect differ in many details. It is not even certain whether the taboos in Colossae were concerned with what is the most important area of debate for today, that of sexuality (v. on v 21). Conversely, abstaining from food on religious grounds plays hardly any role today. And if particular days are differentiated from others, then it is on account of an unlucky number or the constellation of the stars, not because they are festivals. Yet incense and the fear of demons are quite close to each other. There is not much difference between performing

---

61. Literally: "All this is only a reputation of . . . having, not . . . for the satisfaction . . . ," Hrabanus 526C: "obscure dictum"!

62. So more or less B. Reicke, "Zum sprachlichen Verständnis von Kol 2, 23," *ST* 6 (1953), 51. It would then be a badly abbreviated expression.

63. "Honor" and "fulfilling" (πληροῦσ-θαι, not πλησμονή) would then be slo-

gans used by the opponents (Bornkamm, "Häresie," 151f.).

64. Lightfoot, 204: "yet not really of any value to remedy indulgence of the flesh." But is this linguistically possible?

65. G. Delling, *TDNT* VI, 134 (the phrase is dependent on ἅτινά ἐστιν), where other possibilities are listed.

sacrifices to gods and demigods on specific days, and sacrificing a particular undertaking that one has planned, because of one's fear of the constellation of stars.

Above all, however, the point of concern in Colossae is to keep the soul pure and undefiled by the world, and for the writer of the letter this seems to be comparable to what we call being cramped and repressing our amoral feelings. The writer knows as well that this feeling cannot simply be turned off like a tap. He therefore begins by reminding them that they have died with Christ. This does not mean destruction, such as a widow being burned after the death of her husband. It more closely resembles what often happens in the case of a long and happy marriage. After the death of the husband, everything else (eating, reading the paper, going for a walk) loses its importance for the wife, and she soon follows her husband to the grave.

Through what has come about in Jesus Christ, all those things which seem so important to the Colossians lose their potency. Thus the Colossians become free and can die to the elements ("elemental spirits") of this world, precisely so that they can use these elements freely. For the elements have become elements of this world, and can no longer take the Colossians prisoner, or drive them into fits of aggression or depression. It is exactly this that will liberate us to do the will of Christ and to perform what others expect from us in the way of help and strength.

All these things are no longer important—taboos and demigods, purity of soul adhered to in an inhibiting way, or rapid advance in one's career;[66] and it is because we become free for other people and other things. The person who is basically already "above" with Christ no longer needs to worry about one's "heavenly ascent," either as a status symbol or as a moral superiority over others. For such people then, Christ signifies the exact opposite of depression, or feeling downcast, and below par. It is for this very reason, therefore, that one can allow oneself to "be brought down to the level of the lowly" (Rom. 12:16; rsv "associate with the lowly"). Freedom then does not mean arbitrary action; it is this point which the long section 3:1—4:1 proceeds to develop.

---

66. The fact that thus respect for a deep dimension to life, to which for example the secret of living prayer belongs, is not abandoned but is ex- actly what is being offered should certainly be borne in mind (G. Ebeling, "Das Gebet," ZTK 70 [1973] 206f.).

The Life that Comes from Faith (3:1—4:6)

The New Life as an Undertaking (3:1-4)

Bibliography: Merk, O., *Handeln aus Glauben*, 1968 (MThSt 5), 201-204.

1 If then you have been raised with Christ, seek the things that are above, where Christ is, seated at the right hand of God. 2 Set your minds on things that are above, not on things that are on earth. 3 For you have died, and your life is hid with Christ in God. 4 When Christ who is our life appears, then you also will appear with him in glory.

Analysis

The four verses form a typical transition section[1] linking the first part (1:12—2:23), which is didactic, to the second (3:5—4:6), which is exhortatory. "In Christ" is found exclusively in the first part and "in the Lord" exclusively in the second. This more or less corresponds to what can be ascertained in the case of Paul as well.[2] The believer is spoken of as being deeply rooted "in Christ," but he is summoned to walk "in the Lord."

Verse 1a (and 3a = 2:20) resumes what is said in 2:12f., while vv 1b, 2 summarize the admonitions which follow. (The positive appeals precede the negative warning and are emphasized by means of a Christological quotation, in a way which differs from what is found in 2:8, 16f., 18f.). Verses 3b, 4, by contrast, refer to the Parousia which is still awaited, and thus provide a reason for the tension between indicative ("you have already been raised"; RSV "you have been raised") and imperative ("seek what is above," RSV "seek the things that are above," cf. p. 122). Thus the two expressions in the second person plural are set on either side of the two in the third

---

[1] Zeilinger, *Der Erstgeborene*, 62f., understands it as the conclusion of the polemic, while Lamarche, "Structure," 460f., begins the exhortatory section as early as 2:16. However, 3:1-4 is quite clearly the basis of an admonition that is universally valid and that goes far beyond the specific case of the danger threatening in Colossae; hence it is better to begin the third main section

with this. Especially dubious is Lamarche's arrangement of the verses in the sections 2:16-3:2/3:3-17, which completely destroys the unity of 3:1-4. [2] Ludwig, *Verfasser*, 56f., 105-7; but cf. pp. 122f. of this commentary. Even outside this formula, "Lord" appears in Colossians almost exclusively in an exhoratory context.

singular, while otherwise vv 3 and 4 are completely parallel as far
as their form is concerned.[3]

This reference to the Parousia is unique in Colossians, although
there is an occasional allusion made to "hope" (1:5, 23). However,
whereas this hope is otherwise viewed as already having been given
to the believer, that is as providing the basis for the certainty of the
new life, the point emphasized here is that the new life still possesses a concealed character so that the admonition necessarily
results from it. The glory which already distinguishes God and Christ
at present (1:11, 27) will thus only be shared with the Colossians
at a later stage (3:4).[4]

Interpretation

[1] It is by means of the reference to being raised with Christ that
what is said in 2:12 is taken up as the basis of the call. The distinction, then, can be formulated in this way: in the gospel the call to
obedience is *because* one has already been saved and created anew,
while in the law, by contrast, it is *in order that* one may become so.[5]

The link with the preceding section, by means of "then" corresponds to Rom. 12:1 (cf. Eph. 4:1). The astounding assertion of
2:20, that they no longer live in the world, is accordingly to be understood in the sense that they can no longer understand the world
as the purpose and meaning to their life. The way this statement
is developed in 3:5—4:1 shows that it is not an escape from the
world that the writer recommends. On the contrary, it is only in the
world and their life within it that they can hold fast to this purpose
and meaning (and, since Christ's exaltation, both the world and their
life have, so to speak, been "brought to their proper home").[6]

The divine world lies "above" in the Hellenistic conception of the
world, especially as it is defined by Plato (cf. p. 131). However,

3. Zeilinger, *Der Erstgeborene*, 61
(the opposite pole to the Colossian
philosophy is the exalted Christ) and
62 (3b, 4b "your life"; 3d, 4d "in
God/in glory"); ibid., 147: vv 3f. = a
double expression typical of the style
of a hymn.
4. Cf. 1:27 "hope (or even: advance
gift) of glory."
5. De Boor, 243. The fact that resurrection is mentioned before dying (v

3) and that the state of being hidden
with Christ is expressed in the perfect,
in other words that it is not related to
a once and for all event, perhaps
shows that the symbolism of baptism
is no longer consciously maintained
(Schnackenburg, *Baptism* [v. note 34
to 2:8-15], 72). Cf. also above p. 180
along with note 21 to this section.
6. Ernst, 221.

according to Gen. 11:5 "the Lord came down to see the city and the
tower" (cf. Exod. 19:20; Ps. 14[13]:2); and according to Exod.
24:9f. Moses and those with him went up to see the God of Israel,
at whose feet the heaven was spread out like a pavement of sap-
phire stone. According to Ezek. 1:26, the throne of the Lord stands
above the firmaments of heaven; in Dan. 7:13 "one like a son of
man" appears on the clouds of heaven. Again, according to Eth. En.
17:2, Enoch is led to a mountain whose peak reaches up into heaven,
and according to 71:1 he does himself go up into heaven.

As early as Jub. 2:2, 11, 30 the contrast between heaven and earth
is combined with that between the spiritual and carnal natures.[7]
In Sir. 51:9f. the worshiper prays "from the earth" to his Father for
"deliverance" and indeed already offers thanks for this (vv 11f.).[8]
This idea is found still more distinctly in the Qumran community.
In their worship they have the experience of already living in the
"eternal height," "with the host of the saints" and "with the congregation of the heavenly ones." Yet apart from this link with "heaven"
in their worship, this is only true insofar as the individuals know
that they are predestined for salvation (cf. note 19 to 2:16-23).

Paul speaks of the "Jerusalem above" as distinct from that which
is "present (!)" or of the "upward call" as distinct from the future (!)
resurrection from the dead. Thus Paul uses his spatial concepts only
to interpret the eschatological difference (Gal. 4:25f.; Phil. 3:13).[9]
True, the idea of a resurrection that is already experienced goes
beyond this. Yet in this case the event that is expressed in the aorist
must also be given expression in one's life; hence it is that the
imperative is joined to the indicative. The truth promised in the
word can only come to life in the process of "seeking."

This truth might merely be appropriated by one accepting it intellectually, or even being convinced of the magical effect of the sacraments; or conversely the process of seeking might no longer be
rooted in the promise of the gospel. In either case, it would be as
absurd as if a person merely wanted to make a mental note of the
love she had experienced, in order that she could get back to her
everyday business again; or else, conversely, that a person should
try his hardest to love without admitting that he did himself need

7. E. Schweizer, *TDNT* VII, 109
along with the passages mentioned on
line 20; p. 120.
8. Cf. Sanders, *Hymns*, 135.

9. These concepts are used in a more
markedly dualistic manner in John
8:23: "You are from below, I am from
above."

love as well. What is said in 3:5–4:1 makes it clear that all this is in no sense intended as a merely individualistic matter.

This world above is characterized by means of Christ being seated at the right hand of God. This shows that the reference is to the basic confession; to be precise this reference is made by means of a phrase closely resembling a quotation from Ps. 110(109):1, probably the most frequently cited verse in the whole of the New Testament. In Rom. 8:34, sitting at the right hand of God involves interceding for humanity, while in 1 Cor. 15:25 the second half of this verse from Ps. 110 describes Christ's lordship over his enemies. Mark 12:36 (16:19), the Lukan corpus; Hebrews and 1 Peter 3:22 all use Ps. 110(109):1 to describe the Exalted One's position as Lord. Hence, in the use of this quotation here, one is clearly inclined to see a reference to Christ's lordship.

The main point of this reference is presumably Christ's authority over all spiritual powers (Col. 2:10). But there is also an echo here of the idea that he is Lord over those who are obedient to him, and who seek that which is "above." Resurrection is thus interpreted simply as exaltation; in other words, the primary concept here is not the overcoming of death, although that is also included. Rather it is the breakthrough which has been made into God's world, an achievement which is also effective for those who have been raised from the dead with Christ. It is noteworty that here, as in 1 Cor. 15:22-28, exaltation and Parousia are closely connected.[10]

[2] The verb used here means "to think," "to judge"; yet what this actually means is the orientation of one's whole way of life toward something specific. Clearly "above" and "on earth" are not actual topographical descriptions. Rather they designate a sphere in terms of which one can determine one's position. That is parallel to Paul's description of the sphere of the "flesh" and the sphere of the "spirit."[11] Paul's terminology is clearer in the sense that it includes, without further qualification, the possibility that God's spirit

10. This is surely the case with Paul in Phil. 2:9-11 as well, and was probably already so for the text that is taken over there. Further discussion of this theme is given in W. Thüsing, *Erhöhungsvorstellung und Parusieerwartung in der ältesten nachösterlichen Christologie*, 1969 (SBS 42), esp. 88-

99; E. Schweizer, *TDNT* VIII, 370-71.
11. Cf. Rom. 8:5 Τὰ τῆς σαρκὸς φρονεῖν, but in Phil. 3:19 τὰ ἐπίγεια φρονεῖν (in contrast to the πολίτευμα in heaven); the contrast is expressed more generally in Rom. 12:3; Phil. 2:2, 5 etc.

is operative in the life of the "flesh" on earth. It is admittedly more complex in the sense that what Paul wants to devaluate is not life "in the flesh," since all flesh is created by God, but only the state in which one's life is totally orientated toward the flesh (v. p. 162).

The situation is similar here where the language of the Colossian philosophy, with its ardent desire to escape from the "world" to the "above" makes its influence felt. The conflict between the Colossian philosophy and the author of the letter thus concerns the definition of the two spheres. The Colossian philosophy, probably in the course of the reawakening Platonism, evaluated everything material negatively and as a hindrance to the incorporeal soul. The higher one ascended through the elements, from earth to water, to air and the fiery region, the more one discarded everything material, until one attained in the "ether," the pure world of ideas (cf. pp. 131ff.).

The philosophy, then, understood "above" in a topographical or literal sense. The author of the letter, by contrast, begins, like Paul, from the Old Testament perspective. This, as it was further developed in early Judaism, had already mixed together, along with the contrast between flesh and spirit, that between earth and heaven; the world below and the world above as well. Yet the carnal natures are still basically God's good creation. The real trouble lies with one's own spirit, which rebels against God and refuses to accept the limitation of all humans as created beings. In other words, it is the way one thinks or is oriented that is to blame. Hence it is that Col. 3:2 calls them to return to where they should be, to direct their minds wholly toward God, and not to separate off the spiritual life from the corporeal. It is in their corporeal body that the community should be oriented toward God's will, and thus, as v 4 goes on to say, toward God's future consummation.

[3] The idea that the Colossians have "died," as it has already been formulated in 2:20 (taking up 2:12), provides the basis for v 2; hence it is that they belong no longer to the earth but to the world above. The sequel, however, is quite astonishing; the new life is a hidden reality. The sense of this really must not be weakened and merely translated by "stored"(12)for in the parallel expres-

___

(12) So more or less Moule, 112. C. H. Dodd (according to an oral communication, ibid.) even considers the possibility that all we have here is the image of death and burial as being concealed in the earth, over against which the believer affirms that he is hidden in God.

sion in 2:3 as well, the writer at least retains the mysterious character of what is not simply manifest. Here, in similar fashion to the
commentary on the hymn in 1:23, the following proviso is applied,
over against the danger that in their enthusiasm they will ignore the
realities of the situation: what is said is valid only when it is lived
out in faith.

Although the Epistle to the Colossians is formally acquainted
with the assertion (rejected in 2 Tim. 2:18) that the resurrection
has already happened, it maintains that this is so only in faith. In
other words, the new resurrection life remains firmly bound to
Christ, and hence cannot simply be at their disposal. The open-
ended nature of the process which begins with their dying in baptism is thus preserved. "The world knows neither Christ nor Christians, but neither do Christians really know themselves." [13] The
formulation "with Christ in God" is striking. "With Christ" is used
in v 4, as quite often in Paul, to express the fellowship between
Christ and those that are his, at the Parousia and in the consummation connected with this. Perhaps there are still some traces of this
usage here, although v 3 in fact describes the period between baptism and consummation. At any rate, "with Christ," together with
"in God," (a phrase conspicuous by its absence in Paul),[14] is described here as the guarantee of their new life. God's faithfulness
gives here and now a guarantee of that life which one day will
appear. In this way the writer expresses here what was said in 1:5
about the hope already laid up in heaven.

[4] This is the only verse in which the expectation of the Parousia
is still clearly given prominence. Since the crucial point in the context is the contrast between the life which now is hidden but which
one day will "appear," the same verb is used for the future appearance both of Christ and also of the believers. This verb is used by
Paul as a rule, to refer to the proclamation of the gospel. It is only
in a passing reference to the judgment that he emphasizes the moment at which something now hidden will become visible in the

13. Bengel, 821, and frequently cited.
14. Moule *RevExp* 70, 485, who also
refers to the non-Pauline usage of the
formula "with Christ" for non-escha-
tological circumstances, and to the
concept of being already raised from
the dead. In fact only Rom. 5:11
would be a parallel, but there ἐν is
dependent on the verb (likewise 1
John 4:15f.). In 1 (and 2) Thess.
1:1 the article is lacking and πατρί
stands alongside (likewise Jude 1);
cf. also I Thess. 2:2 (ἐν τῷ θεῷ ἡμῶν
λαλῆσαι).

future (1 Cor. 4:5).[15] In Col. 1:26 as well, the discussion relates to the revelation which has already taken place, although there it is connected with the schema of revelation, according to which God's wisdom, hidden for generations, has appeared in the gospel (thus, similarly 2 Tim. 1:9f.; Titus 1:2f.; 1 Peter 1:20). It is not otherwise used of the Parousia until 1 Peter 5:4; 1 John 2:28.[16]

This reticence concerning the revelation which is still awaited is essential in two respects. In the first place it forms the basis for the summons to a practical realization of faith in terms compatible with their life. Secondly it also maintains that Christ never becomes something we can possess or simply have at our disposal. It is he alone who will disclose, at some point in the future who we really are.

This disclosure is circumscribed by means of the concept of "glory." The fact that the community will at some point live in glory is what distinguishes their future consummation from the present, in which this is only promised to them. Glory, according to 1:11, 27 is the world of Christ or God, which, also according to 1:27, still awaits the community, even if it has already been granted them through Christ as a gift in advance. The qualitative difference of the life that is to come is provided by the fact that the future participating in Christ's life will unconditionally determine their lives and will denote full and complete fellowship with him. This gift of participation does of course remain in his sovereign right however much the community may put their trust in his faithfuness and be certain of it. This point is made explicit when the writer says that Christ alone is "our life." [17]

Life in its deepest sense then is not what is to be found in us, but what he, Christ, imprints upon us. Paul has the same idea in Gal. 2:20: "It is no longer I who live, but Christ who lives in me." [18]

15. Cf. also Rom. 1:19 (revelation in the creation) and R. Bultmann/D. Lührmann, *TDNT* IX, 4.

16. Here also, in 1 John 3:2, it is connected with the revelation of the real being of the believers. In 1 Tim. 3:16 it is the earthly appearance that is meant.

17. Whether it is "your" or "our" life that is spoken of makes little difference; the former is rather better attested, but the accommodation of the phrase to the second person plural that has dominated since 2:16, and to the same expression in 3:3, is more easily to be understood as a correction.

18. Phil. 1:21 is probably to be understood differently: life means, for Paul, to exist completely for Christ. Related passages are 1 John 5:12 ("He who has the Son has life");

But Paul is not familiar with the formulation by means of a substantive as it is found in this verse. In Colossians as a whole it is the spatial terminology of above and below which predominates; yet this verse interprets these terms as temporal categories. What has already been accomplished "above," that is in God's world, will only become visible "on earth" at some point in the future. Therefore the community lives fully orientated upwards, "above," where their future lies. That is, they look to their Lord for everything, for it is he who at some point will lay bare and fulfil what is already effective for them now; and they live in expectation of this by abandoning everything that vv 5-11 describe as negative and by performing everything that vv 12-15 set out as positive.[19]

Conclusion

This transition section links the promise of salvation (1:12–2:23) with the call to a new life which results from this (3:5–4:6). It is set in terms of the concept of the two spheres. In contrast to the Colossian philosophy, however, these two spheres are not understood as spiritual and material respectively. Hence the descriptions "on earth" (or "in the world," 2:20) and "above" are not to be conceived of in actual topographical terms, as though what were meant by salvation was the ascent from a constricted earth up through spheres which are less and less subject to material restrictions the higher one goes. Everything that is created is still God's good creation, even if, in contrast to the creator, it is limited and threatened. The fault lies not with what is corporeal, for even the exalted Christ and the angels are thought of in corporeal terms. The fault lies with the spirit of the individual, which is orientated completely toward the creature rather than the creator, so much so that the person looks to the former for the fulfillment of life.

Paradoxically, those who wish, by means of every kind of regulation concerning abstinence, to protect themselves from this world and sever themselves from it are the very ones who take it too seriously and look for salvation and disaster from it. Conversely, those who look to God alone for salvation become free to use this world (2:22), and are free to be of service within it (3:11-14). So the fact

---

Ign. *Eph.* 3:2; (7:2); *Smyrn.* 4:1; *Magn.* 1:2: Christ our unshakeable (reliable, perpetual) life (ζῆν).

19. On the relationship between eschatology and exhortation cf. pp. 230ff.

that he is no longer living in the world (2:20) and that he has
already been raised from the dead (3:1), is not then a position that
can be perceived in a verifiable way, as could, for instance, our being
on the top of a mountain, or even our elation in an experience of
ecstasy or meditation. Life "above" is described as a process of "seeking" life in the world which is totally shaped by the Risen Christ—
a life that looks to Christ for help and direction in every sense.

Thus the concept of spheres is set free from a purely individualistic interpretation. It is by means of baptism that the individual is
incorporated into the community, that is, into a company which has
this meaning imprinted on its life. In the same way, the "world" or
"earth" is always defined by the view that holds sway in it. However,
a warning is issued against any oversimplified division between
church and world. This is given in the statement that the new life
is "hidden" and will only "appear" at the Parousia. That means that
this life is not simply measurable, provable, demonstrable, however
much it must be lived out in specific acts (3:5–4:1). The most that
can be said about it is that the members of the community let their
lives be governed from "above," that is by the will of Christ. Thus
they are governed by what this will holds for them in the future. As
long as they do not allow themselves to be shifted from this (1:23),
the future, already fulfilled "above" (1:5), is a power which is
present in their lives.

Yet there is still more to be said. If their life is hidden with Christ
in God, if Christ himself is indeed their life, then that really must
mean that life in its full sense can only be what the Lord will one
day make of it, when he gives his "yes" to his disciple; it cannot
simply be what people already have on earth. So also with what a
person is—what is it that can convey that once that person has died?
The corpse certainly can't, no matter how beautifully decked out it
is; nor can one's posthumous reputation, no matter how glowing
this may be; nor can the memories that linger in the hearts of one's
friends and relations, no matter how happy those memories are.
Not even what in psychological terms it would have been conceivable for one to become, if an early childhood trauma or a misguided
education had not impeded one's development—not even this could
tell us. Least of all can the person's self-concept and self-image tell
us this. There is only one thing that can tell us what a person is, and
that is the verdict given by the Lord who will at that time appear.

The free and undeserved grace of God bestows true life and real existence upon the person.

The Epistle to the Colossians foregoes any description of the Lord's "appearing," as it is attempted in 1 Thess. 4:16f. and Mark 13:24-27. That which is inaccessible to the human imagination is not depicted. This is helpful at a time when our conception of the world leads us to recognize that the portrayal of a Parousia from heaven is a metaphorical way of speaking about something which cannot be described. On the other hand the point is still made that a faith not orientated toward a future consummation would not be a faith firmly rooted above.[20]

Both these points do, of course, belong together. When I learned to swim, the swimming instructor stood far above me and held me firmly by a rope. Way up above me was the person who held me safe and pulled me, the person from whom all the directions came. Both of these together decided my "future," that is, my being able to swim. In other words, the community possesses its future not so that it can have it at its disposal, but so that it can be motivated again and again by it. Its life thus remains something that is concealed until the final fulfillment. The community remains dependent on the word of its Lord which assigns to it what the community cannot detect simply by looking at itself; that is, the fact that it is accepted by him, that it is a settler in his world, and hence that it is always defined by that fact.

It may be noted that baptism is not mentioned again either in 2:20 or 3:1-4, and that the new life is portrayed here as being hidden in God. This shows that the community's dying and rising again in Christ has taken place, and that they are (through baptism) joined closely "with him." In other words, they have been brought by God into the new "world" which since Good Friday and Easter is given its definition by him.[21] To believe this means, in concrete terms, to live on that basis. It is this theme which is developed in the following section.

---

20. Cf. P. Stuhlmacher, *Schriftausle-gung auf dem Wege zur biblischen Theologie*, Göttingen 1975, 180. Zeil-inger, *Der Erstgeborene*, 149, does indeed also note this, but emphasizes the fact that the world "above" embraces heaven and earth and means rather what we term "desecularizing"

(so F. J. Steinmetz, *Protologische Heilszuversicht. Die Strukturen des soteriologischen und christologischen Denkens im Kolosser- und Epheser-brief*, 1969 [FThST 2], 31).

21. Cf. Lohmeyer, 127: "**In the death** of Christ . . . have all the faithful died." Cf. note 5 to this section.

The Old and the New Man (3:5-11)

Bibliography: Easton, B. S., "New Testament Ethical Lists," *JBL* 51 (1932) 1-12; Fischer (note 78 to 1:15-20) 58-62; Käsemann (note 25 to 2:8-15) 33-49; Kamlah, *Form*, 31-34; 122-126; Merk (p. 171), 204-224; Schweizer, "Lasterkataloge"; id., "Die Sünde in den Gliedern," in: *Abraham unser Vater, Festschrift O. Michel*, 1963 (AGSU 5), 437-439; Vögtle, *Lasterkataloge;* Wibbing, S., *Die Tugend- und Lasterkataloge im Neuen Testament und ihre Traditionsgeschichte unter besonderer Berücksichtigung der Qumran-Texte*, 1959 (BZNW 25).

5   Put to death therefore what is earthly in you: immorality, impurity, passion, evil desire, and covetousness, which is idolatry. 6   On account of these the wrath of God is coming. 7   In these you once walked, when you lived in them. 8   But now put them all away: anger, wrath, malice, slander, and foul talk from your mouth. 9   Do not lie to one another, seeing that you have put off the old nature with its practices 10   and have put on the new nature, which is being renewed in knowledge after the image of its creator. 11   Here there cannot be Greek and Jew, circumcised and uncircumcised, barbarian, Scythian, slave, free man, but Christ is all, and in all.

Analysis

The section is introduced by an imperative prefaced by "then" (cf. p. 122). This serves to draw out the consequences of what has been said thus far, and thus to form a bridge between the dogmatic and ethical sections. Corresponding to "put to death" [1] here is the imperative "put on" in the following section. This is likewise joined by means of "then" and expresses the positive summons parallel to the negative one found here.[2] This first section is further subdivided into two distinct lists of five vices each (vv 5-7/8-11). The first list contains the call to put to death the basic heathen sins (v 5). The motive for this is provided, in line with the traditional formula, by a reference to God's wrath (v 6), but the call is characterized above all by the fact that these vices are viewed as things which the community has already put behind them (v 7). The second list, by contrast, contains sins that are also encountered in the community, and which are "now" to be set aside (v 8). These lists are both summed up in the warning about lying and the basis for them is provided by the reference to the fundamental change from the old to the new

1. Similarly Rom. 8:13 θανατοῦν (νεκροῦν is used only in Rom. 4:19; Heb. 11:12 in a non-metaphorical interpretation of Abraham's or Sarah's body).

2. Ludwig, *Verfasser*, 107f.

person (vv 9f.), which has come about through one's entry into the new world of Christ (v 11). The two sections are skillfully linked together by the pattern of "once" and "but now." Through this, v 8 again takes up, chiastically and in exactly the reverse order, the same structure: specification of time—verb—subject—object.

Interpretation

[5] Just as the imperative "seek the things that are above" follows from the fact that "you have been raised with Christ," so also the admonitions "put to death, therefore . . ." and "put away . . ." (vv 5, 8) follow from the indicative "you have died" (v 3); and so again the positive counterpart, in the form of "put on" (v 10) is in turn added to these admonitions. The concept of the "earthly" is very curious. In order to understand it one should probably take as one's starting point the fact that, according to the Jewish view[3] the "passions . . . are at war in your members" (James 4:1). Paul also speaks of the passions and the law of sin that are at work in the members (Rom. 7:5, 25; cf. 6:13, 19). Again, according to s.Bar. 49:3 it is "the members that are now in sin, and it is by means of them that the sins are committed." According to the rabbis, there are as many commandments and prohibitions in the law as the body has members, so that every member invites man to be obedient to the command of God; but the evil inclination holds sway over 248 members.[4]

But what is the addition of "earthly" supposed to mean? Undoubtedly it is here conceived of cosmically: whereas the community is actually already living "above," certain members are still kept back on earth. All the same, how is this cosmic dimension to be understood? Is it in the wider sense such that the individual person is already living in heaven in his actual self, but is still kept back on earth by a few of his members? Or is it in the narrower sense, so

---

[3] In Hellenistic thought it is, at most, individual parts of the body that are mentioned; thus for example the lusts of the lower part of the body (Cic. *Or. in Pisonem* 66; cf. Philo *Sacr. AC* 33).

[4] Tg. J. I. (Gen. 1:27), ed. M. Ginsburger, Pseudo-Jonathan, Berlin 1903; Aboth R. Nathan 39, and on this Jervell, *IMAGO DEI* (note 6 to 1:15-20), 80; Strack-Billerbeck I, 901 (d); III 94 (b); IV, 472 (b), and on this R.

Meyer, *Hellenistiches in der rabbinischen Anthropologie*, 1937 (BWANT 4/22 88-93. Cf. further Test. R. 2:4-8; 3:3f.; the principle of the punishment of the sinful member is set out already in Wis. 11:16. Further discussion of this question is given in E. Schweizer, "Sünde." Tg. J. I. of Gen. 22:1 is also to be compared: Isaac is ready to give up all his members (and not merely that required for circumcision) to God.

that the members themselves represent the "body of sin," that is, a cosmic force, from which the community has been set free?

In support of the latter, one could adduce the parallel from the Naassene document, where Attis is "taken off," that is separated from the earthly parts (or members) [5] below, and raised up to the eternal essence above, where there is neither male nor female, but a new creation, a new person, which is male and female together (Hipp. *Ref.* V. 7, 15). A similar idea could lie behind the Gospel of Philip 123, according to which circumcision is considered as the destruction of the "flesh . . . of the world." [6] These particular expressions, it is true, are to be dated between one and four centuries later. Indeed, they are probably interpretations of what is said in Paul's letters and in Colossians.

Yet Philo, *Fug.* 110, shows that in fact the cosmic concepts in the narrower sense provide the background here. According to this passage, the High Priest, who has God for his Father and wisdom for his Mother (ibid. 109) represents the Logos when the priest puts on his official dress. For it is the Logos who puts on the cosmos like vestments, putting on first the earth, water, fire, and air, and then on top of this putting on what consists of these elements.[7] Creation, then, is thought of in terms of the Logos, which animates everything. This approximates the Stoic view of the Logos as governing all the elements. This cosmic event is repeated anthropologically in the birth of man, where the individual soul puts on the body, but above all soteriologically in the rebirth, when the reason of the wise man puts on the virtues. This last statement corresponds precisely to what Col. 3:12 demands.

What is presupposed in Philo's formulation is the concept, dominant in Greek thought from Democritus onwards, of the universe as a great human body and of the individual person as a microcosm,[8] such that the human reason in the body corresponds to the divine Logos in the universe. Thus Philo's conception of the world is relatively homogenous with his belief in creation. Just as the divine

5. Μέρη and ｉμέλη frequently interchange: Plat. *Leg.* 795E; Philo *Spec. Leg.* I 210; *Praem. Poen.* 125 (cf. *Rer. Div. Her.* 151); *Corp. Herm.* 12:21.

6. *NHC* II/3 (4/5 cent. A.D.)—W. C. Till, *Das Evangelium nach Philippus,* 1963 (PTS 2), 130, 29f.

7. Presumably it is the ether that is meant by this (*Aet. Mund.* 102); the elucidation of this passage is based on *Spec. Leg.* I 86.

8. Diels II, 153, 8; cf. Philo *Migr. Abr.* 220; *Quaest. in Ex.* 2:74 (members!); also *Abr.* 74. Cf. above note 9 to 1:15-20.

Logos, as mediator in creation, fashions the five elements to form the world, so the soul gives the body its life, and so also the virtues arouse the reason and will of the wise person. So then the virtues, which the person puts on, are exactly parallel to the parts (or members) of the cosmic whole or the human body. Just as the Logos holds together the parts of the cosmic whole (Col. 1:17!), so the soul holds together those of the body; and the virtues hold together those of the reason and will (*Fug.* 112).

However, where this concept was set primarily in Platonic-Pythagorean terms, as at the time of Colossians, the earthly world on the large scale or the human body on the small scale had become an obstacle which held the divine Logos captive. This meant that the virtues, in which the reason and will of the wise have their existence, had to be replaced by the vices, which test and threaten them. Philo himself can certainly speak of the soul, on its ascent to heaven, having to give back to each element what belongs to it (*Rer. Div. Her.* 282), by which he is thinking of something corporeal. However, he can also speak of the carnal element having to be "cut off" or "put to death" by the reason, and it is precisely in this connection that he mentions a list of the five vices, which is opposed to a list of five virtues (*Ebr.* 21, 23f., 69).[9] Thus we have come very close to the picture given in the Naassene document, the only difference being that Philo is clearly thinking in individualistic terms of the particular person in whose soul something earthly still exists.

Thus then the cosmic conception of the Colossians, according to which the soul must forsake the elements of the world and force its way up "above," suggests the idea of a separation (conceived of now in individualistic terms) of the body from its members, and thus from the vices which want to hold it on earth. All the same, there are still some points of detail which are left open. For the concept of the "members" one does not have to go back to the view of the soul deriving from Plato, in which the soul has to separate itself from the body and gather itself (or else, in the terminology of Porphyry ca. A.D. 300: its splintered members) to itself.[10] Still less

---

9. Ἀποκόπτειν τῆς διανοίας (69). By means of ἀναιρεῖν (69) ἀποκτείνειν is taken up from Ex. 32:27 = Ebr. 67. In § 23 the well-known four cardinal virtues take the place of the list of five in § 21. A list of five vices and virtues occurs also in *Virt.* 180, with se-ries of seven and four alongside it (Kamlah, *Form*, 107-114). On *Rer. Div. Her.* 282 cf. p. 131 above.

10. *Phaidon* 67CD; 83A; Porphyr. *Marc.* 10 (281. 1f. Nauck); H. C. Puech, in Hennecke I p. 275; E. Schweizer, *TDNT* VII, 1092-1093.

does one need to look to the way that Gnostic thought took this idea over and applied it to the cosmic man.[11] Nor is there any question here of the concept that sin forms something such as a cosmic body, whose members would then be the individual sins,[12] or the counterpart to these, the seven members of the Logos which represent the divine powers or virtues.[13]

In Col. 2:11, the "body of flesh" should probably be taken to refer to the individual person, and in 3:10 (v. ad loc.) the "new nature" is certainly to be understood in this way. Also it is scarcely conceivable that the idea of a cosmic body, which is in the power of sin and will be destroyed on earth, would be juxtaposed with that of the body of Christ, which likewise exists on earth but actually belongs in heaven, and which is growing (2:9). Again, however, the radical summons given by Jesus and the New Testament community to renounce one's own self [14] can be no more than in the background here, providing a parallel to the content but not enabling us to elucidate the particular image of the members.[15] The Jewish idea, mentioned above, of the vices being located in the members of the body, probably gave rise to the image in Col. 3:5; for the practice of making the elements, as members of the universe, parallel to the members of the human body and the virtues (or vices) was already current, as the evidence from Philo indicates. This explains why these members are classified cosmically as being "on earth" in contrast to the world "above."

As regards the quite remarkable lists of five vices and virtues, one can do little more than offer some conjectures. As far as their content is concerned, the catalogues clearly bear the stamp of a tradition that can be identified only in Paul's writings. That there should be five items in each list is thus probably fortuitous, as it may well

---

11. Fischer, *Tendenz* (v. note 78 to 1:15-20) 58-62: in the Odes of Solomon the image of the person with sense organs = members perhaps already merges into the Pauline image of the person as a member of the body of Christ.

12. Thus Severian, 327; Petrus L., 280B: Gomarus, 562b; Bengel, 821; Abbott, 820; Lohmeyer, 136 n3; cf. Calvin, 155 our nature "quasi massa").

13. Thus perhaps *Corp. Herm.* 13, 8 (2/3 cent. A.D.?) according to the interpretation of Kamlah, *Form*, 122-6.

14. Mark 9:43-8: ἀπόκοψον! Moule, 114f. calls to mind Mark 8:34; Rom. 6:4, 11; Gal. 2:20: 1 Peter 4:1.

15. The topos of cutting off fingernails, hair, and skin, as also diseased parts of the body, in comparisons in ascetic writings, a theme which can be traced from the earliest times up until Porphyry (around A.D. 300, *Marc.* 34 (v. note 10 above), p. 296.7; v. H. Hommel, "Herrenworte im Lichte sokratischer Überlieferung," ZNW 57 [1966], 13-16), plays scarcely any role.

also be with Philo. Here, indeed, one could do no more than suggest that the Colossians had consciously formed lists of five. These had either already been given their distinctive stamp, as far as content was concerned, by the Pauline mission or else had subsequently been accommodated to this tradition by the author of Colossians. The limiting of the list to five points would then be the only feature that would go back to the ideas dominant in Colossae.

What considerations would be relevant in respect of this? In Asia, as Chinese and Iranian instances from before the time of Zoroaster show, a dominant feature was a list of five elements and the parallels drawn between this and the exalted spiritual beings, which represent something such as virtues.[16] This is, in fact, what underlies the Hellenistic concepts, without there being any conscious realization of where they originated. In any case, the first instance is attested to in Diodorus,[17] at the time of Augustus, and the second in the passage from Philo, cited above (*Fug.* 110).

While it is apparent that the sequence dry-moist-cold-warm [18] should also appear alongside the usual sequence earth-water-air-fire (ether), it is more difficult to account for the extraordinary position of the fifth element, the ether.[19] It could, however, have been superimposed, in view of the old cosmic number of five equal elements. Both these series of four appear in a cosmic and anthropological form, in Philo (*Rer. Div. Her.* 282) in the very place in which he recounts how the soul on its ascent gives back what belongs to each element. So then, just as in Philo, the ascending soul left the four

---

16. H. Lommel, "Symbolik der Elemente in der zoroastrischen Religion," in: *Zarathustra*, ed. B. Schlerath, 1970 (WdF 169), 255-7 (a list of five vices as evil spirits ibid., 259); id., "Die Elemente im Verhältnis zu den Amesa Spentas," ibid., 377-84.

17. Diodor. S. I, 11.6 (Diels II, 243.1-5): the five elements: wind—fire—dry—moistness—gaseousness (ibid. 242. 35f.: fire—wind—moistness—dry, both together: air) are as parts of the cosmos comparable to the members of the body.

18. Philo *Rer. Div. Her.* 153; 282; cf. 208; *Sacr. AC* 108 (as elements of the human body alongside those of the cosmos); of Pythagoreans, Diels I, 449.10 alongside the usual ones (ibid.

6). As in Philo (and finally also Diodorus (note 17 above), the cold corresponds to the air here as well.

19. For Diodorus cf. note 17 above. Philo and the frequently-cited Pythagorean text only know series of four; yet in Philo *Fug.* 110; *Aet. Mund.* 102, the ether is mentioned as a fifth element; it does not seem to be transcendent in the strict sense as in other instances. Whether there is any connection at all with the Chinese weather-sequence: wind, warmness, wetness, dryness, coldness (Lommel, "Elemente" [v. note 16 above], 386) is a question that could only be answered if the date of the relevant Chinese texts were known and intermediate links could be indicated.

elements behind it, perhaps likewise in the Colossian philosophy it left behind the five, which were then equated with the vices. In both, however, this has already been taken over and applied to the individual person, where what is spoken of is "putting to death" (Col. 3:5; Ebr. 67) or "cutting off" (Naassenes; Ebr. 69) the carnal element or earthly members.

It was then an obvious step to make the virtues or vices parallel to the elements of the world. But is should also be noted that the number five, which in Pythagorean writings (and also in Schiller's *Piccolomini* II, 1) played a role of considerable importance as the compound total of the first even and the first odd number (2 and 3), was in use as well as the number of the perceptive bodily senses.[20] Manichean speculations, for which we have no evidence before than the third century A.D. at the earliest, scarcely prove anything more than that for the Manicheans the primal man was equated with the five elements of the world. This identification could indeed have been inferred from the passage in Philo, and these speculations are in any case not relevant.[21]

Whatever the influence of the cosmic language and the lists of five virtues and vices may have been, Col. 3:5-14 does in any case refer them all to the individual person (cf. on v 10). So the putting to death of the members, that is of the vices within them, is understood, from the perspective of the Jewish view of sins located in the members, to apply to the individual. The idea that these members exist "on earth," but that the believer is already "above," is (also referring to the individual person) the view usual in Hellenism. The real person (in Greek terms, one's spirit or soul) is already living "above," while it is precisely those members in which sin still takes effect that keep the person here "below."

Plutarch, at a slightly later date, can say that the human spirit is already floating in the firmament above, even if it still remains joined, as though by an anchor chain, to the soul which is life behind

20. Plut. *Is. et Os.* 56; *E. Delph.* 8; *Def. Orac.* 35 (II 374A; 388A-E; 429B-430A); Philo *Plant.* 133 (sense-perception). What the five "fountains" of Empedocles (Diels I, 369.14) are is unfortunately not known; perhaps they also represent the senses. Further discussion of this is given in Schweizer, "Versöhnung," 500, n30. For the

linking together of numbers and virtues cf. Diels I, 452.21f.
21. E. Schweizer, *TDNT* VII, 150 n401. Lohse, 137, thinks of an Iranian background of which the author was not consciously aware; against this, however, v. Schweizer, "Lasterkataloge" notes 40 and 41.
22. *Ser. Num. Vind.* 23f.; *Gen. Socr.*

(on earth). Again, reason is located as a demon outside the body, whereas the soul, in whole or in part, is immersed in this body.[22] According to 4 Macc. 1:29, reason sweeps away the urges that permeate body and soul and cuts them off. Philo (*Det. Pot. Ins.* 85) sees the feet of man as very much rooted on earth, but his spirit as already joined with the eternal circuits of the air and heaven.[23] Hence the terminology of the Epistle to the Colossians, and what it intends to communicate to its readers, probably does not go beyond what could be conceived of from the perspective of Jewish ethics.[24]

The effect of Hellenistic cosmic thought is probably restricted here to the first and broader sense mentioned above, that is, the idea, dominant from Plato onwards, of the soul which is at home above. It appears quite naturally here, since the central problem within the philosophy of the Colossians was precisely that of the soul's ascent from earth to heaven. However, the author does not distinguish between the soul and the body. Two points follow from this: first, the fact that the Colossians have been raised already or are at least orientated toward the world above is taken over and applied to the person as a whole; and second, the fact that they have slipped back into the world is taken to refer to the members in which, according to the Jewish view, sin is resident.

Probably the Colossians had already made the connection between the various vices and the elements, that is the members of the cosmos. Granted this, it is even more likely that they would accept the concept outlined above, even though the author himself certainly no longer understands it in this way. Indeed the continuation shows how little the author had in mind the idea that particular members of the body are evil as such. These "members" which hold one captive are not arms, bones, sexual organs, the belly or whatever, but the vices themselves which are enumerated.[25] Hence the discussion is hardly concerned at all with a straight metaphysical definition of the person,[26] but rather with whether one is molded by the members "on earth" or, alternatively, by the risen Christ.

In view of what has been said in vv 1-4, the world above must

22 (II, 563EF; 564C; 591DE); E. Schweizer, *TDNT* VII, 1041.
23. Further discussion of this is given in Meuzelaar, *Leib* (v. note 51 to 1:15-20) 103-5.
24. J. Horst, *TDNT* IV, 565.
25. On the following cf. the Excursus

"Lasterkataloge" in J. Blank, *Der Brief an die Galater* (EKK) on Gal. 5:19-23 and Schweizer, "Lasterkataloge."
26. So Lohmeyer, 137. It should be added that the character of sin or of the flesh (2:11) and the division into two classes of people (v. on 3:7) has

thus be understood primarily as the world which God will create
in the consummation at the end of time. The expression does, however, affirm that this world has already become present "above,"
that is where the community and its entire thinking abides, and
toward which it is orientated. The community is, in fact, already living "above" insofar as they direct their lives toward this world to
come and allow themselves to be directed by it in all the specific
questions of the present moment. The fact that their existence is
"hid with Christ in God" does indeed mean that the Risen One,
with his claim to be their Lord, is set over them and over everything
that they do, say, think, and feel. But at the same time it also means
that he becomes alive again and again among them with his help,
direction, grace, and forgiveness. It is in this sense that they may
even anticipate, by means of real experiences, something of the world
above which is still awaited and is not simply visibly demonstrable.

Hence what it is they experience is shown in the fact that they are
set free from actions that are ethically irresponsible. This liberation
certainly cannot yet be discerned in its full scope, but it is at least
in evidence here and there. Among the vices mentioned in 3:5 and
8, those of unchastity and idolatry, already interrelated with one
another in Judaism, along with that of avarice, which derives from
the Hellenistic parenesis, form a traditional group.[27] This group is
found in effect as early as 1 Thess. 4:3-6, as the content of the first
instruction given to the community, and in 1 Cor. 5:10 it is supplemented by "robbers." It is the absence of these vices which serves
to distinguish the community from the pagan world.

However, in 1 Cor. 5:11 this list has already been extended by
vices which could have infiltrated the community easier, such as
abuse and drunkenness. This is likewise the case in 1 Cor. 6:9f.,

---

to be heeded (cf. note 35 to 2:16-23).
Comarus, 570a explains that what we
have here is only a metaphor, on the
grounds that otherwise the commandment "You shall not kill" would be
annulled.

27. Vögtle, *Lasterkataloge*, 38f. Unchastity is a direct consequence of
idolatry (Wis. 14:12, 22-7; Ep. Jer.
43f.). Abomination of the heathen,
avarice, and unchastity occur together
in Test. D. 5:5-7, unchastity and avarice in Test. Jud. 18:2 (with idolatry
as their consequence: 19:1), unchasti-

ty, wealth, and defilement of the sanctuary in Damasc. 4:17f. (cf. 1QS
4:9f.). Gr. Bar. 8:5; 13:4 have presumably been subjected to Christian
influence. Lohmeyer, 138 n2 cites a
Rabbinic utterance which links together avarice, prostitution, and idolatry;
otherwise in the Rabbinic sources the
cardinal vices are idolatry, unchastity,
and shedding of blood, to which, however, in T. Men 13:22; S. Lv. 18:3f.
(Strack-Billerbeck I, 937; IV, 473)
avarice is added.

where unchastity is also enlarged on by three further ideas, and theft is added. Above all, 2 Cor. 12:20f., where Paul mentions only those sins which he fears he may encounter in the community, provides a completely different list, introduced by the triad of "strife (RSV "quarreling"), jealousy, and anger." This triad is repeated in Gal. 5:20 and in similar fashion in Rom. 13:13 and Col. 3:8 as well.[28] It corresponds also to the lists at Qumran, where the discussion is likewise concerned with modes of conduct within the community. Gal. 5:19b, 20a also, like Col. 3:5, goes back primarily to the basic community parenesis which pronounces the heathen rites of unchastity, idolatry (and avarice) impossible. Yet the summons "put to death" does indeed indicate a recognition that these vices could again infiltrate into the community (v. on v 8). The reference to previous instruction and the warning about the wrath of God are linked stylistically with the catalogue of vices (cf. on v 6, with note 35 to 3:5-11).

It is not certain whether or how one is supposed to distinguish the particular vices from one another. "Immorality" probably means illegitimate sexual intercourse, especially with a prostitute;[29] "impurity" means every kind of sexual excess; while "passion" is perhaps to be understood in the meaning given by a Hellenistic Jew: Eros is not a god but, in fact, destructive (or furtive) passion,[30] and "covetousness" is again intended to denote sexual lust that is wrongly directed.[31] The first of these expressions is enlarged upon by the other three. This is shown by the fact that the fifth ("covetousness") is separated from these four by means of "and" together with the definite article.

It is also clear that the old schema still exercised a strong hold on the author here. This schema connected idolatry with immorality and avarice; yet whereas idolatry was not a live issue in Colossae, the author still added it. Idolatry is, of course, a word which the

---

28. They are already mentioned in Stoicism (Vögtle, *Lasterkataloge*, 199f.), but they are found in more pregnant fashion in LXX (Sir. 40:4b; 28:10f.; cf. Prov. 6:34; 27:4; also Ezek. 16:38).

29. Further detailed discussion is given in B. Malina, "Does Porneia Mean Fornication?" *NT* 14 (1972), 10-17.

30. Pseud.-Phocylides, *Fragmenta* (note 20 to 2:8-15) 149-56, 194.

31. Cf. Gal. 5:16. Perhaps "evil" is to be deleted with p46G (cf. on v 6). Although the last two concepts are very much Hellenistic, the combination of them with the first two, as also the addition of "evil" (if this original), would not be conceivable in Hellenistic thought (Vögtle, *Lasterkataloge*, 208f.).

Old Testament uses synonymously and metaphorically for avarice, and it is joined on here by means of "which is," which is itself a typical stylistic flourish of the author.[32] The implications raised for present-day thought by this ethical devaluation of sexuality and covetousness will have to be considered in the conclusion.

[6] What is meant by the "wrath of God" [33] is the consummation of the final judgment. This is something which catalogues of vices readily refer to. The emphasis is in no sense on wrath as an emotion. So, for example, the whole section Rom. 1:18-32 speaks of the wrath of God and the death that is thereby threatening man. So also 1 Thess. 4:6 refers to God as the avenger of all wrong; 1 Cor. 5:13 refers to his judgment, and 6:9f. and Gal. 5:21 to the inheriting or not inheriting of the kingdom of God; while Rom. 13:11f. speaks of the "day" and "salvation" which have drawn near. In Eph. 5:5f., the promise of inheriting the kingdom of God and of Christ is linked with the threat of the wrath of God and of death;[34] a very similar formula is found in Rev. 21:7f., while 22:14f. speaks of entering God's city or of being excluded from it.[35]

[7] Corresponding to what was said in v 5, the sins mentioned there are now qualified as belonging to the past. The division of humanity into two classes is expressed particularly pointedly in 2 Cor. 6:14-16 (v. note 12 to 1:12-14). This interpolated section uses the key concepts righteousness-lawlessness, light-darkness (Col. 1:12f.), Christ-Belial, temple of God-idols. Rom. 13:12-14 as well, speaks of light-darkness, Christ-flesh. The eschatological component is certainly clear enough in Romans, while Eph. 5:8 links the con-

---

32. Yet Philo *Spec. Leg.* I, 23-5 also designates avarice as idolatry; for the Rabbinic material v. Strack-Billerbeck III, 606f.; cf. further note 27 to this section and, as far as content is concerned, Matt. 6:24 as well (Ernst, 225).

33. With Paul, the genitive "of God" is lacking on 13 occasions; it is found in Rom. 1:18, but there without the article. With the article it occurs only in Col. 3:6; Eph. 5:6; John 3:36; Rev. 19:15.

34. In Col. 3:6 it can be seen how strong the tendency is in the manuscript transmission for texts to be adapted to other writings that are even better known. Apart from in p[46] and a few of the church fathers, this verse has in the whole textual tradition been supplemented according to Eph. 5:6.

35. Cf. also 1 Peter 4:15-17; for this usage in Judaism, cf. Wis. 14:30f.; 1QS 4:11-14; Sl. En. 10:6 (with the key word "inheritance"; on this v. p. 226). 1 Thess. 4:2; 1 Cor. 5:9; 6:9; Gal. 5:21.

trast between light and darkness with that between "once" and "now," which is the dominant theme here as well.[36]

In Col. 1:21f., as here, this contrast distinguishes the situation before one believes from the situation when one is living in the faith. In 1:26, however, the distinction made between the time of salvation and the time of perdition preceding it is much more far-reaching. The force of this is still felt here. The world in which they live has become a new world; as they once lived "in" the vices, so now they live "in" God (v 3) or "in" Christ (2:10f.).[37] There is thus a fundamental process of turning toward Christ, and it is this which brings people into the new "world."

Just as this turning toward Christ quite naturally does away with any dependence on other gods, in other words idolatry, so also it renders it impossible that they should be bound to the forces of sexuality and money. 2:21f. has already affirmed that this turning toward Christ sets one free to use these things properly; it does not lead to some kind of cramped, abstemious existence. The fact that other things no longer have authority as gods or powers over us means precisely this, that we can use these things properly. They lose their sinister fascination and become natural objects which are provided for our use and which will also pass away again at some point.

[8] The really astonishing feature here, however, is that instead of an indicative introduced by "now, however . . . ," parallel to the indicative of the previous verse and denoting their state of salvation, it is a new imperative that follows. However, the transition provided here by means of an imperative is as striking and shocking as what we find at Rom. 6:4, where a statement about a resurrection which has already taken place is given up in favor of a reference to the way of life of the Christian community. Thus the novelty of the community's position cannot be described as though it was something which one could simply establish as a fact. It can only be recognized in the way that they go about their daily life.[38] Hence

---

36. Cf. "inside-outside" 1 Cor. 5:12f. For the superimposing of a basically differently conceived contrast between the two classes of persons (cf. note 35 to 2:16-23) by means of eschatological views in Judaism, cf. Schweizer,

"Menschensohn" (v. note 79 to 1:15-20) 110-12.
37. Cf. 1 Cor. 6:11 and, on the schema, Kamlah, *Form*, 31f.
38. This is a corrective against an "enthusiastic" misunderstanding (P.

those who read the letter are appealed to personally on this point by means of "you also." [39]

The list of the fundamental vices, which are now behind them, is distinguished as such from the list of those sins which could also appear within the community and which are now enumerated (cf. on v 5). This distinction may well be reflected in the choice of the slightly less severe expression here (that is, "put away" instead of "put to death"). However, "all" primarily serves to recall the things that have already been recounted, that is the list of v 5, so the writer probably intends to suggest that in the failings mentioned in v 8 there is still something that refers again to what has been put away once and for all. Thus the unity of indicative and imperative, which we have already remarked upon at 2:6, is in evidence here as well. "Put off" marks the transition to the image of clothing (vv 9-12).

In good Greek style, the adverbial phrase "from your mouth" ought to be connected with the verb. However, in this present passage it is presumably intended to be taken only with the last mentioned substantive or the last two. [40] Clearly the vices mentioned are those which affect relations between people and which endanger the community. "Wrath" denotes a continuous, smoldering condition, and "anger" appears alongside it as suggesting the outbreak of this wrath. [41] "Malice" is the basic problem, and probably refers to the dealings that people have with one another. "Slander" is otherwise used in relation to God, but in the context here, as in Titus 3:2 where the verb is found, what is meant appears to be the deliberate act of putting someone else to shame, perhaps in the form of a direct attack. It thus differs from "foul talk," which denotes spreading malicious gossip behind a person's back, but these distinctions of meaning are not clear cut.

[9] All this perverted behavior directed against others, particularly in the verbal form it takes, can be summed up by the term "lying." This is probably the case as well in Rev. 21:8; 22:15 and indicates

Tachau, "*Einst*" und "*Jetzt*" im Neuen Testament, Göttingen 1972, 125; he also notes the chiastic arrangement of vv 7f., ibid., 124).
39. Within the totality of Gentile Christians; in other words, is the traditional enumeration applied to them in particular?

40. So also Lohse, 140; cf. the frequent modal adverbial phrases with *en* (above, note 14 to Introduction).
41. Lightfoot, 212, with reference to passages from Stoic writers (Diog. *Laert*. VII, 114, etc.).

that lying in this general sense has become accepted usage.[42] However, the decisive point here is the summons to put off the old nature and put on the new.[43]

   The terms in which this expression is couched are exceptional. We are familiar from the Old Testament and the Rabbinic writings with this verb being linked with substantives such as power (Isa. 51:9; 52:1), righteousness (Ps. 132(131):9), salvation (2 Chron. 6:41), and shame (Ps. 35(34):26); they can also speak of the putting away of hypocrisy.[44] This could explain the expression in Col. 3:8, 12,[45] but not the image of the old or new person along with one's "members." Nor is any further help afforded by the classical usage of the assuming of a dramatic role or discarding the body in death and putting a new body on in the transmigration of souls. Linguistically, perhaps the phrase "put off the . . . nature," meaning "to become free from oneself" approximates Col. 3:9.[46] But this cannot be shown to be any more than a linguistic possibility; for the in-

42. Cf. Kamlah, *Form*, 33, n2. Apart from Eph. 4:25 (Rom. 1:25; 1 Peter 2:1), Ep. Jer. 44 should also be compared.

43. Ἀπεκδύεσθαι is a form found only in Colossians; Paul uses ἐκδύεσθαι. One could understand the participles in the sense that they describe what has happened in baptism (Ch. Maurer, *TDNT* VI, 644 n5, along with those scholars mentioned there). In favor of this is the fact that the continual renewal is distinguished from this by means of the present. However, since an imperative certainly occurs in v. 12, here as well they probably designate the way and means in and by which the overriding admonition "Do not lie!" (present imperative) has to be carried out. Nonetheless, the decisive character of the putting on and putting off is thus more strongly emphasized (inceptive aorist), because this forms the basis which has to be kept in a continual process of applying it to individual problems as they arise.

44. Strack-Billerbeck II, 301; Jos. *Ant.* 13, 220. Cf. also Plato, *Resp.* V 6 (457A): "putting virtue instead of clothing around himself (ἀμφιεννύ-ναι)"; all the evidence for the follow-ing is given in P. W. van der Horst, "Observations on a Pauline Expression," *NTS* 19 (1972/3), 181-6 and Pr.-Bauer s.v.

45. Similarly also Test. L. 18:14; 1 Peter 2:1; James 1:21; 1 Clem. 13:1; 57:2; Herm. v. III, 12:3; s. IX 16:2. From the Greek usage (Demosth. *Or.* 8, 46; Plut. *Coriolanus* 19:4: "to put away anger") similar expressions make their way into Judaism (*Ep. Ar.* 122: "to put away harshness and hardness of heart"); cf. Odes Sol. 11:10f. Kamlah, *Form*, 188, knows only one non-Christian passage which links ἀπόθου with a catalogue, and that is specifically in connection with the ascent of the soul through the spheres: Luc. *Dialogi mortuorum* 10:8 (although this is missing in the older manuscripts and only derives from the mid-second century A.D.).

46. The expression stems from the third century B.C., but is only attested first of all in a collection of the second century A.D., transmitted by Euseb. *Praep. Ev.* XIV, 18:26. It seems to have been well known, since it also appears in *Diog. L.* 9, 66 (van der Horst, "Observations" (v. note 44 to this section), 184-6). Perhaps all that

stances where this phrase occurs are not concerned with the putting
off of the "old" nature and the putting on of the "new."[47]

It is interesting to note that this passage is closely connected with
Rom. 13:12-14. In Romans, the summons is given to "cast off" the
works of darkness and to "put on" the armor of light. Thus this summons uses the same verbs as in Colossians (3:8, 10) and likewise
provides the framework for a catalogue of vices; it also conforms
to the expression "put on the breastplate of faith" (1 Thess. 5:8) and
the Old Testament parallels. However, the summons is taken up in
Rom. 13:14 by the call "to put on the Lord Jesus." This shows that
the ethical admonition to put off a wrong mode of life and put on a
right one (and this admonition is a relatively obvious development
from the Old Testament background), is in fact fulfilled by a com-
pletley different concept, which speaks of putting on Jesus Christ
himself.

According to Gal. 3:27f., this putting on of Christ is achieved in
baptism,[48] and results in a new world in which there exists neither
Jew nor Gentile, neither slave nor free, neither male nor female, but
all are one in Christ Jesus;[49] that is, the world of which Col. 3:11
likewise speaks. Rom. 13:12 points to this as well by speaking of
light and darkness, that is of two mutually opposed spheres in which
one can choose to settle; so also does Rom. 6:6, according to which
the "old self" was crucified (with Christ).

This has the idea in common with Gnostic thought that the believer receives a share in the destiny of his redeemer. In Gnosticism,
however, there can be no question of the believers as a whole dying
with him, in the sense of the "old" person being destroyed and a

---

is meant there, however, is "to flee
from the (cowardly) man (within
us)" (so Moule, *RevExp* 70, 489).
For ἀποτίθεσθαι one should compare
Max. *Tyr.* I, 4E (end of second century A.D.): "to leave off being a spec-
tator and to become a contestant oneself."

47. Strictly speaking, νέος means
"new" in the sense of "fresh, young";
however, καινός, in the sense of the
qualitative, eschatological new person,
the one who is of a "different nature,"
could not readily be used here because
of the verb ἀνακαινοῦσθαι.

48. R. Scroggs and K. I. Groff, "Bap-

tism in Mark: Dying and Rising with
Christ," *JBL* 92 (1973), 537, assume
that a change of clothing took place in
the early Christian baptismal rite.

49. An expression still more suitable
than "new world" would be "new
aeon," since it can be understood in
both a temporal and a spatial sense.
But this expression is so imprecise
that it is better to speak of "world,"
especially since the spatial dimension
is predominant in the metaphor. The
masculine form of "one" here shows
how much this "world" is thought of
as identical with Christ himself.

50. Certainly the images do overlap.

"new" one created. In Gnosticism the concern is that we in our
actual, innermost being, become free from what has hitherto hin-
dered us from really understanding ourselves. Again, in Col. 3:9, we
are close to the passage in Philo, discussed on pp. 183f., according
to which the Logos "puts on" the world as the wise man "puts on"
virtues. True, in Paul it is not a matter of the (Christ-) Logos entering a world and, as a unifying force, holding it together. This is
much more the case in the hymn in Col. 1:15-18. By contrast, what
we do find in Paul, as in Col. 3, is an analogy to the second half of
the Philonic image, which describes the believer's entry into a new
world.[50] Yet Gal. 3:28 and Col. 3:11 presuppose a "world" and not
of a series of virtues which indicates that the background to the
image still has clear cosmological and mythical traces.

[10] Here this background has been made fully ethical and been
given its significance in terms of putting on the virtues (v 12). This
shows a certain difference from the Pauline prototypes. Paul says,
on the one hand, of baptism that in this the believer puts on Christ
and thus enters a new world, the very world of Christ, and the
consequence of this is that these old antitheses previously in operation are now annulled through the all-justifying grace of God (Gal.
3:27f.). On the other hand, he summons those who have already
been baptized to put on Christ. The consequence of this is that other
desires cease (Rom. 13:14), and putting on Christ is identical with
putting on the armor of light.

In Col. 3:5-14 both these aspects are combined. The context is
clearly ethical, in the same way as Rom. 13:12-14; but v 11 takes
over from Gal. 3:28 the picture of what baptism really means. There
can be no question here of a repetition of baptism,[51] even if the
writer may have baptismal experiences in the back of his mind
(2:11f.). What the passage is in fact concerned with is the exhortation to really live out of the event (which is valid once and for
all) of having been called into the new world. This means an ethical
fulfillment of this way of life, in which the antitheses mentioned in
v 11 are overcome. In v 8 it is the vices (summarized by "all") and

---

Whereas Gal. 2:20b describes Paul's
life in the world, in 2:20a the formulation is the other way round: "Christ
lives in me"; cf. Rom. 8:1, 9f.: "Christ
in you/(you) in Christ—the Spirit in
you/you in the Spirit."
51. J.D.G. Dunn, *Baptism in the Holy
Spirit, London*, SCM, 1970 (SBT II/
15), 158.

in v 12 a list of five virtues that are the objects of this putting off and putting on.

The old nature can thus only mean the individual person (before one becomes a Christian) along with all that one does.[52] Likewise the new person (or nature) must denote the individual person who lives in faith; for continual renewal in knowledge is not an expression that could be used of either Christ himself or of the body of Christ.[53] Moreover, the act of putting off here precedes that of putting on, thus corresponding to the ethical admonition of Rom. 13:12, while putting on the Lord Christ (in spite of Rom. 13:14) actually comes before both of these. To be sure, the question of putting on Christ is not explicitly dealt with in Col. 3, since the section concentrates on the ethical renewal of the new person.

One may then ask whether the writer really adheres to Paul's view of the matter, namely, that this ethical renewal can consist in nothing other than a renewed return into the reality brought in by Christ and granted to all people, a return into the righteousness which has been given to believers and which wishes to assert itself fully in them. Yet in Col. 3:1-4 the same correlation is preserved in different terms. In effect, the act of putting on the new nature, understood in an ethical way here, is nothing other than what Paul calls entering into the world of Christ, and putting on Jesus Christ.

It is for this reason that the writer explicitly mentions that the renewal takes place according to the image of the creator. Thus on the one hand he affirms that it is a question of a new creation, and not just giving up a few vices and accepting a few virtues. On the other hand, he says it should lead to knowledge. But this expression, characteristic of Colossians, means ethical understanding. In no sense is it a matter of Gnostic insight into the nothingness of the material world. Above all, however, behind this metaphor (which is understood in an ethical sense) there appears a completely dif-

---

52. This must be the case for Rom. 6:6 as well ("our[!] old self was crucified with him").

53. Present participle! With U. Luz, "Das Gottesbild in Christus und im Menschen im Neuen Testament," *Concilium* 5 (1969), 765f.; against S. Hanson, *The Unity of the Church in the New Testament. Colossians and Ephesians*, 1946 (ASNU 14) 144f.,

and (more cautiously) C. K. Barrett, *From First Adam to Last*, London 1962, 97-9, who think of the new humanity. On the question of "knowledge" cf. pp. 40f. Rom. 1:21-3, 28 portrays those who do not have this knowledge in a blasphemous reversal, they present God according to their own human image (P. Schwanz, *Imago Dei*, Halle 1970, 53f.).

ferent message. The "image of the invisible God," [54] according to 1:15, is Christ.[55] This is also indicated by what follows; in any case, the world described in v 11 has, according to Gal. 3:27f., become an effective reality in Christ.

However, the idea is not carried through completely, for in the first place Christ is never depicted as creator in the New Testament apart from the Old Testament quotation inserted in Heb. 1:10, while in the second place, the phrase "its creator" can only refer to the (new?) nature, and certainly not to Christ. Presumably then one must understand this in the sense that the image of the one who created human beings (that is, God) is present in pure form in Christ alone. The new person is constantly assimilated to him, and is renewed again and again by him.

Thus it is not the old nature that is renewed; it dies! In faith, the believer enters a new world and puts on Christ—or, in terms of what happens to the individual, puts on the new nature. However, this is not a finished product; it is not "ready-to-wear," but is tried on again and again in the course of one's life to see if it fits. In other words, what is meant is not a mere wrapping, but a living person who is continually growing. It is to this "inner nature" that Paul refers (2 Cor. 4:16) when he explains that he is renewed every day, that is, in carrying out his apostolic duty and in suffering the afflictions that are part and parcel of this renewal.

[11] This is made clear once again in v 11. What is said here is not expected in this context; it recalls the fact that the prototype, from

---

54. On the linking together of the concepts of clothing with those of the image (of God) cf. J. S. Vos, *Traditionsgeschichtliche Untersuchungen zur paulinischen Pneumatologie*, Assen (1973) 96f.

55. In 1 Cor. 11:7 man (as male) can indeed be understood in the traditional way as the image of God (Gen. 1:26); yet 1 Cor. 15:49, where there is likewise an interpretation of Adam's creation (although according to Gen. 2, it is true), does distinguish the image of the earthly man from that of the heavenly, who has already become actual in the risen Christ. According to 2 Cor. 4:4 as well, it is only Christ

who is the 'image of God." It is in this way then that Col. 3:10 must be understood, and not merely as a repetition of the creation of Gen. 1 (Moule *RevExp* 70, 490 offers both views for discussion; Lightfoot, 214 thinks of the new creation in baptism). Verse 11 also argues for the reference to Christ as the image of God. He is thus probably both copy of God *and* prototype of the new person (Zeilinger, *Der Erstgeborene*, 155f.). For the patristic and medieval discussion cf. p. 283, for the idea of the new creation cf. H. Schwantes, *Schöpfung der Endzeit*, 1962 (*AzTh* I/12), 26-31, who also adduces Rabbinic material.

which such a renewal comes about, is the new world in which old
laws have vanished.[56] The one man who according to Gal. 3:28 the
community has become is Christ; in other words it is the new
world which Christ includes in himself and into which the believer
enters at baptism. This new world thus characterizes the believer
in the sense that, as an individual, the believer becomes the new
person who represents the image of God as it was intended to be
at creation.

The first and last pairs, "Greek and Jew," [57] "slave and free man"
are also found in Gal. 3:28 and 1 Cor. 12:13. The contrast between
"male and female" in Gal. 3:28 is found only there [58] perhaps because it was a phrase which helped to bolster an exaggerated enthusiasm. One new feature here is the explicit interpretation of the
first pair by means of circumcision and uncircumcision.[59] This points
to the fact that the issue here is concerned with more than merely
national barriers. The continuation by means of "barbarian, Scythian" is remarkable. To take this to indicate four nations set in the
west, east, south, and north respectively [60] is difficult, in spite of
the fact that the expression "barbarian" is occasionally applied to
Africans. The word rather denotes (especially in conjunction with
"Greek" at the beginning of the verse) anyone who is a non-Greek;
and for the west, the Romans would be more obvious than the
Greeks. Thus it is hardly a racial contrast between black and white
that the writer has in mind here.

The point in Col. 3:11 is to modernize and secularize the old religious contrast, perhaps for the very reason that being circumcised
or uncircumcised is no longer a contemporary issue. Thus the more
important theme here is the contrast between nations apparently
superior or inferior (according to the view of the time) in cultural
terms. Barbarian is then the term used to make this contrast, and
since a second member has to be added, a very far-off race and one
frequently designated as being especially barbaric, is chosen.[61] The

56. If the usage of the "putting off" of
the vices belonged to the myth of the
ascending soul, which leaves the cosmos and its elements behind it (but
cf. note 45 to this section and pp.
183f.), the link between vv 8-10 and
v 11 would be intelligible.
57. Paul has (but certainly with theological emphasis: Rom. 1:16; 2:9; cf.
3:9): "Jew(s) and Greek(s)."

58. D°G insert it again in Col. 3:11.
59. Perhaps it is influenced by Gal.
6:15, where the "new creation" occurs
in the abolition of this contrast.
60. Bengel, 822.
61. H. Windisch, *TDNT* I, 552-553.
Jos. *Ap.* II, 269: "differing hardly at
all from wild beasts." At any rate, the
new world corresponds to that before

tendency, already evident in 1:23, 27, to move the world mission, as representing Christ's triumphal possession, into the center of the events of salvation, is operative here as well.

There is a problem thinly veiled by this list. A person is born male or female and neither can nor should change this. This objection holds for the first three pairs here, at least if circumcision is no longer simply a sign of membership of God's people, and the so-called step of civilization is not seen as decisive. Nevertheless the Gentile can accept circumcision, or the Jew remove it (1 Cor. 7:18); the Greek can give up his culture, while the barbarian can adopt it. Hence consideration must be given to the question of whether in the community of Christ it should not basically be made possible for everyone, even those who are originally Jews, to give up circumcision, and correspondingly for everyone to have access to culture (or even to be set free from it!).

The last pair still more describes a human situation created by the social order, which is set on a different level to the natural division between male and female, and can be completely changed.[62] Clearly the main point is, simply, that in the new world characterized by Christ all these differences become unimportant, and hence where a person is encumbered by them they must disappear, as far as that is possible. Thus what is said here is not based on the Stoic view of a world citizenship in which only the inner person and one's spiritual life counts, so that all differences of nationality or class are, by comparison, insignificant. These differences are very much in evidence in Paul, and in Col. 3:11 as well; but they are set under the lordship of Christ, and are therefore no longer allowed to dominate, wherever others are suffering under them. Only Christ should count. He is the measure by which everything is to be defined. He is all in all.[63] In 1 Cor. 15:28 the same phrase is applied to God.

Underlying this formula is the Hellenistic and Stoic view of the world as entirely ruled and completely surrounded by God (v. p. 69f), a view which could eventually lead to making God and the world the same (v. note 38 to 1:15-20). True, it is not found as an actual formula until relatively late instances such as the invocation

---

the Tower of Babel (Kamlah, *Form*, 33f.

62. On this cf. Stuhlmacher, *Philemon*, esp. 67-9.

63. B א DG add the article, probably

through recollection of 1:16f.; here, however, the point under discussion is not the universe but the contrasts that have been adduced.

"You are *one* goddess, you who are all, Isis," or the hymn of praise to Heracles as "the sun (taking effect) in all and (penetrating) through all."[64] But without doubt similar phrases were mediated to the New Testament authors via Hellenistic Judaism, as is obvious from for example Philo's account in *Spec. Leg.* I, 208, according to which "the universe is one or from one and toward one." However, even in this passage alongside the statement about being, the statement about becoming also appears, specifying the origin and purpose of the being; and all the more in Col. 1:15-18 the biblical belief in creation and fulfillment takes effect.

In Col. 3:11, the clause which says that Christ is "all" refers to the antitheses already mentioned. These are limited, in historical terms, and are overcome by the fact that Christ lives and takes effect in all.[65] Here, as in the address to Heracles cited above, "all" can be understood as masculine or neuter, that is, it can be taken to refer to people or things. Probably then it ought to be understood in the sense that Christ, who has become human, has taken upon himself everything that is involved in being a human, has become everything, and in the cross and resurrection (2:14f.) has overcome everything that could stand in opposition to being one. This much we may say, even if we may not go so far as to interpret the phrase as "Christ lives in relation to all and within all."[66]

Conclusion

Underlying this passage there are some great Pauline themes, those which conceive of an entirely new world, which has already become an effective reality in Jesus Christ, a world which overcomes religious, national, and social differences and in which heaven has already broken through. It is into this world that the believer is removed. However, everything is now expressed in ethical categories.

64. Dessau *Inscr. Lat. Select. II*, 4362 (date?); Macrob. *Sat.* I, 20:11 (c. 400 A.D.).

65. R. Schnackenburg, "Der Neue Mensch—Mitte christlichen Weltverständnisses, Kol 3, 9-11" in id., *Schriften zum Neuen Testament*, Munich 1971, understands this as masculine, "in everyone" (cf. Severian 327: in all who are obedient to him). Over against every kind of effusive equating of church and glorious state he also emphasizes that Christ is both the image and also the goal (ibid., 404f.), and hence that one has to differentiate Christ and church, however much they are bound together (id., *Gestalt und Kirche nach dem Epheserbrief*; ibid., 273f.; cf. pp. 282ff. of this commentary).

66. Greek accusative; v. W. Thüsing. *Per Christum in Deum* 1965 (*NTA* I) 244.

The discussion is no longer exclusively concerned with Christ, whom the candidate for baptism "puts on," but rather with the "new nature," that is the form to which Christ wants the individual, to progress. Moreover it is affirmed that this new creation is not something settled once and for all at baptism; rather, the new person must be daily renewed. In baptism the old Adam is indeed drowned; but the scoundrel can still swim!

In a certain sense, then, one can speak of the theme being made trivial here; but it is precisely this "trivial" aspect that is decisive. What has happened on a cosmic scale in the Christ event cannot simply be appropriated as knowledge. It only comes alive as it is made to apply at every point in the everyday life of the community, where for instance one meets one's neighbors and talks to them, or else talks about them in their absence. It is for this reason that in addition to the list of those pagan vices which the believers have left behind them, there is a further list of misdeeds which they must still struggle to subdue. These misdeeds cannot merely be defined as pagan, nor can they simply be exposed as abhorrent; and yet they so often make the common life of the community difficult or even impossible.

The point about all these misdeeds is that:

- gnawing anger can strain lifelong relationships
- wrath can explode, throw off all constraints, and utter ill-considered sentiments which cannot be taken back
- malice forces one's life to be lived to the detriment of one's neighbor
- wickedness hurls abuse at someone without knowing how much distress it causes
- gossip lurks behind people's backs and is impossible to pin down, but makes life virtually unlivable.

These are the ways the old and earthly world—although brought to an end by Christ—still reasserts itself in individuals and in groups. It is not enough simply to raise an accusing finger against these misdeeds. They should all be cast aside, just as on a hot day children throw off their clothes so that they can be completely free and unrestricted (v. on v 7).[67]

---

67. I cannot resist recalling a pun that defies translation from the closing lines of a superb poem by Eugen Roth, which depicts a scholar at an open-air bathing spot who ". . . zieht wieder, was er abgetan, die Kleider

The same proviso also applies to the list of vices enumerated in
v 5, according to the traditional pattern. They are primarily concerned with sexual misconduct, and they express the point of view
of an age which is not the same as our own. However, the continuation of this theme in the following verses (6-11) shows that at least
the point of the passage is not a "pure soul" or the perfection of
the individual. Rather, it is the possibility of a common life in which
other people are caused as little harm and suffering as possible. It is
as relevant today as it was at the time of the Epistle that sexual behavior, in which one has no real interest in the other person, turns
out to be shallow and disconsolate.

That this genuine interest in the other person must be effective
beyond the confines of the community is not explicitly considered
here. Rom. 12, on the other hand, proceeds from discussion of conduct which is purely internal to the community (vv 3-8, 11-13), or
where the limits are not very clearly defined (vv 9f.), to consideration specifically of conduct vis-à-vis those who stand outside the
community (vv 14f.; cf. p. 243). A new life of this kind is not possible except in the knowledge that the community continue to live
"in Christ"; that they dwell, so to speak, in the atmosphere which
allows them to live and which permeates them completely. Christ
is the image that fashions their entire life, just as the mother's
image which the baby sees every day governs it to such an extent
that it could not live without it, even if all the nourishment and
medical care it needed were otherwise provided.

So then, every single aspect of our lives, all the limitations set on
us by our birth, upbringing or class, in every point of our lives, are
seen to be unimportant. Neither an inferiority complex on the part
of the uncircumcised nor arrogance on the part of the circumcised
has any place. For assistance will no longer be patronizingly dispensed; instead it will be taken for granted in dealings between
two people who both know that they derive their life only from the
One who "is all, and in all."

Life in Christ's World (3:12-17)

12 Put on then, as God's chosen ones, holy and beloved, compassion, kindness, lowliness, meekness, and patience, **13** forbearing

---

und den Doktor an und macht sich,
weil er fehl am Ort, zwar nicht sehr

galtend, aber fort" (*Ein Mensch*, Wei-
mar[9] 1937, 119).

one another and, if one has a complaint against another, forgiving each other; as the Lord has forgiven you, so you also must forgive. 14 And above all these put on love, which binds everything together in perfect harmony. 15 And let the peace of Christ rule in your hearts, to which indeed you were called in the one body. And be thankful. 16 Let the word of Christ dwell in you richly, as you teach and admonish one another in all wisdom, and as you sing psalms and hymns and spiritual songs with thankfulness in your hearts to God. 17 And whatever you do, in word or deed, do everything in the name of the Lord Jesus, giving thanks to God the Father through him.

Analysis

This section, like the preceding one, begins with an imperative introduced by "then." In contrast to the negative inference drawn from the portrayal of salvation in Christ and faith in him, the positive aspect is now presented. Again a list of five nouns follows, but this time it is a list of virtues. In v 13 this list is applied to particular relationships within the community, while in v 14 it is summed up in the call to love. This roughly corresponds to the summary in v 9, which consists of a warning about lying.[1] Then in vv 15-17 [2] the author blesses them by proclaiming peace to them by a formulation which elsewhere is found at the end of a letter instead. These verses also include a summons to a proper life of worship, and this summons is set within the framework of an exhortation to give thanks to God (vv 15-17).

Interpretation

[12] Continuing the image of putting off and putting on, the author appeals to his readers to choose the way of love. The verb in the aorist emphasizes the actual moment at which this commitment is made, although the commitment should lead to appropriate conduct being put further into practice. If as in v 5, "then" refers back to the promise of salvation in the preceding section, so also the summons here, by recalling their position as "God's chosen ones" (or "elect"), is anchored explicitly in what has already happened to them. Since they have been saved they should prove faithful.

---

1. Cf. also "idolatry" in v 5, although there it is ascribed only to the last member of the list.

2. Ludwig, *Verfasser*, 108 takes this to be a third section (after vv 5-11/12-14).

The adjective "elect" is found in Paul only in Rom. 8:39; 16:13, specifically in relation to the person who believes in Christ, while the noun "election" features significantly in the discussion of Israel's destiny (Rom. 9:11; 11:5, 7, 28). It is her election by God that sets Israel apart from the nations. The adjective is certainly used in this traditional way here, but without involving the idea that the Colossians, in their ethical behavior, should become like the Jews or, still less, like the heavenly company of angels.[3] They are called "holy" as in 1:2 (v. ad loc.). "Beloved (brothers)" is found in this precise form only in 1 Thess. 1:4, 2 Thess. 2:13; but the same three terms are mentioned in Rom. 1:7, although in somewhat different expressions and in a different order. Once again then there is some evidence of assimilation to Pauline style, without this lapsing into slavish imitation.[4] All these designations emphasize the way the community is made separate by the love of God which he has bestowed upon them. Their conduct is characterized by compassion,[5] kindness,[6] humility[7] (RSV "lowliness"), weakness[8] and patience (cf. p. 44).

The second concept and the last two appear in the catalogue in Gal. 5:22f. as well. In themselves all these terms are already current.

---

3. Against Lohmeyer, 145; ὡς here means "as" not "like." Cf. 1 Chron. 16:13; Ps. 105(104):6; 1QpHab. 10: 13, etc.; in 1 Peter 2:9 the adjective is used referring back to Israel; otherwise it occurs in the Synoptics and the Pastorals. For the verb v. 1 Cor. 1:27f.; it is not found otherwise in Paul.

4. Ludwig, Verfasser, 50f.

5. Phil. 2:1 σπλάγχνα καὶ οἰκτιρμοί; cf. further Luke 1:78; Test. Zeb. 7:3; 8:2 (6 [bg]) σπλάγχνα ἐλέους. In Hellenism there is no evidence to be found for the "bowels" as a seat of mercy (cf. "heart" in English) before New Testament times (H. Köster, TDNT VII, 549; cf. p. 556; for the Old Testament background cf. also G. Sellin, "Lukas als Gleichniserzähler," ZNW 66 (1975), 49f.

6. As a Greek virtue in this sense (K. Weiss, TDNT IX, 484; 489) it is found already in Philo alongside the graciousness of God attested in the Old Testament (ibid., 490). It is

found in Pauline lists in Gal. 5:22; 2 Cor. 6:6 (Eph. 4:32).

7. cf. p. 158f. In context of 3:12 it is not fasting but conduct toward other people that is to be thought of. Over against a boastful, self-obtrusive "humility" (2:18), the splendid saying of Max Scheler (cited by de Boor, 237, on 2:18) should be called to mind; there are virtues which may only be glimpsed on the back of the one who is putting them into practice; here the "doing" is to be emphasized just as much as is the fact that one only discovers in retrospect what has been done. In the Greek-speaking world the concept is negatively evaluated (W. Grundmann, TDNT VIII, 1-4; 11-12).

8. This is, contrary to the humility, highly esteemed among the Greeks, although it is true that it is set within certain limits (F. Hauck & S. Schulz, TDNT VI, 646). It is used of Christ in 2 Cor. 10:1).

in Hellenistic Judaism; but the next verse indicates the distinctive New Testament emphasis. It is also noteworthy that whereas the four Greek cardinal virtues certainly appear in Wis. 8:7, they are not found in the New Testament.[9] The list in 1QS 4:3, by contrast, provides a certain parallel to Colossians, since it begins with "lowliness, patience, rich compassion, eternal kindness," has "intelligence, insight, wisdom" (Col. 3:10; 2:2f.) following, and also mentions (4:5) "love" (but only in relation to the sons of truth!).

Thus traditionally catalogues of vices are formulated in much stronger terms; a warning about evil is easier to set in concrete terms than is a positive summons to good. This not only corresponds to general human experience; it is also required theologically. Thus in Gal. 5:19-23, in contrast to the "plain works of the flesh" we find the "fruit of the Spirit," which is only in the singular, and cannot be called either "plain" or a "work."[10] This fruit certainly grows in particular actions, but it cannot simply be displayed and defined. Thus one can detect a certain novelty in the New Testament, vis-à-vis non-Christian lists, in that the triad "faith, hope, love" (1 Cor. 13:13; 1 Thess. 1:3; 5:8) appears again, (although connected with other virtues, it is true), as "faith, love, forbearance (or patience)" in the catalogue of virtues in Gal. 5:22f.; 1 Tim. 6:11; 2 Peter 1:5-7; 1 Clem. 62:2. In Col. 3:12 as in 2 Cor. 4:6-7, faith does not appear, while in v 14 love is adduced as the all-inclusive concept (v. ad loc.). Likewise, there is no mention here of knowledge (but see v 10), and abstinence, (or moderation; RSV "self-control"), which are connected in (2 Cor. 6:6f.), 2 Peter 1:5-7; Barn. 2:2f. with the remaining two or three expressions.[11]

[13] All five ways of life are also ascribed by Paul to God or Christ.[12] Thus all five are intended to lead on from the way that God acts toward his people to the way that people act toward one

9. Σωφροσύνη, φρόνησις, δικαιοσύνη, ἀνδρεία (instances in Kamlah, Form, 139-44) also occur in Philo Ebr. 23 (v. above note 9 to 3:5-11). Other sequences of virtues are given in H. D. Betz, Lukian von Samosata und das NT, 1961 (TU 76) 206-11.
10. In typical fashion, however, the reference to the Spirit is lacking in Col. 3:12 (v. pp. 38f.).
11. Gal. 5:22; 2 Cor. 6:6; Col. 3:12

(cf. 1 Clem. 62:2) μακροθυμία; 1 Tim. 6:22; Titus 2:2; 2 Peter 1:6; 1 Clem. 62:2 (cf. 2 Cor. 6:4) ὑπομονή; 2 Tim. 3:10; Barn. 2:2 both; γνῶσις, μακροθυμία, ἀγάπη, int. al. in 2 Cor. 6:6. Ἐγκράτεια is linked with faith, hope, love in Gal 5:23; 1 Clem. 62:2 (cf. 2 Cor. 6:4f. for the content).
12. Rom. 12:1; 2 Cor. 1:3/Rom. 2:4; 11:22/Phil 2:8/2 Cor. 10:1/Rom. 2:4; 9:22.

another. This point is now set out explicitly and thematically. Their forgiving should flow from the gracious way in which the Lord bestows forgiveness.[13] The "Lord" is the exalted one whose forgiveness the community has experienced; it does not mean the earthly Jesus whose activity they know about only through reports they have heard. The idea already expressed by means of the present tense ("forgiving") is further underlined by the formulation "forbearing one another" and by the reference to the "complaint" which they might make against one another. In other words, it is a matter not of a single unique act of forgiveness, but of going on forgiving in this way at every moment of their daily life.

[14] The writer, by making Christ's activity the basis for his admonition, has already introduced the unequivocally New Testament aspect; and so now he uses the concept of "love" to sum up the five modes of conduct already mentioned. In Rom. 13:8-10 as well, the love command is used to sum up, comprehensively, the call to cast off the works of darkness and to put on the armor of light, that is Jesus Christ himself (13:11-14). Likewise in Gal. 5:14, the love command dominates the enumeration of the works of the flesh and the fruit of the spirit (5:19-24). In itself the command means that love should be put on (v 12) in addition to everything that was enumerated in vv 12f. However, the addition "bond of perfection"[15] (RSV "which binds everything together in perfect harmony") does indeed show that love is not simply a further item brought in alongside the others; rather it is the source from which all those qualities hitherto mentioned derive their existence.

It is very doubtful whether there is still any lingering trace here of the cosmic concept of that which holds together the whole new world of Christ (as Christ, according to 1:17, holds the universe to-

---

13. Christ as subject is completely exceptional; even Col. 2:13 speaks of God's forgiveness. "God" (א °) or "God in Christ" (33arm) is probably an adaptation to Eph. 4:32; "Christ" (א᪅Cא etc.) is no doubt an interpretation of the original "Lord" (p⁴⁶B etc.) and at the same time an approximation to the Pauline formula καθὼς καὶ ὁ Χριστός (Rom. 15:7; Eph. 5:2, 25, 29; cf. Rom. 15:3; Mark

10:45; 1 Peter 2:21; 3:18; Dahl, "Beobachtungen" [v. p. 99] 6f.).

14. As for other passages, cf. Rom. 12:9; 1 Cor. 13; Matt. 22:39f. etc. and this present chapter from v. 12 to the end. To be a Christian means then not to be faultless but to be able to live properly with mistakes (Caird, 207).

15. In place of ὁ א °D° read ὅς, and א ἥτις; cf. note 17 to 1:15-20.

gether).[16] In light of v 13, one must surely think in terms of love binding together the community (and not the various virtues).[17] However, it is true that this peace is in fact created only by the world which is portrayed in v 11 and which has come about in Christ. Further, it is this peace that brings about the abolition of the class distinctions which mislead the community into identifying (higher class with higher value. It makes no great difference whether one understands the genitive "in perfect harmony" as qualitative the perfect [perfectly binding] bond),[18] or as in apposition ("that is perfection")[19] or perhaps better as objective ("that leads to perfection (or creates it)").[20] In one way or the other, love makes the community into a unity and is described as the fulfillment of all that has been portrayed.

[15] At this point the writer abandons the set of images about putting garments on and off, along with its cosmic implications. This verse not only has the function of expressing a prayer for peace (as does the expression which appears at the end of the Pauline Epistles).[21] The peace mentioned is, in context of vv 13f., that peace which belongs specifically in the common life of the community. True, it is designated, in the sense of v 11, as peace which is given by Christ and brought about by him. For that reason one can only be "called" into it. The "one body" in which this takes place is therefore most probably the body of Christ, the church, (1:18, 24; 2:19), although this expression, without the article and without the genitive "of Christ," can also designate, metaphorically the unity of a group.[22]

16. Moule, 124 mentions it as a possibility; Calvin, 158; the perfect bond, which embraces all virtues. Corp. Herm. 13:14 knows the idea of a "body which is made up of the powers of (God)", and Plat. Polit. 47 (310A) calls the noble mind a divine bond which holds together the various, divergent parts of human virtue (ξύνδεσμος ἀρετῆς); according to Simplicius, (sixth century A.D.!) in Epict. 208A (S. 89, 15-17), the Pythagoreans consider φιλία (love between friends) to be a bond of all virtues.
17. So Lohse, 148f.
18. Masson, 146 n7 considers this as

a possibility, as does Moule, 123 ("the bond which completes them"). The article can be found even in the case of a genitive of quality (BFD 165 and appendages to this).
19. Lohmeyer, 147: the unity is perfection (on this concept cf. p. 112).
20. BDF 163 appendage; Dibelius-Greeven, 43f. (with linguistic parallels); Lohse, 149 (final genitive).
21. In Phil. 4:7, 9 it is likewise somewhat earlier in the composition of the letter.
22. The divided Peloponnese should become "one body" (E. Schweizer, TDNT VII, 1041; cf. 1039).

The distinctive feature here is that stress is laid on the fact that this peace must enter the hearts of the members of the community; that is, it must enter their feelings, thoughts and wills,[23] and must begin to reign there and set their priorities in order.[24] In this way what is in Christ can become real in the actual way that the community lives.[25]. As already in 1:12; 2:7, and again in 3:17, the writer summons them to thanksgiving (*eucharist* in Greek). Verse 16, inserted between this verse and v 17, shows that such thanksgiving should manifest itself in the community's worship.

[16] The subject of this worship is not in fact the community, although the verse, as it continues, goes directly over into the plural; rather, it is the word of Christ itself.[26] It is what Paul calls the "gospel," although this should not be thought of as a definite sum of fixed phrases such as is found, for instance, in a book, but as the living event of the proclamation, in which the exalted Lord is himself at work, rousing people to action and thus making his way through the world. It is for this reason that the writer can speak of the word dwelling "in you richly." The word of Christ is not something that one becomes aware of and then possesses; it is something that "dwells" in a person, and can do so either richly or feebly. In other words, its presence can make itself felt either hardly at all or else by completely permeating a person. It lives then for the very reason that Christ himself lives in it.

In a similar way, Ps. 37(36):31 speaks of the law dwelling in the

---

23. So in the Old Testament; since it is the whole person that is thus paraphrased, "in you" (v 16) can likewise properly be said.

24. The word describes the apportioning of a prize in sport; that is, the peace of God that comes alive in the individual distinguishes what is of primary from what is of secondary importance and so on. This happens in such a way that, with reference to the heavenly Lord firmly in mind, the desire is no longer to gain as much profit as possible from one's slave, but instead to do what is just and fair (assimilating them to their master; 4:1). Thus peace becomes the arbiter, taking the place of the disqualified

arbiter of 2:18 (so already Severian 328).

25. So also Phil. 2:5. The idea that this must grow out beyond the confines of the community is not yet conceived of here, but for the present day it undoubtedly has to be borne in mind.

26. Paul speaks of the "word of God" (as in Col. 1:25) or, in accordance with the content, of the "word of the cross" or "of reconciliation"; but he does speak once as well, in 1 Thess. 1:8, of the "word of the Lord" (in 4:15 the reference is presumably to the earthly Jesus). The genitive can then designate originator and content (the latter is to be preferred here; Houlden, 206).

hearts of people.[27] As in 4:5 (cf. 1:9-11) the phrase "in all wisdom" is better taken with what follows, as a more precise definition of the community's activity.[28] Because the word of Christ is present in the living event of the proclamation, the writer can speak without further ado of teaching and admonishing. Here also the fundamental practice of the apostle (1:28) is taken over as the function not of some official within the community, but of the community as a whole. Presumably the dual expression (teaching and admonishing) embraces both the proclamation of God's saving activity and also the admonition to live on the basis of that; nor is it possible to separate the two from each other.

Alongside this expression "singing" appears. Since in the Greek there is no "and" in between, one could understand this to mean that the teaching and admonition take place in the singing. But it is explicitly stated that the singing be directed toward God, whereas the teaching-admonishing is related to members of the community. So very probably these three expressions (the dwelling of the word, teaching and admonishing, singing), although juxtaposed, are not subordinated to each other. Psalms, hymns and spiritual songs clearly cannot readily be distinguished from one another.

Rev. 19:1-8 shows that the community there, presumably spontaneously, sang phrases and themes from the Old Testament in a contemporary form adapted to their present situation.[29] However, definite hymns with a more fixed form, as in Col. 1:15-20, had also grown up, although perhaps only gradually. These hymns are probably called "spiritual" simply to distinguish them from secular songs, without this involving the explicit notion of the spirit being at work in them (cf. note 19 to 1:3-8). However, "spiritual" is also probably intended to emphasize the fact that these hymns are deeply rooted in their hearts (cf. v 15) and directed towards God.[30]

It is not clear how one should translate the further phrase that

---

27. Cf. 1 John 2:14 "the word of God abides in you." John 15:7 says exactly the same of the words of Christ as 15:5 etc. say of Christ himself (cf. 8:31: to continue in his word). 28. Moule, 125, discusses the question of whether it does not depend on λόγος as it does on ἐπίγνωσις in 1:9. On the ethical orientation of wisdom cf. pp. 40f. Chrysostom IX, 1 (361) identifies it with virtue.

29. Kraft, HNT 16a (note 23 to 2:16-23), 243; cf. p. 281 of this commentary.
30. Christ is not mentioned here; but 1:15-20 actually and Rev. 5:9f. expressly, are both addressed to the exalted One, so that the *carmina Christi*, the songs to Christ (Plin. d.J. X 96:7; cf. Ign. *Eph.* 4:1) in fact already have their roots in the New Testament.

follows. The word used here mostly denotes the grace (of God) as at 1:6. However, it can also mean graciousness, and could be understood thus in 4:6. It could also be interpreted in this way here, if the article did not originally belong to the verse.[31] In the context here the more obvious meaning seems to be "saying grace."[32] However, since the article, although somewhat difficult, is probably original, it is best to think of "(God's) grace." This is the phrase with which (likewise without the genitive "of God") the whole letter comes to a close. But one should not forget the fact that all these interpretations represent a range of meaning which for the readers was covered by one and the same word. Hence all one can ask is which nuance was central for them here. The phrase does at any rate include the idea that all graciousness, and even more so, all genuine thanksgiving, flows from God's grace, and knows God's grace as the purpose of every song of praise.

[17] The conclusion, which summarizes this section, sets all that they do under the name of Jesus and thus within the thanks given to God. The divine service is carried on in their everyday life, in worship which is intelligible to everyone and in accord with reason and intellect (Rom. 12:1). The name of God (or Christ) does at the same time convey his mighty presence, as when it is invoked at baptism (1 Cor. 6:11; Acts 10:48) in prayer (Phil. 2:10; John 14:13f. etc.), in healing (Luke 10:17; Acts 3:6; 4:7 and frequently), or when a plan of action is confirmed (1 Cor. 5:4, judgment of a sinner; 2 Thess. 3:6, admonition).[33] Thus yet again the writer explicitly affirms that the whole life of the community flown forth from the Lord Jesus Christ himself. Thus also, however, he provides the heading for the section on household rules attached at this point.

Conclusion

Verse 12 lists ways of life which are otherwise ascribed to God or Christ; but at the same time it summons the readers to put on this way of life that belongs to Christ. In fact underlying this is the image

---

31. It is found in P⁴⁶BD* etc.
32. The passage most closely related to this is 1 Cor. 10:30; it is almost always used in a construction with ἔχειν and/or connected with θεῷ as object.

33. As well as the ἐν-formula used here, εἰς, ἐπί and plain dative are also found. "To call on the name (of Christ)" means to be a Christian (Acts 2:21 [Joel 3:5!]; 9:14, 21; 22:16; 1 Cor. 1:2; 2 Tim. 2:22[?]).

of the reader entering into Christ, and thus into the world refashioned by him. The decisive point is that all the concepts describe
a kind of encounter between people. Thus it is in this encounter
that the stream of love flowing from God to humankind via Christ
makes its effect felt further. It is for this reason as well (v 15) that
priorities can only properly be established by means of the peace
of Christ (not in the sense of the subjective state of one's soul, but
as salvation objectively established). That is, only the peace of
Christ can lead people in their vulnerable state and yearning to be
loved, and in spite of all their stubborn opposition, set them where
they really belong (v 13).

It is for this reason that worship, in which the Exalted One can
become alive in his word and thus lead a person into singing and
thanksgiving (vv. 16f.), is so important; for it is thus the place in
which this kind of self-giving on God's part is accomplished again
and again, and becomes in the individual the source from which one
can also give oneself to others. In light of all this then it follows that
the life of the community can only consist of giving thanks to God.
In this understanding, everything is said that needs to be said—
those who live in thanksgiving live out God's will; they have attained what God intended in his creation (v 10!) and have become
the creation in whom God's stream of love flows back in response to
him who is its source.

/ 16

Christ in the Sphere of Marriage, Family, and Work (3:18—4:1)

Bibliography: Crouch, *Origin;* Dibelius-Greeven, 48-50; Goppelt, L.,
"Jesus und die 'Haustafel'-Tradition," in: *Orientierung an Jesus, Festschr. J. Schmid,* Freiburg (1973) 93-106; Lillie, W., "The Pauline House-
tables," *ExpTim* 86 (1975) 179-83; Merk (p. 171) 214-24; Schrage,
"Ethik"; Schröder, *Haustafeln;* Schweizer, *Haustafeln;* Weidinger, *Haustafeln;* Wendland, "Bedeutung."

18 Wives, be subject to your husbands, as is fitting in the Lord.
19 Husbands, love your wives, and do not be harsh with them.
20 Children, obey your parents in everything, for this pleases the
Lord. 21 Fathers, do not provoke your children, lest they become)
discouraged. 22 Slaves, obey in everything those who are your
earthly masters, not with eyeservice, as men-pleasers, but in singleness of heart, fearing the Lord. 23 Whatever your task, work heart-
ily, as serving the Lord and not men, 24 knowing that from the

Lord you will receive the inheritance as your reward; you are serving the Lord Christ. 25 For the wrongdoer will be paid back for the wrong he has done, and there is no partiality. 1 Masters, treat your slaves justly and fairly, knowing that you also have a Master in heaven.

Excursus: The Household Rules

Col. 3:18–4:1 is the first Christian Household rule, a compilation of short admonitions to the various divisions, to men and women, parents and children, masters and slaves. Eph. 5:22–6:9; 1 Peter 2:13–3:7; Titus 2:2-10; 3:1f.; 1 Clem. 21:6-8; Ign. *Pol.* 4:1–6:2; Pol. 4:2–6:1, should all be compared with this passage. The form here is the product of a long process of development.[1]

Already in *Greek literature*, above all in Stoicism and the authors dependent on it,[2] admonitions of this kind are found in combination. Thus the three groups mentioned here, although certainly along with others as well, appear in Aristotle, Seneca, and Plutarch.[3] However, it is almost always only *the male, adult and free person* who is thus addressed, and he is told how he should behave in relation to women, children and slaves.[4] The idea that women, children and slaves could also act in an ethically responsible way is scarcely even considered.[5] Indeed, the master is recommended to treat his

[1] Cf. most recently Crouch, *Origin*, 13-31; on the whole question v. Schweizer, *Haustafeln*.

2. On this v. above all Dibelius-Greeven, 48f.; Weidinger *Haustafeln*, 27-40.

[3] Aristotle *Pol.* I, 2:1 (1253b, 7ff.): master and slave, husband and wife, father and children; yet the difference involved in these relationships is made especially prominent (I, 1:5 [125b, 1ff.]; 5:1 [1259a, 38ff.]). The higher unity of civic community and state remains paramount (I, 1:7f., 11 [1252b, 15ff.; 1253a, 19ff.]). Sen. *Ep.* 94:1 uses the question of how the husband should behave toward his wife, the father bring up his children, and the master govern his slaves, as examples for the Stoic discussion of whether ethics that differentiate in this manner belong to the task of philosophy; 94:3 mentions only wife and son, 94:5 father and wife; 94:11 uses the categories of friend, citizen and comrade as examples; 94:8 speaks of that which properly belongs to the husband, to the wife, to those who are married, and to those who are single; in 94:14ff. yet further differentiations are introduced. Plut. *Lib. Educ.* 10 (II, 7E) ranks woman, children, and slaves behind gods, parents, laws, authorities, and friends (cf. notes 47 and 51 to this section). This is always formulated as an admonition to the free man (except in the incidental remark in Sen. *Ep.* 94:8).

[4] Weidinger, *Haustafeln*, 27-39; Schroeder, *Haustafeln*, 38; e.g. Epict., *Diss.* II, 10, 3:7: how the reader should conduct himself as a man, citizen, son, and brother.

5. Crouch, *Origin*, 116f. A dual admonition to superior and subordinate

slave well because it is in his own interests.[6] Above all, this kind of conduct is given a basis in the cosmic order.[7] As a citizen of the world, as a man among men, the free man adapts himself to the ordered life of the universe.[8]

This way of referring various kinds of human relationship to a comprehensive ethical admonition undergoes a decisive transformation in *Judaism*. Indeed, it is alien to the nature of Judaism, since the law has no need of any new formulation of this kind. It is for this reason as well, then, that the Hellenistic prototype can still be clearly detected. In Philo and Josephus, as in Hellenism, the list usually begins with God and one's native country, and friends and relations are then added.[9] But the relationships between husbands and wives, parents and children, and masters and slaves are now more noticeably prominent.[10] Perhaps this was because the commandment in the Decalogue about honoring one's parents was extended to apply to the other two cases as well, and perhaps occasionally another commandment, belonging to the Noachite commandments and thus obligatory also for the Gentiles, was also appended.[11] This at any rate would explain the point about subordination (which is now especially prominent) and the way the exhortations are arranged in pairs.[12] Even so, it must be said that actual household rules, by which is meant collections in short paragraphs of those counsels where preeminence and subordintion are the decisive themes, are still not found even in Hellenistic Judaism.

Certainly for the New Testament instances it is *Jesus' proclamation* and the whole of his activity which have become determinative. Indeed, it could not be forgotten that the person who wants to be great must become a servant, and whoever wants to be first must become the slave of all, because the Son of Man himself came not to be

groups is found in Sen., *Ben.* II, 18:1f. (ibid. 55, cf. 72 for Hecaton). An exception is perhaps provided by the emancipated slave Epictetus, who sees himself spiritually however as one who is baptized (that is as a Jew; II, 9:20f.). On the expression τὸ καθῆκον etc. cf. notes 39 and 40 to this section).

6. Plato, Aristotle (Weidinger, *Haustafeln*, 53).

7. This is found already in Aristotle, *Pol.* I, 2:7 (1254a, 14ff.); hence the slave also belongs to the master as an

object (ibid. 2:6 [9ff.]). Cf. below, note 54 to this section.

8. Schroeder, *Haustafeln*, 55-67.

9. *Vit. Mos.* II, 198; *Mut. Nom.* 40; *Deus Imm.* 17-19; *Plant.* 146; *Ebr.* 17; Jos. *Ap.* II, 199-209. Cf. note 47 to this section.

10. Philo, *Poster. C.* 181; Pseud.-Phocylides, op. cit. (v. note 30 to 3:5-11), 175-227.

11. Crouch, *Origin*, 84-101, 106; cf. Schroeder, *Haustafeln*, 30, 92f.

12. Philo *Decal.* 165-7; cf. *Spec. Leg.* II, 226f.

served but to serve and to give his life as a ransom for many (Mark 10:43-45).[13] Again, the fact that this formulation of household rules seems to begin with the theme of marriage [14] may derive from the fact that Jesus spoke of marriage (Mark 10:1-9; Matt. 5:27f.). But it is extremely improbable that there is any direct dependence on sayings of Jesus in the other two instances, however much the dominant theme there (that true greatness is attained in the very act of serving) is still determined by reference to Jesus.[15] The idea of a widespread primitive Christian catechism, which would have contained this sort of household rule,[16] must be abandoned; for such household rules appear neither in the genuine Pauline Epistles nor in those writings that have nothing to do with Paul. However, it is likely that a misunderstanding of the Pauline proclamation about freedom could have played an important role in these rules being introduced. "Everything is permitted" was of course the solution proposed by the Corinthians, who in doing so presumably appealed to Pauline formulations such as that in Gal. 3:28 ("There is neither Jew nor Greek, there is neither slave nor free, there is neither male nor female"). The fact that this formulation also appears in Col. 3:11 could suggest that this same context is still relevant. The formulation in Colossians, however, has been modified, in the sense that the emphasis is now on the tension (theologically no longer dangerous) between circumcision and uncircumcision, and on an international outlook extolled in the Hellenistic world. But the perilous move of equating husband and wife has been abandoned. However, the ethical ideas of the day were definitely not the sole source

---

13. Cf. Pol. 5:1.
14. Col. 3:18f.; in Eph. 5:22-33 marriage alone is expressly discussed and given a christological basis; in 1 Peter it is set at the end but, like the admonition to slaves, it is strongly emphasized. Eph. 5:25, 29 is echoed in Ign. *Pol.* 5:1, and Pol. 4:2 begins with the call to wives to love their husbands; in the Pastorals and in 1 Clem. by contrast, marriage is scarcely given any prominence.
15. This point nevertheless has to be made over against L. Goppelt who derives these from the earthly Jesus. Mark 7:10 would still be a possibility for the topos parents/children, but it

remains uncertain whether it is a saying of Jesus that we have there.
16. A. Seeberg, *Der Katechismus der Urchristenheit,* 1966 (*TB* 26), Vorwort, 1-9, 246-73 etc.; E. G. Selwyn, *The First Epistle of St. Peter,* (London 1958) 18-23; Thompson, 156.
17. Cf. Crouch, *Origin,* 104, 149-51, 157f.; Lillie, "House-tables," 180, 183. The idea that the eschatological aspect would have led to the adoption of the ethics of the household rule, is improbable in Col. because the expectation of an early Parousia makes a new order of society unnecessary. (Merk, *Handeln,* 223).

for these rules, since the emancipation of children was not an issue at the time, and in the household rules both parties are always addressed.[17]

The fact that the Epistle to the Colossians, which lays such strong emphasis on life "above" (2:21; 3:2), contains a household rule of this kind indicates a healthy and sensible New Testament involvement in the world, however questionable this might be in particular detail. In this way, in face of every kind of ascetic withdrawal from the world, a positive appraisal is offered for creation, marriage, the family and work. The question raised here is rather this: whether setting the difference (inherent in nature) between parents and children alongside the difference (created by man) between masters and slaves [18] does not pave the way for a disastrous development. True it must be maintained, even without taking account of the completely different situation prevailing at that time,[19] that the situation in the Epistle to the Colossians is much more concerned with personal than purely functional structures.[20]

Above all, there is no question whatever here of anchoring the differences in the natural order, which is more or less what happens in Aristotle.[21] Any kind of identity between God, nature, and human reason is never even hinted at. For this reason there is also a complete absence of the argument that taking one's correct position in the cosmic system is to one's own advantage. Therefore, at least in Col. 3:18–4:1, the admonitions are not framed by those of respect for the state and for God.[22] As distinct from Hellenistic, even Jewish-Hellenistic, parallels, it is only the will of the "Lord" that they are reminded of. The style of the diatribe, which seeks to convince the reader by means of references to the reasonableness of this cosmic order,[23] is altogether absent. Of course, merely to use a form of words expressing subordination to the "Lord" does not amount to

---

18. On this cf. above p. 199. Aristotle does indeed clearly distinguish the different levels; however, he does this in such a way that the slave as the "property" of his master is still set far below women and children (cf. note 3 to this section: I, 1:5; 2:6 [1252b, 1ff.; 1254a, 9ff.]).
19. Cf. Stuhlmacher, *Philemon*, 46-8, and below, note 52 to this section.
20. Wendland, "Bedeutung," 114.

21. Cf. note 3 to this section and Schroeder, *Haustafeln*, 55-67.
22. Cf. Dibelius-Greeven, 49; Merk, *Handeln*, 221; Lillie, "House-tables," 180.
23. Schroeder, *Haustafeln*, 39-41; thus e.g. Philo, *Decal.* 165-7 (ibid., 74).
24. H. Preisker, *Christentum und Ehe in den ersten drei Jahrhunderten*, (Berlin 1927), 139 n118.

much, if it does not effect a corresponding change in the content as a whole.[24]

But at least the point is made clearly enough that neither love nor parenthood nor authority, nor the world order which provides the basis for these is deified; the circumstances of human life are simply accepted as they are found. However, on the positive side one should also recognize the extent to which consideration for others, especially those who are weaker, has become determinative. This is indeed shown by the fact that the weaker party is considered as a completely proper *subject* of ethical action.[25] The household rule is introduced by a summons to the members of the community to daily worship, and in this way they are all called to proclamation, teaching, ministry, and sacrifice of praise (3:16f.).[26] Therefore it is perfectly natural for both partners to be addressed. In the individual formulations also, this consideration for the weak, inculcated already by the Old Testament, is in evidence.[27]

A survey of later Christian household rules shows how Christianizing and paganizing go hand in hand. The dual character of the admonitions is no longer kept up in every case. In Titus 2:4f. and Pol. 4:2, only the wives are required to be subordinate to their husbands and to bring up children, without there being any corresponding word to husbands (cf. 1 Clem. 21:6). The theme of parents and children is not found in 1 Peter and Ign. *Pol.*, nor is there any admonition to children in Titus 2:4; Did. 4:9; 1 Clem. 21:6, 8; Pol. 4:2. In

---

25. Aristotle *Pol.* I, 5:8f. (1260a, 20ff.) sharply distinguishes the different ethical quality (ἠθικὴ ἀρετή) not only of the master vis-à-vis the group of subordinates, but also of each member of that group vis-à-vis the others in the same group.

26. Merk, *Handeln*, 222. This is also the case in Eph. 5:21 (on this v. H. Schlier, *Der Brief an die Epheser*, Düsseldorf 2nd edn. 1958, 250); 1 Peter 2:13 is introduced in similar fashion in the form of a heading with a general admonition, so that the appeals made in the household rule only appear as special applications of the basic principle, although that does not mean that one should interpret this simply as a criticism of the form of the household rule (as does J. P.

Sampley, "*And the Two shall become one Flesh*," 1971 [MSSNTS 16], 117). The first injunction in the household rule in Eph. 5:22 is even grammatically dependent on v 21. The key concept of the general priesthood appears literally in 1 Peter 2:9f. as the introduction to 2:11–3:7; yet the idea there is not of priestly service within the community, as it is in Col. 3:16f., but of its effect on the non-believing world (likewise Col. 4:5f.; Titus 2:5, 8, 10).

27. Cf. on v 21b; cf. further 1 Peter 3:7; Tobit 10:13; Pseud.-Phocylides (note 30 to 3:5-11) 207; Eccles. 7:21ff. (W. Zimmerman, *Grundriss der alttestamentlichen Theologie*, Stuttgart 1972 [ThW 3], 143) and Crouch, *Origin*, 113-16.

the exhortation to slaves (which is not mentioned at all in Pol. 4 or 1 Clem. 21) in 1 Peter and Titus 2 there is no direction given to their masters.[28]

The household rule is incorporated into the all-embracing rule of the state in 1 Peter 2:13-17,[29] in proximity to the preeminence of God, a fatal proximity in view of the effect that this association has subsequently had.[30] Still more important is the emergence of the community hierarchy. In 1 Peter 5:1-5, this is still kept separate from the household rule. Titus 2:2-8, set alongside 1:5ff. and in the light of Titus' self-ascribed position, is certainly to be taken in terms of actual hierarchical ranks within the community.[31] Advice is given, by means of phrases drawn from household rules, in 1 Clem. 21:6 (as in 1:3) on the position of superiors and presbyters, and in Ign. Pol. 6:1 and Pol. 4:2–6:1 on that of bishops and deacons (along with widows and others). Above all, however, actually adopting biblical and Christian ideas might be understood as providing the basis for an eternally fixed divine world order.

In Eph. 5:22-23, the deeply-rooted understanding of marriage as love which offers itself in service could in fact also lead to the idea of a fixed hierarchy characterizing the relationship between husband and wife, corresponding to that between Christ and the community (cf. Paul in 1 Cor. 11:3). Again, the explicit quotation from the Decalogue, "Honor your father and mother" (as the first commandment with a promise, Eph. 6:2f.), could set the seal on the subordination of children to the authority of their parents as representing the divine ordering of nature. This subordination to authority is indeed described, in phrases drawn almost straight from the Old Testament, as "the discipline and instruction of the Lord." Nevertheless, one must stress the fact that in Eph. 5f. the sovereignty of Christ is understood completely as service, while conversely in 1 Peter 2:18-25 the slave is made parallel to Christ, and in 3:1 it is

---

28. Cf. 1 Tim. 6:1f. This is emphasized, by contrast, in Did. 4:10; Ign. Pol. 4:2.

29. This, however, is done in such a way that the subordination to the emperor and to governors is seen as a special case of the subordination proper to all human creatures (2:13) and the call to respect God and emperor goes back to Prov. 24:21.

30. Cf. also Titus 3:1f., framed by Christological and theological excursuses (2:11-14 and 3:3-7) and separated from the other parts of the household rule (2:2-10).

31. Cf. also the transition from 1 Tim. 5 to 6:1f., and Col. 3:16 set before 17ff. (J. Gnilka, "Paränetische Traditionen im Epheserbrief," in Melanges Bibliques für B. Rigaux. 1969, 408); Eph. 5:18-21; 1 Peter 2:4-10.

the wife herself to whom the writer assigns the really active role
(v. pp. 228f.).

A more calamitous development is the way the idea of service is
gradually distorted. Viewed properly, it is to be rendered not to
other people but to the Lord (Col. 3:23). Originally what this en-
visaged was nothing less than complete liberation from every human
master. But as early as Eph. 6:5 it is formulated in a way which
is very much open to abuse: "be obedient to those who are your
earthly masters . . . as to Christ." Moreover the slaves are no longer,
as in Col. 3:22, called in general terms to fear God but rather with
fear and trembling to be obedient to their masters.[32] The fact that
1 Peter 2:21-25 offers Christ to the slaves as their prototype, without
their masters being mentioned at all (possibly because there are no
slave owners in the communities that are addressed ?) could lead
mistakenly to equating of service for Christ with service rendered
to the next class up in the social order.

Indeed, Titus 2:9 changes the sense of Col. 3:20; instead of the
idea that one must do what is well-pleasing to the Lord it says that
slaves should be well-pleasing to their masters. Finally, in Did. 4:11
masters become for their slaves the "type" of God, and in Barn. 19:7
this is even extended to all kinds of masters. In both places this is
linked with characteristically biblical expressions about fear of God
and trust in him. In Pol. 5:3 presbyters and deacons, to whom one
should be subordinate, are found in place of God. In Ign. Pol. 6:2
the image of a military hierarchy is used. In 1 Clem. 20f. the paganizing process is almost completely achieved by means of subordi-
nating the household rule to the cosmic order, which prescribes for
every star its course.[33]

Bound up with this is the fact that the difference in style from the
Hellenistic prototypes has clearly diminished. Titus 2:1ff. is already,
in its essence, an admonition which governs the reader's attitude
toward various groups. This is still more emphatically so in Did.
4:9f. In 1 Clem. 1:3; 21:6-8 as well, the admonition to wives and
children are couched in the form of an address to husbands.[34] In
Ign. Pol. 4-6, only Polycarp is instructed concerning his duties vis-

---

32. Yet on account of this the reference to the Judge is more clearly related to the masters. The danger is
well perceived by Wengst, "Versöhnung," 25f.

33. The fact that conscience takes the
place of the divine commandment (1
Peter 2:19; 1 Clem. 1:3) may also
belong here.

34. Cf. the relationship to Polyb.
XVIII, 41:8 (Weidinger, Haustafeln,
56).

à-vis widows, slaves, wives and husbands, while emphasis is also
laid on subordination to the bishop, before whom each marriage
must be contracted, and to presbyters and deacons. Arrangement by
means of pairs is now found only in 5:1, and that in rudimentary
fashion. The content there shows that it is only slaves and not their
masters who are admonished; the form, by contrast, shows that increasingly it is the male, adult, free individual who again becomes
the person addressed. Both reveal how the reciprocal exhortation,
intended to help both parties find their respective place, more and
more turns into the proclamation of a fixed order, in which the husband should prove his worth in relation to all other persons, while
wives, children and especially slaves should be subordinate.

Thus the process of Christianizing and paganizing go hand in hand
in a remarkable and precarious manner. Ironically, what has been
lost in this process of development is precisely the healthy worldliness of the sets of rules, taken over more or less unthinkably from
the surrounding milieu. For it is this worldliness that guarantees that
the rules make only relative not absolute demands. It is indeed
still clearly present in Col. 3:18—4:1, and indicates the distinctively
Christian aspect of this first Christian household rule.

Analysis

Wives and husbands, children and parents, slaves and masters
are set in contrast to each other in three groups. Each injunction
begins with the vocative of the person addressed, followed by the
imperative. In the first member of each pair respectively, the basis
for what is said is provided by means of a reference to the "Lord."
In the second member this happens only in the case of the admonition to masters; that to parents is provided with a different motive,
while that to husbands is supplemented only by a further imperative. The admonition to slaves is considerably extended in v 22, and
above all in vv 23-25 by means of a general reference to judgment.
And it is certainly worth asking whether this judgment is intended
to apply to the masters, or to both groups together.

Interpretation

[18] In the New Testament, in contrast to the Hellenistic prototypes, wives, children, and slaves also appear in these rules. This is
all the more remarkable since from 3:1 onwards the discussion has

been concerned with the life of those who are already risen, who are living "above" and are no longer in the world (2:20; 3:2, 5). Furthermore, it was said in 3:11 that all differences of religion, nationality, and status have been done away with. But it was probably in face of exactly this sort of misunderstanding on the part of an enthusiasm that has lost all sense of limits that the author wrote instructions of this kind, expounding the basic tenet of v 17. The community's life of worship finds its continuation in the everyday world of marriage, family, and work.[35]

Subordination is demanded of wives, although this should be distinguished from the obedience required of children and slaves.[36] The verb used of the wife denotes voluntary self-disposition, as when it is used of Christ in relation to the Father (1 Cor. 15:28).[37] Furthermore, the demand made on husbands provides a decisive counter-balance. Nevertheless, the fact remains that the position ascribed to the wife in marriage assumes a different form from that given to the husband.[38] This point will be considered further in the conclusion.

The grounds for this subordination of the wife are provided first of all by reference to custom. Greek and especially Stoic thought had over a long period discussed what this subordination should actually comprise. Zeno wrote an entire book entitled *Concerning That Which Is Fitting.*[39] This Greek thought was mediated to the New Testament writers via Hellenistic Judaism.[40] In Col. 3:18, 20 however it is defined more precisely by means of the phrase "in the

---

35. Community and house are closely connected with each other (Gnilka, "Traditionen" [v. note 31 to this section] 408).

36. In 1 Peter 2:18; 3:1 the word is used for both household servants and wives; "obey" is found only in 3:6 (of Sarah vis-à-vis Abraham). The prefix is common to both expressions.

37. The passive describes, in the same verse, the subjugation (brought about by God) of the powers to Christ.

38. In Titus 2:4 the wives are also instructed to love their husbands (φίλανδροι); that husbands should likewise be subordinate to their wives is never said.

39. Περὶ τοῦ καθήκοντος, von Arnim I, 55 (cf. III, 30 plural, etc.); on this v. Schroeder, *Haustafeln*, 44.

40. Τὰ ἀνήκοντα seems only to be found with an indication of that to which something "is due" or "belongs" in a few papyri and inscriptions, and also in 1 Macc. 10:42 (Liddell-Scott, 137b, s.v.); καθῆκεν (imperfect as here!) occurs in Ep. Arist. 54; 149 (with the following infinitive likewise in the present: Pseud.-Phocylides, op. cit. [note 30 to 3:5-11] 80), and τὸ καθῆκον in Ep. Arist. 227; 245, etc.; and in Jos. *Ant.* 13, 66 in an absolute sense (cf. ibid. 7,131; 12,259). In Philemon 8 τὸ ἀνῆκον is found in an absolute sense.

Lord." Indeed, in this instance the admonition would have been completely accepted outside the community as well. But the writer of the letter thus emphasizes the fact that the Lord [41] alone provides the criteria for what can be taken over unchanged from the generally accepted ethic, and what must be reformulated or abandoned. Thus the vital points here are first that the writer does not simply presuppose a natural order valid everywhere and at all times which would determine relationships for all spheres and ages on earth, and second that he only provides a summons to the fundamental relationship, and leaves the detailed working out of this as something still open to discussion.

[19] Husbands are admonished to love. This is an innovation, simply by virtue of its concentration on this one act and in the choice of this verb which is especially favored in the New Testament.[42] The extensive Christological justification set forth in Eph. 5:25-33 shows how strong the special character of this love still was. In a practical and sensible way, the call to love is developed into a warning against becoming bitter [43] (a development found also in the Rabbis of the third century A.D.).[44]

41. The "Lord" is "Christ," the one who gives ethical injunctions and establishes salvation: v. pp. 171f. along with note 2 to 3:1-4. It is true that v 20 shows how much of a set formula this reference has already become. To connect "in the Lord" with "be subject to" would be difficult in view of the word order (thus, correctly, Calvin, 160).

42. It is by means of στέργειν that in Pseud.-Phocylides (note 30 to 3:5-11) 195-7, after lengthy remarks about adultery and sexual perversions, the call is made for mutual love between husband and wife. Philo (*Poster. C.* 181), in a sort of household rule, speaks of ἐπιμέλεια for the wife, and in *Deus Imm.* 19 the wife appears alongside many others for whom one should be at hand. In Hellenism there occurs here and there already in Alexis Fr. 70 (*CAF* II, 320) the demand for a spiritual marriage partnership that goes beyond merely carnal lust (for further discussion of this for the New

Testament period, v. E. Schweizer, *TDNT* VII, 1039f.). Something similar appears in the wedding speech in Plut. *Praec. Coniug.* 34 (II, 142F): the contrast to ἐρᾶν is provided by a marriage for a dowry or the procreation of children or a marriage to satisfy lust (or, textually uncertain, without sexual intercourse); in any case, a married woman and a courtesan exercise completely different functions (ibid. 29—II, 142C). It is a constant presupposition throughout that the wife must "listen" to her husband, be under his control, have neither friends nor gods of her own, nor speak in public (ibid. 6; 11; 19; 31—II, 139AD; 140D; 142CD).

43. Since Plut., *De coibenda ira* 8 (II, 457A), also speaks of "being embittered against (πρός) women," it is not to be concluded from this construction that it is particularly those cases where the wife gave no occasion for bitterness that are intended (discussion in W. Michaelis, *TDNT* VI, 125 n16).

[20] It is remarkable that children are addressed at all, that they are treated as fully human beings in their own right.[44] True, they even more than wives are called to be obedient, and the point is further emphasized by the addition "in everything." The verb "obey" is used by Paul only of conduct vis-à-vis Christ, the gospel and the apostle, that is, toward the Lord himself and the proclamation concerning him. Not until post-Pauline and deutero-Pauline writings is the call to obedience found in relation to human authorities.[46] As in v 18 (v. ad loc.), the writer refers back to a general ethical principle,[47] (to what is "well-pleasing") but at the same time he says that this is also valid "in the Lord." This addition is made by means of a customary formula (cf. p. 171); what one would actually expect is well-pleasing "to" (instead of "in") the Lord.[48]

[21] It is not clear who is being addressed in what follows. All that is certain is that it is the "fathers" (thus literally) whom the writer has most of all in mind, since he does not choose the normal word for "parents" as he does in v 20. But even so, "fathers" in the plural can also frequently include both parents (Heb. 11:23),[49] and since they appear in v 20 as the object of the children's obedience, presumably the writer really has both of them in mind here as well, even if he is thinking primarily of the father. For the father, of course, stands in greater danger of provoking or embittering the children by bringing them up in an autocratic way. Parallels can be

---

44. Strack-Billerbeck III, 631; however, it is impressed upon the husband that he should be careful because the tears of the wife could punish him.
45. Of course, there are also grown-up children; here, however, it is those children who are in the process of growing up that are thought of.
46. W. Schenk, "Die Gerechtigkeit Gottes und der Glaube Christi," TLZ 97 (1972), 165.
47. Honoring one's parents is found for example in Plut. Lib. Educ. 10 (II, 7E) after worship of the gods at the beginning of a catalogue, and is subordinated to the love of one's country in Stob. Ecl. III, 39:34 (I, 731, 1-3); it is found as a call to obedience in everything in Epict. II, 10, 7. It is, of course, very much emphasized in Ju-

daism: Philo derives everything from the commandment to honor one's parents (Decal. 165-7; as first member in Mut. Nom. 40; it is placed after the worship of God in Vit. Mos. II, 198; similarly in Poster. C. 181, where the worship of God is set as the climax at the end, and in Plant. 146 where, according to the Hellenistic model, the love of one's country precedes it [in Ebr. 17 it is the other way round]); also in Jos. Ap. II, 206 this commandment follows that of the worship of God and leads to further admonitions. Cf. above, notes 3, 9, 10 to this section.
48. It is corrected in this way in 81 al.
49. So Pr.-Bauer for this passage as well; instances from classical usage are also given there.

found in Greek and Hellenistic-Jewish authors.[50] However, the reason the writer gives for this admonition is astounding. Again the child is viewed in an almost modern psychological way; faced with an upbringing of this kind, he could lose the courage to become himself.[51]

[22] The admonition to slaves at first runs parallel to that given to the children.[52] It is true that because the emphasis here is so strongly on the Lord (vv 18, 20, 22f.), the masters (*kyrios* in Greek) have to be designated as bodily or "earthly," indeed literally as those "according to the flesh." [53] The point of this is not to evaluate them negatively but to set limits to their significance. They are masters (lords) only within the earthly domain. Yet this exhortation is considerably extended as compared with the others. Partly this could be because Onesimus is one of those who conveys the letter. However, the exhortation is necessitated above all by the fact that hardly any parallel existed for admonitions to slaves.[54] Thus it was precisely in this sphere that the problems were the most pressing.

50. Plut. *Lib. Educ.* 12 (II, 8F) explains that blows and torture are suitable for slaves but not for free children, and ibid. 18 (II, 13E) that hotheaded anger should quickly die down. Menander (*Stob. Ecl.* IV, 26:3-5 [II, 651, 11-19]) also advises reasoning rather than being angry with a child. Pseud.-Phocylides (note 30 to 3:5-11) warns against being severe and advises reprimanding through the mother, but beware of maidens in firmly closeted chambers!

51. Plutarch wrote an entire treatise on the bringing up of children in a sort of household rule (v. Excursus), he appealed to men to be sensible toward their wives, to love their children, and not to offend their slaves inordinately (*Lib. Educ.* 10 [II, 7E]; cf. note 47 to this section). He exhorts them to use sensible words and admonitions, praise and reproof, and especially to behave in an exemplary way (ibid. 7, 12, 16, 20 [II, 4C, 8F, 9A, 12C, 14A]). Thus this Christian instruction is not unique (so, correctly, Moule, 129). Pseud.-Phocylides (note 30 to 3:5-11) 184-7 fights against infanticide, the exposure of children and castration, and in ibid. 177 he recalls the sorrow children suffer when their parents are divorced. Jos. *Ap.* II, 204 advises parents to exercise restraint during birthday parties and to give instruction in reading. Philo mentions upbringing and care of children only incidentally (*Poster. C.* 181; *Deus Imm.* 19; *Plant.* 146).

52. On the problem of slavery cf. Stuhlmacher, *Philemon*, esp. 40-8, 65-9. The fact that 1 Cor. 7:21 is a call to accept emancipation if it should come (above all this is so on account of the aorist) has now been further shown by J. B. Bauer in his discussion of S. S. Bartchy, ΜΑΛΛΟΝ ΧΡΗ-ΣΑΙ. *First-Century Slavery and the Interpretation of 1 Corinthians 7:21* (SBLDS 11) in *TLZ* 71 (1975), 462f.

53. It can be questioned whether Paul himself would have formulated it thus. In Philemon 16 "in the flesh" stands alongside "in the Lord"; Rom. 9:5 has Χριστὸς τὸ κατὰ σάρκα.

54. In Hellenistic and, above all, Stoic

What did it mean to say that the slave was now a brother, specifically "in the flesh" and "in the Lord" (Philem. 16)? According
to this passage, what it means for the slave is that his obedience includes more than what is obviously required, that is, the minimum
possible to avoid punishment or to receive his reward; in other
words it is not merely "eyeservice." His service should not be done
with one eye on the approval of others, especially of his master; it
should be carried out with singleness of heart. What this denotes
is a disposition and mode of action (cf. note 23 to 3:12-17) with a
clear sense of direction, not trying to do several things all at the
same time. It denotes also an attitude which in the case of conflict
sees what really needs to be done, and not simply what is spectacu-
lar and likely to gain approval or reward.

It is in such conduct that the fear of the Lord is evidenced. Fear
should certainly not be thought of as the opposite of trust; this is
shown by the fact that in Ps. 33(32):18, for example, it is equated
with hoping for God's grace. What fear really means is a way of
living which is afraid of nothing except of losing this one Lord, in
the same way that a person who is in love fears nothing so much as
losing the affection of the beloved.

[23] From here on, the admonition becomes clarified: they should
do everything from the heart (literally: from [the whole] soul),
that is for the Lord and not to please men. This enlarges on what
is said in v 17 to all the members of the community. But notice what
a change there would be in the sense if the phrase "as [55] to the Lord"
were taken to mean that the earthly master takes the place of the
heavenly, and that every act of service performed for the earthly
master is service for Christ (cf. p. 219)! However, this cannot be
the point here. There is a liberating aspect to this summons. The
power of the masters is explicitly limited to the earthly domain, and
all service should, as far as possible, be directed to the particular
matter at hand, and not to the impression it will make on these
masters.

---

parallels, the admonition to masters to
behave properly toward their slaves
(thus Pseud.-Phocylides [note 30 to
3:5-11], 224-7) seldom occurs because
slavery is overcome at least theoreti-
cally. (Schroeder, Haustafeln, 50f.).

This shows that oftentimes the more
something is reflected upon intellectually the less the practical problems are
felt. Cf. also note 7 to this section.
55. BDF 425,4.

[24] What has been said is reinforced by the reference to the judgment (cf. p. 191). Thus by taking up the concept of "inheritance" (cf. p. 50), the writer emphasizes the extent to which what is to come is guaranteed for them. The Old Testament concept of the inheritance of the land promised to Israel had already been given an eschatological interpretation in Judaism and set in terms of eternal life. Thus both aspects are emphasized: the transfer which has already been made by God and is therefore assured, and the fulfillment which is still awaited and will only become visible at the consummation.[56]

The clause, "you are serving the Lord Christ," is probably to be taken as an imperative, not as an indicative. Indeed it is expressed in such general terms that one may ask whether (as is probable) it is directed only at the slaves, whether in other words it simply repeats in summary fashion what has already been said; or whether, as in Rom. 12:11 where almost the same formulation is found, it may be interpolated in a more general way, and be intended as an address to the masters as well.

[25] The question of who exactly is being addressed here is even more relevant in this case where the reason for the admonition is given and reference is made to the judge. Even if one takes this as addressed only to slaves, since the new form of address does not follow until 4:1, one may still ask whether it is not primarily intended to comfort them by pointing out that God is completely aware of the injustice that may have been inflicted on them.[57] In support of this one may perhaps adduce the fact that consideration for the person is, as far as we can see, always mentioned in favor of the weak; for such consideration could not be permitted by an earthly

---

56. Cf. above pp. 176f. J. Herrmann, *TDNT* III, 769-776, shows that the motif of the promise and the gracious apportioning of the land is stronger than that of the inheritance (774f.); cf. W. Foerster, ibid. 779f. It is already interpreted in an eschatological sense in Ps. 36:9 LXX, and in terms of eternal life in Ps. Sol. 14:10, Eth. En. 40:9, etc. Calvin, 160, emphasizes the character of the gracious reward; the inheritance is based on the filial

relationship that has been bestowed. On the striking lack of the article in ἀπὸ κυρίου (alongside usage which is otherwise determinate) cf. BDF 254, 1.

57. Eph. 6:9 inserts the warning about God, who has no regard for the status of a person, into the admonition to the masters. Chrysostom X, 2 (368) takes the dictum to be addressed formally to the slaves but, in fact, to be meant for the masters.

judge nor expected of the heavenly judge.[58] Perhaps the question
of who is being addressed is deliberately left open because what is
said is valid for everyone. The admonition may give a warning to
the masters and may comfort those who suffer injustice, but at the
same time it may remind the slaves that they also will one day stand
before the judge, and that they should not simply set their hopes on
God's partiality.

[1] One certain fact is that the admonition to the slaves is counter-
balanced by that addressed to the masters, of which there were
presumably not many in the community at that time. An important
point here is that what is asked of them is not that they should show
mercy, as if this were a specific merit, but that they should grant
what is fair and just. Thus the rights of slaves are defended; it is
not simply a feeling of pity for them that is aroused. Literally translated, the fairness that should be accorded them, in fact, means
equality, and it should certainly be understood in this way in 2 Cor.
8:13f. (!). The word is very common in Greek law and political science. There also the concept is intended to protect a person's proper
rights against the encroachment of a stronger party. In this, the
increasingly dominant idea is that if the standard is not the same
for everyone, it must be adjusted so that the sum of what should
belong to each individual brings the same benefit to all.

This concept is almost synonymous with that of justice; and Philo
often describes equality as the mother or source of righteousness.[59]
In the New Testament as a whole, the main emphasis is on the basic
equality of all believers before God, not on a social equality regu-
lated by some external force (3:22). However, the point here is that
the fundamental equality before God, expressed in 3:11 as the basis
for every admonition, must lead to a mode of conduct in which the
stronger party does not assert its rights by means of the authority
it possesses, but on the contrary defends the rights of the weak. So
everyone, both those who are weaker and those who are stronger

58. Thus the stranger (Deut. 10:17f.;
cf. 1:17), the poor, the widow, and
the orphan (Deut. 10:17f.; Sir. 32:15-
18 [35:13-15 LXX]; James 2:1-9),
the person who neither offers nor can
offer a bribe (Deut. 10:17; 16:19; 2
Chron. 19:7), and the Gentile (Rom.
2:11; Acts 10:34) are all protected
(cf. also Gal. 2:6). Only Lev. 19:15
(Deut. 1:17) warns against showing
partiality to both strong and weak, and
the dictum in 1 Peter 1:17 does not
stand in any direct relation to the
context.
59. G. Stählin, TDNT III, 345-48;
354.

in social terms should receive a share in that which helps them to
live. And they should also share, in the same way, in bearing the
burdens that must be endured. Precisely because the word chosen
for this purpose is general but all-inclusive, every age has to consider what righteousness and fairness might mean in their particular
situation. The admonition takes on its solemn tone because of the
fact that the slave owners also have a master (or lord) before whom
they must answer for all that they do.

Conclusion

The writer explains in detail, with reference to three examples,
what the principle of v 17 means in the social life of the community.
Quite clearly these instructions cannot simply be taken over and
applied to an age and a society which have developed in a quite
different way. Here we may suggest an analogy: just before a dangerous bend on a road, you may still come across a sign, left there
from the time when horse-drawn carriages were used, warning you
to go "Dead Slow." Quite clearly you will no longer understand this
literally; but you will not ignore it and take no notice of what it
says. Rather, you will adapt its warning to suit present-day circumstances, and you will certainly reduce your speed considerably.

Just as in this instance the important point is the basic warning
about a sharp bend in the road, which one ignores at one's peril, so
also here in Colossians it is the basic directions which matter, not the
specific individual commands which have to some extent become
obsolete for the present day. Even if an admonition of this kind in
the New Testament era had more clearly brought about a new social
order and a new social justice, these would have long since become
outmoded. Moreover, because of the interdependence between external order guaranteed and enforced by state law and inner readi-
ness to act according to a justice that applies equally to all, no
modification of relationships would be accomplished with lasting
effect unless the individual person were transformed. Slavery still
exists in both capitalist and socialist systems, even where it is no
longer permitted by the law; it merely assumes a different name.
But on this question one needs to compare the interpretation of the
Epistle to Philemon.

If wives, children, and slaves are exhorted to be subordinate or
obedient, this does not in itself rule out equality of status. It is pos-

sible that precisely in this function of being subordinate or obedient
they play the decisive role; at any rate, according to 1 Peter 3:1, the
wives, who should win over their husbands without a word, represent the active half of the married state. And the fact that a child
can live happily only when it is given direction and example does
not in itself limit its equal rights. The child can even in an extreme
instance thus become the member of the family with the most rights.
Similarly, slaves are set free from the very situation in which they
are constantly, stubbornly orientated toward their masters and
employers. Slaves who know of the highest lord (or master) of all,
can observe the behavior of another master with proper humor and
some irony.

Certainly all this can be said only if the counterbalance of an
admonition to those who are socially superior is maintained. Otherwise the whole thing collapses. It is like a modern bridge, held in
position on a high pier, set up on only one side, by means of a corresponding counterbalance; as soon as this counterbalance breaks
off, the bridge collapses. Wherever he is summoned to love, a husband can never play off his own rights against those of his wife. He
can thus never become bitter against her like a wine in which the
bitter sediment gradually increases to such an extent that the wine
is completely ruined. Where parents see it as their main duty to
protect the courage of a child, they neither crush the child by angry
outbursts or punishments, nor by a stifling concern which never
allows the child to live a life of its own. When master (or lords)
and employers are set under their lord (or master) to whom they
owe responsibility, that is to whom they are directly answerable,
then they will not take advantage of their superiority. This indeed
is because part of their responsibility is to have the rights of their
subordinates at heart, to care for the rights of those who in spite of
their different social standing have the same fundamental status.

However, the fact that this household rule still attempts to make
specific proposals for its own time challenges us to draw the necessary practical conclusions for our own time as well. In the New
Testament community above all, the courage to look for solutions
which are not ideal but pragmatic and restricted to a specific situation and time should not be stifled by statements of a purely ideal
and general fashion. True, the paramount duty of the community
remains the proclamation of the Lord who challenges people to
protect the rights of others. But this still does not mean that, in their

faith, the community should simply withdraw into a charmed circle of like-minded people, where it is enough simply to mention their common Lord. They must accept their responsibility without any illusions or utopian dreams. They must do so even where what is necessary for the rights of the weak is enforced by law, for example, on the basis of a majority decision which is also binding on the minority.

Again it is this very kind of household rule which may remind us of the importance of the tasks which await us in our family and place of work, in hospitals, institutions, and homes for the handicapped and incurable; for these tasks are not taken into account by programs whose scope is grandiose and worldwide. At the same time, set over this perspective is the recollection of the new world of Christ (3:11) and this will guard against making the limits too narrow. In such a sense, the basic tenet of 3:17 is set over the household rule: a life which understands itself as thanksgiving, which flows back to God via Christ, will in word and deed be the expression of that torrent of love which has, through God in Jesus Christ, poured into the creation and sustaining of the world, and will flow on yet further into God's creatures, as love for one another.

The Call to Intercession and Missionary Responsibility (4:2-6)

2 Continue steadfastly in prayer, being watchful in it with thanksgiving;   3 and pray for us also, that God may open to us a door for the word, to declare the mystery of Christ, on account of which I am in prison,   4 that I may make it clear, as I ought to speak. 5 Conduct yourselves wisely toward outsiders, making the most of the time. 6 Let your speech always be gracious, seasoned with salt, so that you may know how you ought to answer every one.

Analysis

Similar series of individual admonitions are found in 1 Thess. 5:12-22; Gal. 5:26—6:6; Phil. 4:8f. toward the end of the letter. Here also the admonitions are used to return from the household rule to the general exhortation. Hence the characteristic marks of the author's style, participles, appended relative clauses, infinitives, and circumstantial descriptive phrases ("with thanksgiving," v 2; cf. note

14 to Introduction), are again more noticeably evident. As far as content is concerned, most of this section is reminiscent of the Pauline Epistles—thus for instance, the admonition to pray and be vigilant, and to intercede for the apostle whose ministry is described in terms characteristic of Colossians, as also the reference to his imprisonment. The final two verses have been thoroughly remolded. Verses 2 and 5 form, by means of an imperative and a participle that takes up the sense of this, the framework within which are set the more personal references to the work and fate of the apostle in vv 3f.[1]

Interpretation

[2] The letter, in summarizing all the admonitions, now points the community toward prayer; more precisely, it is prayer in which they should persevere, and which they should not restrict to situations of special need. This same phrase ("be constant in prayer") is found in Rom. 12:12. The participle can be used almost as an imperative (v. note 4 to 1:12-14); indeed one such participle appears also in v 5 alongside an imperative in order to describe the precise way in which this imperative should be interpreted. The prayer should thus take the form of "watching." It is in basically the same way that 1 Thess. 5:4-6 shows how one should fervently direct one's attention to the coming day of the Lord.

Much the same point is made in the Parable of the Watchman, who had to keep watching at night since his master could return at any time from the feast (Luke 12:36-8). In Luke 21:34-6, however, the call is given to watch "at all times," that is so that they do not let themselves be taken captive by all kinds of things and so that the day of the Lord should not find them unprepared. In Mark 13:34f., the master (or lord) in the parable is away on a journey, and the main emphasis falls on the exemplary conduct of the servants in the meantime. This conduct is designated, in a figurative way, as "watching," although the traditional image of the door-keeper is still appended in v 34, and the return of the lord from his journey in vv 35f. is, strangely, expected only at various hours of the night. In the parallel parable in Matt. 24:48 the evil servant reckons on his master being away for a long time. In Matt. 25:1-12

1. Ludwig, *Verfasser*, 123-6; Zeilinger, *Der Erstgeborene*, 70.

conversely it is the wise virgins who are prepared for a delayed arrival of the bridegroom.

Thus the meaning of "watching" moves more and more noticeably in this direction: to begin with it has the connotation of being constantly orientated toward the coming day of the Lord, which could occur at any time; it then takes on the sense that one should use the intervening period responsibly, having regard for the responsibility which will be laid aside at the day of the Lord, whenever this may come; and finally it comes to mean perservering in using one's time positively over a much longer period. Col. 4:2 lacks any reference to the coming day of the Lord; so also, as early as 1 Thess. 5:5-8 and in spite of the heightened expectation of the Parousia, the watching is described as living in the light and in sobriety, in faith, love, and hope. Thus the weight of emphasis shifts to a certain extent because of the experience of a period that stretches on ahead, although the basic attitude is not changed (cf. p. 176).

[3] Prayer can never be contained exclusively within the confines of a single individual; it must always include others as well. Thus intercession for the apostle and his fellow workers [2] is at the same time an entreaty for the main concern, that is the progress of the gospel. The image of the open door is common. In Hellenism it denotes the freedom to turn in every direction, for example, even with one's literary work. In Judaism, by contrast, it is the actual opening of the door which is emphasized, either in the sense that one opens one's self to God in penitence, or else in the sense that God grants people the opportunity for prayer or repentance, or even that he grants them his grace.

In the New Testament, the important point is that the door is opened by God's grace. In Acts 14:27 this is so in the sense that God makes people open to his message; and in 1 Cor. 16:9; 2 Cor. 2:12; Rev. 3:8 in the sense that God gives the apostle or the community the chance to proclaim the gospel. For Paul presumably the idea is especially that of his word being given effective power, whereas here it is the possibility of exercising his apostolic ministry

2. This is how the plural (alongside the singular in v 3 at the end and v 4 at the beginning) is probably to be understood.
3. Only in Rev. 3:20 is it expected of

the believer that he should open the door to the Lord. Yet there the idea is probably of the eschatological coming of the Lord, as it is in the parable of the doorkeeper (v. on v 2).

in the outside world again, by means of his release from prison. In
any case, the apostle petitions for the door to be opened not for
himself personally but for the word which he represents.[4] The content of this word is described as "the mystery of Christ" (cf. on 1:27;
2:2). In 1:24 it has already been made clear how much the apostle's
suffering in imprisonment, in fact, belongs to this.

[4] It is characteristic of Colossians that the writer speaks of revelation or unveiling, and not proclamation. Thus the apostle is set in
the place of God or of Christ (1:26).[5] Prominent in this concept is
the idea of the wisdom of God (2:2f.), which normally is hidden
but which has now been disclosed by the proclamation of the gospel.
Yet it is this very wisdom which retains its mysterious character. It
cannot simply be taught like a theorem in mathematics; whether
or not it is recognized always depends on God giving it. If the
emphasis at the end of the phrase is on the conjunction *how* (RSV
"as"), then the main point is that the proclamation only really
reaches its hearers when it is delivered in the right mode and manner, that is as it is bestowed on the apostle by God himself. If instead
the emphasis is on *must* (RSV "ought to"), then one may also see
a reference to the idea that the apostle cannot keep silent about his
commission but has to speak. In their intercession, the community
is involved in the event of the proclamation and is responsible for it.

[5] The mention of the outsiders also belongs to the terminology
proper to the mystery that is revealed by God alone. However, as
distinct from Mark 4:11f., the point here is not their hardness of
heart but rather that they may attain this mystery. The expression
is indeed found most notably in 1 Thess. 4:12 in the same connection
as here; there, in fact, it appears in context of the ethical distinction
between the Gentiles and the people of God, a distinction which is
characterized by the list of vices (v. on 3:5). The context is the
same for 1 Cor. 5:12f., although there at least there is no emphasis
placed on this distinction.[6] Thus the Pauline passages provide the
paradigm as far as the language is concerned here.

---

4. Calvin ad loc.

5. Lohmeyer, 162; Ernst, 239. Καταγ-
γέλλειν is the word found in 1 Cor.
2:1; cf. Rom. 1:2; λαλεῖν in 1 Cor. 2:7;
εὐαγγελίζεσθαι in Rom. 15:20; Gal.
1:8; ἱερουργεῖν in Rom. 15:16; πλη-

ροῦν in Rom. 15:19, etc. With Paul,
φανεροῦν in the active is used only
in relation to God (2 Cor. 2:14: this
happens through the apostle).

6. This does happen in Paul in 1 Cor.
2:14f.; 3:1, 3f. by means of the dis-

However, the precise understanding offered by the writer is also fashioned by concepts such as those that appear in Mark 4:11f.; Col. 1:26. The wisdom to which they are called is the wisdom belonging to conduct, that is, ethically correct insight into God's will (v. p. 41). "To buy out the time" (RSV "making the most of the time") probably means to take advantage of every opportunity.[7] The expression in Greek, in fact, describes not a never-ending period but a specific period of time, in other words one which is given by God, a time span kept open by him for his work.

[6] In the case of the description of the "speech," it is presumably a current idiom that is taken over. Salt, which can be the seasoning and aroma of food, is designated by some as the food's "charm."[8] Hence although the word can in itself mean God's grace, that is scarcely the idea here, especially since there is no article (v. p. 211). However, the writer's point of view is not a purely rhetorical one, in which eloquence is something worth striving for simply for its own sake. As in vv 4f., the main interest is the missionary responsibility concerning questions raised by those who are outside the community. This objective becomes more and more important at a time when the community of Jesus, although not actually persecuted, is living in the midst of a population that thinks differently and by which the community is called into question (1 Peter 3:15). It is only God himself who can convict, not the community or the apostle (v 3); but they should be a witness to their Lord before every one. It is not altogether a matter of chance that the writer speaks of answering or replying here. In fact, this shows that the

---

tinction made between the "spiritual" man and the "unspiritual" or man "according to the flesh" (thus frequently), or simply "man" on its own. Rabbinic parallels are given in Strack-Billerbeck III, 362.

7. In Dan. 2:8 LXX the expression means "to seek to gain time." Here what is meant by "buy out" is probably the exhausting of every opportunity that is afforded (F. Büchsel, TDNT I, 128; Zwingli, 227).

8. Plut. Quaest. Conv. V, 10:2 (II, 685A): ἅλες, χάριτες; similarly De Garrulitate 23 (II, 514F): "to convey a certain grace (χάριν) by means of

words as with salt (ἁλσί)." Cf. Mark 9:49f. W. Nauck, "Salt as a Metaphor in Instructions for Discipleship," ST 6 (1952), 165-78, understands salt as an image for wisdom at the time of the eschatological fulfillment. Zwingli, 227: "Salted speech, brave, wise, powerful, tasty, not indifferent, resounding." Λόγος τῆς (!) χάριτος in Acts 14:3; 20: (24), 30 means "word of grace"; in Luke 4:22 (where it is found in the plural) the idea is rather more that of "graceful" or "charming" words. Yet there, as in Col. 4:6, there may be echoes of the recollection of God's grace.

point is not to inaugurate a propaganda campaign for Christ, but to be prepared to face all those who ask about him.

Conclusion

The section first provides a call to prayer, and then to responsibility vis-à-vis those who are outside the community; that is, it directs the community first of all toward God and thence toward their neighbors, especially those outside the community. Like a child who tags along behind his mother in a shopping center, never letting her out of his sight even if she has not looked back at him for a long while, so also the community in its prayer should remain completely orientated toward God. Thus the dialogue between God and his people opened up by Christ should be given practical application. It is for this reason that the emphasis on thanksgiving also permeates this closing section as it does the whole letter (1:3, 12; 2:7; 3:15, 17). It is for this reason as well that they are again reminded that only God can open closed doors. The kind of prayer which this implies is especially intercession.

This sets the people free from the danger of being caught up completely in the narrow and restricted world of their own relationships, cares, and joys; instead it links them to their real concern, that is their interest in the progress of Christ's message throughout the world. So the exhortation proceeds quite naturally to the theme of their responsibility for others. Again, this is not something that one can simply "do." In any case, converse with God in intercession takes precedence over all converse with human beings. Thus also, first and foremost, it is the community in every facet of its existence, not just its words, that would take effect. For their way of life is the most important factor in the mission. Indeed, the point is expressed succinctly by what an Indian is once supposed to have remarked to a European: "What you are shouts so loud that I can no longer hear what you say."

In this respect, the statement that "the time" should be used to full effect is intended to make two points: first, that one is able to wait for the right time, and second, that one should then use the given time for a decisive discussion. Their word should not be vague, but seasoned with salt, pungent and provocative, yet also healing and beneficent, full of daring in order to come to grips with urgent questions. Yet it can be this and still not lose its character as mystery. It is only God who can open up this understanding for another person as well; hence the main concern is to bring others to an individual experience of God's gift. This provides courage for responsible discussion, and correspondingly warns against false, obtrusive propaganda.

The Conclusion of the Letter (4:7-18)

7 Tychicus will tell you all about my affairs; he is a beloved brother and faithful minister and fellow servant in the Lord. 8 I have sent him to you for this very purpose, that you may know how we are and that he may encourage your hearts, 9 and with him Onesimus, the faithful and beloved brother, who is one of yourselves. They will tell you of everything that has taken place here. 10 Aristarchus my fellow prisoner greets you, and Mark the cousin of Barnabas (concerning whom you have received instructions—if he comes to you, receive him), 11 and Jesus who is called Justus. These are the only men of the circumcision among my fellow workers for the kingdom of God, and they have been a comfort to me. 12 Epaphras, who is one of yourselves, a servant of Christ Jesus, greets you, always remembering you earnestly in his prayers, that you may stand mature and fully assured in all the will of God. 13 For I bear him witness that he has worked hard for you and for those in Laodicea and in Hierapolis. 14 Luke the beloved physician and Demas greet you. 15 Give my greetings to the brethren at Laodicea, and to Nympha and the church in her house. 16 And when this letter has been read among you, have it read also in the church of the Laodiceans; and see that you read also the letter from Laodicea. 17 And say to Archippus, "See that you fulfil the ministry which you have received in the Lord." 18 I, Paul, write this greeting with my own hand. Remember my fetters. Grace be with you.

Analysis

The section is composed of short communications (vv 7-9), a fairly long list of greetings (vv 10-17), and the concluding greeting (v 18). In context of the letter as a whole, this section is longer than the corresponding sections in the Pauline Epistles. The characteristic idiosyncracies of the author noticeably diminish, but do not disappear altogether.[1] In vv 7-9 the bearers of the letter are com-

---

1. The formulation "faithful minister" (4:7) also appears in 1:7, likewise connected with "beloved" and "fellow servant" (only "brother" is lacking there); "faithful brother" (4:9; cf. 4:7) is found also in 1:2 (in the plural), and for this it is true that 1 Cor. 4:17 (Timothy, "beloved and faithful

mended to the Colossians, while in vv 10-17 those who send greetings are first of all mentioned and described. Only in the case of the last two who are mentioned (v 14) is this detailed description omitted completely or almost completely. Next is attached a greeting to the brethren in Laodicea, along with the recommendation for an exchange of letters; then an admonition to Archippus [2] forms the conclusion. No one apart from Nympha is greeted by name, but conversely the fellow workers staying with the apostle are introduced at great length. This is connected with the fact that the letter is directed to a community which Paul does not know. In v 18 the apostle's greeting with his own hand concludes the letter, as it does in 1 Cor. 16:21; 2 Thess. 3:17 (cf. Gal. 6:11; Philem. 19). This is followed by a reminder of his imprisonment and the promise of grace, in an abbreviated form [3] which is both unPauline and which is also found in 1 Tim. 6:21; 2 Tim. 4:22 (Titus 3:15), likewise specifically as the very last thing to be mentioned.

Interpretation

[7] By means of the formulation "what concerns me" (as in Phil. 1:12; RSV here "my affairs"), and a verb especially favored by Paul, reference is made to the fact that Tychicus will report on everything necessary (cf. similarly Epaphras in 1:7; v. p. 37). As a "fellow-servant" he is set at the apostle's side; both carry out their ministry together "in the Lord,'" as it is expressed by this phrase which the author of Colossians particularly favors. Tychicus otherwise appears only in the post-Pauline Epistles. He is however mentioned in Acts 20:4 on the relief mission, as a companion of Paul, and originating from Asia Minor.

---

child" of Paul "in the Lord") is to be compared, as the only instance (Bujard, *Untersuchungen*, 99, 175). The addition of πᾶν to θέλημα τοῦ θεοῦ in 4:12 (similarly 1:9) is plerophoric (ibid., 159f.). Other features that could also be mentioned are appended relative clauses which are not specific in themselves but carry on from one another (4, 8, 9, 11; ibid., 68f.; Ludwig, 127), perhaps also the duplication of the designation, unfamiliar in Paul, of the community as "mature and fully assured" (4:12; cf. 1:28;

2:10; 3:14), and a participial construction, not especially striking it is true, in 4:12 (Ludwig, ibid.).
2. On the agreement of the names with those in Philemon cf. pp. 20f. In Paul, those sending greetings and those receiving them may also stand in reverse sequence, and the closing blessing can be shorter or longer (Ernst, 240).
3. All of Paul's letters close: ἡ χάρις *tou* κυρίου (ἡμῶν) Ἰησοῦ (Χριστοῦ) μεθ' (or μετὰ τοῦ πνεύματος) . ὑμῶν, possibly further supplemented with other terms (2 Cor. 13:13).

[8] Information about the apostle's personal circumstances is viewed as an important matter.[4] It should also afford encouragement for their hearts (v. p. 116). The figure of the apostle should not be allowed to evaporate into some sort of mythical or ideal object. The community's link with the apostle should be made real precisely by their knowing of the circumstances, whether important or merely trivial and incidental, of his human existence. Indeed, the intercession requested in vv 3f. cannot effectively be realized without a vivid association of this kind, which includes all aspects of human life, both significant and insignificant. In antiquity, the writer of a letter would put himself into the place of the reader and say (as here), "I have sent," even if he is thinking of a "sending" which at this precise moment, at the actual time of writing, is still to follow and which we must therefore translate by the present tense.

[9] Onesimus can hardly be taken to mean anyone else except the person mentioned in Philemon, both because he is introduced as a brother who comes from Colossae, although not as a fellow worker, and also because the names in the list of those who send greetings correspond almost completely with the list of names in Philemon. It is understandable that nothing is said of his flight, if the letter was indeed, as is probable, composed shortly after (or even at the same time as) that to Philemon, in which case everything that needed to be said would have been dealt with in this more private communication; or else, if Colossians comes from a later time, it would be at a stage when this particular case would no longer be of interest.

[10] The list of greetings is extraordinarily long, and in this respect can be compared only with Rom. 16. Yet it is almost exclusively a matter of greetings sent from Paul's fellow workers and friends to the community as a whole. Certainly the Colossians Epaphras and Onesimus are staying with the apostle. However, the apostle and probably also the writer of the letter (Timothy?), who is staying with Paul as well, do not know the community personally; hence

---

4. p[46]C, etc., as also Chrysostom XI, 1 (375), formulate this the other way round, that is that he should seek news concerning Colossae. However, the textual attestation and Eph. 6:22 argue in favor of the rendering given here; for Ephesians often repeats phrases from Colossians, so that the equivalence here does not depend on assimilation by a copyist.

there is hardly any mention of individuals in Colossae by name, but instead the apostle's fellow workers are introduced. This is done in a way that distinguishes them from each other very clearly.

Aristarchus is presented as a "fellow prisoner," which is what is said of Epaphras (Col. 4:12) in Philemon 23. That is, he shares with Paul the fate of being imprisoned, whereas the others are presumably free and can only come on visits. As for the Thessalonian called Aristarchus (Acts 19:29; 20:4; 27:2), he is clearly the same person as here, since he also appears, both before and after the relief visit (v. on v 7), in Ephesus, where Colossians was presumably written, and again as a companion of Paul on the journey to Rome.

Mark is introduced as the cousin of Barnabas, who is apparently known to the community. In spite of the difficulties connected with the person of Mark in Gal. 2:13; Acts 13:13, 15, 37-9, Barnabas at any rate is also known to the Corinthians (1 Cor. 9:6); his connection with Mark is mentioned in Acts 15:37, 39, without any reference to their being related. Since Mark is also mentioned in Philemon 24,[6] it is clear that the disagreement did not bring about a lasting separation between Paul and Mark or Barnabas. Letters of recommendation were necessary at that time, and used extensively, since one did, of course, have to stay with friends and take meals with them, but they also needed to be protected from impostors. In this case these letters have perhaps reached the community from some other source, or else Paul has written them earlier, without Mark's proposed journey having hitherto taken place.[7]

[11] Jesus Justus is the only one who does not appear in Philemon, unless it is his name that should be read in v 23 there (cf. pp. 20f.). A second name, intelligible in Greek or Latin, was frequently used alongside the Semitic one. Justus, "the just," was for this purpose especially favored by the Jews.[8] The three people mentioned here

5. A purely metaphorical conception (2 Cor. 10:5) is surely not possible here, where there is no reference to Christ, although otherwise the word does rather denote a prisoner-of-war (Caird, 211).

6. If this were not the case, the name would count as an indication of the unauthenticity of the letter, since Mark, after the separation of Acts 15:39, never appears together with Paul (except in 2 Tim. 4:11). Cf. also note 25 to Introduction.

7. The assumption that these letters would have given warning about Mark, but that meanwhile the reconciliation took place (Thomas Aquinas, 554b), is extremely improbable since in that case something would have had to be said of this.

8. Instances are given in Pr.-Bauer, s.v.; Lightfoot, 236. Chrysostom XI, 2

are specified as the only Jewish Christians (literally: "those of the circumcision") who have remained faithful to God in the apostle's ministry for the kingdom of God,[9] and have thus become a "comfort" [10] to him in his plight. "They alone" [11] is set on its own at the end, and its position makes it the more emphatic. The battles about the law had of course been fought through in Galatians and Romans, and the repercussions of these can still be felt even in Ephesians and James, although later all traces completely disappear; here the fight is carried on in a certain isolation from the apostle. These three are "fellow workers," probably of Paul (as in Philemon 24), not of God (as in 1 Cor. 3:9).

[12] Epaphras is obviously a Colossian who has won people for Christ in his home town (1:7) and now (voluntarily?) shares Paul's imprisonment (Philemon 23). He is given an epithet which usually belongs to Paul (but cf. James 1:1; 2 Peter 1:1; Jude 1): "slave of Christ"; yet in Phil. 1:1 Timothy is also described in this way along with Paul, and 1 Cor. 7:22 suggests, although admittedly in context of the problem concerning the slave and the free man, that it applied more generally. However, the participial clause also largely corresponds to what 2:1 and 1:3 say of the apostle himself. Once again it is impressed upon the community that they should remain perfect and "fully assured"[12] specifically, they should be oriented toward the whole will of God, as Colossians characteristically expresses it (v. p. 41).

[13] The pains [13] or trouble (RSV, "he has worked hard") that Epaphras has taken for the Colossians and the neighboring com-

---

(375) wonders whether it is the person mentioned in Acts 18:7.

9. The phrase "the kingdom of God" is used only sparsely by Paul, and mostly in a traditional, eschatological manner; yet Rom. 14:17; 1 Cor. 4:20 show that this phrase would not be impossible for him.

10) Παρηγορία is found only here in the New Testament and, like παράκλησις (18 times in Paul including Philemon 7), denotes the response that can be both admonition and consolation. The verb παρακαλεῖν appears in Col. 2:2; 4:8.

11. Should one see Tychicus also as a Jewish Christian or conversely exclude Aristarchus (on account of Acts 19:29; 27:2; cf. Houlden, 220)? For Calvin, 164 and Beza, 421a, 27-30, this proves that Peter was not in Rome.

12. Cf. pp. 111 and 139. Possibly it can also be translated "and completely convinced by."

13. The textual variants introduce in place of this concept those which avoid this nuance with its slightly negative effect, but which do not really change the sense.

munities can be taken to refer to his involvement in intercession and his concern for the well-being of the community. It is not necessary, therefore, to assume that the place of his imprisonment was geographically so close to the community that constant visits were possible, although there is some hint of such proximity. It is also conceivable that Epaphras had encountered difficulties, and hence had had to withdraw and return to Paul.[14]

[14] Here alone is Luke, who like Mark is mentioned along with Paul in Philemon 24, given the designation "doctor." He is a Gentile Christian, as v 11 shows. Demes later, in 2 Tim. 4:10, is reproached for having fallen away from Paul.

[15] Next there follow greetings from the apostle himself, first of all to the community at Laodicea. This lies only sixteen kilometers from Colossae, and the instruction to greet them should help to strengthen mutual relationships. It is true that the Laodiceans are themselves being sent a special letter (that to Philemon?) or indeed have already received it; but some time may already have elapsed since this letter was sent (cf. pp. 24f.). Whether or not this is the case, the instruction to greet them is readily intelligible, since the apostle suggests that messengers should go to the neighboring community with this letter.

The house community addressed here is probably based in Laodicea. Whether a man, Nymphas, or a woman, Nympha, is meant depends on what one considers to be the original reading for the personal pronoun. Perhaps an original "her" was subsequently changed to "his," because at a later stage it could not be conceived of that a woman might be responsible for an entire house community.[15] In the New Testament the same word denotes both an (extended) family gathered together in faith and also the worldwide church.[16] Wherever people meet together in the name of Jesus, they are a "church" without the necessity of any quorum at all, not even the minimum number of ten, as in the case of the Jewish synagogue service.[17] Perhaps the writer even has in mind here the whole Lao-

---

14. Cf. Lohse, 174.

15. "Her" Bsy[h], etc., "his" א DG, etc.; the Hesychian group read "their," presumably because both readings already existed. On the house community cf. Stuhlmacher, *Philemon*, 70-5.

The feminine accusative form of the proper name is not the usual one (Caird,, 212; hence he prefers the masculine version).

16. Lohse *NTS* 11, 214.

17. F. Hahn, *Des urchristliche Gottes-*

dicean community which meets in this house, since to begin with
certainly private houses represented the sole possibility for a common meeting place.

[16] The proposal to exchange letters is probably the first hint
anywhere of a collection of Pauline letters, assuming that the communities did in fact begin to make copies of other letters. It is possible that in this case only the most important parts were copied and
kept together with their own letter, and perhaps later both were also
written out together (cf. pp. 21f.). The philosophical ideas that had
infiltrated Colossae had presumably gained a hold in the neighboring
regions as well, so that the exchange of the two letters would thus
prove all the more important. Of course, the letter from Laodicea is
likewise a letter of Paul, which should come to them "from" this
community, and not a letter that the Laodiceans had written.[18] It
has not been preserved for us, unless in fact the letter in question
is that to Philemon. Much later, someone pieced together a letter
of this kind from various Pauline phrases.[19]

[17] Archippus is also mentioned in Philemon 2 as a fellow com-
batant of the apostle, dwelling in the community addressed there
(Laodicea?). We can no longer say for certain what he is admonished to do. The word used here denotes quite generally any kind of
"ministry," not specifically for instance the office of a deacon. The
fact that he has undertaken it "in the Lord" does however show that
it must be a ministry of some importance. Except for Philemon and
Apphia, to whom the letter to Philemon is addressed, all those mentioned in Philemon appear in the Epistle to the Colossians as well.
Apart from the doubtful case of Jesus Justus (v. on v 11), along
with Tychicus (v 7) and Nympha(s) (who according to v 15 is
probably in Laodicea) there is no one in Colossians who is not also
found in Philemon.

[18] It was customary to use a greeting from one's own hand in

dienst, 1967 (JLH 12), 19 (cf. Matt.
18:20).
18. So e.g. Chrysostom XII 1 (382,
as the opinion of some); Theodoret
625CD (perhaps with complaints
about the Colossian error); Photius
632 = Oecumenius 53D; Hrabanus

540; Zwingli, 228 (because otherwise
Col. 4:15 would be impossible!); Bullinger, 269; Beza 421b, 13-18: not 1
Timothy (John of Damascus 904C));
likewise Gomarus 575a; Calov 848a
(not Ephesians).
19. Hennecke II, 128-32.

order to acknowledge that one had written a letter (cf. 1 Cor. 16:21; Gal. 6:11). The request to remember the apostle and thus to associate oneself closely with him is also to be found in 1 Thess. 2:9; it is given still greater emphasis here by the reference to his imprisonment. 4:3f. shows that the community should remember not only his personal suffering but also their share in his task of proclaiming the gospel. The last word, however, properly belongs to grace; for it is grace that represents the sole source of all effective power and help for both parties, the one who sends the letter and those who receive it.

Conclusion

A striking feature of this last section is that so much is said throughout about purely human affairs. It indicates that there was a considerable amount of coming and going, as well as of visiting and bringing news in person. Tychicus comes to Colossae as does Onesimus, who had perhaps returned to Paul again after the journey that had been announced in Philemon. Epaphras has at some point returned from Colossae and now sends greetings. As regards Mark, they have received news from someone—perhaps the apostle himself—he will travel to them later. Messengers should come to them from Laodicea and bring back from there a letter from the apostle. There is a prolific activity—correspondence, reading of letters, talking, praying, and thinking of one another—going on between the apostle and the community, between one community and another, and even between individuals who belong to the small group that gathers together in a house. Reciprocal exchange and sympathy of this sort is of crucial importance. People need one another in the community; even the apostle needs brethren and friends. Hence it is that the writer speaks of their "hearts," of a "beloved brother," of "fellow prisoners; fellow servants, and fellow workers."

One can only "lay claim" to the gospel when one knows and takes seriously other people and their situation. The banal, everyday world, which at root is not so banal at all, thus takes on importance; and the community must learn to open themselves to others without trying to keep up appearances. Indeed, the sending of Tychicus is "for this very purpose" of giving the Colossians an idea of what really happens in the apostle's everyday life. It is worth taking the trouble to write, to set out to see someone, to give oneself time to think of others. It is worthwhile when all this is carried out before the one Lord who is worshiped in common; thus all human contact takes on the dimension of prayer. Such contact becomes all the more essential where there is obvious need, as perhaps during Paul's detention. Glowing coals are put out the moment they are no longer touching other coals. Hence it is that prayer can even become a struggle and self-exertion in which one may indeed live through a difficult period with another person, expose oneself to various kinds of afflictions, and in which one can no longer shield oneself from anything unpleasant. In all this, one's concern will be with God's kingdom and God's will (vv 11f.). And it is for this reason that there will be tremendous confidence in being together, because then everyone can encourage each other with the blessing "Grace be with you."

The Impact of Colossians

I

Introduction

The impact which a work has had is shown not so much in commentaries as in systematic presentations, attempts to understand the text in one's contemporary situation, and above all in the life of the church. Hence one ought to look fully into all of those in order to arrive at any conclusions. This can be done here only in a very fragmentary way.[1] Moreover for the early period it is difficult to decide to what extent ideas that are prior to or in close affinity with the New Testament have had on Colossians. For the later period as well, it is equally difficult always to ascertain whether the New Testament text itself has been the source of fresh developments or whether it has merely provided additional support for such developments.

The most important impact that Colossians has had is the fact that the Epistle to the Ephesians came to be written (cf. note 6 to the Introduction). Ephesians, therefore, ought to be included in an account of the impact of Colossians. But a detailed discussion of this point will have to be left to a commentary on Ephesians. Often the interpreter cannot be certain whether it is a passage from Colos-

---

1. Especially helpful were: *Biblia Patristica (Des origenes à Clément d'Alexandrie et Tertullien,* Paris 1975); Staehelin, *Verkündigung;* the references in Lightfoot and Abbott and the Indices in modern editions. R. R. Brinkmann, *The Prototokos Title (Col. 1:15) and the Beginnings of Its Exegesis,* Rome 1954 (Diss. Gregoriana), is unfortunately not available in Switzerland, and hence I have not used it.

sians or the corresponding one from Ephesians that has exercised
influence in a particular case.

There is no passage in the New Testament, apart from the Prologue to the Fourth Gospel and Heb. 1:3, whose roots can be traced
so clearly to Jewish Wisdom literature as the hymn in Col. 1:15-20.
This fact has important theological repercussions. It is much more
striking in Colossians than in the Fourth Gospel or Hebrews how
these expressions from Wisdom literature are combined with the
interpretation of the author of the Epistle. The result is that statements about the Pre-existent One are set directly alongside those
about the human Jesus and his death on the cross. This has had a
forceful effect in the further development of statements about
Christ. Indeed, it is this which must have given rise to the propo-
sition concerning the fullness of the divine being actually dwelling
in Christ, making him head over all authorities and bringing him
victory over them (2:9f., 14f.).

In Colossians as well there emerges for the first time the concept
of the "economy" of God (1:25), which was soon understood as part
of the plan of salvation history. Likewise the household rule (3:18–
4:1) appears here for the first time, and has exercised a strong influence especially in more recent times. Finally the proclamation of
the reconciliation of the universe (1:20) has had an extraordinary
impact in various ways, although it is true that these have often
developed more noticeably in underground movements and outside
the official teaching of the church.

In Colossians as well the abrupt juxtaposition of the hymnic experience concerning reconciliation in heaven and on earth with the
way that the redactor restricts this to the body of believers becomes
a problem which is difficult to resolve. And also in Colossians various questions are raised concerning the relationship between the
world and the church, between nature and the church, and between
creation and redemption.

II

Christology: The Father and the Son

1. Christ as the Wisdom of God

The two verses, Col. 1:15, 18b, provide the first instance where
the influence of Colossians is clearly felt. Here, at the beginning of

two parallel strophes, both verses have their roots in the wisdom
tradition and serve to provide a more precise definition of the significance of Christ.

JUSTIN, given a philosophical training in Ephesus on the west
coast of Asia Minor, takes the "first-born of all creation" (*Dial.* 85:2,
without the article as Col. 1:15) or "of all creatures" (*Dial.* 128:3,
cf. 84:2), correctly in the sense of Jewish Logos theology, to refer to
the one who exists "before all creatures" (*Dial.* 100:2). Above all
Justin is still aware of the import of such expressions, which are intended to describe God's movement toward humankind for their salvation. It is for this reason that he speaks immediately of the miracle
of the incarnation; and the juxtaposition of the "first-born of all creation" and "beginning," at the start of the two strophes of the hymn,
in Colossians, reminds him of the way in which the first and second
creations are made parallel (as can be shown to be the case in
Philo).

Thus, in PHILO, Noah is, vis-à-vis Adam, "the progenitor of a new
human race," the "leader of rebirth";[1] so also in Justin, Noah becomes a type of Christ, the "beginning of a new human race, born
again of him" (*Dial.* 138:2). This is the theology which one also finds
in *the Epistle to Diognetus* (7): God sent not only a man, but the
holy Logos, the creator and maker of the universe, through whom
everything has been created and keeps its order, a God as man.

This view still persists in IRENAEUS, who likewise was trained on
the west coast of Asia Minor, in Smyrna. The key word of Col. 1:25,
now understood in the sense of the divine plan of salvation, for him
serves to describe the work of the Logos which has already taken
place before the incarnation, and its fulfillment in it, as God's movement toward his people to bring salvation. By the incarnation the
shepherd comes to his lost sheep [2] and restores again the dispensation of salvation, by saving "Adam" who is created according to
the image and form of God.[3] Thus according to God's dispensation

---

1. *Abr.* 46; *Vit. Mos.* II, 60; 65; on
this v. E. Schweizer, "Menschensohn
und eschatologischer Mensch im Frühjudentum," in: *Jesus und der Menschensohn,* ed. R. Pesch and R. Schnackenburg, Freiburg 1975 (Festschr. A.
Vögtle) esp. 104. As Col. 1:18, so
also Justin *Dial,* 138:1 links this with
the resurrection of Jesus (and with

deliverance at the Judgment. Ibid 3).
2. This image has had its repercussions; the remaining ninety-nine sheep
have been identified with the world
and nature outside the church, which
have likewise been brought into the
salvation of God (Eudokimov *KD* 11,
9; similarly in John Scotus, v. p. 266).
3. III, 32, 2 (23,1) – II, 124; cf. III,

of salvation, the flesh is accorded salvation, since it has come to partake in incorruptibility, through the fact that according to Col. 1:14, 21f.; 2:13-15, 19, the Logos took on human form and restored man whole again.[4]

In the Logos, God has become what we are in order to make us into what he is (V praef. — II 314). It is in the "body of flesh" that he has suffered, according to Col. 1:22, because the flesh taken on by God has thus redeemed our flesh (V 14, 3 (2) — II 362). According to Col. 1:18, he has gone through death in order that, as Adam was the beginning of those who die, so he may become the beginning of those who live, the "first-born from the dead" and thus also Lord of those who are beneath the earth.[5] Thus beginning and end have come together; the commingling and uniting of man with God has become a reality (IV 34, 4 (20, 4) — II 215). Here also then the interest still lies completely with God's gift of salvation to the world; this will be discussed under III 2a. But the really basic Christological questions have already been opened up.

The situation is similar with the Alexandrian writers. Here the Hellenistic-Jewish world of ideas is still a basic presupposition for their concepts. This is so of CLEMENT [6] and especially of ORIGEN. For Origen, Christ is seen as the expression of the substance of subsistence of God, his revelation, "word," and "wisdom," "pure and perfect power," [7] God's "emanation" and the "beginning of his ways." [8] Again, "image," precisely because it is connected with the "invis-

19, 1 (18,1) and the ethical consequences deriving from this on the basis of Col. 3:5, 9f. in V, 12, 3f. — II, 352f.

4. V, 2,1 (2,2); 14,2-4 (14,2-5) — II, 318f.; 362f.: dispositio (= οἰκονομία, I, 1,11 (6,1)—I, 52). In V, 12, 4 — II, 353f. Col. 3:10 proves that the person living in the flesh is also the one born again through the "restoration."

5. III, 32,1 (22.4); II, 33,2 (22,4) — II, 124; I 330; IV, 34.2 (20.2) — II, 214.

6. Strom. V, 38,7 (353,1): as "image of the invisible God" (Col. 1:15) he is the principle of all things and everything is created according to him; cf. further VII, 12,2,5; 34,4; cf. 6,1 (9, 26-8; 10,2-5; 27, 5-8; 6,8-10).

7. Virtus: Hom. in Gen. 6:2f. (69:10-13); Comm. in Joh. 1:22 (27:32f.); in Princ. I 2:1; 7:25f. (28:8-12) Col. 1:15 and 1 Cor. 1:24 are already combined together: Christ is wisdom and power; cf. the trinity as "power" in 4:3 (65:9-12). The same combination of Col. 1:15 with 1 Cor. 1:24 is found in Athanasius, c.Arian, II, 62f. (280AB); Cyril, c. Nest. 2 (68B: "creator of the world, wisdom and power (1 Cor. 1:24), image (Col. 1:15) and reflection (Wis. 7:26) of the hypostasis of the Father"); John of Damascus 888C; cf. Basil, c.Eunom. 4 (PG 29, 701B-704A; Prov. 8:22; 705A).

8. I, 2:9 (39:12—40:7): ἀπόρροια (Wis. 7:25f.); IV, 4:1 (349:11-15): Prov. 8:22.

ible image" which the Pre-existent One represents,[9] is understood
first and foremost as a revelatory event, in other words dynamically.[10]

Then again there is the notion, which is originally rooted in Platonic concepts of the Logos as the place in which all God's ideas
are found.[11] This notion, which in Philo serves to make intelligible
the role of wisdom in creation (note 30 to 1:15-20), was expressed
at about the same time by one of the disciples of Irenaeus: the
Logos is the sum total of the divine ideas, in which the whole cosmos dwelt already before the creation of the world.[12]

This concept was later taken up by THOMAS AQUINAS (535ab),
and plays its part in cosmological disputes; it was rejected, ironically, by ERASMUS (885 C), but has been reiterated up until recent
times. There is at present an animated complaint about this doctrine
of the Logos (perhaps mediated by Apollos) which has infiltrated
the New Testament only in this sole instance of the hymn in Colossians.[13] Luecken calls it "one of the most disastrous developments"
in which "philosophy has stifled religion" and "the Savior recedes
behind the idea expressed in the Logos." [14] But this is not valid at
least for this early stage of the debate. On the contrary, the rediscov-
ery in more recent times of these sources for the concept has served
the purpose of finding a way from an abstract Christology to one
related directly to human beings and their world.[15]

---

9. E.g. Orig., *Princ.* I, 1:8; II, 4:3;
IV, 4:1 (25:3-7; 130; 3-131:23; 349:
5f.); according to *Comm. in Joh.*
XXVIII, 18,159 (412) this, it goes
without saying, is the Logos who, in
turn, is God.
10. As a manifestation of God: Orig.,
Comm. in Joh. VI, 19 (110, 18-24),
with reference to John 14:9 which is
everywhere reiterated; Tertullian,
Marc. V, 19, 13 (721, 13-18). According to Basil *Ep.* 38,3 (340A-C) it is
"image of his goodness"; "form and
πρόσωπον(countenance) of the knowledge of God."
11. The instances for Cl. Al. are assembled in E. F. Osborn, *The Philosophy of Clement of Alexandria*, 1957
(TaS) 41-4. Cf. the resumption of these
ideas in note 54 to C IV Ethics.
12. Hipp. *Ref.* X, 33,2 (289,8-11);

Tertullian, *c. Hermogenem*, 18,5 (411,
20–412,9); *c. Praxeam* 6, 3:7,1 (1165,
5-20) with reference to Prov. 8:22.
Cf. note 39 to 1:15-20 and notes 30
and 50 to C III Soteriology.
13. Scott, 12; cf. 20 (similarly at a
later stage in the Prologue to the
Fourth Gospel) and 22 (on 1:17: the
religious interest is forgotten).
14. Luecken, 344.
15. Apart from those mentioned on
pp. 257f., 286f., cf. also amongst modern writers Mussner, 39f.; however, cf.
also the link with the Johannine Prologue and the view of Christ as wisdom in person in Petrus L. 264A (cf.
267B; 269B; 273B), or the reference
to Heb. 1:3 and Wis. 7:25 in Melanchthon (*Enarratio*, [Introduction to
Col. 1:1] 326).

2. First-Born of All Creation, Image of the Invisible God (Col. 1:15)

The Arian controversy brings this phrase into prominence. The formulation "first-born of all creation" was bound to lead to the false idea of Christ being seen as the first creature.[16] Against this, ATHA-NASIUS and, of his followers, above all THEODORE made the point that 1:18a does indeed speak of the "head of the church," that is, of the incarnate one. They then used the argument to refer the passage unhesitatingly to the human form of Jesus that the Logos assumes.[17] MARCELLUS explicitly claimed this also for the description "image of God." [18]

The background of the Hellenistic-Jewish world of ideas has by now vanished almost completely, and the Church Fathers at this stage could not conceive of attributing 1:18a to a redactional interpretation on the part of the author of Colossians. So the question whether Col. 1:15 should be taken to refer to the Preexistent One, or better still to the Incarnate One,[19] has never been settled despite centuries of debate. Right from the beginning, of course, the difficulties could not be overlooked. Indeed Theodore was already forced to draw the obvious conclusion, that is, to take Col. 1:15-17

16. Athanasius, c. Arian. II, 62f. (277C-281C); Hilary, Ex opere historico fragmentum 3,30 (655C-656A). The patristic discussion is explicitly treated in Gomarus 550a.

17. 262,4-9; 263,4-264,13 with reference to the "image of God" in Gen. 1:27; 1 Cor. 11:7; the repercussions of this can be seen in Augustine, Expos. ad Rom. 56 (2077); it is explicitly contested in the Catena (Cramer, 302 on 1:13).

18. This view is still given in the Jerusalem Bible p. 343 note (e); it is disputed by Euseb., De ecclesiastica theologia I, 20, 14 (PG 24, 885C-888A).

19. So e.g. Hrabanus 511A-512C; Calvin 129 (with the remark that it was only the anti-Arian stand that was responsible for the interpretation in terms of the Pre-existent One); Beza, 403a, 30ff.; Grotius, 672a-673a (against this, Calov, 803b); Flatt,

168 ("attributes of God in a gentle image appropriate to us"); de Wette, 24 (with reference to the connection with 1:14(!): in the one who has become man, the two natures are united); Schleiermacher, Predigt IV, 236f. (against Luther); 240 (what profit would the Colossians have gained from propositions concerning preexistence?); TSK V/I, 505-12 (with reference to Col. 1:18a!). According to Bengel (on the "image of God") 811, Christ is invisible according to his divine nature, and visible according to his human nature. Gomarus 549b makes the distinction: he is identical in nature, to the Father always indeed, and to us as the Incarnate One (thus Gomarus parries the Arian position); Zanchi, 261 speaks of the invisible which has however become visible in the incarnation. This remains the normal explanation.

to refer to the new creation. But in doing so he has to acknowledge vv 16d, 17a to be an exception.[20] If one were not happy with
this, then one would at the very least have to interpret "powers and
authorities" in terms of earthly lords; and this had political consequences in the post-Reformation period.[21]

Hence this interpretation has largely been abandoned. However,
in order to refute the Arian arguments. the suggestion was even
made that by moving the Greek accent the text could be made to
read "first progenitor" instead of "first-born." [22] This was untenable,
both linguistically and also in view of 1:18b. However, from Athanasius onwards, the point was repeated countless times that what
is spoken of here is the "first-born" and not the "first created"; [23]
and likewise that the formulation in 1:17 specifically has "is" and
not "became." [24]

This was emphasized especially in the struggle against PAUL OF
SAMOSATA, and the claim that "brothers born after" and equal to
him was rejected.[25] Again, as far as the concept of the "image of God"
was concerned, the idea of a replica, as represented for example by
images of wood or wax or by statues and coins, had to be averted.[26]
Col. 1:15 is taken to mean the invisible image of the Preexistent

20. 267, 13-17 (Greek); 277, 1f.; on
the exception v. 272,3-273,11 (cf.
274, 19-27, Greek); cf. note 26 to C
III Soteriology.
21. Theodoret 600B refers to the angels of the nations, John of Damascus
(896B on 2:15) to the ruling powers
on earth who crucified Jesus; likewise
Flatt, 219. The idea is limited to
"thrones and dominions" in Crell 529a,
and rejected by Gomarus 550b-551a
(he also on 551-3 adduces a great deal
of material concerning the hierarchies
of angels); it is carried through to its
logical conclusions in Schleiermacher,
TSK V/I, 514, cf. 532. Augustine, ad
Oros. 14 (678) already conducts a
polemic against speculations concerning hierarchies of angels on the basis
of Col. 1:16. Cf. further note 60 to C
III Soteriology and note 40 to C IV
Ethics.
22. Isidore, Ep. III, 31 (749CD); cf.
Basil, c. Eunom. IV (PG 29, 701C).
23. Athanasius, Expositio 3 (204C-

205A); Chrysostom III, 2 (318);
Theodore 263, 8f. as an assertion on
the part of the opponents; Theodoret
579CD; Ambrosiaster 172,1; Petrus
L. 263B; Calov 803a etc. Cf. also note
30 to 1:15-20.
24. Basil, c. Eunom. IV (701BC);
Theodoret 600C; Photius 631; Theophylact 1224A; Bengel, 812 etc.
25. Chrysostom III, 2 (320, cf. 319);
cf. Theophylact 1224A. Basil seems
to have done this with reference to
Rom. 8:29 (so already Theodore 263,
14-264,5) and Mark 3:35, and Cyril
seems to have based something similar in the incarnation of the Logos
(catena in Cramer, 305f.).
26. Theodoret 597B; Oecumenius
453f.; Petrus L. 263B; Dionysius 99F.
The repelling of the Arians is constantly repeated, e.g. in Theophylact
1220B; Thomas Aquinas 535a; Erasmus 885C; Beza 403b, 15-18; Calov
802b.

One, who also, as the one who has become incarnate, can be perceived not physically but only in a special act of intellect as the image of God.[27] This image is "consubstantial" with God,[28] although it can become material, like the incorporeal light in the sun which shines upon all.[29] Even the expression about consubstantiality has to be admitted to be inadequate, as AUGUSTINE shows by using the illustration of eggs that are equal to one another, an analogy that has been used time and again ever since; the provenance from the archetype, therefore, has also to be included.[30] Even so, the image of God (Col. 1:15) is identical with the "Son of his love" (Col. 1:13; RSV "his beloved Son"), and thus the expression of the hymn and the redactional formulation were again united.

This redactional formula "Son of his love" still served to provide Theodore with the means for an adoptionist Christology, according to which Christ was worthy of the love of God in exactly the same way as were those who believed (v. III 1); however, it was very soon realized that this formula was merely a Hebraism, meaning nothing more than "beloved Son." This fact has also been reiterated again and again ever since.[31] Once more it is Augustine who, while assenting to this, yet understands love as the "nature and substance" of God, out of which the Son has grown.[32]

3. The Two Natures

We have thus arrived at the doctrine of the two natures of Christ. This would certainly have grown up without the Epistle to the

27. Chrysostom III, 1 (318); Ambroisiaster 170, 23f.; 171, 18-25; Theophylact 1220 AB (since he is invisible he is not merely a man; since he is the image of God he is not merely an angel); Bullinger, 235 ("ipsissimus deus").

28. Ὁμοούσιος, Theodoret 597B; Ambrosiaster 171, 14f.; Oecumenius 455 (on 3:17); John of Damascus 893B (on 2:9: with the Father and the Spirit).

29. Oecumenius 454 (on 2:9).

30. Augustine, Divers. Quaest. 74 (213f.); Greg. Naz., Or. Theol. 30,20 (129); John of Damascus, De Imagine 1.9 (PG 94,240); further Crell 527ab

(seen in a strongly dynamic sense, as the ray which reveals a luminous body cf. note 29 to this section).

31. E.g. Theodoret 597A; Severian 318 (not merely a physical son); Oecumenius 17C and 453; Lanfranc 321 (I 9); Theophylact 1217C; Dionysius 99E; Erasmus 884D; Grotius 672a; cf. pp. 53 and 259.

32. Trin. 15,19 (at the end, 514, 155-69); Hrabanus 510B; Petrus L. 262D; Thomas Aquinas 534b; it is still cited verbatim in Zanchi, 260, with the addition that thus the undiminished love of God is in store for us.

Colossians; but Col. 1:15-20 was nevertheless one of the most important New Testament passages in which both propositions could be found. This passage has thus been appraised up to the present day as one of the weightiest pieces of evidence for the doctrine of the two natures.[33] Whereas, against Theodore, it was affirmed that Col. 1:15 describes the Pre-existent One, yet Theodore's interest in the humanity was still something to be defended.

The juxtaposition of the opening lines in the two strophes, in particular the redactional reinterpretation in 1:18a, was bound to lead to a dual formulation. Redemption depends not only on Christ's consubstantiality with God, but likewise on his consubstantiality with the human being who is to be redeemed. It is precisely the Preexistent One of 1:15 who is at the same time the Incarnate One, and who yet at the same time bears the whole divine being in himself [34] and is head of the angels, but who is also head of the church and consubstantial with us.[35] So along with Col. 1:19, the other passage (2:9) also assumes importance since it speaks of the indwelling of the whole fullness of the divine being in Christ.[36]

Given that Wisdom Christology was understood in a dynamic sense, then it was possible to speak of the indwelling of the "powers" of God (notes 7 and 11 to C Christology), and thus to conceive of these as God's mighty presence in the Son. This was a concept whose repercussions continued to be felt for a long while afterwards, and which has been revived especially in more recent times (cf. note 54 to C IV Ethics).[37]

Yet in the early period, this conception soon proved inadequate, and the expositions of Col. 1:19; 2:9 resort more and more notice-

---

33. Huby, 43.
34. This is still emphasized in Bullinger, 236 (on 1:18a).
35. Theodoret 600D; 601A (cf. on 2:9: 608C; 609A); Cassian, c. Nestorium de incarnatione Christi 5, 7 (CSEL 17, 312, 9-30 on 1:15/18b, 20); for Gnosticism cf. III, 2b along with note 20 too C III Soteriology.
36. The addition "of the deity" has infiltrated from 2:9 into 1:19 as well as in the Latin versions.
37. Cf. Ambrosiaster 174, 13f. (deus perfectus); 179, 1 (on 1:19; 2:2). He wishes to see in the incarnation neither a diminution in the case of the Father nor an increase in the case of the Son (172, 19f. on 1:16). Cf. further Petrus L. 264CD (1:18a according to his divinity and humanity; indwelling of the trinity in Christ as the "fullness of all wisdom and power," Col. 1:19); on Thomas Aquinas v. p. 249. Beza (405a, 2-13) speaks of divine grace, while Melanchthon (Enarratio 346 [cf. 337f.] on 2:9) and de Wette, 29, 44 (against this Meyer, 238) talk of the divine gifts and attributes, and Grotius (673b on 1:19) of the fullness of the divine powers. On Schleiermacher cf. pp. 287f.

ably to the key ideas of a unity of the two natures which is "not accidental" but "pertaining to the essence," "unalloyed and undifferentiated." [38] The union between the godhead and the human body is, according to Col. 1:17, so close that it was even effective for the three days in the grave, during which the soul was already detached. [39] The common point of interest is clear for all these attempts at a solution: Christ's divine rank (Col. 1:15-17) should be upheld in exactly the same way as should his human kindness (1:18-20). This brings us to those problems that are posed for our modern era. [40]

In the course of this debate, the meaning of the adverb "bodily" or "incarnate" (2:9) has naturally been the subject of particular controversy. ATHANASIUS, as one would expect, took it to refer to the incarnation. [41] Others saw in it a reference to the "body of Christ," the church. [42] AUGUSTINE helped bring about a breakthrough for the interpretation in terms of a "real" indwelling (in contrast to one that is purely shadowy, as in the Old Testament; Col. 2:17) by means of the (dubious) argument that the deity could not be corporeal. [43] Others then spoke, in a dogmatically more pointed

38. Origen, *Princ.* II, 6, 2 (144, 4-7): substantialis; Isidore, *Ep.* IV, 166 (1256AB): οὐσιωδῶς; Oecumenius 21AB; 32D/33A; cf. 454f. (on 1:19 and 2:9), appealing to Cyril, Nestorius II (65A-69A); likewise Theophylact 1224D (not only the "powers"); cf. further John of Damascus 893B; Dionysius 101C; Grotius 673a (on 1:19); Melanchthon, *Enarratio* 346; Beza 409b, 8-28; Calov 802a; 805a/806a (Calvinistic-Lutheran discussion).
39. Greg. Nyss., *Trid. Spat* 9 (293, 3-294,13); Theophylact 1240C (in agreement with Cyril); against this Erasmus 889B.
40. Theophylact 1224A (in exactly the same way Prat, *theologie* I, 343, note 1; 588, assigns 1:15-17 to the divine and 1:18-20 to the human life of Christ); cf. also Calov 804b. In the Middle Ages, effective causes in the divine nature and instrumental causes in the human nature were differentiated from one another (Dionysius 99B on 1:2).
41. *Expositio* 4 (205B); likewise Hra-

banus 522C; Petrus L. 273A; Calov 818b (image of the temple, although with reference, it is true, to Augustine; note 43 to this section). In more recent writers the point has been emphasized that the Exalted One is thought of in bodily terms: de Wette, 44; Abbott, 249; von Soden, 45 (in contrast to the mere θειότης in Rom. 1:20).
42. Against this, Chrysostom VI, 2 (339); cf. notes 30 and 31 to C III Soteriology. Tertullian, *Marc.* V, 19, 6 (722, 22-5), even conducts a polemic against an interpretation of the "body of flesh" (Col. 1:22) in terms of the church.
43. *Ep.* 149, 25 (371, 9-12); *Gen. ad litt.* 12, 7 (388, 14-23); Hrabanus 522B (the body as a temple); Lanfranc 324 (II, 7); Petrus L. 272C; Zwingli 223; Bullinger, 249 (cf. 253 on 2:17); Grotius 678ab; Ewald, 371 (against a purely dynamic indwelling).
44. Cf. note 38 to this section; similarly Hilary, *Trin.* 8, 54 (277A): in the fullness of the deity. Cassian, *c. Nest.* (note 35 to this section) 5, 7

manner, of an indwelling "in substance," [44] and in the course of the history of the church, this distinction has been formulated more and more precisely.[45]

4. Christ in the Old Testament

The earliest clear impact exercised by Colossians, as pointed out by Justin, already spoke of Noah as a second Adam, the type of Jesus; and these ideas are developed further in Irenaeus. In particular, the equating of Christ with the Logos helped to see God's work in the Old Testament in the image of Jesus, and thus to understand God as the one who was active in both Old and New Testaments, fundamentally "in Christ" (v. II 1).

In contrast to this, the GNOSTICS saw in the expression about the mystery "now" revealed (Col. 1:26) proof of the fact that the prophets had still had no knowledge of this, and that it could only have been the Demiurge who was at work in the Old Testament.[46] In face of this danger, Irenaeus used Col. 1:15, 18b to defend the unity of the whole "dispensation of salvation," and this concept was put to further use in the interpretation of Colossians in order to overcome the problem of the unity of God's work.[47] Irenaeus sees in Col. 2:11

---

adduces Col. 1:12-20 against Nestorius to show the absolute unity of the Son of God, whom one cannot divide up into two persons (313, 4-9); cf. further John of Damascus 893B; Beza 410a, 1-34.

45. As an example: Musculus 134 on 1:15: to be distinguished are (1) what belongs only to the divine nature, (2) what belongs to the person of the Son or the Logos, (3) what is common to both, (4) what belongs to the Incarnate One. He understands "bodily" (2:9) as in contrast to the indwelling of the "power" of God = "really," in the sense of ipsissimus deus, and not in some such sense that thereby a non-human, divine body were to be understood. Gomarus 560b makes the distinction: (1) essential, ruling in all things, (2) as a special presence of divine grace in the temple, etc., (3) as a unique grace dwell-

ing in Christ. On 560b/561a there follow the various possibilities for interpreting "bodily" in which Augustine is appealed to against the Ubiquitarians.

46. For Valentinians v. Hipp. *Ref.* VI, 35, 1 (164, 7-11); similarly *Ev. Veritatis* (18(7), 15f. In ibid. 2 0(11), 25-7 the "command" (διάταγμα) of the Father even seems, with reference back to Col. 2:14, to be understood as the hitherto unknown book of revelation, which was nailed with him to the cross. Cf. already Cl. Al. *Strom.* 60-2 (366, 18-368, 2) on Col. 1:9-11, 25-8; 2:2f.; 4:2: there is also wisdom for those who are perfect. Marcion deletes the statements about creation in 1:15-17 (Tertullian *Marc.* V, 19, 4 (721, 24)).

47. Irenaeus III, 17, 2 (16,3)–II, 84; Theodoret 604CD; cf. 605C; 628A (on 1:26f.; 2:2; 4:18).

a reference to the provisional nature of the Old Testament laws, which do, however, as shadows (Col. 2:17) point to the redemption in Christ; and Tertullian uses this same verse (2:17) to explain, against Marcion, that the shadows can never be separated from the "body." [48]

AMBROSIASTER, in his interpretation of 2:17, evaluates Jewish monotheism very positively as a first step in the Christian faith (185b, 1-9 on 2:13); although he expresses this in such a way that the Mosaic law subsequently becomes unnecessary, just as the image of the Emperor is rendered superfluous when the Emperor himself arrives (188.18-24, on 2:17). Nevertheless, he still holds that the Gentiles who have not received this law (184b.19-26; 175. 7-19, on 2:13; 1:21f.) should love God all the more, since more must be forgiven them (185b.9-26, on 2:13). For Ambrosiaster it is clear that Moses has already proclaimed Christ, who appeared to him at the burning bush (171.6-11; 176.19-24, on 1:15, 23).

For HIPPOLYTUS as well, the prophets have already supplemented the sufferings of Christ (as has Paul, according to Col. 1:24).[49] CHRYSOSTOM enumerates an abundance of Old Testament passages that point to Col. 2:1-4, and expounds God's salvation history as a pedagogy which advances step by step; that this was not necessary for the Gentiles can only be understood as a special miracle of God.[50] From the great plethora of interpretations of Old Testament events in terms of Christ only a few instances can be adduced. The idea is found already in JUSTIN (Dial. 138:1) that the eight people in the ark refer to the eighth day, on which Christ rose from the dead. According to IRENAEUS (V 17.3 — II 371), using Col. 2:14 as a basis, the wood (of the cross) saves man, who became guilty through the wood (of the tree of knowledge, Gen. 3:6), and the paradigm for the "first-born of all" (Col. 1:15) was already provided in Jacob (IV 35.2(21.2) — II 226).

---

48. Irenaeus IV, 27, 1(16, 1); 21, 4 (11, 4)—II, 189, 176; Tertullian, Marc. V, 19, 9 (723, 1-9); cf. I, 16, 4 (458, 19-28), appealing to Col. 1:16, and c. Valent. 16, 1(766, 15-20). Similarly Pseud.-Hippolytus, Easter Homily 2, 1 (SC 27, 119, 13-15) understands the Old Testament as a prefiguring shadow: the Passover points to the cross).

49. Hippolytus, David and Goliath 3, 1 (G. N. Botwetsch, Drei georgisch erhaltene Schriften von Hippolyt, 1904 [TU 26] 80. 1-4—CSCO 264, 2, 1-4). 50. V, 4 (336-8); IV, 3f.; V, 1 on 1:25f. (328-32). The question why Christ did not come earlier is explicitly treated (IV, 3; V, 1; X, 3 on 1:25; 2:2; 4:4 (328-30, 332, 369)).

Similarly, the Paschal Homily of MELITO of Sardis sees in the Old Testament a glimpse of Christ, who "includes all things in himself" (5f. [SC 123.62-4]). ORIGEN detects Christ as the "power" of God underlying Gen. 20:14 (note 7 to C II Christology), a passage that tells of Sarah remaining with Abraham. The understanding of the temple as the prefiguration of the indwelling of God in Christ (Col. 2:9) was a particularly favorite theme.[51] These and other similar interpretations can of course be traced throughout the Middle Ages and right up into modern times.[52]

5. The Function of the Statements About Christ

In Colossians, the statements concerning the sole and full sufficiency of Christ were introduced into the specific situation of the community as the answer to their problems. As far as the interpretation is concerned, the commentator's own historical situation has always made its influence felt. This point, however, is to be discussed particularly in Section IV. Here what we are concerned to observe is the fundamental change that came about with the emergence of the Christological discussion concerning the understanding of the two natures. The more emphatically this distinction had to be made, the less evident became the significance of these formulations for the individual in one's temporal and eternal existence.

The emphasis, dominant in Justin, Irenaeus, and Clement, on the activity of God, who encounters his people through the events recorded in the Old and New Testaments, gives way more and more to the description of the eternal being of Christ. THEODORET shows that he still feels this to be a problem, when he explains that Col. 1:18 forms a transition from "theology" (1:15-17) to "economy," to God's saving activity (p. 600C). CALVIN's observations on Col. 1:15 very perceptibly mark the beginnings of the reaction against this.

51. Pseud.-Hippolytus (v. note 48 to this section) 9, 6 (137, 8f.); Pseud.-Justin, *Expositio rectae fidei* 13, 9 (386B); cf. 17, 11f. (389B) = *Opera*, ed. J. C. Th. de Otto III/I, Jena 3rd edn. 1880, 52, 64; Hrabanus 522BC; Petrus L. 272C; 273A etc. (this idea is still found in Calov, note 41 to this section).
52. Hrabanus 518D on 1:24; Petrus L. 264BC on 1:15f. (Job as a symbol of Christ; the church begins with Abel) = ibid. 275C; Dionysius 101D; Beza 411b, 30f. (the note of debt = Gen. 2:17) etc. = Lanfranc 324, 326 (II 9, 19): circumcision on the eighth day points to the day of the resurrection, the new moon to the new life, the Sabbath to the eternal rest, the Passover to Christ; there are many further examples, e.g. in Rupert, in the Index (vol. 24).

He explains that in fact the early church had become predominantly one-sided, through its struggle against the Arians. In fact the hymn in Colossians was in no sense intended to provide information about the nature of Christ, understood in a physical sense. Rather it was intended to describe his relation to us as the one who reveals, the one who becomes visible. The crucial point is not what Christ is in himself, but what he brings about in others.

Calvin thus, provocatively and with powerful effect, gave formal expression to what LUTHER had already said: in the whole of Colossians the main concern is the wisdom once hidden but now brought forth. The one who has been crucified for us (Ch. 1), who is set against all merely human doctrines (Ch. 2), leads us in pure faith into every kind of good work (Ch. 3) and into prayer (Ch. 4).[53] MELANCHTHON's now famous distinction between the "person" and "benefits" of Christ is along the same lines, and has been emphatically taken up again in recent times by BULTMANN.[54] Calvin's exegesis has had considerable impact; it has often been reiterated and has been both attacked[55] and defended equally vigorously.[56]

Thus the way was again opened up for conceiving of God's indwelling in Christ, in the sense of the Early Fathers and the Alexandrians, as the indwelling of God's saving might, of his power and his grace (v. notes 7 and 37 to C II Christology).[57] The interpretation found in SCHLEIERMACHER will prove to be completely consistent with this.[58] However, we have thus already arrived at the question of the salvation brought about through Christ.

---

53. *Vorreden,* 98f.

54. *Beneficia, Enarratio* 326 (also 340); cf. the strong emphasis on justification by grace alone *(Scholia* 211f.); also Bullinger, 230 (argumentum) etc.; Bultmann, *Faith and Understanding,* London 1969, 279, and on this G. Ebeling, *Wort* II, 343-71 (esp. 348 n12), and on Melanchthon ibid. 279-81.

55. E.g. Calov 802b on 1:15.

56. Crell, 527b, points to John 1:18 (it is in his proclamation, not in his being or his person, that Christ reveals God). Musculus (153 on 1:28) to the "Papists" that they proclaim the only begotten Son of God, the true God, the one who is consubstantial with the Father and yet true man, but that they do not proclaim him as our only righteousness and only mediator; this means then that what is in fact a false Soteriology can be linked with a Christology that is completely correct. De Witte (24, note) defends Calvin, because Calvin presupposes as a matter of course the divine nature of Christ.

57. Gomarus 554a makes the distinction: 1:19 speaks of the indwelling of the deity, not merely of grace and faithfulness, while it is only in 1:20 that the effect evoked by this is spoken of.

58. *Predigten* IV, 240, on 1:15.

III

Soteriology: The Son and the World

1. Incarnation of the Logos as Salvation for the World

As early as JUSTIN, Col. 1:15, 18b was seen as evidence for the miracle of the incarnation of the Logos, and this theme occupies a central place in the thought of IRENAEUS. This is all the more so with THEODORE (v. II 3). For him, Col. 1:15-17 spoke of the new creation which had come about through the incarnation. The overall context (which he was not of course able to separate off, as redactional material, from the hymn itself) forced him into this position; for 1:13 undoubtedly spoke of the earthly Jesus as the "son of his love." The solidarity between the Logos, which has put on humanity, and the humanity which is to be redeemed was important to him in that he interpreted the phrase "son of his love" in the sense that the Logos was thought worthy of sonship in the same way as were the elect.[1]

Salvation is thus understood as the redemption of mortality. This mortality is destroyed in the circumcision of Col. 2:11, that is in baptism; this is a theme that, via AUGUSTINE, persisted right into the Middle Ages.[2] It was helped by the fact that Latin texts of Col. 2:15 have the rendering: Christ has put off "the flesh."[3] In this connection, the mythical language of the "power of darkness" (Col. 1:13), arising from the terminology of conversion, suggested the idea of a struggle against the "tyranny of the devil;"[4] and subsequently SEVERIAN (p. 324), probably conditioned to some extent by Gnostic thought (note 22 to this section), understands the incarnation of the Logos, on the basis of Col. 2:15, explicitly as a means to deceive by Satan. This idea was also readily taken up,[5] and was later linked

1. 259,15-260,11 (Greek) on 1:13 (on the correction of this view cf. notes 31 and 32 to C II Christology); the repercussions of this view can be seen in Theophylact 1248B (on 2:17). De Wette, 23 still formulates it thus: "the Son, who possesses his (God's) love."

2. 287, 12f.; 289, 21f. (Greek) on 2:11, 13; cf. already Tertullian, *Resurrectio* 7, 7 (930, 26) on 2:11: annihilation of the flesh; then Augustine, *Faust,* 16, 29 (474, 20-7); Hrabanus

523AB (cf. 518A on 1:21f.); Lanfranc 324 (II, 8); Petrus L. 276A on 2:15.

3. So Augustine (note 2 to this section and *Ep.* 149, 26 (372, 20; 373, 1)); further discussion is given in Lightfoot, 188. Hippolytus *Ref.* VIII, 10, 17 (230, 19-23) is already doing battle with docetic ideas which attach themselves to Col. 2:11, 15.

4. Chrysostom II, 3; cf. V, 1 (312, 332).

5. Theophylact 1245AB: as Satan

with the doctrine of the descent into Hades, in the course of which the pious ones of the Old Testament were also stolen back from the power of the devil.[6]

2. *Universal Redemption?*

(a) Justin, Irenaeus, Hippolytus, Origen

The statement concerning the redemption of the universe, a redemption spoken of as already attained, is the expression that above all characterizes Colossians and is unique in the New Testament; it is clear therefore that it was bound subsequently to exercise strong influence. Here indeed we have the source of what is probably the most important consequence of Colossians. As long as no distinction was drawn between the hymn and the letter, there were really only two alternatives. Either supreme prominence would have to be given to the universalism of this expression, although a proper place could not then be allowed to what is said immediately afterwards about faith and obedience; or else the emphasis would have to be laid on this latter point instead, but at the expense of dropping the idea of the redemption of the universe. Thus either the concept of the universe would be severely restricted, or else the idea of redemption would be understood in a much weaker sense.

The conception of Christ according to the paradigm of the expressions concerning wisdom or the Logos, discussed under II 1 above, included the view of a creation already achieved "in Christ." The question remains, however, whether the idea of the creation being restored by redemption is thus also expressed, and who exactly belongs to this new creation?

As early as JUSTIN there is speculation concerning the sign of the cross which has set its mark on the whole of nature, representing Christ's power penetrating everything (*Apol.* 55:2-4; cf. 35:2); yet it seems that this is said without any direct reference at all to Colos-

---

thought he had the Crucified One, he lost even that which he rightfully possessed already; therefore he sent the Docetists, who deny Jesus' death! Cf. Rupert, *Div. offic.* 9, 6 (251AB); but cf. also, already, Augustine *Enchiridion* 14 (49): the devil, vanquished because he puts to death the innocent, loses that to which he would

have a right (76, 21-5); furthermore cf. Petrus L. 275B; 276A and on 1:13: 262B; 263A; Sasbout, 170 (on Col. 2:10); Musculus, 131f.; 172 on 1:13; 2:15; Calov 801a-802a on 1:13 and further Brunner II, 335f. on Col. 1:13; 2:15.

6. Lanfranc, 325 (II, 13f.); against this Calov 827a.

sians (an Epistle which Justin knew). IRENAEUS, by contrast, although educated in the same part of the world, takes up the idea in connection with Col. 1:17, according to which the universe is given its stability in Christ. The cross which has set its mark on nature provides evidence for nature having been permeated by the invisible Logos.[7] In GREGORY OF NYSSA the idea of the cosmos being completely penetrated in all its spheres, in heaven, on earth, under the earth, and beyond the limits of the earth, still appears but is now connected with Eph. 3:18f.[8]

The key concept of the "restoration" or once and for all summing up of the creation in the Christ event was introduced by Irenaeus.[9] In his writings this concept refers simply to the new creation which brings redemption, while for future developments it is an idea that takes on extraordinary importance. According to HIPPOLYTUS, the Logos, the fourth person in the burning fiery furnace (Dan. 3:25), bears in himself the whole creation and simultaneously, as the first-born (Col. 1:15), takes on in himself Adam, the first created being. This interpretation also serves to express the restoration of man.[10]

If the incarnation has brought the flesh as such back again to God (cf. II 1 above), then all the patriarchs are also brought back again into the divine womb and born again. Then, with the incarnation of wisdom, God's sovereignty is restored to all spheres (Col. 1:15-20). If the head has risen from the dead, then so also the body of every person is risen as soon as that person's time of condemnation is past.[11] Yet here it is still only the individual that is spoken of.

Pseudo-Hippolytus, by contrast, sees in Col. 2:15 the ascension as the ascent of the "image" (= the whole image of God in Christ, Col. 1:15; 2:9) and as the taking captive of the powers, an action which again imparts life and stability to the entire universe.[12] On this view, the powers are excluded from redemption. Yet ORIGEN's explanation specifically holds that the reuniting of divine and human

---

7. *Demonstratio* 34 (19f.).

8. *Trid. Spat.* (299, 13-302, 6).

9. *Recapitulatio* e.g. V, 12, 4 (II, 353) on 3:10 (against contempt of the flesh); cf. note 3 to C II Christology. Cf. further the ἀποκατάστασις, in which angels attain to the status of the 'thrones' (Col. 1:16); Cl. Al. *Eclogae* 57, 1 (153, 25f.); κατορθοῦν in Chrysostom IV, 3 (328), and for Ambrosiaster v. note 40 to this section.

10. In Dan. II, 30, 3-6; IV, 11, 5 (100, 3-102, 4; 215, 1-7 (176,9-30; 284, 1-9)).

11. Cf. note 5 to C II Christology and III, 20, 3 (19, 3)—II, 124, 214, 105.

12. 61; 55 (SC 27, 187, 17-189, 1; 181, 20-183, 21).

13. *Cels.* 3:28 (226, 13f.).

14. *Princ.* I, 6, 1-3 (79, 3-84, 21), *Comm. in Joh.* 1, 16 (20, 11-18);

nature [13] will bring redemption even to the devils.[14] His disciples then affirmed that in light of Col. 2:9 everything is brought to unity in Christ, and that nothing is any longer outside;[15] and that God, who lives in all, has taken on a similar name to us.[16]

(b) The Gnostic Doctrine of the "Fulness" in the Redeemer

It is in Gnosticism that statements about the universe are taken over in their strongest form. Those formulas according to which the universe comes from God or from the redeemer and remains in him probably derive from the same basic source as do the corresponding verses in Colossians (cf. notes 36-42 to 1:15-20).[17] Yet in Gnosticism, as also in the school of Origen, the fulness (the "Pleroma") was limited to the restored world, and the material element was excluded from it. Thus METHODIUS the Olympian regards the descent of the redeemer from the "fulness of the divine being" (Col. 1:19; 2:9) as a deprivation.[18]

According to the VALENTINIANS, the Father and the "fulness" send the "angel of the decree," in which the meaning of Col. 1:16 is realized.[19] In the descending redeemer, the "good pleasure" (Col. 1:19; RSV "pleased to [dwell]"), there dwells bodily "the whole fulness" (Col. 2:9), that is the "seeds" (= the Gnostics) which suffer with him and which he, in his body, consubstantial with the church (v. note 35 to C II Christology), hoists up, as a "head" (Col. 1:18; 2:10) upon his shoulders, into the fulness once more. Thus he is the "first-born" (Col. 1:15, 18b) in the world of the "fulness" and of those chosen for it.[20] It is in this sense that Valentinus can equate the redeemer with the universe, by appealing to Col. 2:9; 3:11; and

---

other relevant passages are given in G. Müller, "Origenes und die Apokatastasis," *TZ* 14 (1958) 180-9. Augustine, *Enchiridion*, affirms against this that the evil angels may indeed still live through God's goodness, but that there is no recovery for them. They are replaced by men who have been converted (8f. [27-9]); cf. note 36 to this section.

15. Didymus the Blind, *In Zachariam* 268, 21-5 (SC 84, 778); here eschatologically understood? (Cf. note 33 to this section.)

16. Julius Africanus, *Chronica*, ed. M.

J. Routh, 2nd edn. Oxford 1846 (*Reliquiae Sacrae* 2), 239.

17. *Ev. Thomae* 77a; *Ev. Veritatis* 17 (5), 4-7; 18 (7), 33-5; 19 (9), 7-10.

18. *Convivium* 202 (SC 95, 230).

19. Cf. Irenaeus I, 1, 8 (4, 5)–I, 38 (the Paraclete, whom Christ who has returned into the Pleroma sends), and *Apocryphon of John* 51 (143), 8f. (sending of the αὐτογενής on the basis of the decree of salvation (Col. 1:19)).

20. Cl. Al., *Exc. Theod.* 43:2f.; 31:1; 42:2f. (120, 10-14; 117, 4-6; 120, 3-7). Cf. above, note 18 to 2:8-15 and espe-

by this means the uniquely born one in the Pleroma becomes the first-born in the creation.[21]

According to BASILIDES, the whole creation has failed to discover the incarnation in the perfect man of Col. 1:28 (cf. III 1 at the end); and yet included in him are all the forms of which the four elements are made up.[22] For the PERATAE the three parts of the world, the full deity of the triad (Col. 2:9), are joined together in him.[23] This provides the basis for the redemption which leads to unity with the "powers" [24] and to being restored to a position equal to the angels.[25]

(c) The New Creation in Theodore and His Followers

THEODORE's interpretation of Col. 1:15-17 in terms of a new creation instead of the first creation [26] has taken on crucial importance even in commentaries of medieval and modern times. If salvation for him is redemption from mortality through the flesh put on by God's Logos, then the fulness dwelling in Christ (Col. 2:9) embraces both the church and the universe, and represents the whole of nature restored in Christ and united with God; that is, the new creation made fit for resurrection and immortality.[27] He explicitly lays special emphasis on the relationship between the universe and the individual, who consists of the four elements and whose soul is joined together with the invisible powers.[28] This view was championed by

cially note 27 to 3:12-17. Cf. also *TDNT* VII, 1088.

21. Irenaeus I, 1, 5 (3, 4)—I, 28f. (Greek); Cl. Al., *Exc. Theod* 7:3; cf. 8:2f.; 10:5; 19:4 (108, 12f., 26f., 110,1; 113, 6-10).

22. Hipp. *Ref.* VIII, 13:3; 14:2 (233, 7-11, 24-8); cf. further V, 19:21; VII, 25:3 (120, 22-4; 203, 4-9).

23. Ibid. V, 12; 4f.; X, 10:3f. (105, 4-8; 269, 12-17); cf. VII, 13:1f. (232, 27-233, 7: all figures are included in him).

24. Thus the baptismal formula of the Marcosians in Irenaeus I, 14, 2 (21, 3)—I, 183.

25. Thus the Valentinians in Cl. Al *Exc. Theod.* 22:3 (114, 4): "who also have the angels"; cf. 36:1 (118, 20f.): "our angels, who came forth from one, are one."

26. V. p. 251 along with note 20 to C

II Christology; this view is still held in Crell 527b-528a and in modern commentators (v. note 8 to 1:15-20).

27. On Col. 1:19 v. 275, 11-276, 4; cf. 276, 8-12; on Col. 2:9 v. 286, 3-8; on Col. 2:15 v. 292, 1 ("all" was connected with the resurrection; in fact however, he was speaking of the believers). The repercussions of this can be seen in Theophylact 1224B (on 1:18), who emphasizes the resurrection, the death (1245A on 2:15), and the incarnation (1248B on 2:17); cf. also Hrabanus 516CD; Petrus L. 264C (on 1:18b: the resurrection as the restoration of the creation).

28. 268, 6-8; the repercussions of this can be seen in Hrabanus 512D; 514C; Rupert, *Div. offic.* 9, 6 (252D/253A): man as microcosm (!) determines the cosmos and even the angels.

the Nestorians, and even as late as the thirteenth century references to Theodore can be found in Nestorian works.[29]

Many of Theodore's ideas were preserved in the Byzantine church as well. JOHN OF DAMASCUS still knows of the basic source of these ideas in wisdom theology: all things were created in Christ (Col. 1:16), because it says in Ps. 104(103):24 that God has created all things "in wisdom" (that is, according to Col. 1:24, in Christ; cf. notes 7 and 12 to C II Christology); hence in Christ as well all things were snatched from destruction, because the breach between Creator and creature (Eph. 2:13f.) has been repaired by means of the nature taken on by the Logos.[30]

In the West, this line of interpretation was cut short. Thus in THEODORET [31] and SEVERIAN [32] the fulness of Col. 1:19 was interpreted, in light of Eph. 1:23, as applying only to the church. Even so, the possibility remains that the church will at some point in the eschatological fulfillment include the whole of humanity. This interpretation was suggested above all by Rom. 8:19-23, and has had its advocates right up to the present day.[33] AUGUSTINE explicitly rejected a doctrine of the restorian of all things, which even included stars and angels. He understood Rom. 8:19-23 in the sense that the whole creation lives in human beings and is thus also redeemed with them (ad Oros. 10-12 [674-7]).

29. Solomon of Basra, *The Book of the Bee* 60f., ed. E. A. W. Budge, *Anecdota Oxoniensia*, Oxford 1886 (Semitic Series 1/2), 139-42. There may be echoes of Col. 1:16 in ibid. 5 (p. 9). The development along these lines, and above all its significance for the modern conception of the solidarity of God with the world, is traced in Kasper, *Jesus*, 219-25; 233-5.

30. 888CD. As a modern representative of the Orthodox view of a divinization process set in motion through the incarnation, embracing both mankind and the cosmos, and in which matter moves into the Pleroma, cf. Eudokimov, 9-13, 17-20 (there are echoes of Col. 3:9f. and 2 Cor. 4:16 on p. 7). Completely different is the emphasis in Küng, 445f., that in the "lofty words" of Phil. 2:6-11 and Col.

1:15-20 the cross on both occasions appears as the decisive declaration.

31. 601A on 1:19 (in 608C; 609A this interpretation rejected for 2:9); against this Chrysostom VI, 2 (339: God, not the church, dwells in Christ; also it is not the Father who is under discussion, as some think); Hrabanus 516C (church and universe). Cf. note 42 to C II Christology.

32. 320; 322. In 319 (on 1:18) it is explicitly said that not all will be raised as brothers of Christ. Cf. Lanfranc 322 (I, 15).

33. Cf. note 15 to this section and p. 269. Cf. also Theophylact 1224B (on 1:18); Dionysius 100B (on 1:20 and 2 Cor. 5:19, along with others). Hrabanus 516C; Dionysius 100B take the verse to refer to the eschatological resurrection promised to all. Huby, 37, 47 (cf. note 35 to this section) ex-

However, the extending of redemption in this way to what is in heaven and what is on earth (Col. 1:20) did cause difficulties. This means available to exegesis right up to the present time for resolving this dilemma are given in outline form already at an early stage.[34] Thus, first, the idea can be taken to refer to angels and people. This can be done in such a way that one discovers here, contrary to what the text says, the reconciliation with humans of those angels set at enmity with them because of human offense,[35] or even the replacement of the fallen angels by people who have been converted.[36] This view has been accepted by commentators even in recent times in the sense that, for the sake of harmony with 2:14 and 1 Cor. 15:24, Col. 1:20 is seen as no more than a process of pacification which does also force into submission those who are unwilling to respond.[37] Or, one can perceive in Col. 1:20, on the basis of Eph. 2:11-22, the redemption of Jews (to whom heaven was already promised) and of Gentiles.[38]

One may, however, keep to the meaning of reconciliation and understand it, according to what the text actually says, as that between God and everything in heaven and on earth. Yet in that case, unless one were willing to interpret this in terms of the dead

---

plains it in the sense of Rom. 8:19-23. Synge, 71f. takes it in a purely potential sense, since in Col. 1:21-3 the discussion is concerned simply with the church. J. Munck explains that according to Col. 1:22-9 Paul understood himself as the instrument of an eschatological plan, according to which "the fullness of the Gentiles" must attain to salvation (*Paul and the Salvation of Mankind*, ET London, SCM, 1959, 41, 48, 155).

34. These are assembled in Gomarus, 554f.

35. Chrysostom III, 3 (321); Theodoret 601B; John of Damascus 889A (with reference to Luke 2:14); Maximus Confessor, PG 90, 877B; Theophylact 1225BC (with reference to Paul's heavenly journey, 2 Cor. 12:2); Dionysius 100B; Crell 530a (for the good angels need no reconciliation, while the evil angels receive none); Grotius 672b (on 1:16; cf. 673b/674a); Calov 807b (with reference to

Gen. 3:24 and Luke 2:14; in 808a created things that lack reason and devils are explicitly excluded); Bengel, 813; Flatt, 177ff.; Huby, 47f. (cf. note 33 to this section).

36. Augustine, *Enchiridion* 16 (61f., 82, 16-46); Gregory, *In primum Regum expositiones* III, 5 on 7:13 (PL 79, 214A); this has frequently been reiterated.

37. E.g. O'Brien, *RTR* 33, 45-53; similarly G. S. O'Collins and T. M. McNulty, "St. Paul and the Language of Reconciliation," *Colloquium* 6 (1973) 6 "to make to conform (to the divine plan)." Ewald, 332f. does indeed also interpret Col. 1:20, with explicit reference to Col. 2:10, 15 and to the impossibility of the apostle contradicting his own statement, as "to bring . . . into ordered relationships," and he even considers the conjecture ἀποκατατάξαι.

38. Petrus L. 264D; Thomas Aquinas 537b.

(those already in heaven) and the living (those still on earth),[39] one would be forced to admit that there is error even in heaven. This point could be conceded if one were prepared to argue that the reference is to the stars, that is the "carnal" heaven, the purely topographical parts of the cosmos, to be found above the earth;[40] or else that it is to the angels, who are also not completely pure. This line of interpretation certainly goes back before CALVIN, but it was through him that it achieved particular effect.[41]

(d) The Western Understanding of the Doctrine of the Real Redemption of the Universe

Col. 1:20 and Eph. 1:10 exercise further influence, particularly outside the mainstream development of thought and doctrine, right through the medieval and postreformation period. JOHN SCOTUS speaks of the return of all things, one of which is still to be distinguished as special and as leading to supernatural glory (1001AB). But at any rate, it is now the whole of humanity that is restored in Christ, not just one section of it. Further, human nature becomes equal to that of the nine classes of angels and fulfils the role of these (1005C-1006A; cf. 1002CD). All this is proved by the parables of Luke 15 (cf. note 2 to C II Christology). Hence the whole human race will go redeemed into the heavenly Jerusalem (1007C). The devil's dominion will be destroyed, even though he could return whenever he wanted (1002BC); at the judgment every creature will acknowledge God (1003A).

During the Reformation, it was especially individuals on the

39. E.g. Petrus L. 265A; Alting 395a; Bengel p. 813 (but cf. note 35 to this section).

40. Hieronymus (PL 26, 493BC on Eph. 1:22, alluding to Col. 1:20): the stars, which before God are also not pure. Ibid. 507A-508A; in 515A he seems to include the heavenly powers and angels (more cautiously expressed in 535CD). Ambrosiaster (173, 14-25; 174, 17-23): As the first being in the creation and the new creation Christ restores everything, even the heavenly order. Musculus (141f. on Col. 1:15-20) protests against this (while simultaneously taking issue with Chryssostom). He does indeed defend the restoration of all things, but at the same time explains that unbelievers have no part in this. Both views are set alongside each other, because humans can have no idea of the events of the end.

41. Augustine ad Oros. 13 (677); Calvin, 132 (against him, Calov, 808a); de Wette, 30; Luecken, 345; Meyer, 202. The question is raised in the Handbuch, 410, whether, between completely good and completely evil angels, there is not a middle rank.

periphery of the movement who upheld the universal hope, often
by appealing to Col. 1:20; thus HANS DENCK [42] and, following MAR-
TIN BUCER,[43] J. BRADFORD.[44] The diary of GEORGE FOX for 1648 [45]
lays bare again the basic roots of this hope in a remarkable way.
Fox sees the putting on of the new nature (Col. 3:10) as a return to
the position of Adam before the Fall, and in the process of this
putting on, the whole creation is opened up to the believer. This
idea is still found in the writings of the PLYMOUTH BRETHREN[46] and
in 1784 Col. 1:26 appears as the title of a publication of CHARLES
CHAUNCY concerning the reconciliation of the universe.

In Switzerland, MARIE HUBER finds in Col. 1:19f. the promise of
the salvation of all people.[47] For LAVATER, the dual statement in
Colossians about Christ and the individual as the image of God is
proof of a universal reconciliation to come. For how could God bring
about what no civilized human being could tolerate, that is eternal
damnation? [48] A particularly prolific source of such views was the
Pietism of Württemberg. Col. 1:20, linked with the statements about
Christ as the "head of men and of angels," allows OETINGER to see
the mystery of God (Col. 1:26f.), the great transaction of redemption for the whole creation, in the fact that Christ will again reconcile everything to himself (Col. 1:18a, 20; 2:10); and Col. 2:3 enables
him to look ahead to that golden era, when all knowledge will be

42. *Briefe und Akten zum Leben Oekolampads*, ed. E. Staehelin, II Leipzig (1934), 52f. (Nikolaus Thoma to Oekolompad on 1 April 1527): appealing to Col. 1:20; the everlasting fire is only a threat necessary for the godless. Cf. note 50 to this section, at the end.

43. I, 343 (Strassburg 1536), mentioned in Bradford, 355: it is true that this is only in the sense of Rom. 8:19-23 (cf. note 33 to this section).

44. Pp. 350-64. He appeals to Col. 1:20 (ibid. 352f., 357) and to Augustine and Thomas Aquinas, who both taught at least a partial restoration of nature.

45. P. 69.

46. J. N. Darby. *L'attente actuelle de l'eglise*, Geneva 1840, (Evening 2) 25f.: Col. 1:20 teaches the already

accomplished reconciliation of the church and the still outstanding reconciliation of all things (as they are enumerated in 1:16) right down to the last blade of grass; otherwise the Devil would indeed have a success to set on record.

47. *Le sisteme des Theologiens sur l'état des âmes séparées des corps*, London 1739 (Letter 2): Col. 1:19f. (pp. 52f.) and Eph. 1:9f. (p. 54) show that God's grace is so great that at the end all sin will be annihilated (p. 58); thus the way to heaven has become broad and the way to hell has become narrow (Letter 6, 105).

48. *Aussichten in die Ewigkeit III*, Zurich 1773, Letter 23, 274f.; cf. 266 and 262-4 (Letter 22, toward the end).

joined together in Christ. This understanding will only fall to the lot of the believer in his spiritual age.[49]

The BERLENBURG BIBLE interprets Col. 1:20 in the sense that the world may be brought back from its disorder to proper order again (although not all at once, but everything in its own time), so that "finally a universal joy and an unending, eternal praise of God may be awakened amongst the whole creation," and in this even the fallen angels will participate (1016f.). HAHN sees in the mystery of Col. 1:26f. the reconciliation of the universe, and according to 1:20 this "purifies and renews all creatures and leads them to higher levels of life" so that "this heavenly water of the transfigured humanity of Jesus damps down the blazing fire of the wrath of God." [50]

Hahn's first point is also considered valid by THEREMIN, who uses Col. 2:2f. as evidence for it. Yet in his writings a further development of the idea is already set under way, and this will be dealt with under IV 5. The "summing up of all beings in heaven and on earth" is, in fact, "a great social alliance extending through the visible and invisible world" (Col. 1:13f.), and according to Col. 1:16 this also includes in Christ's saving will "the state and civil society," until "everything dissolves in the one unending kingdom of God" (8f., 13f.). CHR. BLUMHARDT concludes a morning meditation on Col. 1:12-20 for Easter 1899 thus: certainly there are hells, and he himself

---

49) *Grundbegriffe des NT*, Reutlingen, 1852, sermon on Passion Sunday about Heb. 9:11-15, 145 (Col. 2:2) and 149. Cf. *Biblisches und emblematisches Wörterbuch*, no place of publication given, 1776, s.v. "Versöhnen" (according to Col. 1:20, "everything is brought into its original state," even the "physical being," 664f.), and "Wiederbringung," 683. Also found there, s.v. "Leib," 407, is the famous sentence about corporeality as the "end of the works (not "ways"!) of God" and the expectation of the annihilation of the "serpent's nature introduced into the creation." In the Preface he understands Col. 2:9 as the essential, bodily revelation.

50. P. 60 (Address 26); 47-9 (Address 20). On 43 (Address 19), there appears again the old theme of wisdom as God's architectural plan (cf.

note 12 to C II Christology). Hahn does indeed speak of eternal judgment (61), but he maintains that the consummation will only be when "the elevated and anointed spirit of man shall have spread out into all worlds and shall have become the house of the triune God" (45, Address 19). Cf. further the paraphrase of Col. 1:15-20 "Principalities and authorities, powers which keep watch on the throne" = Col. 1:16) in Ph. F. Hiller's (1699-1769, Württemberg) "Jesus Christ rules as King" (Gesangbuch [v. note 44 to 1:24-9] no. 336), and for the further development v. G. Müller, *Apokalypsis panton, A Bibliography*, published by the author (Basler Missionsbuchhandlung), Basel 1969, IX (from 1800; on H. Denck v. Appendix II 1); also in id., *Identität und Immanenz*, Zurich 1968.

knows of them very well, but they will come to an end since according to Col. 1:13 all people already belong to God (III, 271f.). E. F. STROTER also explicitly treats of the reconciliation of the universe.[51]

(e) Modern Attempts to Deal with the Question

On the Catholic side, free will is much more strongly emphasized, even if it is affirmed in the sense of Rom. 8:19-23 (cf. note 33 to C III Soteriology), that what happens in the case of humans should permeate the whole of nature as well.[52] Interestingly, however, at this very point there emerges a solution which has assumed importance in recent decades in the Protestant, and especially Anglo-Saxon and Reformed, sphere. From the perspective of Col. 1:20, especially if one's free will is evaluated so positively, even those who stand outside the church are still children of the church, provided that the words of a poem of Goethe apply to them: "whoever strives and exerts himself . . . ."[53]

In the more recent period, M. A. WAGENFUHRER, by excising v 18a from the original hymn, has seen Christ as the head of the universe and has thus also understood 1:20 as God's reconciliation with the universe. Further, this universe includes humankind and the spirit world, so that the powers become "divine organs."[54] P. PRAT speaks of the worldwide restrospective effect of the cosmic role of Christ, who is indeed already, as Logos, the "place" of the future cosmos (note 39 to 1:15-20). As a rule, he says, God's saving will does indeed embrace only humanity, but Col. 1:19f. goes further. It is true that what Col. 1:19f. means is not reconciliation to God but reconciliation to one another. This is, however, directed "to him," so that the original unity will eventually be attained again under the leadership of Christ (II, 107-9).

Much more cautiously, F. MUSSNER speaks of the depths of space and of souls, and of the powers of history, which are embraced by

51. *Das Evangelium Gottes von der Allversöhnung in Christus*, Chemnitz, no date, (1915), esp. 326-84: Col. 1:15, 18 is proof of the victory of the imperishable life in Christ, Col. 2:15 of the triumph on the cross (379, 364):
52. Thus J. N. Schneider, *Die Versöhnung des Weltalls durch das Blut Christi nach Kol. 1.20*, Schaffhausen (1856), 121-4, 227-31, but effective for deliverance or condemnation.
53. Ibid., 178f.
54. *Die Bedeutung Christi für Welt und Kirche*, Leipzig (1941), 61, 63, 68f. (in Gabathuler, *Jesus Christus* pp. 150f., 168-70).

Christ. He draws attention to the fact that natural objects such as light, wax, fire, and incense are included in the worship of the church, in whose liturgy the creation is restored to its proper place (41f. on 1:16). Again, the JERUSALEM BIBLE understands the fulness of Col. 1:19 as the universe which is caught up in salvation (NT, p. 345; cf. p. 347 note on 2:9). It solves the problem of 1:20 thus: heaven and earth return to God collectively, but those who do not desire this are forced to belong to the new order.[55]

From a Reformed perspective, EMIL BRUNNER sees the final gathering up of the universe in Christ as being God's purpose, certainly, but at the same time he also emphasizes that not every creature will attain this; hence universal reconciliation is a doctrine that stands in contradiction to the Bible and must be abandoned absolutely.[56] OSCAR CULLMANN takes it for granted that Col. 1:20 should be understood as referring to Jews and Gentiles being united within the church as the purpose of salvation history. He is equally aware of the solidarity of the creation (Rom. 8:19-23; note 33 to C III Soteriology) with the whole saving event and of the way in which from eternity the powers have been brought within the Christ event.[57]

By contrast, KARL BARTH has recourse to the Reformers' understanding of the all-sufficiency of Jesus Christ, and thus comes again and again to an idea of the Christ event that is all-embracing. The positive response of the community can only be a provisional confession uttered on behalf of every creature. If God dwells in Christ, then he also dwells in the creation, for in Christ the creator becomes the creature, without the distinction between them being dissolved. So one can, without qualification, speak of cosmic peace which extends over all beings both in heaven and on earth.[58] From this, then, one may conclude that faith is not merely an inner event, but consists in liberation for the entire cosmos. Yet Christ has united our human nature with his divine person in order that it may thus find its real self in him.[59] However, in this case one has to take note of the fact

---

55. Col. 2:14 is taken to refer to the law and the angelic powers that mediate it (Jerusalem Bible, NT, p. 347 note m).

56. Dogmatik I, 248, 363; II, 181; cf. also II. 68: Col. 3:10 shows that while the regaining of the very image of God is promised to faith, it is also not the whole of salvation as Gnosti-

cism understood it to be (ibid. 118).
57. Salvation, 118, 146; cf. Christ 186, also 91.
58. Dogmatics IV/1, 501f. (on Col. 1:13); II/1, 486 (on 1:19; 2:9); IV/2, 257 (on 1:20 and 2:14f., with emphasis on the saving death of Jesus).
59. Dogmatics III/4, 491f.; I/2, 391f. (on 1:21f.).

that the powers mentioned in Col. 1:16 though not being identical
with earthly rulers (cf. note 21 to C II Christology), are at least their
"originals," so that the redemption which has come about also takes
on political significance.[60] According to Col. 2:14f., the universe has
been deprived of its divinized status. This then leads to a much
more calm and open attitude on the part of the people of God in
relation to the world than is the case in the Old Testament with its
religious wars.[61] This leads Barth finally to call to mind, in the case
of Col. 1:15-20, Calvin's doctrine of the Holy Spirit as the principle
of life, which also rules over the whole world, and at least to ask
whether the Advent hymn about the Savior who should "spring from
the earth" does not represent a biblical understanding.[62]

This idea of Barth's has been developed further, although in altogether different ways. W. H. G. THOMAS sees in Col. 1:15 the fusion
of nature and grace which causes God's goodness to be "linked
physically and eternally with the whole universe"; that is, it renders
possible a belief in providence which allows the physical unity of
the universe, as demonstrated by science, to be understood in a
moral and spiritual sense as well. However, he concludes from this
unity of nature and grace that "order is heaven's first law," which
as a matter of course includes proper authority and discipline.[63]

For SYNGE as well, the cosmic work of Christ, the Incarnation, by
which the whole universe is affected, in practice consists in the order
of those who are ruled and those who rule, both of whom should
exercise their office in the service of Christ (p. 70 on 1:15f.). BAR-
CLAY (Christ, 61-5) even goes so far as to make reference to Heraclitus' Logos as the regulating principle of the world; the order
restored by the Spirit of Christ in the universe ought to make its
effect felt as well in society, in the church, and among nations, in
different races and social classes living harmoniously together.
Hence one can speak of an evolution in which all people attain the
fulness of Christ, an end which God, as the one who orders history,
dreams of (ibid., 66f.).

LIGHTFOOT explains the physical law of gravitation itself as being
the expression of the Spirit of Jesus, because it preserves the world
from chaos (p. 154 on 1:17). SCOTT understands Col. 1:20 as the

---

60. *Dogmatics* III/3, 457-9 (cf. note
21 to C II Christology and note 40 to
C IV Ethics).
61. *Dogmatics* I/2, 106f.

62. *Dogmatics* IV/3, 756.
63. Pp. 53-5 on 1:15; 122f. on 3:18,
21; on this conclusion cf. pp. 283ff.

reconciliation of the universe, caught up in a struggle with itself, and its mysterious powers; the alienation of man, mentioned in Col. 1:21, is only a consequence of this situation. Thus a "stupendous history set towards the future" is opened up to the believer (pp. 26f.).[64] If that is right, then one is certainly delivered up to the natural process of evolution which comes to an end without human agency; now, however, this is understood in a completely positive sense. This approximates the position of those early apocalypses which look for salvation not in one's conversion but in the earth being transformed into Paradise, a view which is supported by the curious notion that in a good environment everything works in the best possible way for humans as well. This, however, will be discussed under (f) below.

Among New Testament scholars, BULTMANN finds in Col. 1:15-20; 2:15; 3:1-4 evidence of the Gnostic idea of the primal man, who does indeed determine the fate of the entire cosmos, suggesting at the same time that this must be interpreted in an existential way.[65] STAUFFER, by contrast, simply speaks of the "homecoming of the universe." It is true that alongside this, in the New Testament, there appears the expectation of eternal damnation. Yet according to Jesus' words, the church's authority and intercession reach out beyond this life and this world (§ 57, pp. 222f.). It is in Col. 1:15-20 that the theology of creation is most clearly distinctive. Christ, as the basis for the existence of the universe, indeed, of all thrones, dominions, powers, and authorities, is also the one who reconciles the universe, who certainly disarms but does not destroy the powers of hell (Col. 2:15; ibid. 224f.). *The weath is also the recreator*

W. MICHAELIS, in a monograph on this theme, attempts to find a

---

64. De Boor, 189-91 (on 1:20) thinks, in agreement with Scott, that one ought not to dismiss what is said as mere mythology, but that in fact industrialization and world wars may show how dependent people are on the creation and its condition. In completely the opposite way to Scott, von Allmen emphasizes the clear primacy of the anthropological affirmations. What the mission and social work of the church can do is set up signs for the fulfillment that will only come with the parousia; it can set up signs in so-cial life, science, technology, and the arts, so that the modern "powers" may be exposed (RHPR 48, 44f.). On Col. 1:15-20 as an example of the translation into a new culture (e.g., "Africanization"), cf. id., "Pour une theologie grecque?" Flambeau 25 (1970), 20-3, 26-33.

65. Theology I, 132f., 175f., 178f. (here he also discusses the redaction of the passage), cf. 303; Exegetica 250, cf. 406 (this background causes—contra Cullmann—the very scandal of the cross to disappear, ibid. 366).

New Testament basis for the reconciliation of the universe; and Col.
1:20, along with Eph. 1:10, still serves as the fundamental source
for this.[66] His solution is based on the fact that "eternal" damnation
is nowhere spoken of in the New Testament, since this is not
what the Greek, and underlying Hebrew, terms express.[67] Finally,
E. STAEHELIN has traced the idea of the reconciliation of the universe
through the entire course of the history of the church.[68]

(f) Cosmic Christology?

All this has been given new relevance by the work of TEILHARD
DE CHARDIN.[69] Again, what happens when the discussion fails to distinguish between the hymn and the commentary becomes clear in
the writings of O. A. DILSCHNEIDER. In 1953 he advocated, in opposition to the whole process of secularization, the theology (preserved
in the Eastern Church but forgotten in the West) of nature and history, with its understanding of Christ Pantocrator (cf. III 2c and
note 2 to C II Christology); this idea would then result in a consciously Christian university.[70] It was in the year of the New Delhi
Ecumenical Conference that Dilschneider developed this into a
pleromatic Christology, which proclaims the hierarchy of Christ in
the sphere of the aeons.[71]

66. *Versöhnung*, 24-7; against Benoit
(Jerusalem Bible), it is not merely a
partially enforced pacification that is
spoken of (28-30).

67. Αἰών and αἰώνιος denote an indefi-
nite length of time, but not eternity in
the modern sense (ibid. 41-8); this
latter idea is difficult to maintain, exegetically, on account of verses such as
Mark 9:48.

68. *Die Wiederbringung aller Dinge*,
1960 (Balser Universitätsreden 45);
no instances are given here, but most
of them are to be found (even if the
references are imprecise) in id., *Verkündigung*.

69. Explicit references to him are relatively seldom; cf. the instances assembled in Ahrens, *Diskussion: P. Teilhard de Chardin, Der Mensch in Kos-
mos*, München [7]1967, 247ff.; S. M.
Daecke, *Teilhard de Chardin und die*

*evangelische Theologie, Die Weltlich-
keit Gottes und die Weltlichkeit der
Welt*, Göttingen 1967; W. Dantine,
"Schöpfung und Erlösung: Versuch
einer theologischen Interpretation im
Blick auf das gegenwärtige Weltver-
ständnis," *KD* 11 (1965), 41; H. Ried-
linger, "Die kosmische Königsherr-
schaft Christi," *ConcD* 2 (1966), 53-
62; O. Rousseau, "Die Idee des König-
tums Christi," ibid. 63-9; J. Wille-
brands, in: *Christus, Zeichen und Ur-
sprung der Einheit in einer geteilten
Welt*, Zurich 1970, 20-4.

70. *Gefesselte Kirche. Not und Ver-
heissung*, Stuttgart 1953, 139f., 146f.
(in Gabathuler, *Jesus Christus*, 152-4).

71. *Christus Pantokrator. Vom Kolosserbrief zur Oekumene*, Berlin 1962,
31f., 41, 49 (in Gabathuler, *Jesus
Christus*, 154-6; in Ahrens, *Diskussion*,
104-7).

However, the most important repercussions were those that came
from the conference itself, and especially the paper of J. SITTLER,
who bases his argument on Col. 1:15-20.[72] He directs himself against
the dualistic separation of church and world in Augustine, and
appeals to Irenaeus (cf. above II 1): nature and grace are one; redemption embraces both history and also nature, which is threatened
at present; but equally, it embraces the world of politics, business,
and the arts as well. In a fascinating way, the paper appears to show
how "even the furthest corners of the world are filled with the energy
and substance of Christ." [73]

H. J. GABATHULER has entered into debate with Sittler, making use
of the fruits of exegetical work,[74] and TH. AHRENS has given a summary, up to 1965, of the long and often complicated discussion of his
thesis.[75] Essentially, it is in the fields of the theology of missions and
of historical and natural theology that the conclusions have been
drawn: Christ is present—unacknowledged certainly but no less effectively for all that—among the non-Christians who are addressed.[76]
The Holy Spirit teaches us to recognize history as developing toward
universal history, into which the church, growing together into unity,
ought to be incorporated; and again, nature can be understood as
an evolution toward the kingdom of God.[77] An energetic warning
was also issued against falling into a syncretism where the intention
is to detect Christ, as the Holy Spirit, in the heart of every person.
This warning was also directed against recognizing God's provi-
dential action in history, without making any mention of sin and
forgiveness. Above all, it was directed against the complete confu-
sion of belief in God with belief in the world. In particular, the
theology of the cross is appealed to in order to counter the threat
of a theology of glory.[78]

---

72. "Zur Einheit berufen," in: *Neu
Delhi 1961*, ed. W. A. Visser't Hooft,
Stuttgart 1962, 512-23 (in Gabathuler,
Jesus Christus, 159-63).
73. R. Scheffbuch, "Die Herausforde-
rung von New Delhi," *LM* 1 (1962),
Vol. 1,7.
74. Gabathuler, *Jesus Christus*, 163-7,
180f.
75. *Diskussion*, esp. 90-199.
76. So e.g. also in de Boor, 182 on
1:16 (he does, however, warn against
a Christian natural philosophy, since

Jesus is the personal Savior; ibid. 184).
77. Also de Boor, 183 (along with
note 13) does not wish fundamentally
to reject the idea of evolution: the universe finds its fulfillment in Jesus, in
order then, when it has attained its
goal, "to be cast aside like a garment"
(on 1:17). Thus, however, the problem is overplayed.
78. The point has frequently been
made that salvation is indeed open to
everyone but is not accepted by everyone: e.g., Melanchthon, *Enarratio*,

Of very great interest is the report which J. REUMANN presents on the discussion in North America.[79] That the question of the relation between creation and redemption has been raised by the reconsideration of Col. 1:15-20 at the New Delhi Conference, and is still at issue is stated already in the report of the Conference on Faith and Order in Montreal (1963; ibid. 126). There is general agreement that Christ's sovereignty over the true church is a reality at present, whereas his sovereignty over the world will only become apparent in the future. However, the question remains, whether there is any real continuity between the original expressions of the hymn in Col. 1:15-20 and the way the hymn is taken over by the author of the letter, who makes this proviso clear; whether, in other words, it is permissible or necessary to teach a cosmic Christology according to which Christ is hidden outside the church, but is at work there is no less real a way, embracing the whole world within his reconciliation, or at least leading it toward this.

Another contentious issue is that between the view which identifies the secular order with God's order (or Christ's order) which is immanent in the world (W. HAMILTON, T. ALTIZER, D. MILLER), and the opposite view according to which the secular order is perverted and is already falling apart (G. VAHANIAN; ibid., 146). The evaluation of religions and of so-called "anonymous Christians" (ibid., 147-51) is also an open issue, as is the significance of Christ for the world of nature, right down to the "harmless neutrons." According to J. W. HEIKINNEN, the kingdom of Christ lays claim to the powers in order to bring everything to the telos (ibid., 156f.), and J. C. COOPER links the "God is dead" theology, its mysticism and its social sensibility, with Teilhard de Chardin and his Omega-point (ibid., 160f.). The global view of Chardin, with its evolutionary optimism, as also a song of praise to the great secular city, can be traced throughout this discussion (ibid., 181). Over against all this, the author of the report has to confess that in his view it is only by recognizing, sensibly, the two layers of the statements in Col. 1:12-23 that one can guard against fanciful interpretations.[80]

327; Beza 404a, 45-b, 45 (1:18 as a corrective to the statements about the universe); von Soden, 30, 51 (on 1:20, with reference to 1 Cor. 15:24, and on 2:15); de Boor, 189 (on 1:20);

W. H. G. Thomas, 55 (on 1:15-20); J. Schneider, TLZ 77 (1952) 160f. (discussion of W. Michaelis).
79. Humanität, 120-89.
80. Ibid. 162-79, with reference to

Thus indications have already been given of the most recent development, which was discussed above on pp. 125f. Since the methods of the history of religions school came into fashion, it has become increasingly clear that the position which Colossians is fighting against is not simply "Judaizing." In other words, the message of Colossians is not merely justification by faith as opposed to justification by works. Instead it is apparently directed against some enthusiastic trend. Naturally, such a movement was perturbed by fears of all sorts of invisible powers. No matter how one specifies the history of religions background of Colossians, it is obvious that interpreters see analogies to our modern anxieties and dubious efforts to find security.[81]

More important is the fact that the statements of the hymn, with their "lofty viewpoint," [82] are now understood as an already existing tradition which the writer of the letter takes over critically; the hymn has been labeled by some interpreters as a pre-Christian Gnostic tradition [83] while other interpreters regard it as a tradition of Christian enthusiasts.[84] However, if it is recognized that language works on various levels and has to be formulated in a different way in a song of praise than it does in doctrine, this recognition has, I hope, meant a further step toward the proper understanding of both sets of statements, the hymnic and the dogmatic (v. pp. 86f. and 96f). In this way, the point has been reached at which it becomes clear that a *doctrine* of the redemption of the universe cannot be based on Colossians. Instead, the community in its song of praise cannot abstain from reminding God, over and over again, of his boundless grace, and thus including everyone and everything in their

---

Schnackenburg, EKK I, and Schweizer, EKK I.
81. Particular points that are mentioned include helplessness vis-á-vis a world which is governed by mechanical laws, genetics, milieu, and social and economic factors (Scott, 19. 50, on 1:15-17; 2:15; Thompson, 170); the meaninglessness of life (ibid., 171); horoscopes (ibid., 143 on 2:8; 170 and de Boor, 171, 225, 232, on 1:13; 2:16-23); Spiritualism and Moral Rearmament (Barclay, 134f.); modern syncretism in general (ibid., 132; Thompson, 121 [on 2:9]; 168).

82. Luecken: hence many exclude them as unauthentic.
83. Käsemann, *Baptismal Liturgy*, 152-9 (37-43); this view is echoed in Sanders, *Hymns*, 97f. (cf. 126, n3), but it is no longer maintained with any certainty; simply for the raw materials for this concept, v. Schenke, "Christologie," 221f.
84. E.g., Schweizer, *Neotestamentica*, 297, 303-5, 310-13 (without directly identifying it with the "Enthusiasm"); likewise Gabathuler, *Jesus Christus*, 139-42.

praise and petition.[85] This point will be discussed in the final section, D "Outlook."

IV

Ethics

1. General

As far as the ethical sections of Colossians are concerned, it should first of all be noted that there is little in the way of new ideas. CLEMENT OF ALEXANDRIA uses Col. 2:11; 3:1-10, 16f., in his attack on luxury, worldliness, and passions;[1] in TERTULLIAN, the rigorous commands are stressed.[2] The extensive moral admonitions which provide the focal point of CHRYSOSTOM's sermons would as a rule be given without the textual basis being attached. The spiritual love of Col. 1:8 offers an invitation to the poor and brings greater happiness than does worldly love, especially in a society with a glut of material goods, where it is more difficult to endure two days of being full than twenty days of hunger, and where the sight of beautiful dancing girls merely intensifies the torment of not being able to possess them (I 3-6, esp. 5 [306]). The new nature of Col. 3:10 is the free will which overcomes the old nature (VIII 1 [352f.]); the putting to death of the members on earth (Col. 3:5) is directed against every kind of extravagance (VII 3-5; VIII 1 [346-53]): where there are flute players, Christ no longer has any place (XII 6 [389]). In the comment on 4;3, women are admonished to think of the chains of Paul's imprisonment rather than golden chains around their necks (X 4f.; XII 3 [371-4; 383]).

As for the discussion in the medieval period, the sacramental basis of ethics is the main characteristic theme. This is linked with the fact that the "mystery" of Col. 1:26f.; 2:2 was translated by "sacramentum" in Latin.[3] How could the mouth that has received the sacrament give utterance to those vices which, according to Col. 3:8,

---

85. Cf. Schneider (note 78 to this section), 161 with reference to Col. 1:20 (2:15), 160: "Whether the reconciliation of the universe is a final possibility open to God and concealed in grace is something that is beyond our knowledge." The distinction between song of praise and doctrine also has something essential to say on the prob-

lem of "indigenization" (v. note 64 to this section, at the end).
1. *Paed.* III, 71:1-3; II, 43:1-4 (275, 7-17; 183, 16-184, 26); *Strom.* III, 43:3-5 (216, 4-17).
2. *Pudicitia* 17:8 (1317, 73-8).
3. This leads Dionysius 100E to the definition of Christ as the material substance of the sacrament (it also more-

come from the mouth (Theophylact, 1256C)! The chief problem, however, was constituted by the extreme moral demands. The perfection required by Col. 1:22, 28; 3:17 is either a state which one can only look forward to in the future,[4] or else it must be limited to a minority which takes on itself a way of life that exceeds the demands made for everyone in general, but that then also serves vicariously for the benefit of others.[5]

It was in this context that Col. 1:24 exercised an especially forceful influence. Hence in this connection Thomas Aquinas distinguishes between carnal and spiritual sins and considers where these count as mortal sins.[6] Obviously the Reformers registered their protest on this point in particular.[7] In this respect, Zwingli offers the decisive insight, by explaining the demand for perfection in a philologically correct manner from Hebrew usage and the Old Testament background.[8] Nevertheless, it is precisely in this area of debate that the actual polemical sections of Colossians take on importance.

2. The Polemical Sections

(a) 2:8 Against the Philosophy

Clement of Alexandria understands the philosophy as still having a place as a "preparatory school," or, with reference to the "elements" of Col. 2:8, as an "elementary school" for the faith. True,

---

over leads him to the interpretation of the threefold sprinkling at baptism in terms of Christ's three days of lying in the grave; 101D on 2:12); and it leads Erasmus to ridicule the fact that an eighth sacrament would thus be introduced, if one did not know the original Greek text itself (887D, reiterated Beza 407b, 29-32).

4. Lanfranc, 323 (I 22).

5. Thomas Aquinas 540b (perfectio supererogationis, on Col. 1:28); Dionysius 100D (thus the "treasure of the church" is daily enlarged; on Col. 1:24). Cf. note 15 below.

6. He concludes that this is only when they are consciously committed, and even then not when the basic attitude is opposed to the particular deed (549a on Col. 3:8; 552ab on 3:17).

7. Zwingli, 221f. (on 1:24); Calvin,

129, 134, 144 on 1:14 (against doctrines of satisfaction); 1:22 (against Pelagianism); 2:10 (against infused perfection); Melanchthon, *Enarratio* 340 (on 2:8 against Pelagianism); 354f. (on 2:21f., against Osiander's essential justification); Beza, 417a, 51-3 (against works of supererogation); Gomarus, 556a (on 1:22b, against justification by works); 557a (on 1:24, against doctrines of satisfaction); 558a (on 1:28, against Catharists and other perfectionists); Meyer, 296 (on 3:14), etc.

8. P. 222 on Col. 1:28; cf. also Gomarus, 558ab. Zanchi, 254 explains Col. 1:10 in the sense that one can be pleasing to God only in Christ, that is precisely in our imperfection which was covered by his obedience.

one no longer needs to go back to this school once one has discovered the perfect understanding.[9] TERTULLIAN by contrast, fights against the philosophy,[10] and AMBROSIASTER issues a polemic against all wordly sciences in general.[11] Both of these positions are found in the writings of the Reformers and in much more recent works as well.[12] An example of the former is G. EBELING, who is provoked by this same verse, Col. 2:8, into emphasizing the claim that the tradition has though, it remains relative.[13]

(b) 2:16-23 Against Ascetic Practices

IRENAEUS sees in Col. 2:16 a summons for the church to be united against all ascetic demands and the separations they caused (Greek Fragment II p. 505f.). CLEMENT OF ALEXANDRIA uses 2:18, 23 to contest the demand for Christians to remain celibate, although he does recommend continence (*Strom.* III 51.3 [p. 219.31f.]). Chrysostom's argument (XIII 6 [pp. 388f.]) is also pertinent here. As ascetic conduct attracted more adherents, the demands of the opponents, which are rejected in Col. 2:21, were openly put about as being Pauline commands; and it is this argument that AUGUSTINE energetically disputes.[14] GREGORY THE GREAT uses Col. 2:23 to issue a warning against the arrogance of the ascetics, although it is true that he understands Col. 3:3 as a description of the person who approaches perfection, and for whom the world has passed away completely.[15]

---

9. *Strom.* VI, 62 1-3 (463, 1-14); 117, 1 (490, 27-30); I, 50, 4-52, 2 (33, 3-34, 9); V, 60-2; 80, 5 (366, 18-368, 10; 379, 15-17 on Col. 1:26f.; 2:2f.); I, 15, 3-5 (11, 21-8 on Col. 1:28, parallel to the Old Testament for the Jews).

10. *Praescript.* 7, 7 (192, 21-193, 40), *An.* 3-6 (785, 1-790, 79); *Marc.* V, 19, 7f. (722, 3-24); *Apol.* 46-8 (160-8).

11. 179, 21-7; 189, 7-12 on 2:2, 18; it is repeated verbatim, in part, in Petrus L. 269C-270B (on 2:2f.; but against this Erasmus 892B on 2:19). Also according to John of Damascus 893A (on 2:8), human reason always remains dependent on the elements.

12. A positive appraisal is given by Calvin, 143; Bullinger, 243-8 (on 2: 3f., 8); Gomarus, 560b, etc. A nega-tive warning is issued by Melanchthon, *Scholia,* 230-44 (more cautiously in *Enarratio,* 343). As an instance of a modern attitude, that of de Boor is interesting: although human thought is to be given its proper due in contrast to man, "no dog ever asks how it could go about becoming a proper dog" (216) . . . yet it does not lead to the goal (217-9).

13. "Wort Gottes und Tradition," *Ki-Konf* 7 (1964), 141.

14. Augustine *Ep.* 149, 23 (369, 7-17). Real asceticism is also rejected in *Conf.* 10.31 (46), by means of using Col. 2:16 (274).

15. *Regula pastoralis* III, 19 (62)—*PL* 77, 81D/82A; *Moralia* VIII, 26 (45) (264)—*PL* 75, 829B and V, 6 (9) (142f.)—684BC.

For the Reformers, the whole section 2:16-23 serves as a welcome aid in the battle against all ascetic precepts.[16] K. BARTH stands firmly in this tradition when he argues that a person can be a nonsmoker, a teetotaler, and a vegetarian, and yet still be called Adolf Hitler.[17] LUTHER, by contrast, can understand this same section, Col. 2:18, as a rejection of all "rabbles," who have neither scripture nor experience on their side;[18] while FLATT is of the opinion that, in the licentious situation of his time, one ought to urge exactly the opposite of freedom from asceticism (*Observationes* I 11f.).

(c) 2:18 Against the Angel-Cult

This verse took on contemporary relevance when a new angel-cult grew up in the church; for this cult was then promptly equated with that already repudiated by the apostle.[19] This polemic dominates the interpretation of the whole letter in CHRYSOSTOM, and is often repeated by later writers.[20] It was taken up afresh in the Reformation protest against the cult of saints,[21] veneration of ecclesiastical

16. Erasmus, 892E (on Col. 2:22); cf. 893E (on 2:23); Melanchthon, *Enarratio*, 340, 342, 353f.; Bullinger, 260 on 2:21 (not against moderate fasting which one does not understand as a means of one's salvation); Beza, 416a, 7; 416b, 48-55; 417a, 24-36; 417b, 21f.; Gomarus, 567b/568a; Luecken, 353 (against the infernal arrogance of the ascetics). Calvin, 163, by contrast, uses Col. 4:6 (cf. on 3:16) to combat the use of worldly jokes.

17. *Dogmatics* III/4, 348.

18. WA 36, 504, 10ff. (he reads "has not seen"!).

19. On this v. A. von Harnack, *Dogmengeschichte*, 7th edn 1931 (*GThW* IV/3), 199, 272-5, along with note 1; F. Scheidweiler, *RGG* 3rd edn II, 465f.

20. I, 2 (302) = Oecumenius, 13C and very frequently; Theodoret, 613AB on 2:18, with reference to the Synod of Laodicea (this reference is likewise made still in Calov, 831a); 620D on 3:17; Theophylact 1205B; 1208A (the person who does not believe in the parousia must be content,

as in the Old Testament, with being led home by angels); cf. Ambrosiaster, 176, 15-17; 189, 16-20.

21. Calvin, 149f.; cf. *Institutio* III, 20, 20 (Col. 4:3 shows that the apostle solicits the intercession of the community, and not vice-versa) and I, 14, 10 (Col. 1:16, 20, against angel worship); Beza, 414b, 12-27, with reference to the (neo-)Platonic background (as already Calvin). Musculus, 135f. does battle against the use of pictures and images of saints by using the argument that Christ is the unique image of God and the image of the apostle is his teaching; cf. further Gomarus, taking issue with Bellarmin (565b-566a, 568a); Bengel, 819 (referring to the Synod of Laodicea); Luecken, 352. Since 2:18 was, in light of Gal. 4:3, 8-10, taken to refer to the angels of the law, other verses of Colossians are usually quoted as evidence for the protest against the cult of saints (e.g., in addition to the passages quoted above, 1:24; 3:5 in Zwingli, 221, 226; 2:20-3 in the *Handbuch*, 413).

authorities, and reverence vis-à-vis the "angelic" way of life in celibacy.[22] K. BARTH does indeed use what is said in Col. 2:8, 20 to attack the confessional cult of Lutheranism and Calvinism.[23]

3. The Call to Worship Addressed to All the Members of the Community

The admonition that singing should form part of the service causes Chrysostom to complain of the fact that the children now know only secular songs by heart, and can no longer remember a single psalm (IX 2 [362]). Eusebius (*Hist. Eccl.* V 28:5) attests to the fact that Christological psalms were composed by the "brethren." CLEMENT OF ALEXANDRIA recommends the singing of psalms even for social gatherings not intended as worship (*Paed.* 2.4 [183.20-184.26]), and TERTULLIAN likewise suggests this for the common domestic life of a husband and wife (*Ux.* 8.8 [394.53f.]).

This theme also takes on a new aspect in the period of the Reformation. Col. 2:16-23 is universally understood as a renunciation of all ceremonies.[24] This certainly leads to some difficulties as far as defending Sunday and the (two) sacraments are concerned.[25] Much more important than this is the abolition of the distinction between clergy and laity.[26] This, it is true, does nothing to prevent the ecclesiastical hierarchy, especially now that it has a good grounding in theological education, from infiltrating again and rediscovering itself

22. Calvin, 149; Melanchthon, *Scholien*, 255, cf. 243.

23. *Dogmatics* I/2, 617.

24. Zwingli, 227 (on 4:2, against murmuring as part of prayer); Calvin, 143, 146f., 157 (on 2:8-14; 3:11; but without directing a polemic against anything in his own day).

25. Calvin (148f. on 2:16f.) uses good order as the justification for the observance of Sunday (cf. Bengel, 818: such observance is necessary for those who work hard, but otherwise it is left relatively open for someone to choose what to do), while he justifies the New Testament sacraments on the grounds of their function as "pictures," which do not merely remain shadowy outlines as do the Old Testament ceremonies (Beza, 413a, 13-18: "shadows of the Christ who has already come," not only of things to come in the future).

26. Cf. note 22 above; Zwingli, 220f., 227 (on 1:1, 18; 3:14 against bishops, the pope, and monks who have grown rich); Calvin, 158 (on 3:16 for the right to read the Bible; likewise Musculus, 201, appealing to Jerome and Chrysostom; Gomarus, 568ab; 574a taking issue with Catholic attacks; Calov, 842b); Schleiermacher, *Predigt* XVI (398f. on 4:17: ministers of the congregation should be set not over but under it); Thompson, 155 (3:16 parallel to 1 Cor. 14:26); de Boor, 262 (the activity of the apostle in 1:28 is ascribed to the community in 3:16).

in the "joints and ligaments" of Col. 2:19.[27] Both these approaches
can be traced in the subsequent interpretation of Colossians; whereas
on the one hand the church is understood as a "larger incarnation"
of Christ.[28] On the other hand the Quaker service is praised for
being especially close to the Bible, and on the basis of this a warning
is issued against allowing music in worship to become the worship
of music.[29] In the case of the noted formulation "the circumcision
of Christ" (Col. 2:11),[30] from the Reformation onward the emphasis
has been laid on the importance of this happening inwardly "within
the heart" (Calvin, 144), in other words on the importance of faith;
and thus the idea of a sacrament effective *ex opere operato* is rejected (Beza, 411a.3f.). Finally, it leads BARTH to deny that baptism
is what is meant by this phrase.[31]

4. The Household Rule

The approach demonstrated in the Excursus on the Household
Rule (3:18–4:1), of using the household rule to cement together
more and more firmly a God-given order, seems at first not to be
taken any further. CLEMENT OF ALEXANDRIA recognizes in the household rule the antiascetic position, and makes it clear above all that
the church on earth must become an image of that in heaven, one
in which differences of sex, race, and status have come to an end
(Col. 3:11). It is indeed for this very reason that one prays daily
that God's will may be done on earth as it is in heaven.[32] CHRYSOS-
TOM recommends an open discussion on marriage problems without
any false shame vis-à-vis taboos; and he lays special emphasis on

27. Grotius, 682a. Already Theodoret,
613C/D had seen in this phrase apostles, prophets, and teachers of the
church, while Gregory the Great
(*Homiliae in Ezechielem* I, 6-8–PL
76, 832B [1216]) had found there
apostles, martyrs, pastors, and doctors,
and John of Damascus (896D) teachers of the word; for more recent interpretations cf. note 41 to 2:16-23. Melanchthon, in the *Scholien*, explicitly
defends the relative rights of the civil
and ecclesiastical authorities 260-77).
28. Scott, 24 (on 1:18a); Zeilinger,

Der Erstgeborene, 159 (the church as
"Christ living, on").
29. Thomas 86 on 2:8.
30. As early as Justin *Dial.* 43:2, baptism is designated as the "spiritual"
circumcision; the fact that he is thinking of this verse in Colossians is shown
by 28:4, where the "Scythian" (Col.
3:11) appears as an example of the
"good and useful circumcision."
31. Barth, *Dogmatics* IV/4, 118-20;
cf. 14, 160.
32. *Strom.* IV, 64-6 (277, 17-278, 21),
esp. 66, 1 (278, 10-12).

the equal status of the wife, especially in spiritual service.[33] Otherwise, the household rule is accepted as a matter of course, certainly, but it is not given much attention. In the writings of JOHN OF DAMASCUS, this is the only section which is left without any commentary at all.[34]

The Stoic watchword, that the soul of the slave always remains free, is repeated by CHRYSOSTOM[35] THEODORET (621B), and OECUMENIUS (48D) on Col. 3:23. The idea that 4:1 should not be taken to mean the abandoning of all class distinctions can be found as early as THEODORE (306.21), and recurs over and over again right into the twentieth century.[36] The requirement of obedience, it is true, is limited in those cases where God's commands would thereby be broken.[37] Although AUGUSTINE rejects rigorous asceticism, he is nevertheless of the opinion that the family life described in the household rule poses a greater threat to people than does that of those who are unmarried (*Civ. D.* I 9 [9:42-53]). AMBROSIASTER emphasizes the slave's reward in the next world (201.14f.), and the subordination of the wife, already taught in Gen. 3:16 (199.24-6 on Col. 3:18). However, one remark of his is above all fraught with significance for future interpretation; this is where he says that the "image of the creator" in Col. 3:10 differs from what is said in Gen. 1:27 and 1 Cor. 11:7 by including the wife as well (196.18-25). This comment is frequently repeated in the medieval period and related to the human faculty of reasoning,[38] although with the addition, that dominion over wives belongs to husbands because of their superiority in reason.[39]

In the Reformation and post-Reformation period, the household

---

33. XII, 6 (388f.); cf. PG 62, 659 on 2 Tim. 4:21; also Hrabanus, 536C.
34. Theophylact, 1264D thinks that the household rule is lacking in earlier Epistles because in these the more important dogmatic discussions were crucial.
35. X, 2 (367); here, nevertheless, it is illustrated by means of the example of Paul in bondage (ibid. 3[370]) and buttressed by the fact that they do their work so willingly that supervision becomes superfluous.
36. Abbott, 296, appealing to Theodoret; cf. notes 42 and 44 below.
37. E.g., Theophylact, 1265B; also

1272B on 4:6, where respect for kings is otherwise thoroughly recommended; Musculus, 206, etc.
38. Hrabanus, 536B; Lanfranc, 328 (III, 8); Petrus L. 282A-C.
39. Petrus L. 285A; Thomas Aquinas, 552ab on 3:17 ("the law of love does not annul the natural law but fulfills it"); here he also shows considerable psychological insight into the repercussions of childhood experiences (Col. 3:21); according to Wis. 13:1, the "elements of the world" should already have led to the knowledge of God; ibid. 542b on 2:8).

rule serves not merely to illustrate worship in everyday life but also to reject an exaggerated enthusiasm. Certainly the point is also emphasized, in opposing abuses of power on the part of magistrates, that no government can prohibit what Christ permits (ZWINGLI 223 on 2:10); and SCHLIERMACHER is aware that even proper authorities can behave like slave owners (*Predigt* XIII, 357f.). Yet he interprets the powers (Col. 1:16), created and preserved in Christ, in terms of wordly officials, and the reconciliation between "heaven" and "earth" (Col. 1:20) in terms of "religious" and "worldly relationships." [40]

Thus by and large, the household rule is used "to counteract the abuse of Christian freedom and equality." [41] Christ's righteousness and the political order should not be made mutually interchangeable; the equality of Col. 4:1 has to be understood not arithmetically but in the sense of a geometrical relationship that is, of finding one's place in relation to each other. [42] CALOV explains that there are certainly limits to proper chastisement, but that one ought not to become lax. [43] VON SODEN even goes so far as to think that the admonition to husbands (3:19) "reflects on the natural weakness of the female character" (64), and the hierarchy of authority provided by nature, which grants to the husband the position of master, is defended right up into the twentieth century (Huby, 100). What the household rule teaches is the opposite of militant revolution and emancipation; [44] for the sake of religion itself, a social revolution must be shunned. [45] The "inward enrichment of the individual soul"

---

40. *TSK* V/I, 514-6, 532f.; in *Predigt* VIII (293f.), he explains, on the other hand, that the powers dealt with by Christ (Col. 2:15) are not something such as the civil princes and magistrates but the angels of the law.

41. De Wette, 68.

42. Melanchthon, *Enarratio*, 361, 351 and 364 (cf. notes 27 and 36 above); in particular he lays emphasis almost exclusively on Col. 3:16 as a warning against exaggerated enthusiasm (357; cf. 362), and expressly against Anabaptists (329, 343, cf. 352); Bullinger, 256f. (on 2:18, against Anabaptists); 260 (on 2:21). On the problem of the doctrine of the two kingdoms cf. Ebeling, *Wort* III, 574-92 (*ZTK* 69 [1972], 331-49).

43. Similarly Musculus, 207. Bengel, 823, by contrast, knows that "a broken spirit is the plague of youth"; similarly Flatt, 258; de Wette, 70; Huby, 101, who warns against training a child as though it were an animal.

44. *Handbuch*, 414. Beza, 420b, 40-5 takes issue against the Anabaptists, who disturb the good order. Musculus, 205, deduces the subordination of servants to their masters or citizens to the authorities from that of wives to their husbands and children to their parents; Schleiermacher (*Predigt* XIII, 360) asserts that it is love that is demanded, not disruption of the proper order.

45. Luecken, 356; similarly Synge, 92; Thompson, 158; de Boor, 271 (who

is more important than the "external" factor of payment, although the apostle does acknowledge the injustice of unpaid slave labor (Scott, 81, on 3:23f.). So the household rule, as the moral ordering of the home and of the well-regulated state, is according to 19th and 20th century interpreters, the actual working out of reconciliation, while the Christian family and, consequent on this, the reconstruction of the whole of human society is the most profound change brought about by Christianity.[46]

All this is set into sharp relief only when one recognizes how closely these conclusions are bound up with a Christology and Soteriology based on the hymn. That is, as soon as one interprets the reconciliation of the universe, as expressed in Col. 1:20, in a merely political and ethical manner, then one is committed to the doctrine of a continual evolution of the status quo (and this can, of course, be a status attained by means of revolution) toward an ever more perfect order; and thus one arrives at the standpoint outlined above at the end of III 2 (e). All the more striking is the volteface of the last few years. This is also bound up with the fact that we have learned to distinguish the language of the hymn from the prosaic style of the writer of the letter, but at the same time to take seriously the real dimension of the salvation proclaimed in the hymn. So for HANS KUNG (543f.) the point is that the New Testament has, in the household rule, taken over a secular ethic, even if this is not left unaltered.[47] EDWARD SCHILLEBEECKX (*Jesus*) is aware of the problem of different "languages" and warns against a "christologizing" of Jesus of Nazareth which makes him into a "great icon" and could destroy "the critical aspect of his prophecy, which has consequences that are altogether social and political." In fact, he is (as Schillebeeckx puts it, following formulations such as Col. 1:18b) "the first-born and leader of a new humanity." Finally, in 1976 it can even be claimed that the whole polemic of Colossians is aimed di-

does, however, take seriously the equality or fairness of Col. 4:1, and properly affirms that great rallying cries are merely cheap as long as others are supposed to carry out what they say).

46. Schneider, *Versöhnung* (note 52 to C III Soteriology), 182-5; Scott, 77.
47. On this problem cf. Ebeling, "Die Evidenz des Ethischen und die The-

ologie," II, 1-41, where on p. 15 (= ZTK 57 [1960], 332) the commandment to honor one's parents is used as an example; cf. also H. Schürmann, "Haben die paulinischen Wertungen und Weisungen Modellcharakter? Beobachtungen und Anmerkungen zur Frage nach ihrer formalen Eigenart und inhaltlichen Verbindlichkeit," *Gr.* 56 (1975), 237-71.

rectly against adapting oneself to the existing structures of the status quo.[48] The fundamental question raised by this must now be discussed further.

5. Ethical Implications

In these specific ideas and opinions there is concealed a development which has its beginnings in the early period, with the Alexandrians, and which is taken up again in the thought of the Reformers. With the Reformers, in fact, a shift of emphasis can be observed; here the idea moves from an abstract doctrine about Christ to expressions concerning his relation to and significance for us (II-5). The effect of this is that propositions concerning the two natures of Christ and his relationship to the Father are pushed into the background, and that correspondingly his influence on the life of the believer is thrust into the foreground. True, the Reformers are here thinking of the central promises of salvation in the narrower sense, that is, of justification and the situation at the last judgment. However, the modern positions, cited immediately above, vis-à-vis the ethical problems do indeed show how markedly the main focus now falls more and more on sanctification, the new ethical life of the believer, finally of human beings in general. It is not possible to illustrate this point in any greater detail here; however, a few main tendencies do emerge.

Discussion of a resurrection that has already taken place is found for the first time in Col. 2:12; 3:1-4. Hence, of course, already in the Early Church it is interpreted by means of the distinction between a spiritual resurrection that has already occurred but is not yet visible and a resurrection of the body or the flesh, apportioned to everyone; the idea of the resurrection which had already happened is then protected against its possible consequences.[49] It gains classic status through AUGUSTINE's identification of the kingdom of Christ and the kingdom of heaven with the church. Here a completely different kind of reign in the future kingdom of God is a point that

---

48. Wengst, "Versöhnung"; this is an attempted solution which bases itself on the traditional equating of the "elements" with the "angels" worshiped in Colossae, but it can scarcely be upheld exegetically, since it was precisely the worldly "structures" that the Co-

lossians wished to escape, and hence ascetically to separate themselves from (cf. pp. 131ff.).

49. Theodoret 609C; 616C (on 2:12; 3:3f.); Severian 322f.; John of Damascus 893D; Ambrosiater 192, 13-16; Hrabanus 531A.

is firmly maintained.[50] On this view, the first resurrection is at an early stage understood in particular as an awakening to an ethically new way of life.[51]

In the later period, and in particular in the sixteenth and seventeenth centuries, this is unfolded in many different ways.[52] Finally, in the nineteenth century moral renewal is considered to be "the sublime purpose" and "the ultimate goal of Jesus' death." Thus the message of Col. 2:12 is thought to be simply this: "You have thus vividly felt the punishment and abomination which your sins deserve, as if (!) you had yourselves suffered the death that Christ endured," and therefore "you have resolved, firmly and frankly, to renounce sin, as though (!) you had been raised with Christ." [53] The Christology corresponds to this. An indwelling of God in Christ that is to be understood in an ontological way is completely out of the question. Origen's interpretation of the fulness of the divine attributes and powers again comes to the fore. Now, however, it simply means the profound union between the earthly Jesus and God.[54] Through him "a hitherto unknown feeling of God's nearness is awakened." [55]

This point is emphasized most clearly of all by SCHLEIERMACHER, who develops Theodore's exegesis to its logical conclusion; he takes the whole of the first strophe of the hymn Col. 1:15-18a) to refer to the person being recreated (which is now understood in a moral sense) by the earthly Jesus, that is to "the spiritual kingdom of the Son," as, for Schleiermacher the context suggests (1:13f.).[56] Accord-

---

50. *Civ. D.* 20, 9 (716, 39-51 = Beda, *Explanatio Apocalypsis* 20, PG 93, 192B); *ad Oros.* 8 (673f.).

51. Oecumenius 36A (on 2:13); Theophylact 1241C (on 2:12); against this Meyer 245, 247 (on 2:12, 13), cf. 280 (on 3:3).

52. E. Sarcerius, *Expositiones in epistolas dominicales et festivales*, Frankfurt 1538, 55f., uses Col. 3:1-4 to defend the importance of good works, which are only possible, however, on the basis of justification. Gomarus 549a (on 1:13) differentiates very precisely between justification and sanctification, the kingdom of grace and the kingdom of glory; also, we are already transposed into the latter, partly *de facto* (that is, in Christ), partly *de iure*

and in hope (similarly 569a on 3:1-4).

53. Flatt, 182 (on 1:22); 211f.; similarly *Observationes II*, 18f.; cf. de Wette, 45-8, 56, 62, 68 (on 2:12-15; 3:1, 9, 17), also 47 (on 2:14: it is not guilt but the consciousness of guilt that is annulled).

54. De Wette, 29f., 44 (on 1:19; 2:9, now also in the hearts of believers); cf. notes 7, 11, 37 to C II Christology.

55. Luecken, 347 (on 1:22); cf. 350.

56. *TSK* V/1, 518, 521; *Predigten IV* (238 on 1:15: the spiritual world, in which everything has come to its proper being); V (252 on 1:22a: the life of Jesus, not merely his death; similarly on this point also Ewald, 386 on 2:14); VIII (295 on 2:15: "completely set free from the letter, and

ing to him, this demands a genuinely ecumenical attitude within
the church,[57] and it also leads to a continual development of the
whole human race towards a higher nature.[58] Indeed, "the kingdom
of God is consolidated, and the name of the redeemer has become
an object of veneration in every corner of the earth." [59] This can also
be expressed in the words of modern English-speaking scholars:
the raising of Jesus from the dead denotes God's confirmation of the
fact that Jesus' view of the matter, which leads the individual to
a higher level of life, was correct.[60] Christianity is sanctity, a holy
way of leading one's life, for which redemption through the "divine
person" of Jesus is indeed still necessary.[61]

In the case of Schleiermacher, it is true to say that the actual eschatological expectation no longer plays an essential role alongside the
hope of a more or less continual advancement of humanity. The
same development becomes more and more clear in the work of
writers whom we have already mentioned, in particular representatives of Anglo-Saxon scholarship.[62] In a systematic presentation of
the evidence, C. H. DODD as early as 1936 brought together Col. 2:12,
20; 3:1-4, and in particular the phrase about the life hidden in God
(3:3), in order to designate as sheer illusion all apocalyptic, whether
ancient or modern, along with Utopian dreams of a social evolution
toward paradise on earth. Dodd's point, in agreement with Toynbee, was also that one could only speak of an encounter that takes
place in history between two "personalities" (although in Dodd's
case it must be said that these are superhuman and therefore definitely conclusive); an encounter, that is, between Yahweh and the serpent, and one which has ushered in a new epoch once and for all in
Jesus.[63]

brought back only to that which is
spiritual"; cf. 287f.: divine grace as
"the greatest spiritual good").
57. *Predigten* XV (376-87 on 4:5f.).
58. *TSK* V/1, 522f.; *Predigten* IV
(241-3 on 1:15: everything that is human is taken over more and more into
the community).
59. *Predigten* VI (262 on 1:24: suffering for his sake may only now occur
at the most as a rare exception in distant lands); IX (305 on 2:21: the
spiritual body is meant to encompass
the whole human race).

60. Thompson, 150 on 3:1f.
61. Thomas, 143f.
62. E.g., Lightfoot, 140 (on 1:13;
morally and spiritually, even if it may
perhaps be seen especially distinctively
in the world to come); completely different (if also not without its dangers) is the argument in Mussner, 44
(on 1:18): "in the body of Christ, the
'habitat' of God reaches already into
this world, 'heaven' is already present."
63. *The Apostolic Preaching and Its
Developments*, London 71951 = 1936,

However, we cannot conclude our account of the impact that
Colossians has had without acknowledging that a possibly still more
important area has not been dealt with at all; that is, the effect and
impact that Colossians has exercised within the arts. Simply to
illustrate this point, we wish to conclude this section with an extract
from Thomas Wolfe. He speaks of the "huge great wall of loneliness," as it looms up in Job and in its ultimate fulfillment in the life
of Christ. However, he thus discovers how true are the Beatitudes
of Matt. 5:3-10, and how the same loneliness can lead to "wild songs
of jubilation" as well as to "bitter grief"; how also the "glory of joy
springs from pain, the bitter pain and loneliness of man," so that
Job's "song to pain is at the same time a song to joy." He concludes
with the formulation found in written form for the first time in
Colossians: "We who were dead have been raised," and interprets
it thus: "We who were lost have been found again; we had sold
our ability, passion, and youth to a death not of the body; we had
perished deep down in our hearts; our talents had been squandered
and our hope was gone—but in bloody struggle in loneliness and
darkness we have regained our life." [64]

79-96 (the passages from Colossians
are given on 88).
64. *Hinter jenen Bergen*, ro-ro-ro, Tas-
chenbuch, Hamburg 1956, 142.

Whether and to what extent this corresponds to what is meant in Colossians is something which cannot be
discussed further here.

Outlook

Three new insights for understanding Colossians have become clearer in recent years. First, history of religions research has helped us recognize the particular problems that arose in Colossae. Second, it has been recognized that the ethical injunctions, in particular the household rule (3:18–4:1), derive from Hellenism and Hellenistic Judaism. Finally, in the case of the hymn (1:15-20), tradition and redactional material have been distinguished from one another.

The Epistle to the Colossians in History

As long as it was not recognized that Colossians poses a problem in terms of the history of religious background not only of the author but also of the hymn and the recipients of the letter, we find that this letter remained in the shadow of Galatians and Ephesians. Interpreters then had two choices: First, they could understand Colossians from the perspective of Paul's doctrine of justification and interpret the Colossian Christology as if it consisted in doctrinal formulations meant to combat legalism (or else one could focus in the ethical statements of Colossians in order to counteract the emphasis on the doctrine of justification). Second, interpreters could view everything that Colossians says about the world outside of the Christian community, including the references to the universe, as if the church were meant. Thus the world receives the stamp of the

church and non-believers are labeled as "anonymous Christians."
Both approaches in understanding Colossians could assign a crucial significance to the ethical statements of this letter, regard them
as its genuine Christian substance and develop them into a timeless
system which is supposed to usher in paradise. However, difficulties
arose with either approach as soon as it was recognized that it is
necessary to distinguish different levels of language, namely the
traditional hymn of praise must be distinguished from its interpretation by the author of this letter.

1. In the *doctrine of Christ* the lofty notions (note 83 to C III Soteriology) of the Christological hymn in 1:15-20 were further considered and developed. The concern to speak as objectively as possible about the nature of Christ and his significance for salvation led
to distinctions that became more and more abstract. Thus increasingly, care had to be taken to differentiate between the Father and
the Son (and the Holy Spirit). In this process, different epochs, that
is the time before creation, the time after creation, and in particular
the Old Testament salvation history, the Incarnation, and the final
consummation, had to be distinguished from one another. The uniting of the divine and human natures in Christ became a problematic theme and gave rise to the question of whether the godhead
remained united with the corpse of Jesus, even though his soul had
left his body (note 39 to C II Christology). This line of thought is
to be found above all in the Catholic tradition, where the hymn in
Colossians was treasured as "one of the strongest arguments for the
doctrine of the two natures" (note 33 to C II Christology); by contrast, in the opinion of a Protestant writer the hymn has brought
about "one of the most disastrous developments, in which philosophy has stifled religion" (note 14 to C II Christology).

2. Concerning the *significance for salvation,* the doctrine of the redemption of the universe is the logical consequence as soon as the
statements of the hymn are interpreted as a doctrinal system. It is
a development that has come about above all in the exaggerated
enthusiasm of Pietism, and of the Anglo-Saxon Free Churches. This
development led to great difficulties, and strange theories had to be
devised concerning the redemption of good, bad, or middling angels (notes 14, 35, 36, 41 to C III Soteriology). Alternatively, every
possible interpretation had to be brought in to harmonize this doc-

trine with statements about judgment and condemnation (notes 34, 37-40 to C III Soteriology).

The more emphatically salvation was identified with the new life that can be experienced here, the more clearly there grew up, out of the doctrine of the reconciliation of the universe, the conviction of an objectively progressive moral evolution. In this evolution, the order of the kingdom of God asserts itself in civic propriety far beyond the church and yet is embraced by it. This order is guaranteed by the well-founded authority of those who rule until paradise on earth for all is attained and "order as heaven's first law" (note 63 to C III Soteriology) is finally established. The fact that in more recent times, the expectation has been of a revolutionary rather than a civic order makes little difference to the concept as a whole. In fact this theme necessarily leads to the idea of the Spirit of God being at work even outside the church (note 62 to C III Soteriology), and to the concept of "anonymous Christians" (note 53 to C III Soteriology.

It is precisely at this point that the confessional boundaries are done away with. The hope of a transformation of nature, a transformation objectively based in the incarnation of Christ, does of course have its roots in the notions of the Alexandrians and Theodore of Mopsuestia, along with the influence that these notions exercised in the case of the Nestorians and the Eastern Church. On the Catholic side, this has achieved a considerable impact through the work of Teilhard de Chardin. It has subsequently been taken up especially by Protestant and Orthodox theologians, and has finally been sanctified, so to speak, by a meeting of the Ecumenical Council. Reference was made back to Heraclitus' Logos as the principle that sets the cosmos in order. This idea, along with the actual understanding of the natural laws as consequences of the Christ event, have thus come dangerously close to creating a "theology of order" which justifies the status quo because it believes in an inevitable progression toward good.

The crucial question is whether one's salvation depends on an objective, external, progressive transformation of the world, or even of the universe, or whether the position is in fact the reverse of this. Even within one and the same confession this question has been answered in diametrically opposite ways (cf. note 64 to C III Soteriology). Likewise, the doctrine of the redemption of the universe has been both defended and contested equally vigorously (notes 56, 58, 65, 66 to C III Soteriology).

3. In the case of the *ethical statements,* an important role has been played both by the warnings given against an ascetic flight from the world at least as far as it was evaluated positively in itself) and also by the instructions provided for the spheres of marriage, the family, and work (as set out especially in the household rule). These admonitions became fraught with fateful consequences wherever the proper counterbalance to them was not explicitly and earnestly held; the counterbalance, that is, of being prepared to undertake active service for the gospel, even where this might involve some self-sacrifice, and of serving others, even where this might mean renouncing one's own rights. The danger arises, in other words, where an injunction expressed within a specific situation is then transferred to a general system divorced from it. This threat came to a climax in the development (portrayed in 2 above) into a moralism which equated salvation and a new morality with each another, and which was thus considerably and emphatically controlled by nothing other than those ideals that were current and in accordance with the prevailing fashion.

The Epistle to the Colossians in Its Setting

see p 125ᵗ

The findings of the history of religions research have enabled us to perceive more clearly what the questions at Colossae revolve around, even if it is impossible to attain absolute certainty in this matter. It can at least be said that at the time Colossians was writen there was a general fear and anxiety concerning the world. The earth was no longer the firm foundation on which one could gain a secure footing. It had became fragile. All the elements were in uproar, and it was only the precarious balance in the struggle of all against all that to a certain extent held the world together.

Natural catastrophes gave cause for concern about what could happen if one of the elements gained the upper hand—if, for instance, earth became an arid desert, if water turned into a flood, if fire took the form of a volcanic eruption, or if air took the form of a cyclone. Who gave any guarantee that the elements would not be completely set loose from their order, a process which would result

in the entire universe being rent asunder in a terrible cosmic conflagration or a totally annihilating tidal wave?

It was this kind of catastrophe that the Stoic philosophy awaited;
and Stoic theories, in a very popularized form, dominated the
thoughts of people almost everywhere. True, it also offered consolation with its belief in the freedom of the soul over against every
external threat. So also, in a different way, did middle Platonism
which was gaining ground at that time. It knew of an unimpaired
world "above," from which the human soul originated and to which
it should again return. Accordingly, salvation was to be found in
transcendence; one's real home was in the world beyond, although
admittedly it could be experienced here and now in the innermost
depths of the soul. Pythagoras and Empedocles, those prophets who
spoke of a primitive antiquity less impaired than the present, had
pointed the way to this development. Strict asceticism succeeded in
setting the soul free from the earthly world and its elements; purificatory baths enabled it to become more and more pure; veneration
of the gods and of celestial heroes linked it here and now to that
heavenly world. After the death of the body, the soul would come
to partake in that unimpaired world above for ever (cf. Excursus
to 2:8, pp. 125-134).

1.9 It was in this situation that the Colossians had heard the message
of Jesus Christ, the Risen and Exalted One; that is, they had heard
of the one who had already left this evil and fragile world behind,
and who had gone on ahead and shown the way to glory. This message thus offered certainty. Jesus was the guarantee for the fact that
the world above existed and that those who belonged to him ought
at some point to partake of it. The problem of a world utterly im-
periled and breaking apart was thus to be resolved by escaping
from this problematic position in due time. One needed only to
retreat into the world of the religious. Various stipulated practices
helped promote physical experiences in which one was set loose from
the world and withdrew into the realm of the soul, and perhaps indeed experienced in advance a real heavenly ascent. The only remaining question was whether the soul was pure enough, inwardly
detached enough, to ascend once and for all into the higher and
better regions.

Over against this, the writer of Colossians has set first and most
importantly that hymn which the Colossians sang in their own wor-

ship (1:15-20). He has thus consciously taken over and set firmly at the beginning of the letter that which they themselves, in their song of praise, expressed about the majesty of Jesus Christ. He is completely in agreement with the community on this point, that it is impossible to begin in any other way except by speaking of Jesus Christ, that is, of the one who is Lord of the creation and the new creation.

(2) In this hymn, however, this present world as well was set forth, in a manner markedly molded by the Old Testament, as God's creation, and was indeed explicitly understood as the work of a creator who continually loves it. Thus when the problem ought not to be solved simply by abandoning the earthly world and withdrawing into the experiences of one's own soul and to a world above. Marcion's solution, which emerged some decades later and, at least according to Hippolytus' account, rested on exactly the same philosophical presuppositions, offered no real way out (cf. note 11 on Excursus: The Colossian Philosophy). In a sublime, all-embracing view, the hymn extolled God's positive acceptance of this earthly world itself and promised it his faithfulness.

This certainly went further than anything that Paul had formulated, and yet it only drew out the full implications of themes that were already to be found in Paul. The theme of this song was not simply that God had in Jesus Christ inclined himself completely to sinners and redeemed them. Its theme was that love and redemption really were universal, embracing everything including the universe. In face of the flight from the world that appeared so tempting in Colossae, it was not enough to call to mind that God looked in this world for individual, reconciled sinners, in other words, for pure souls or something very much like them; it had now to be articulated clearly that he wished to create a new world or, more precisely, to have the old world made new under his love. This world had indeed already been created "in Jesus Christ," that is, by the God who had become visible in Jesus as a movement of love. It had also been reconciled in him, brought back from its state of separation and united again with God. So also then its true goal could only be Jesus Christ, God's seal of approval.

In no sense could this goal be sheer catastrophe or nothingness. This then is the positive formulation that the hymn, along with Paul, offers. It goes far beyond anything that is to be found in Stoicism, which at best provides only the first steps toward such a view. Those singing the hymn experienced this goal and purpose already in advance in the jubilant song of praise in their worship, since it was here that the presence of the Exalted One became so real that it brought both community and world, both people and things into union with one another, and joined them together with God. For God's creation and once and for all reconciliation were now both set in relation to Christ. How then could there be anything for which they were not valid? How could anything at all be excluded from their scope?

Yet the words of the hymn had to be interpreted. It could certainly not be a matter of suggesting to the Colossians a different view of the world. There could be no question of simply offering a substitute for the Platonic-Pythagorean view, according to which the earth was evil and ephemeral and only the world above was eternal and unimpaired; of replacing it, that is, with the Stoic view, according to which God's creative spirit flowed through the entire cosmos, so that even everything apparently afflicted and imperfect was yet incorporated into the one good world of God. It could also not simply be a matter of linking this Stoic view with the biblical belief in creation and of providing this optimistic Stoic outlook, orientated toward earth, with an additional guarantee through the proclamation of Jesus Christ.

Something like this had happened to the Colossians (or to some of them) with regard to their Platonic outlook, when they saw in the exalted Christ the guarantee of the existence of the heavenly world above. Merely exchanging this with Stoicism was not enough. True, it was essential to perceive that the God of the Old Testament was the God of the entire creation. There was then no way in which one could detach oneself from this earth and all created life within it. Similarly, on no account could God's commandments be used (or abused) as the means of escape for an ascetic retreat from the earth, its tasks and responsibilities, into a world beyond or into the otherworldly experiences of the individual soul.

3. However, the crucial point about the hymn remained the fact that it was sung by a believing community. Here in the very act of singing its confession of faith actually became life. Therefore the Colossians had to be helped to bring to fulfillment their view of Christ, not only in the time set aside for worship but also in their everyday

life. In the end it mattered little whether the conceptual framework
was Platonic-Pythagorean or Stoic; in both cases the belief was in
the last resort ahistorical. In one way or another it was a timelessly
valid theory which existed independently of the conduct of the believer and was intended simply to explain the world. Therefore the
emphasis now had to be laid on the event which depicted the historical bond of faith in its most shocking form: the putting to death
of Jesus on the cross. Hence there had also to be an emphatic reference to the faith of the Colossians in the historical context of their
change from their earlier pagan state of being "in evil works" to
their present position of being reconciled, and at the same time of
the necessity for their faith to be tried and tested in the future
(1:21-3). Therefore, finally, there had to be an emphatic presentation as well of the attempt to dispute the Platonic-Pythagorean philosophy current in Colossae at the time and its ascetic rules intent
on separation from everything earthly (2:8-23).

Once again it must be noted that this confrontation with the philosophy was not conducted in such a way that the Stoic view of the
world (standing close to the Old Testament belief in creation)
could now simply dominate everything. What is set at the start of
the exhortation sounds almost as though the one who is admonishing
is an advocate of the "philosophy" being contested; for he calls those
whom he addresses to seek that which is "above" and to "put to
death" what is still "on earth," because they have already been raised
with Christ and thus are settled "above" (3:1-5). And yet this is not
a summons to flee from the world. This conduct should be lived out
in the world.

Hence this point is illustrated, in an almost shockingly banal way,
by the taking over of a traditional catalogue of vices and above all
of the household rule, which appears here for the first time in the
New Testament (3:5, 8, 18—4:1). The fact that the whole world
actually belongs to Christ can thus only be thought, said, and perceived by allowing him to become Lord in this world. Only thus
can both points be set out; first that the world is not their real lord,
but rather he who already holds sway "above" in perfection and to
whom those who believe already belong as his body (2:18f.). Second, it is this Lord who reclaims for himself the entire world with
everything that belongs to it; he has not written it off. For this very
reason, then, there is gathered a host of believers who allow their

complete freedom from obligations *to* this world to be offered only
as service *for* it.

The Epistle to the Colossians Today

This situation in Colossians as portrayed by the history of religions
school is to be treated seriously. People today are neither Platonic
nor Stoic; still more is Pythagorean asceticism alien to them. In
this respect they are a whole world removed from the Epistle to the
Colossians. However, the experience of the fragile nature of the
world and the fear and dread of its disintegration not only afflict
people today but cut them to the quick. Hence it may indeed be
asked whether the fascination that the cosmic Christology exercises
is so very far removed from the fascination evoked at that time by
the Stoic view (with a veneer of the Old Testament creation belief)
of the whole world being penetrated by the divine Logos. It may
likewise be asked whether that comparable fascination, which loves
to engage in every kind of meditation, is far removed from the fascination aroused at that time by middle Platonism (bolstered by
means of Pythagorean ascetic practices) with its conviction of an
unimpaired, transcendent world which could be experienced and
attained in the mind.

It has been recognized in recent scholarship that the hymn and
the commentary belong to different linguistic spheres. The hymn is
set in the situation of worship, that is of making approach to God.
The commentary has its place in context of the discussion with the
community which is addressed, that is of making approach to one's
fellow-man. This realization has opened the way to a new understanding of what Colossians says.

The hymn in 1:15-20 speaks of *Jesus Christ*, who is Lord over the
community and the world. If this is not to lead to any illusions, for
instance the theory that the whole world is already taken up into
him, or else that the church has already in him been separated once
and for all from the impure world, then one must reckon seriously
with the fact that the hymn invites all people to offer praise. The
community must certainly on no account allow themselves to be
deprived of this act of praise. For in this praise which is part of
their worship, they must risk using expressions for what is inex-
pressible. In this they will always be mindful of the fact that they

speak in inadequate images. However, in the living encounter with the one who transcends all human words, worshipers may speak of what he means for them, for all the world, and for all time. This needs to be said, in just the same way as the faltering words to one's beloved need to be said, even though they cannot contain everything that one wants to say. So God's gracious activity in Jesus Christ must also consciously be taken over, considered, and expressed by the community. Thus they can never forego their worship, as the source of their power and their means of entry into the world; and the strong emphasis traditionally placed on worship, especially from the Catholic side, is to be carefully preserved.

In this sense then the community must speak in Christological terms. It has to do this conscious of the fact that its words are not something that can simply be taught. That is, these words are not simply at the community's disposal; they cannot be communicated directly to others. The tremendous words of the hymn are true only when those encountered, moved, and comforted by God allows what they have experienced to flow back through the words they utter. Therefore the community also knows that it can never simply possess and pass on the "results" without God's love in Christ really coming about. Thus they cannot control and communicate the "results" as they could for instance in the case of an infallible method of salvation with efficacious rites, or an ethical system that derives from this but lacks its link to faith in Christ. To put this in theological terms: they know that Christology must always be the basis for Soteriology and Ethics.

This distinction drawn between the language of worship and the language of doctrine is vitally important. In his experience of his father's all-forgiving love, the prodigal son who has returned can burst out with these words of praise: "Father, your love is boundless; there is really nothing that you would not forgive" (v. p. 87). *Prod su* What is said here would be quite false as doctrine for the brother, who would similarly like to use his father's money to enjoy life ("Do as I have; squeeze as much money out of him as you can. His love is boundless; there is really nothing that he would not forgive."); for as soon as one reckons on this love as something to be taken for granted, it is no longer the free love of the father. However, it would also be false as a moral maxim to the brother ("It is simply not as easy as that; for you would have to come back contritely as I did"); the father's action would then be dependent on

cf presumption si.

the son showing penitence, and again therefore would no longer be love. There are thus expressions which come alive only as they are experienced in the praise offered for what has been freely given; they cannot be encased in an objective doctrine valid for all time.

2. However, the case is similar with the events of salvation history brought about for humankind by God. Here again it has to be noted that everything said about these events has its roots in worship. The community must not abuse their praise of the one who has reconciled everything in such a way that they take this reconciliation over into their own charge and guarantee it to those who submit to their rites. Nor must they abuse this praise in such a way that they either become concerned only with the salvation of their own souls, or withdraw complacently into a theory of the reconciliation of the universe. When they take over into their worship the tremendous expressions of the hymn, then they will bring again and again before God all their needs and all the sufferings of their neighbors and indeed of the whole creation. They may, indeed they must, thus hold God to his promise, and they must also understand this promise as boundless. They will therefore bring again and again before God everyone and everything, believers and non-believers, human and non-human creation, and demand his love for them.

They will, in doing this, never tie up God's freedom within their own system, and construct a doctrine of the redemption of the universe which fixes limits to God's activity from now until the final consummation. On the contrary, they will find that it is a liberating experience not to have to know everything, but to be able to leave to God what properly belongs to him alone. It trusts God's love; it does not prescribe for him what this love should be. Therefore also they will not forcibly persuade "anonymous Christians" and reclaim them against their will.

An elder son, still remembering well his exemplary father now long since dead, would not think that his younger brother, who no longer had such memories, was for that reason obviously a worse son. In just the same way, the community will not pretend that this is the postion for those who do not know their Father. However, the converse also holds: the elder son will remain thankful for the rest of his life that he was given this relationship with his father and that he can draw on reminiscences of it to sustain his life for the future. Likewise, the community will be joyful that it can see and recognize its Father in Jesus, and will therefore never obscure this distinction from others or cease to tell of the one who has encountered them in Jesus Christ.

3. They can do this only in the sense of bearing witness in such a way that, roused by God's coming, they do their best to involve him in the whole sphere of their ethical activity. The stress which the Protestant Church has traditionally placed on this must never be forgotten. Indeed, the realization that many of the ethical directives in Colossians have been taken over from the contemporary milieu will serve to guard against devising a system valid for everyone and for all time. It will instead lead one to take seriously the particular situation and circumstances which one finds oneself in, and then on the basis of faith to do exactly what is necessary. Openness to the modern world will thus be a characteristic of the community's ethics.

Various misunderstandings have resulted from the admonitions in Colossians, although in this connection one ought not to forget how much specific help has also emanated from these injunctions. However, these misunderstandings have only had fatal consequences when they have been linked with a doctrine (expressed with final authority) concerning an evolution which is set in motion by Christ and which is moving towards a paradisiacal order of the universe. Properly understood, all the ethical maxims given to the Colossians are no more than a witness to God's loving will. Obviously this witness is expressed in the language of its time, and can therefore only be reiterated by a serious attempt to reformulate it for the whole world today, an attempt that demands the involvement of the whole person.

This sets one free to say and do, in an uninhibited way, precisely what is necessary and helpful. Even a problematic section such as the household rule sets one free for a healthy worldliness. It brings the liberating insight that one does not have to do everything but only what is assigned and given to one to do. The person thus liberated will do this without a false inferiority or superiority complex. This will be so whether it is a matter of service for the church in the narrower sense or whether it is a so-called secular ministry; whether it is preaching a sermon or whether it is involving oneself in protection of the environment or social welfare work.

4. Thus from the Epistle to the Colossians the present-day community can say that God has shown his face in Jesus Christ (1:15), and that this very secret of his, hidden for generations, is now disclosed; it cannot, however, be put at one's disposal but can only be witnessed to as a mystery (1:26f.). This favorable countenance of God's bringing life not destruction, is set over the whole of creation, over its origin, its continuing existence, and its end (1:16f., 20). Those who are roused by this can no longer conceive of it or teach it as a mere understanding of the world. They can, according to Colossians itself, believe it in no other sense than that in the midst of this world they are orientated toward God's world, and that every single part of them is given this new direction and purpose (3:1-17).

The belief in a world which has meaning because it is beloved by God can only be lived out, both in the small circle of husband and wife, parents and children, employers and employees (3:18–4:1), and also in the much wider sphere in which something of the new world will become reality, where there are no naturally religious and non-religious people, civilized and primitive nations, tyrants and tyrannized (3:11). This cannot come about without the power of the word which again and again offers the world God's promise, even if many know nothing about it. This promise given by God is the concealed vital energy (3:3) of the world, which the community knows about and by which both community and world are borne until God at last brings the consummation (3:4).

It is for this reason that worship, in which praise and adoration are reawakened again and again, is still the source of real, world-renewing power. This worship can only be ecumenical, uniting Catholic and Protestant traditions and hopes, not obscuring what is distinctive about them both but bringing them together in the perfect bond of love (3:14-16). Thus the Epistle to the Colossians has set under way a movement which is not yet at an end.

Bibliography

Commentaries

Abbott, T. K., *The Epistles to the Ephesians and to the Colossians*, Edinburgh (1897), 6th ed. 1953 (ICC).

Alting, J. (1618-79, Groningen), *Opera Theologica* IV, Amsterdam (1686), 389-400.

Ambrosiaster (*c.* 380, Rome), *Ambrosiastri qui dicitur commentarius in epistulas Paulinas* (CSEL 81/3).

Athanasius (*c.* 295-373, Alexandria), *Contra Arianos* (PG 26)

——— *Expositio fidei* (PG 25)

Augustine (354-430, Milan and North Africa)

——— *De Civitate Dei* (C. Chr. SL 47/8).

——— *Confessiones*, ed. P. de Labriolle, Paris 1961.

——— *De diversis questionibus* (C. Chr. SL 44A).

——— *Enchiridion* (C. Chr. SL 46).

——— *Epistulae* (CSEL 44).

——— *Expositio ad Romanos* (PL 35).

——— *Contra Faustum* (CSEL 25).

——— *De genesi ad litteram* (CSEL 28/1)

——— *Ad Orosium contra Priscillianistes et Origenistes* (PL 42).

——— *De trinitate* (C. Chr. SL 50A)

Basil (329-79, Caesarea, Cappodocia)

——— *Epistulae* (PG 32).

——— *Contra Eunomium* (PG 29).

Bengel, J. A. (1687-1752, Würrtemberg), *Gnomon Novi Testamenti.* Tübingen 1742.

Berlenburg Bible: *Die Heilige Schrift Neuen Testamentes nebst der buchstäblichen und geheimen Erklärung* (Berlenburg 1735-7). Stuttgart 1859-61.

Beza, Th. (1519-1605, Geneva), *Annotationes maiores in Novum Testamentum*. No place of publication given (1594), 402-21.

Bieder, W., *Der Kolosserbrief* (Prophezei). Zürich 1943.

Blumhardt, Christoph (1842-1919, Bad Boll/Würrtemberg), *Eine Auswahl aus seinen Predigten, Andachten und Schriften*, ed. R. Lejeune. Erlenbach-Zürich 1925-37.

Boor, W. de, *Die Briefe des Paulus an die Philipper und an die Kolosser*. 2nd ed. Wuppertal 1962 (Wuppertaler Studienbibel).

Bradford, J. (c. 1510-55, Cambridge, England). *The Writings of J. B., Sermons, etc.*, ed. A. Townsend. Cambridge 1848.

Bucer, M. (1491-1551, Strassburg), *Metaphrases et enarrationes in epistulam ad Romanos* (VIII). Strassburg 1536.

Bullinger, H. (1504-75, Zürich), *In Divi apostoli Pauli ad Galatos, Ephesios, Philippenses et Colossenses epistulas commentarii*. Zürich (1535), 230-71.

Caird, G. B., *Paul's Letters from Prison*. London, Oxford, 1976 (NCB).

Calov, A. (1612-86, Königsberg), *Biblia Novi Testamenti illustrata* II. Frankfurt (1676), 796-850.

Calvin, J. (1509-64, Geneva), *In Novi Testamenti epistulas commentarii* II, ed. A. Tholuck VI/2. Berlin, no date (1831).

Chrysostom, John (354-407, Antioch and Constantinople), *Homilies on Colossians* (PG 62, col. 299-392).

Clement of Alexandria (ob. c. 215, Alexandria),

——— *Eclogae ex scripturis propheticis* (GCS 2nd edn 17/2)

——— *Excerpta e Theodoto* (GCS 2nd ed 17/2)

——— *Paedagogus* (GCS 2nd ed 12)

——— *Stromata* (GCS 52 and 2nd ed 17/2)

Conzelmann, H., *Der Brief an die Kolosser*, in: J. Becker/H. Conzelmann/G. Friedrich, *Die Briefe an die Galater, Epheser, Philipper, Kolosser, Thessalonischer und Philemon*. 16th edn 1976 (NTD 8).

Cramer, J. A., *Catenae in Novum Testamentum* VI. Oxford (1842), 294-330.

Crell, J. (1590-1631, Holland), *Opera omnia exegetica* I. Amsterdam (1656), 539-43.

Cyril of Alexandria (ob. 444, Alexandria), *Contra Nestorium* (PG 76).

Dibelius, M. and Greenven, H., *An die Kolosser, Epheser, an Philemon*. Tübingen 1953 (HNT 12).

Dionysius the Carthusian (1402-71, Roermond), *In omnes beati Pauli epistulas commentaria*. Cologne 1545.

Erasmus (1469-1536, Basel), *Opera omnia* VI. (Leiden 1705) London 1962), 881-98.

Ernst, J., *Die Briefe an die Philipper, an Philemon, an die Kolosser, an die Epheser*. Regensburg 1974 (RNT).

Ewald, P., *Die Briefe des Paulus an die Epheser, Kolosser und Philemon*. Leipzig 1910 (KNT).

Flatt, J. F. von, *Vorlesungen über die Briefe Pauli an die Philipper, Kolosser, Thessalonicher und an Philemon*, ed. C. F. Kling. Tübingen 1829.
——— *Observationum ad epistulam ad Colossenses pertinentium particula prima/secunda*. Tübingen 1814/15.

Gomarus, F. (1563-1641, Leiden), *Opera theologica omnia*. Amsterdam (1664), 547-76.
Gregory of Nazianzus (329-90, Constantinople and Nazianzus), *Orationes* (PG 36).
Gregory of Nyssa (330-95), *De tridui spatio*, in: *Opera*, ed. W. Jaeger and H. Langerbeck, IX. Leiden 1967.
Grotius, H. (1583-1645), *Annotationes in Novum Testamentum* II. Erlangen (1756), 669-92.

Hahn, P. M., *Erbauungsreden über den Brief an die Kolosser*. Stuttgart 1845.
Handbuch der Bibelerklärung, ed. Calwer Verlagsverein III. Calw 1900.
Hilary of Poitiers (315-67, Gaul and Asia Minor), *De Trinitate* (PL 10).
Hippolytus (beginning of C3, Rome), *In Danielem* (GCS 1/1).
Houlden, J. L., *Paul's Letters from Prison*. Harmondsworth, Penguin, 1970 (PGC).
Hrabanus Maurus (780-856, Fulda and Mainz) (PL 112, pp. 507-40).
Huby, J., *Saint Paul. Les Epitres de la captivité*. 2nd ed, Paris 1974 (VS 8).
Hugedé, N., *Commentaire de l'Epitre aux Colossiens*. Geneva 1968.

Irenaeus (end of 2nd cent., Lyon), *Demonstratio* (= Epid., cited in *TDNT*).
——— *Adversus haereses*, ed. W. Harvey. Cambridge 1857 (alternative numeration given in brackets).
Isidore of Pelusium (*c.* 360-435, Egypt), *Epistulae* (PG 78).

The Jerusalem Bible
John of Damascus (670-750, Jerusalem), (PG 95, 883-904).
John the Scot (ob. *c.* 870, France), *De divisione naturae* (PL 122).

Lanfranc (1005-89, Le Bec, Canterbury), (PL 150, col. 319-32).
Lightfoot, J. B. *St. Paul's Epistles to the Colossians and to Philemon*. 3rd ed, London 1879.
Loane, M. L., *Three Letters from Prison*. Waco, Texas, 1972.
Lohmeyer, E., *Die Briefe an der Philipper, an die Kolosser und an Philemon*. 8th edn, Göttingen 1930 (KEK 9).
Lohse, E., *Colossians and Philemon*. Philadelphia, Fortress, 1971.
Luecken, W., *Die Briefe an Philemon, an die Kolosser und an die Epheser*. 3rd ed, Göttingen 1917 (SNT).

Luther, M. (1483-1546, Wittenberg), *Vorreden zur Heiligen Schrift.* Munich 1934.

Martin, R. P., *Colossians and Philemon.* London, Oliphants, 1974 (NCB).
—— *Colossians, The Church's Lord and the Christian's Liberty.* Exeter, Paternoster, 1972.
Masson, C., *L'épitre de S. Paul aux Colossiens.* Neuchatel and Paris 1950 (CNT 10).
Melanchthon, P. (1497-1560, Wittenberg),
—— *Enarratio = Opera* IV. Wittenberg (1577), 326-65.
—— *Scholien = Werke in Auswahl* IV, ed. P. F. Barton. Gütersloh (1963), 209-303 (*Scholia* 1527).
Meinertz, M. and Tillmann, F., *Die Gefangenschaftsbriefe des heiligen Paulus.* Bonn 1917 (HSNT).
Meyer, H. A. W., *Kritisch-exegetisches Handbuch über die Briefe an die Philipper, Kolosser und an Philemon.* 2nd ed, Göttingen 1859 (KEK 9).
Moule, C. F. D., *The Epistles of Paul the Apostle to the Colossians and to Philemon.* Cambridge, CUP, 1957 (CGTC).
Mussner, F., *The Epistle to the Colossians* (along with J. Gnilka, *The Epistle to the Philippians*, in *The New Testament for Spiritual Reading*). London 1971.

Oecumenius (writings collected *c.* 900), (PG 119, col. 9-56 and Staab, *Pauluskommentare*, 453-5).
Origen (185-254, Alexandria and Caesarea),
—— *Contra Celsum* (GCS 2)
—— *In Joannem commentarius* (GCS 10)
—— *De principiis* (GCS 22)

Peter Lombard (*c.* 1100-60, Paris), (PL 192, col. 257-88).
Photius of Constantinople (9th cent. Constantinople), = Staab, *Pauluskommentare*, 631-3.

Rupert of Deutz (1070-1129, Deutz) *De divinis officiis* (C. Chr. CM 24).

Sasbout, A. (1516-53, Louvain), *Opus homiliarum*, ed. M. Vosmerus. Cologne 1613.
Schleiermacher, F. (1768-1834, Halle and Berlin), *Predigten über das Evangelium Marci und den Brief Pauli an die Kolosser*, ed. P. Zabel. Berlin 1835 (second part).
Scott, E. F., *The Epistles of Paul to the Colossians, to Philemon and to the Ephesians.* London, Hodder and Stoughton, 1930 (MNTC).
Severian of Gabula (*c.* 400, Syria), in Staab, *Pauluskommentare*, 314-28.
Soden, H. von, *Die Briefe an die Kolosser, Epheser, Philemon; die Pastoralbriefe.* Freiburg i.B. and Leipzig, 1891 (HC III/I).
Staab, K., *Die Thessalonicherbriefe. Die Gefangenschaftsbriefe.* 5th edn, Regensburg 1959 (RNT 7, 1).
—— *Pauluskommentare aus der griechischen Kirche, aus Katenenhand-*

schriften gesammelt und herausgegeben von Karl Staab. Münster i. W. 1933 (*NTA* 15).

Synge, F. C., *Philippians and Colossians.* London, SCM, 1951 (TBC).

Tertullian (*c.* 160-225, Carthage); *De anima, Apologeticum, Contra Marcionem, De praescriptionibus, De pudicitia, De resurrectione mortuorum, Ad uxorem, Contra Valentinianos* (C. Chr. SL 1-2).

Theodore of Mopsuestia (ob. 428, Cilicia), *Theodori episcopi Mopsuestini in epistolas B. Pauli commentarii. The Latin Version with the Greek Fragments,* ed. H. E. Swete. Vol. 1, Cambridge (1880), 253-312.

Theodoret (*c.* 395-460, Syria), (PG 82, col. 591-628).

Theophylact (*c.* 1050-1108, Constantinople and Bulgaria), (PG 124, col. 1205-78).

Thomas Aquinas (1225-74, Paris and Italy), *Opera Omnia,* XIII. Parma (1862), 530-55.

Thomas, W. H. G., *Studies in Colossians and Philemon.* Grand Rapids, Eerdmans, 1973.

Thompson, G. H. P., *The Letters of Paul to the Ephesians, to the Colossians and to Philemon.* London, CUP, 1967 (CNEB).

Wette, W. M. L. de, *Kurze Erklärung der Briefe an die Colosser, an Philemon, an die Epheser und Philipper.* 2nd edn, Leipzig 1847 (Kurzgefasstes exegetisches Handbuch zum NT II).

Zanchi, Hieronymus (1516-90, Strassbourg, Heidelberg), *Opera theologica* VI. Geneva (1617), 241-360.

Zwingli, H. (1484-1531, Zürich), *Huldrici Zwingli opera completa, editio prima,* edd. M. Schuler and J. Schulthess, VI/2. Zürich (1838), 220-8.

Other Literature

Ahrens, T., *Die ökumenische Diskussion kosmischer Christologie seit 1961. Darstellung und Kritik.* Lübeck 1969 (mimeographically reproduced, Dissertation, Hamburg).

Allmen, D. von, "Réconciliation du monde et christologie cosmique," *RHPR* 48 (1968), 32-45.

Apocryphon Johannis = W. C. Till, *Die gnostischen Schriften des koptischen Papyrus Berolensis 8502.* Berlin 1955 (TU 60).

Barclay, W., *The All-Sufficient Christ: Studies in Paul's Letters to the Colossians.* London 1963.

Barth, K., *Church Dogmatics* I/1-IV/4. ET by G. T. Thomson etc., Edinburgh, T. and T. Clark, 1936-69.

Benoit, P., "Corps, tête et plérôme dans les épitres de la captivité," *RB* 63 (1965), 5-44.

—— "L'hymne christologique de Col. 1.15-20," in: *Christianity, Judaism and Other Greco-Roman Cults.* (Festschrift for M. Smith) ed. J. Neusner, I. Leiden, Brill, 1975 (SJLA 12), 226-63.

Blinzler, J., "Lexicalisches zu dem Terminus τὰ στοιχεῖα τοῦ κόσμου bei Paulus," AnBib 17-18 (1963), 439-41.

Bornkamm, G., "Die Häresis des Kolosserbriefes," in id., *Das Ende des Gesetzes.* Munich 1952 (BEvT 16), pp. 139-56.

—— "Die Hoffnung im Kolosserbrief. Zugleich ein Beitrag zur Frage der Echtheit des Briefes" in : *Studien zum NT und zur Patristik* (Festschrift für E. Klostermann). Berlin 1961 (TU 77), 56-64.

Brunner, E., *Dogmatik* I-III. Zürich 1946-60.

Bujard, W., *Stilanalytische Untersuchungen zum Kolosserbrief als Beitrag zur Methodik von Sprachvergleichen.* Göttingen 1973 (SUNT 11).

Bultmann, R., *Exegetica. Aufsätze zur Erforschung des NT,* ed. E. Dinkler. Tübingen 1967.

—— *Theology of the New Testament.* ET by K. Grobel, 2 vols. London, SCM, 1952-5.

Burger, C., *Schöpfung und Versohnung. Studien zum liturgischen Gut im Kolosserbrief und Epheserbrief.* Göttingen 1975 (WMANT 46).

Burney, C. F., "Christ as the 'ΑΡΧΗ of Creation," *JTS* O.S. 27 (1926), 160-77.

Carr, W., "Two Notes on Colossians," *JTS* N.S. 24 (1973), 492-500.

Crouch, J. E., *The Origin and Intention of the Colossian Haustafel.* Göttingen 1972 (FRLANT 109).

Cullmann, O., *Christ and Time.* ET by F. V. Filson, 3rd ed London, SCM, 1962.

—— *Salvation in History.* ET by S. G. Sowers, London, SCM, 1967.

Deichgräber, R., *Gotteshymnus und Christushymnus in der frühen Christenheit.* Göttingen 1967 (SUNT 5).

Ebeling, G., *Word and Faith.* ET by J. W. Leitch, London 1963.

Eckhart, K.-G., "Exegetische Beobachtungen zu Kol. 1.9-20," *ThViat* 7 (1959/60), 87-106.

—— "Ursprüngliche Tauf- und Ordinationsliturgie," *ThViat* 8 (1961/2), 23-37.

Ernst, J., *Pleroma und Pleroma Christi.* 1970 (BU 5).

Eudokimov, P., "Die Natur," *KuD* 11 (1965), 1-20.

Evangelium Veritatis, edd. M. Malinine, H.-C. Puech, G. Quispel, W. C. Till. Zürich 1956.

Feuillet, A., *Le Christ, sagesse de Dieu d'après les épitres pauliniennes.* Paris 1966 (EBib).

Fischer, K. M., *Tendenz und Absicht des Epheserbriefes.* Göttingen 1973 (FRLANT 111).

Foerster, W., "Die Irrlehrer des Kolosserbriefes," in : *Studia biblica et semitica, Festschrift für Theodore Christian Vriezen.* Wageningen (1966), 71-80.

Francis, F. O., "Humility and Angelic Worship in Col. 2:18," *ST* 16 (1962), 109-34.

Francis, F. O. and Meeks, W. A., *Conflict at Colossae.* Cambridge, Massachussets 1973 (SBLSBS 4).

Fukuchi, M. S., "The Letter of Paul to the Colossians," *BiTod* 60 (1972), 762-76.

Gabathuler, H. J., *Jesus Christus. Haupt der Kirche—Haupt der Welt.* Zürich 1965 (ATANT 45).

Gibbs, J. G., *Creation and Redemption. A Study in Pauline Theology.* 1971 (NovTSup 26).

Glasson, T. F., "Colossians I 18, 15 and Sirach XXIV," *NovT* 11 (1969), 154-6.

Grässer, E., "Kol. 3.1-4 als Beispiel einer Interpretation secundum homines recipientes," *ZTK* 64 (1967), 139-68.

Hegermann, H., *Die Vorstellung vom Schöpfungsmittler im hellenistichen Judentum und Unchristentum.* Berlin 1961 (TU 82).

Hendricks, W. L., "All in All. Theological Themes in Colossians," *South Western Journal of Theology* 16 (1975), 23-35.

Holtzmann, H. J., *Kritik der Epheser- und Kolosserbriefe.* Leipzig 1872.

Hooker, M. D., "Were there False Teachers in Colossae?," in : *Christ and Spirit in the New Testament* (Essays in honour of C. F. D. Moule), edd. B. Lindars and S. S. Smalley. Cambridge (1973), 315-31.

Kamlah, E., *Die Form der katalogischen Paränese im Neuen Testament.* Tübingen 1964 (WUNT 7).

Käsemann, E., "A Primitive Christian Baptismal Liturgy" in id., *Essays on New Testament Themes.* ET by W. J. Montague, London, SCM, 1964 (SBT 1st series 41), 149-168.

Kasper, W., *Jesus the Christ.* ET by V. Green, London 1976.

Kehl, N., *Der Christushymnus im Kolosserbriefe. Eine motivgeschichtliche Untersuchung zu Kol. 1.12-20.* Stuttgart 1967 (SBM 1).

——— "Erniedrigung und Erhöhung in Qumran und Kolossä," *ZKT* 91 (1969), 364-94.

Kremer, J., *Was an den Leiden Christi noch mangelt. Eine interpretationsgeschichtliche und exegetische Untersuchung zu Kol. 1.24b.* Bonn 1956 (BBB 12).

Küng, H., *On Being a Christian.* ET by E. Quinn, London, Collins, 1977.

Lähnemann, J., *Der Kolosserbrief. Komposition, Situation und Argumentation.* Gütersloh 1971 (SNT 3).

Lamarche, P., "Structure de l'épitre aux Colossiens," *Bib.* 56 (1975), 453-63.

Lohse, E., "Christusherrschaft und Kirche im Kolosserbrief," *NTS* 11 (1964/5), 203-16.

Ludwig, H., *Der Verfasser des Kolosserbriefes—ein Schüler des Paulus.* Unpub. diss., Göttingen 1974.
Lyonnet, S., "L'hymne christologique de l'Epitre aux Colossiens et la fête juive de Nouvel An (S. Paul, Col. 1.20 et Philon, De spec. leg. 192), *RSR* 48 (1960), 93-100.

Martin, R. P., "Reconciliation and Forgiveness in the Letter to the Colossians," in: *Reconciliation and Hope* (Essays presented to L. Morris), ed. R. J. Banks. Exeter, Paternoster, (1974), 104-24.
Michaelis, W., *Versöhnung des Alls. Die frohe Botschaft von der Gnade Gottes.* Gümlingen and Bern 1950.
Moule, C. F. D., " 'The New Life' in Colossians 3:1-17," *RevExp* 70 (1973), 481-93.
Münderlein, G., "Die Erwählung durch das Pleroma: Bemerkungen zu Kol i.19," *NTS* 8 (1961/2), 264-76.
Munn, G. L., "Introduction to Colossians," *South Western Journal of Theology* 16 (1973), 9-21.
Munro, W., "Col III.18-IV.2 and Eph. V.21-VI.9. Evidences of a Late Stratum?," *NTS* 18 (1972), 434-47.

Olbricht, T. H., "Colossians and Gnostic Theology," *Restoration Quarterly*, Abilene/Texas, 14 (1971), 65-79.

Percy, E., *Die Probleme der Kolosser- und Epheserbriefe.* Lund 1946 (SHLL 39).
Pöhlmann, W., "Die hymnischen All-Prädikationen in Kol. 1.15-20," *ZNW* 64 (1973), 53-74.
Prat, P., *Theology of St. Paul.* ET, 2 vols. in I, London 1959.

Reicke, B., "The Historical Setting of Colossians," *RevExp* 70 (1973), 429-38.
Reumann, J., "Die Reichweite der Herrschaft Christi," in: *Humanität und Herrschaft Christi,* ed. I. Asheim, Göttingen (1974), 120-89.

Sanders, E. P., "Literary Dependence in Colossians," *JBL* 85 (1966), 28-45.
Sanders, J. T., *The New Testament Christological Hymns. Their Historical Religious Background.* Cambridge 1971 (MSSNTS 15).
Schenke, H. M., "Die neutestamentliche Christologie und der gnostiche Erlöser," in: *Gnosis und NT,* ed. K.-W. Tröger. Berlin 1973, 205-29.
——— "Der Widerstreit gnosticher und kirchlicher Christologie im Spiegel des Kolosserbriefes," *ZTK* 61 (1964), 391-403.
Schillebeeckx, E., *Jesus: an experiment in Christology.* ET by H. Hopkins, New York, Seabury, 1979.
Schleiermacher, F., "Über Koloss. 1.15-20," *TSK* V/1 (1832), 497-537.
Schnackenburg, R., "Die Aufnahme des Christushymnus durch den Verfasser des Kolosserbriefes," in: *EKK Vorarbeiten* 1. Zürich and Neukirchen (1969), 33-50.

—— *God's Rule and Kingdom*. ET by J. Murray, 2nd ed London 1968.

Schrage, W., "Zur Ethik der neutestamentlichen Haustafeln," *NTS* 21 (1975), 1-22.

Schroeder, D., *Die Haustafeln des Neuen Testamentes*. Unpubl. diss. Hamburg 1959 (typewritten).

Schubert, P., *Form and Function of the Pauline Thanksgiving*. 1939 (BZNW 20).

Schweizer, E., "Christianity of the Circumcised and Judaism of the Uncircumcised—The Background of Matthew and Colossians," in: *Jews, Greeks and Christians: Religious Cultures in Late Antiquity* (Essays presented to W. D. Davies), edd. R. G. Hamerton-Kelly and R. Scroggs. Leiden, Brill, 1976.

—— "Christus und Geist im Kolosserbrief," in: *Christ and Spirit in the New Testament* (Essays presented to C. F. D. Moule), edd. B. Lindars and S. S. Smalley. Cambridge 1973.

—— "Die 'Elemente der Welt' Gal 4.3, 9; Kol 2.8, 20," in: *Verborum Veritas* (Festschrift für G. Stählin), 245-59 = id., *Beiträge zur Theologie des Neuen Testaments*. Zürich (1970), 147-63.

—— "Zur neueren Forschung am Kolosserbrief (seit 1970)," in: *Theologische Berichte* 5, edd. J. Pfammatter and F. Furger. Zürich (1976), 163-91.

—— "Gottesgerechtigkeit und Lasterkataloge bei Paulus (inkl. Kol und Eph)," in: *Rechtfertigung* (Festschrift für E. Käsemann), edd. J. Friedrich, W. Pöhlmann and P. Stuhlmacher. Tübingen and Göttingen (1976), 453-77.

—— "Die Weltlichkeit des Neuen Testamentes: die Haustafeln," in: *Beiträge zur alttestamentlichen Theologie* (Festschrift für W. Zimmerli), ed. R. Smend. Göttingen 1977, I, 397-413.

—— "Die Kirche als Leib Christi in den paulinischen Antilegomena," *TLZ* 86 (1961) 241-56 = id., *Neotestamentica*. Zürich (1963), 293-316.

—— "Kolosser 1.15-20," in: *EKK Vorarbeiten* 1. Zürich and Neukirchen (1969), 7-31 = id., *Beiträge zur Theologie des Neuen Testamentes*. Zürich (1970), 113-45 (with additional material).

—— "The Letter to the Colossians—Neither Pauline nor Post-Pauline?," in: *Pluralisme et oecuménisme en recherches théologiques: mélanges offerts au R. P. Dockx*, edd. Y. Congar, G. Dejaijve, H. de Lubac, etc. Paris and Louvain 1976.

—— "Versöhnung des Alls. Kol 1.20," in: *Jesus Christus in Historie und Theologie* (Festschrift für H. Conzelmann), ed. G. Strecker. Tübingen (1975), 487-501.

(Dr. Schweizer's essays on Colossians are included in a collection of his articles published by Vandenhoeck and Ruprecht, 1982).

Staehelin, E., *Die Verkündigung des Reiches Gottes in der Kirche Jesu Christi* I-VII. Basel 1951-65.

Stauffer, E., *New Testament Theology*. ET by J. Marsh, London 1955.

Strugnell, J., "The Angelic Liturgy at Qumran," in: *Congress Volume Oxford 1959, 1960* (VTSup) 7, 318-45.

Stuhlmacher, P., *Der Brief an Philemon*. Zürich and Neukirchen 1975 (EKK).

Trudinger, L. P., "A Further Brief Note on Col. 1:24," *EvQ* 45 (1973), 36-8.

Urban, A., "Kosmische Christologie," *EuA* 47 (1971), 472-86.

Vawter, F. B., "The Colossians Hymn and the Principle of Redaction," *CBQ* 33 (1971), 62-81.

Vögtle, A., *Die Tugend- und Lasterkataloge im Neuen Testament: Exegetisch, religions- und formgeschichtlich untersucht*. Münster i. W. 1936 (*NTA* 16, 4/5).

Wagenführer, M.-A., *Die Bedeutung Christi für Welt und Kirche. Studien zum Klosser- und Epheserbrief*. Leipzig 1941.

Weidinger, K., *Die Haustafeln: Ein Stück urchristlicher Paränese*. Leipzig 1928 (UNT 14).

Weiss, H., "The Law in the Epistle to the Colossians," *CBQ* 34 (1972), 294-314.

Weiss, H.-F., *Untersuchungen zur Kosmologie des hellenistichen und palästinischen Judentums*. Berlin 1966 (TU 97).

Wendland, H.-D., "Zur sozialethischen Bedeutung der neutestamentlichen Haustafeln," in: id., *Botschaft an die sociale Welt*. Hamburg (1959), 104-114.

Wengst, K., *Christologische Formeln und Lieder des Urchristentums*. 2nd edn 1972 (SNT 7).

——— "Versöhnung und Befreiung. Ein Aspekt des Themas 'Schuld und Vergebung' im Lichte des Kolosserbriefes," *EvT* 36 (1976), 14-26.

Zeilinger, F., *Der Erstgeborene der Schöpfung. Untersuchungen zur Formalstruktur und Theologie des Kolosserbriefes*. Vienna 1974.

Index of Subjects

Adam, 67, 247
Admonition, 116, 210, 231
Angels, 60, 68, 81, 126, 132, 137, 264f., 291f.
 worship of, 127, 155, 159f., 280f.
Apocalyptic, 34, 37, 44f., 105, 109, 288
Apostle, 28f., 98, 103-105, 232, 237
 apostolic activity, 100, 111f.
 apostolic proclamation, 110f., 113
 suffering apostle, v. Suffering of the apostle
Asceticism (ascetic), 132f., 166-170, 215, 279f., 293
Authorities, v. Powers

Baptism, 76, 143-148, 165, 179, 196, 282
Body, 59, 72, 91, 103, 156f., 183, 208, 261
 of Christ, 58f., 93, 102, 140, 157, 163f., 185, 208, 254
 of flesh, 91, 138, 178, 261
 resurrection, 138f.
 = world, 68f., 71f., 82f., 183
Bodily, 254

Christ, v. Head; Suffering of Christ
Christians, anonymous, 268f., 275, 291, 300
Church, 58f., 82, 163f., 241f., 262, 264, 282, 286, 298
 divine (triumphant), 97
Circumcision, 140, 157
 of Christ, 142f., 282
 of the heart, 141
Colossae, 13ff.
Consummation, v. Eschatology

Conversion, terminology of, 50
Cosmos, v. World
Creation, 62-88, 130, 178, 183f., 197, 260-263, 270, 275, 295f.
 new, 76, 79, 86, 263ff., 287, 295
Cross, 59f., 149, 153, 261
 blood of the, 59, 62, 83f.
 sign of the, 260
 theology of the, 274
Crucifixion, 138f.

Day of Atonement, 62, 75
Devil, 148, 262, 266
Doctrine, v. Teaching

Elements (of the world), 60, 126f., 131, 151f., 165f., 175, 186f.
Ephesians, 15
Eschatology (eschaton, etc.), 70, 108, 144f., 156, 170, 179f., 231, 288
Ethics (ethical), 45, 94, 110, 268ff., 301
Evolution, 272, 274, 285, 288, 292, 301

Faith, 33f., 53, 94f., 270, 301
 love, hope, 33
First-born, 67-69, 73, 261
 from the dead, 67, 74
Flesh, 174f., 183, 248, 259, 261
 body of, 143, 147, 185, 248
 foreskin of the, 147
 sense of the, 143, 162f.
 works of the, 206
Forgery, 19-22
Fullness, 63, 76-79, 137, 262ff.
 of Christ, 271

313

Gentile, 106-109, 114, 233, 256, 300
  Christians, 147
Glory, 109f., 177
  of God, 43
Gnosticism (Gnostic, etc.), 44, 125f., 152f., 163, 183, 195f., 255, 259, 262f., 272
Gospel, 35, 94f., 100, 107f., 209f., 232f.
Grace, 27, 30, 211, 243

Hands
  made with, 140f.
Head, 72, 163, 261
  = Christ, 58f., 61, 163, 262
  of the world, 72, 83
Heart, 116
Heaven, 51, 71, 81, 138, 173, 175f., 185, 188, 265
Hermeneutic, 86-88, 97, 173, 298-301
Hope (v. also Faith), 33, 39, 95, 176
Household Rule, 213-220, 282-286, 293, 297, 301
Hymn, 47, 55-63, 85-88, 96ff., 247, 259, 276, 285, 291, 294f., 296, 298
  fragment of, 135
  interpretation given by the writer of the letter, 82-88
  original, 63-81
  translation, 57

Image, 56, 63-69, 73f., 248
  of God, 198, 250ff., 283
  prototype, 65, 198
Imprisonment, 19f., 25
Indicative and Imperative, 15, 94, 122-125, 153, 171, 173, 181f., 192
Inheritance, 52, 226
Intercession, 40f., 232

Justification, 91f., 197, 290f.
  Christ's righteousness, 284

Knowledge, 41-45, 117ff.

Laodicea, 20, 24f., 241ff.
Law, 17, 149ff., 155f., 172, 256
Letter, Hellenistic, 32
Logos, 65, 68, 77-81, 137, 183f., 196, 247ff., 255, 259ff., 263f., 269, 292
Lord, 216, 218, 222, 225
  Exalted, 207
  = Christ, 123f., 216
  lordship of Christ, 174
Love (v. also Faith), 33, 116, 131, 205-207, 222, 252, 300

Members, 184-188
Monotheism, 36, 255f.
Mortality, 259, 263
Mystery, 37, 107-110, 117, 176, 233, 267f., 302

Nations, v. Gentiles
Natures of Christ, 252-257, 286, 291
New Year, 75, 129f.

Officials, holders of office, 164, 210, 281
Onesimus, 24, 224, 238, 243
Order, 218, 268, 271, 285, 292
  (dispensation) of salvation, 247, 255f.
  theology of, 292

Parousia, 145, 174, 176, 180, 232
Peace, 27f., 30, 62, 208, 270
  making of, 75, 80f.
Perfection, 111f., 203, 207f., 278f.
Philo (Philonic), 65, 78, 80f., 129-133, 143, 156, 183ff., 196, 201, 214, 249
Philosophy, Colossian, 120, 122f., 125-134, 137f., 154-157, 175, 178, 188, 278f.
Plato (Platonic, etc.), 131f., 136f., 156, 175, 184, 188, 249, 294, 297f.

Pleroma, v. Fullness
Plutarch (Plutarchian), 81, 129, 137, 187, 213
Powers, 16, 51, 60f., 81ff., 126, 151, 251, 261f., 271, 284
Proclamation, 95f., 108, 110, 113, 232f.
Prophet, prophets, 29, 100, 112f., 256
Prototype, v. Image
Put on, put off, 193-198, 208, 267
Pythagoras (Pythagorean), 81, 129-133, 136f., 151, 157, 184, 294, 297f.

Qumran, 50f., 141, 147, 159, 173, 190, 206

Reconciliation, 59-63, 84, 87, 89, 91-93, 264f., 300
of the universe, 79-81, 84, 86, 260-276, 291f.
Requirements, v. Law
Restoration, 261
Resurrection, 144, 173f.
already anticipated, 146f., 173f., 192, 286f.
with Christ, 172-174
Revelation, schema of, 96, 108f., 177
Righteousness, v. Justification

Saints, 51, 108, 280f.
Saving activity of God, 113, 286f., 300
Sin, 90f., 147, 165, 185, 188, 190ff., 278
Social order, 198-203, 213-220, 227-230, 268f., 285, 301f.
Soul, 131f., 139, 143, 157, 161, 163, 184, 186ff., 203, 294f.
Spirit, 18, 38f., 43, 117, 119f., 174, 178, 187, 206, 210
of God, 119, 174f.
Stoicism (Stoic, etc.), 81, 129, 141, 183, 200, 213, 294, 297f.

Structure (of the letter), 18ff.
Style, 18f., 46f., 56, 236f.
Suffering
of Christ, 17, 101-105
of the apostle, 16f., 19f., 100-106

Teaching, 86f., 96f., 110, 210, 276, 299
Thanksgiving, 31ff., 39, 53f.
Timothy, 23, 25, 29f.
Truth, 35, 37

Universal reconciliation, v. reconciliation of the universe
Universe, 72, 183f., 262ff., 295
formula, 69f.
God, 58, 83
temple of the, 140
Upper world (world above), v. Heaven

Vices (catalogue of), 184-191, 193, 202, 206, 297
Virtues, 184-188, 196, 204
cardinal, 206
catalogue of, 207f.

Warning, v. Admonition
Well-pleasing, 42
Wisdom
as hypostasis, 65f., 248f., 260
of God, 118, 261f.
literature, 70, 78
sayings, 86
theology, 264
World, 58f., 68-71, 79f., 82ff., 95f., 163, 165f., 172f., 184, 188f., 195, 199, 212, 250, 261, 270ff., 294f.
cosmic Christology, 273-277
Worship, 209-212, 221, 281f., 298f., 302
in everyday life, 217
Wrath of God, 191, 268

Index of Biblical References

Included here are those verses of Colossians discussed in the Impact of Colossians and Outlook sections. Also included are a number of verses and passages from outside Colossians, which are dealt with in Excursuses and extended discussions (v. Index of Subjects for the particular pages relevant to these themes).

A. Old Testament

Lev. 26:41 ⎫
Deut. 10:16 ⎪
1 Sam. 16:7 ⎬ v. Circumcision of the Heart
Jer. 4:4—9:25 ⎪
Ezek. 44:7, 9 ⎭

B. New Testament

Rom. 1:29-31	v. Vices (Catalogue of)
2:29	v. Circumcision of the Heart
13:11-14	v. Vices (Catalogue of)
1 Cor. 5:9-13	v. Vices (Catalogue of)
6:9-11	v. Vices (Catalogue of)
2 Cor. 6:4-7	v. Virtues (Catalogue of)
12:20f.	v. Vices (Catalogue of)
Gal. 4:3, 8-10	v. Philosophy (Colossians)
5:19-22	v. Vices (Catalogue of)
5:22f.	v. Virtues (Catalogue of)
Eph. 5:5f.	v. Vices (Catalogue of)
5:22—6:9	v. Household Rule

Col.

1:1	note 26 to IV Ethics
2	note 40 to II Christology
5	note 20 to IV Ethics
8	p. 277
9-11	note 46 to II Christology
10	note 18 to IV Ethics
12-20	p. 268; note 44 to II Christology
12-23	p. 274
13	pp. 252, 259, 269; notes 17 to II Christology, 1, 5, 58, 81 to III Soteriology, 52, 62 to IV Ethics

13f.   pp. 268, 287
14   p. 248; notes 19 to II Christology, 7 to IV Ethics
15   pp. 246f., 250ff., 255f., 259, 261, 271; notes 6, 7, 35, 45,
            55, 58 to II Christology, 51 to III Soteriology, 21, 56, 58
            to IV Ethics
15f.   notes 7, 52 to II Christology
15-17   pp. 250f., 254, 257, 259, 263; notes 40 to II Christology,
            81 to III Soteriology
15-18   p. 287
15-20   pp. 246, 253, 261f., 271f., 274f.; notes 30, 40, 50, 64, 78
            to III Soteriology
16   pp. 251, 262, 264, 268, 270f., 284, 290f., 294f., 298,
            302; notes 37 to II Christology, 9, 29, 35, 46, 50, 76 to
            III Soteriology, 21 to IV Ethics
17   pp. 251, 254, 261, 271; notes 13 to II Christology, 77 to
            III Soteriology
18   pp. 246, 248, 250f., 255, 257, 259, 262, 267, 285; notes
            1, 19, 34, 35, 37 to II Christology, 27, 32, 33, 51, 78 to
            III Soteriology, 26, 28, 62 to IV Ethics
18-20   p. 254; note 40 to II Christology
19   pp. 253, 262, 264, 270; notes 36, 37, 38, 57 to II Christol-
            ogy, 19, 27, 31, 58 to III Soteriology, 54 to IV Ethics
19f.   pp. 267, 269; note 47 to III Soteriology
20   pp. 246, 265ff., 268ff., 271ff., 284f., 302; notes 35, 57 to II
            Christology, 33, 37, 40, 42, 44, 46, 49, 52, 58, 64, 78, 85
            to III Soteriology, 21 to IV Ethics
21   p. 272
21f.   pp. 248, 256; notes 2, 59 to III Soteriology
21-3   p. 297; note 33 to III Soteriology
22   pp. 248, 278; notes 42 to II Christology, 7, 53, 55 to IV
            Ethics
22-9   note 33 to III Soteriology
23   p. 256
24   pp. 256, 264, 278; notes 52 to II Christology, 5, 7, 21, 59
            to C IV Ethics
25   pp. 246f.; note 50 to II Christology
25f.   note 50 to II Christology
25-8   note 46 to II Christology
26   pp. 255, 267
26f.   pp. 267f., 277; notes 47 to II Christology, 9 to IV Ethics
28   pp. 263, 278; notes 56 to II Christology, 7, 8, 9, 26 to IV
            Ethics

2:1-4   p. 256
2   p. 277; notes 37, 47, 50 to II Christology, 11 to IV Ethics
2f.   p. 268; notes 46 to II Christology, 9, 11 to IV Ethics
3   p. 267
3f.   note 12 to IV Ethics

8	pp. 278f., 281; notes 81 to III Soteriology, 7, 11, 12, 29, 39 to IV Ethics
8-14	note 24 to IV Ethics
8-23	p. 297
9	pp. 253f., 257, 261ff., 270; notes 28, 29, 36, 37, 38, 45 to II Christology, 27, 31, 49, 58, 81 to III Soteriology, 54 to IV Ethics
9f.	p. 246
10	pp. 262, 267, 284; notes 5, 37 to III Soteriology, 7 to IV Ethics
11	pp. 255, 259, 277, 282; notes 2, 3 to III Soteriology
12	pp. 286, 288; notes 3, 49, 51 to IV Ethics
12-15	note 53 to IV Ethics
13	p. 256; notes 2 to III Soteriology, 51 to IV Ethics
13-15	p. 248
14	p. 265; notes 46 to II Christology, 55 to III Soteriology, 53, 56 to IV Ethics
14f.	pp. 246, 271; note 58 to III Soteriology
15	pp. 259, 261, 272; notes 2, 3, 5, 27, 37, 51, 78, 81, 85 to III Soteriology, 40, 56 to IV Ethics
16	p. 279; note 14 to IV Ethics
16-23	pp. 279-281; note 81 to III Soteriology
17	pp. 254, 256; notes 48 to II Christology, 1, 27 to III Soteriology
18	pp. 279ff., 297; notes 11, 20, 21, 42 to IV Ethics
19	pp. 248, 282; note 11 to IV Ethics
20	pp. 281, 288
20-3	note 21 to IV Ethics
21	p. 279; notes 16, 42, 59 to IV Ethics
21f.	note 7 to IV Ethics
22	note 16 to IV Ethics
23	p. 279; note 16 to IV Ethics
3:1	note 53 to IV Ethics
1f.	note 60 to IV Ethics
1-4	pp. 272, 286, 288; note 52 to IV Ethics
1-5	p. 297
1-10	p. 277
1-17	p. 302
3	p. 279; note 51 to IV Ethics
3f.	note 49 to IV Ethics
4	p. 302
5	pp. 277, 297; notes 3 to II Christology, 21 to IV Ethics
8	pp. 277, 297
9	note 53 to IV Ethics
9f.	notes 3 to II Christology, 30 to III Soteriology
10	pp. 267, 277, 283; notes 4 to II Christology, 9, 56 to III Soteriology

11	pp. 262, 282, 302; notes 24, 30 to IV Ethics
14	notes 7, 26 to IV Ethics
14-16	p. 302
16	notes 16, 26, 42 to IV Ethics
16f.	p. 277
17	p. 278; notes 6, 20, 39, 53 to IV Ethics
18	p. 283; note 63 to III Soteriology
18–4.1	pp. 246, 282-286, 290, 297, 302
19	p. 284
21	notes 63 to III Soteriology, 39 to IV Ethics
23	p. 283
23f.	p. 285
4:1	pp. 283f.; note 45 to IV Ethics
2	notes 46 to II Christology, 24 to IV Ethics
3	p. 277; note 21 to IV Ethics
4	note 50 to II Christology
5f.	note 57 to IV Ethics
6	notes 16, 37 to IV Ethics
17	note 26 to IV Ethics
18	note 47 to II Christology
1 Thess. 4:3-6	v. Vices (Catalogue of)
1 Tim. 6:11	v. Virtues (Catalogue of)
Titus 2:2-10	v. Household Rule
3:1f.	v. Household Rule
1 Peter 2:13–3.7	v. Household Rule
2 Peter 1:5-7	v. Virtues (Catalogue of)
Rev. 21:7f.	v. Vices (Catalogue of)
22:14f.	v. Vices (Catalogue of)

C. Apostolic Fathers

Barn. 2:2f.	v. Virtues (Catalogue of)
1 Clem. 21:6-8	v. Household Rule
62	v. Virtues (Catalogue of)
Ign. *Pol.* 4:1–6.2	v. Household Rule
Pol. 4:2–6:1	v. Household Rule

153 "our world is in danger of being heavenless" i.e. the ...
: ercn. has been lost to us. (Shickery phrase — may use of II Set

Cp50. Achtemei, new Hermeneutic on pleuroena — "if sheer overpowere
198 "God is present in pure form in Xst alone"   wealth of being
Today we're not concerned about reaching God in or thru th heavens
Hence Col. is bizarre. Better then to think of today techniques of trying
reach to God with, or the true Self, etc. Here diet, rituals are being used
262 " In baptism th old adam is indeed drowned : but the swimmer
    can still swim"
205 quotation on humility

196 II Set 1. Putting on th virtues contrast Paul. Putting on Xst   197 too
19   on II Pet 1: 16 f : authorly. The typical view   206 II Set 1: 5-7 "See
                    pseudo   control" = altruism
129 f or bhqs fr Col. 1: 19-20 x

137 x very must on II Set 1 "have escaped   92 II Cor 5:14
138   corruption.." of "Paul she of divine nah²   129 cf II Set 3 — destruct stoic
     (diminishing of late) (see 128 f)   a undeserved assumption world
     Could II Set then reflect same area? date
     of Col.?   unless we can find same theology earlier   152 or Eph 4:8

153 diminizatio in gnostic sense ? II Set 1. Could Pet. show gnost

                                247 on Noah. Cf my view
                                   on I, II Set. on N
                                   (Philo)

                                295 a contrasting v
                                   col II Set 3 — not
                                   destroy, but rea
                                   universe

              filed   177 Phil 1:21 ie 'to
                                  exist completely for'

                                218 f or Eph 5:22-3
                                222

                                232 Rev 3:10 X